The European Union in the Security of Europe

This book examines the European Union's contribution to providing security in Europe amidst an increasingly complex and challenging environment.

In this new and comprehensive guide to the EU's role in security since the end of the Cold War, the authors offer an explanation of EU internal and external security regimes, and argue that the Union has become an important exporter of security within its region. However, the Union's rhetorical ambitions and commitments continue to outstrip its capabilities and it lacks both a common conceptualisation of security and a meaningful, shared strategic culture. Drawing extensively on primary sources the book examines the Union's relations with the US and Russia in a time of shifting geostrategic calculations and priorities. With the EU capacity for enlargement slowing, this text presents a detailed assessment of EU security policies towards Central Europe, the Mediterranean, the Western Balkans, Eastern Europe and Southern Caucasus.

The European Union in the Security of Europe will be of interest to students and scholars of the EU, security studies, and international relations.

Steve Marsh is Reader in International Relations at Cardiff University.

Wyn Rees is Professor of International Security at the University of Nottingham.

The European Union in the Security of Europe

From Cold War to Terror War

Steve Marsh and Wyn Rees

LONDON AND NEW YORK

First published 2012
by Routledge
2 Park Square, Milton Park, Abingdon, Oxon, OX14 4RN

Simultaneously published in the USA and Canada
by Routledge
711 Third Avenue, New York, NY 10017

Routledge is an imprint of the Taylor & Francis Group, an informa business

British Library Cataloguing in Publication Data
A catalogue record for this book is available from the British Library

Library of Congress Cataloging-in-Publication Data
Marsh, Steve, 1967-
The European Union in the security of Europe : from Cold War to terror war /
Steve Marsh and Wyn Rees.
p. cm.
Includes bibliographical references and index.
1. Security, International--European Union countries. 2. National security--
European Union countries. 3. Security, International--Europe. 4. European
Union countries--Foreign relations. I. Rees, G. Wyn, 1963- II. Title.
JZ6009.E94M37 2011
355'.03304--dc22
2011012959

ISBN13: 978-0-415-34122-6 (hbk)
ISBN13: 978-0-415-34123-3 (pbk)
ISBN13: 978-0-203-80304-2 (ebk)

Typeset in Bembo
by Integra Software Services Pvt. Ltd, Pondicherry, India

Contents

List of Abbreviations   viii

1   Introduction: The nature of security   1
    The end of the Cold War in Europe   3
    Global security concerns   6
    Re-ordering the security agenda   9
    A broader security agenda   11
    The approach of this book   14

2   The EU and internal security   18
    Introduction   18
    The institutionalisation of EU internal security   19
    Illegal immigration and asylum   23
    Organised crime and drug trafficking   26
    Drug trafficking   28
    Transnational terrorism   29
    Counter-terrorism co-operation with the US   32
    Conclusion   34

3   The EU and external security relations   35
    Introduction   35
    History and the shaping of EU external relations   36
    EU external relations: policies and competencies   39
    The European Security Strategy (ESS)   47
    The EU and the European security architecture   52
    Conclusion   57

4   The US, European security and EU–US relations:
    'The indispensable nation'?   59
    Managing the EU–US security relationship   60
    American foreign policy and the emergence of transatlantic strategic
        dissonance   63
    America, European security and the EU   65
    The EU, European security and the US   72
    Conclusion   78

5   Russia, European security and relations with the EU:
    The underprivileged strategic partnership?   80
    From agreement on trade and economic and commercial co-operation to
        common spaces: the architecture of a strategic partnership   81
    Russian foreign policy contours   83
    Russia, European security and the EU   88
    The EU, European security and Russia   92
    Conclusion   99

6   EU enlargement to Central and Eastern Europe   101
    The 'Return to Europe'   101
    Enlargement and hard security   103
    The costs of enlargement for the EU   107
    Diversity and reform within the EU   109
    Reform of the new Members   112
    The risk of exclusion   113
    Future enlargements   115
    Conclusion   117

7   The EU and the Eastern arc of instability: The Western Balkans,
    Eastern Europe and Southern Caucasus   119
    A decade of disaster   120
    Taking stock, re-dividing Europe   123
    The division of Europe: inner Europe   125
    The division of Europe: outer Europe   131
    Conclusion   140

8   The EU and its Southern Mediterranean neighbours   142
    Mediterranean challenges   143
    EU approaches and policies towards the Southern Mediterranean rim   147
    Problems and challenges in EU relations with the Southern
        Mediterranean rim   150
    Conclusion   158

9 Conclusion   160
     Hard times ahead?   *163*

Notes   167
Bibliography   210
Index   238

Abbreviations

ACT	Allied Command Transformation
AFSJ	Area of Freedom, Security and Justice
BMD	Ballistic Missile Defence
BRIC	Brazil, Russia, India and China
CARDS	Community Assistance to Reconstruction, Development and Stabilisation
CCP	Common Commercial Policy
CD	Conference on Disarmament
CDP	Capability Development Plan
CEPOL	European Police College
CEEC	Central and East European Countries
C4ISR	command, control, communications, computer, intelligence, surveillance and reconnaissance
CFE	Conventional Forces in Europe
CFSP	The Common Foreign and Security Policy
CIS	Commonwealth of Independent States
CIVCOM	Committee for the Civilian Aspects of Crisis Management
COREPER	Committee of Permanent Representatives
CSCE	Conference on Security and Co-operation in Europe
COTS	commercial off-the-shelf technology
CSDP	Common Security and Defence Policy
CTC	Counter Terrorism Committee
DTIB	Defence Technology Industrial Base
DTSI	Defence Trade Security Initiative
EBO	Effects-Based Operations
ECHO	European Commission Humanitarian Aid and Civil Protection
ECMM	European Community Monitoring Mission

ECSC	European Coal and Steel Community
EDA	European Defence Agency
EDF	European Development Fund
EDTIB	European Defence Technology and Industrial Base
EEAS	European External Action Service
EFTA	European Free Trade Association
EGF	European Gendarmerie Force
EIB	European Investment Bank
EMCDDA	European Monitoring Centre for Drugs and Drug Addiction
EMAA	Euro-Mediterranean Association Agreement
EMP	Euro-Mediterranean Partnership (AKA the Barcelona Process)
ENP	European Neighbourhood Policy
ENPI	European Neighbourhood and Partnership Instrument
EP	European Parliament
EPC	European Political Cooperation
ESDP	European Security and Defence Policy (now CSDP)
ESS	European Security Strategy
EUBAM	European Union Border Assistance Mission
EUJUSTLEX	EU's Rule of Law Mission for Iraq
EULEX	European Rule of Law mission in Kosovo
EUPOL COPPS	EU Police Mission in the Palestinian Territories
EUROFOR	European Union Force
Eurojust	European Judicial Agency
EUROMARFOR	European Maritime Force
Euromed	Euro-Mediterranean Partnership (formerly the Barcelona Process)
Europol	European Police Office
FDI	Foreign Direct Investment
FPC	Foreign Policy Concept of the Russian Federation
FRIDE	(independent European think tank based in Madrid)
Frontex	European Border Agency
FYROM	Former Yugoslav Republic of Macedonia
GSP	Generalised System of Preferences
GWOT	Global War on Terrorism
IAEA	International Atomic Energy Agency
IBRD	International Bank for Reconstruction and Development
INF	Intermediate-range Nuclear Forces treaty
IPA	Instrument for Pre-accession Assistance
ISAF	International Security Assistance Force
JAP	Joint Action Plan
JHA	Justice and Home Affairs
JLS	Justice, Liberty and Security
KFOR	Kosovo Force (NATO led)
MAD	mutual assured destruction
MAP	Membership Action Plan

MEPP	Middle East Peace Process
MNEPR	Multilateral Nuclear Environmental Programme in Russia
MFN	most favoured nation
NPT	Nuclear Non-Proliferation Treaty
NTA	New Transatlantic Agenda
NVA	former East German army
NSS	National Security Strategy
OBNOVA	Programme for assistance to Bosnia and Herzegovina
OSCE	Organisation for Security and Co-operation in Europe
PCAs	Partnership and Cooperation Agreements
PFP	Partnership for Peace programme
PHARE	Programme of assistance (*Pologne et Hongrie assistance à la reconstruction economique*)
pMS	participating Member States
The Quartet	United Nations, the United States, the European Union, and Russia
The Quint	Britain, Germany, France, Italy and the US
RMA	Revolution in Military Affairs
SAA	Stabilisation and Association Agreement
SALW	small arms and light weapons
SAP	Stabilisation and Association Process
SCO	Shanghai Co-operation Organisation
SEA	Single European Act 1986
SIPRI	Stockholm International Peace Research Institute
SIS	Schengen Information System
TAIEX	Technical Assistance and Information Exchange Instrument
TEU	Treaty of European Union
ToA	Treaty of Amsterdam
TREVI	*Terrorisme, Radicalisme et Violence Internationale*
UMEP	Union for the Mediterranean and Eastern Partnership
UNDCP	United Nations Drug Control Programme
UNFIL	United Nations Interim Force in Lebanon
UNMIK	United Nations Interim Mission in Kosovo
UNPROFOR	United Nations Protection Force
VIS	Visa Information System
VISIT	Visitor and Immigrant Status Indicator Technology
WEU	Western European Union

1

INTRODUCTION

The nature of security

'Security' is an inherently vague and indeterminate concept because it is a state of mind. In essence, it represents a feeling of well-being, an absence of fear.[1] For an individual or group to feel secure, there must be a lack of threat to their core values. A sense of insecurity leads to feelings of anxiety and concern and, at worse, can result in panic and irrationality. Security is therefore a prerequisite before other types of constructive and purposeful behaviour can occur. If there is no sense of security then it is unlikely that there will be confidence about the possession of property, the rule of law or the pursuit of peaceful endeavour. The absence of security can lead to societal paralysis.

Security is a relative rather than an absolute concept. A feeling of complete security is not achievable so each actor has to weigh up how much security is enough to satisfy their needs. The resources that will have to be expended to obtain the desired level of security have to be matched against the risks that each is willing to tolerate. Marginal increases in security may only be available at relatively high cost and an actor will have to balance these costs against other priorities. The extent of the threats that are tolerated will usually reflect the size and power of the actor concerned, although major actors also tend to have correspondingly large and diversified interests that have to be protected.

The process by which an issue becomes a security matter has been the subject of considerable academic study. 'Securitisation' involves raising an issue to a special level of priority, thereby justifying a high level of resources and an urgent response. Buzan, Waever and de Wilde have identified three stages in the securitisation process.[2] The first is the elevation of an issue that is perceived subjectively by a community to represent an existential threat to a referent object. The second stage is a speech act that uses the language of security in order to place a subject into this special category. This speech act is carried out by groups within the community that have both responsibility and authority for ensuring security. The third and final stage in the process is the acceptance of this language by a mass audience, with the result that it is granted legitimacy.

The nature of what is perceived to be at risk will vary according to circumstances. The traditional conception of security conceives of States, and their sovereign independence or survival, being put at risk by the military forces of other States. According to this model, the objective of the state is to preserve its own territorial integrity and autonomy of action. Security is thus understood as the preserve of the state – national security – with the aim of protecting its citizens and its homeland. The state is the sole, legitimate possessor of military forces for the purpose of guarding its domestic space from hostile incursion.

However, this approach fails to appreciate that States themselves can be the causes of insecurity. Military preparedness for defence can be interpreted as potentially hostile acts by neighbouring countries. States can misconstrue these as offensive preparations leading to a security dilemma in which each side seeks to counter the defensive preparations of others.[3] A second dimension is that state repression can deny people the exercise of their rights or deprive them of their liberty. States may even use coercion against their own people.[4] A third dimension is that weak or failing States lack the power to provide security for their own people. State disintegration and the inability to deliver basic social services may contribute to the undermining of the internal security of the state and to spillover security challenges for other States.

This has led to discussion of alternative referent objects for security, other than States. An alternative referent object that has been postulated is societal security.[5] Focusing upon society helps to capture some of the non-military threats that can lead people to feel insecure. Societal security places emphasis upon values and sense of identity, as opposed to just territorial integrity, and these can be threatened by a variety of factors. For example, organised criminal activity puts societal security at risk, whilst at the same time co-existing in a parasitical relationship with the state. Similarly, large-scale immigration can generate feelings of insecurity in host societies that fear a loss both of self-identity and of employment prospects. Efforts to increase societal security can be measured in terms of upholding the rule of law, minimising corruption, maintaining the integrity of institutions such as the judiciary and the police, and preserving a sense of shared identity.

Another choice of referent object has been the security of individuals. Rather than concentrate on the security of the state or the more abstract concept of society, the focus of this approach is upon human beings. It has its origins in the work of the United Nations' Development Programme Report of 1994 that assessed security issues that impact on individuals, such as health and welfare as well as poverty and disease.[6] It also takes into consideration what threatens the well-being of people and draws a distinction between security that involves the threat of violence and a broader, non-military, concept encompassing freedom from want.[7]

This introduction aims to explore how the concept of security has evolved for the European Union in the post-Cold War period and to establish a context for the later empirical chapters in the book. The EU is a unique security actor because it is not a conventional state. Unlike a state, it does not have a central source of authority, nor does it possess traditional coercive apparatus such as armed forces or police. The EU exists at a level above that of its Member States, each of which retains national security policies. Nevertheless, a security role has been bestowed upon the Union by its Members as they have recognised their increasing interdependence and the need for a framework to aggregate their responses. This introduction sets out how the EU has been required to find ways, amidst its own process of development, of making itself capable of responding to a broader and more complex post-Cold War security agenda.

The end of the Cold War in Europe

During the Cold War, Europe was the focal point of superpower military confrontation with the armed forces of two major alliance systems drawn up on each side of the inner German border. The end of that confrontation represented a systemic shift in geopolitics as one part of the bipolar structure effectively imploded. The collapse of the Warsaw Pact in 1990 and the break-up of the Soviet Union in 1991 brought to an end the military stand-off between East and West that had dominated security politics for the last forty-five years. Countries in Central and Eastern Europe asserted their independence from Moscow's control, Russian troops found themselves resident on the soil of a re-united Germany and the balance of military power, that had rested upon the presence of both nuclear and conventional forces, appeared increasingly redundant. The relationship between the United States and Western Europe, hitherto one of European security dependency, now lay open to question. The continent was safer than it had been since the end of World War II with no likelihood of territorial aggression against any West European country. Yet how a new security system would emerge remained a subject of intense speculation.

The East–West balance had revolved around military threats to the survival of States. Paradoxically, the latter part of the 1980s had prepared the stage for a down-playing of the importance of military security. The implications of nuclear deterrence had made clear that no side could profit from recourse to war and had engendered a sense of stalemate. It was the 1987 Intermediate-range Nuclear Force (INF) treaty that unlocked the stand-off between the United States and the Soviet Union and paved the way for a radical change in relations. Its significance lay in three areas. First, the treaty resulted in the removal of a whole category of nuclear weaponry, of short- and medium-range, that was potentially de-stabilising to the delicate balance between the two sides. Second, it facilitated deeper reductions on the Soviet side, thereby challenging the traditional notion that arms control had to have equal impact. Third, the treaty provided for intrusive verification procedures by which teams of observers were allowed to visit military sites and oversee the dismantling of nuclear weapons. This helped to overcome the deep mistrust that had been built up over many decades.

Changes to the conventional military balance, in which Warsaw Pact forces had hitherto enjoyed a preponderance, complemented the reductions undertaken in nuclear weaponry. The Conventional Forces in Europe (CFE) treaty heralded massive reductions in the size of Eastern bloc forces before the treaty itself was overtaken by the collapse of the Warsaw Pact. This change in the level of threat was exploited by West European countries which cut their defence spending and sought to realise a peace dividend. Transformations in the configurations of military forces have been achieved more slowly but the move towards smaller, professional armed forces has been inexorable. For example, in 1995 only five European countries had all-volunteer forces whereas ten years later the number had risen to sixteen.[8]

A crucial issue that sprang from the end of the Cold War was the future of East and West Germany. The treatment of Germany had been at the heart of the original post-war division between the three triumphant allied powers and it had been the focus of confrontation for the next forty-five years. The decision by USSR General Secretary Mikhail Gorbachev to allow the unification of the two halves of Germany was the single most important step in overcoming the Cold War antagonism. It was even agreed that a united Germany would continue to be a Member of NATO; thereby reassuring both former adversaries and allies that it would not be a threat to its neighbours. The former East German army (NVA) was folded into its West German counterpart and the overall size of the Bundeswehr was reduced to 370,000 personnel. The Alliance legitimised the continuation of allied forces on German soil and provided a mechanism for a continued American presence on the continent.

The European Community was well placed to adapt to these changed circumstances in Europe after 1989. Although it had been a civilian power during the Cold War, it had been intimately concerned with the security of its Members. The EC had been created as a peace project with the deliberate intention of rendering the use of force redundant amongst the States of Western Europe. Through the creation of supranational structures and the pooling of sovereignty, the interests of its Members had become so intertwined as to represent a 'Security Community'. According to Deutsch, the EC had become a community in which the interests of all parties were resolved peacefully and competition was channelled through institutional relationships into economic affairs.[9] Amidst the chaos and uncertainty that accompanied the end of the Cold War, the EC represented a source of stability. It symbolised the way in which democratic States had transcended military rivalry among themselves and developed a new form of multi-level governance in Europe.

How the EC would develop as a security actor became one of the leading questions facing the organisation. Through the 1993 Treaty of European Union there was a determination amongst its Members to integrate more closely economically and politically, but the ambitions of a future European Union in security and defence were unclear. It would come to depend partly upon the sorts of threats and security challenges that the EU would have to address. The institutions that the EU would construct in matters of foreign and security policy would in turn help to determine the sort of actor it would become. It would also be influenced by the extent to which the US envisaged playing a continuing leadership role in the security of the continent.

While the EU could engineer the institutional arrangements, it was a harder task to infuse its Members with a common security culture. The EU is, in reality, host to a variety of co-existing strategic cultures. France and the UK, for example, have sought to act as global military powers, projecting military forces to far-flung theatres in support of their national interests.[10] In contrast, a country such as Germany, despite possessing sizeable military forces, has been reluctant to employ its capabilities due to the painful legacy of its actions in the Second World War. There are countries within the EU, such as Ireland, Sweden and Austria, that have long adhered to neutralist positions.[11] This spectrum of approaches is evident in the amount of money that EU Members have been willing to allocate to defence, their involvement in military procurement projects and their levels of participation in major military operations. While it is true to say that the Union has taken steps towards a more collective security culture, and even published a European Security Strategy in 2003,[12] it has nevertheless struggled to achieve rapid progress.

In spite of the fact that there was no overt threat to national territories following the end of the Cold War, military security challenges did not disappear altogether. The EU found itself confronting a new security environment, one in which conflict was actually more likely. This was due to the instability that was left behind after the termination of East–West rivalry. Russian troops were in the process of being returned home during the early years of the 1990s, but there was plenty of opportunity for friction with former Soviet republics that had asserted their independence. Tensions with the Baltic States were especially marked due to the presence of large numbers of Russian nationals, and this led to conflict between Russian forces and Latvia. Relations between Russia and Ukraine were acutely sensitive because of strategic missile sites in Ukraine that were returned to Russia, arms industries on Ukrainian soil and the naval base in the Crimea. In Central and Eastern Europe, there were historical sources of tension between some countries that could have led to conflict. As for the Balkans, there were multi-ethnic States such as Yugoslavia that had been held together artificially. Such States as these were at risk of collapsing into civil and ethnic conflict with major implications for neighbouring countries in Europe.

With the risk of major inter-state war having receded, civil and ethnic conflicts represented the sorts of complex emergencies that were more likely in post-Cold War Europe. Unlike the mass mobilisation wars of the twentieth century, these would be intra-state conflicts with ill-defined causes. Western forces would not find themselves fighting well-defined enemies on a distinct battlefield but rather para-military organisations amidst a conflict in which their countries did not have vital interests at stake.[13] With no immediate threat to their own territories, EU countries would be faced with 'conflicts of choice' rather than necessity. The conflict zones were likely to be situated amidst the civilian population and would involve the deliberate targeting of non-combatants. These conflicts would generate regional instability that could spill over onto the territories of EU Members, and could result in the exodus of large numbers of refugees into Western Europe.

Such conflicts present major challenges for the military forces of EU Members. Having configured themselves for high-intensity warfare during the Cold War era, these new sorts of conflicts call for different types of forces trained in different ways. Intra-state emergencies require forces that can be transported to a war zone far from their own countries. These forces need to be relatively lightly armed and adaptable as they are unlikely to be engaging with the armed services of another state. Most importantly, they must be highly trained and capable of acting in a controlled fashion as they will be operating within a highly charged political environment. Restraint over the use of lethal force is vital if the interventionary force is to be part of the solution to the crisis rather than just one of the protagonists.

It has thus been necessary for European forces to prepare for a broad range of contingencies. They may be called upon to engage in a number of tasks that range across the spectrum of conflict. At one end of the spectrum, a symbolic show of force may be designed to prevent hostilities from breaking out in the first place. At the other end, interventionary forces may be required to engage in war-fighting in order to stop an armed group from achieving its strategic objectives. The purpose may be less the defeat of an adversary and more the cessation of hostilities and the restoration of stability. Alternatively, if protagonists have fought themselves to a point of exhaustion or they have been coerced into a cessation of hostilities, an interventionary force might seek to enforce a peace and police a hard-won agreement. The post-1990 period has presented a broader array of conflict scenarios in which EU forces could be called upon to engage.

Post-conflict societies have usually experienced deep-seated trauma and the arousal of enmities between ethnic communities. Outside interventions in such complex emergencies demand long-term engagement rather than just short-term military action. The task is to help rebuild the societies concerned and prevent a return to violence. The EU has been particularly suited to such tasks,[14] drawing upon its history as a non-military power and the diverse strengths and skills of its Member States. The Union has been at the forefront of efforts to develop a capacity for hybrid operations in which it integrates military and civilian agencies to assist in the reconstruction effort. This demands the integration of financial aid, technical assistance, policing skills, judicial and administrative instruments and the oversight of elections. It also draws upon expertise from civil agencies and non-governmental organisations. Since the Feira European Council in 2000 a Committee for the Civilian Aspects of Crisis Management (CIVCOM) has been formed within the European Council and capability conferences have been convened to provide a range of non-military resources.[15] For example, the European Gendarmerie Force (EGF) based in Vicenza, has been assembled as a quick reaction force for policing duties, in addition to judges and administrators being identified for overseas service.

Global security concerns

One of the by-products of the end of the Cold war has been a perception that the security of Europe was now assured from within and that it was time to transfer the collective attention of the West to issues outside of the continent. This rhetoric has been especially strong from the US who felt that their post-war investment in the security of Europe had achieved its objectives and it was now timely to address a variety of global issues. The US considered that the foremost post-Cold War security challenges were no longer in Europe but in the wider world. These included the threat from nuclear proliferation and States that sought to undermine the Western-led order. The 9/11 terrorist attacks and the continuing instability in the Middle East intensified the perception of American policymakers that the most urgent security threats were extra-European in nature. Leading American voices called for a global partnership in which the transatlantic allies addressed the principal sources of threat to international security.[16]

The EU has been reluctant to acquiesce in this US-led agenda. There has been sufficient instability and conflict in Europe since the end of the Cold War for States to conclude that their own backyard should preoccupy their attention. The need to project stability into Central and Eastern Europe and the objective of preventing spill-over from conflicts, such as those in Bosnia and Kosovo, were the primary considerations. To add to this agenda, there was growing concern about security issues arising from neighbouring States in the Mediterranean. While some countries, such as the UK, shared US priorities, others within the EU felt that they had more than enough problems within their own region.

Other considerations have led to misgivings among EU States about adopting a global security agenda. Conducting operations beyond one's home territory is particularly demanding and the expeditionary capabilities of most Union Members are extremely limited. Such operations impose demands of long-range transportation and re-supply, especially in situations where the involvement is of a protracted nature. All conflicts carry the risk of escalation: that a small intervention may result in being drawn into a larger engagement. While the intervening forces can intend only a short and decisive conflict, the enemy can seek to entrap them and suck them into a long-term campaign. Adversaries may deliberately engage Western countries asymmetrically, using insurgency and terrorist tactics to inflict casualties and sap the will to fight, while avoiding set-piece encounters. Western forces have found themselves unable to bring their military superiority to bear and have been forced to modify their tactics and use precision aerial attacks in order to limit their own losses. Insurgency campaigns can tie down Western forces and undermine the willingness of domestic populations to support the campaign. The counter-insurgency campaign in Afghanistan since 2006, when NATO forces went into the South of the country, is a prime example of this.

Western countries have also struggled with the issue of legitimising their expeditionary operations. The EU in particular has wrestled with questions as to how it can reconcile its desire to act ethically with the need to be able to use military force in circumstances other than the defence of national territory. The Report of the UN's High Level Panel in 2004 recommended five criteria that should determine a state's willingness to resort to conflict. First, the use of force needs to be sanctioned explicitly by the Security Council. Second, the action must be a response to a clearly defined threat. Third, the use of force must be the last resort, after all other options have been exhausted. Fourth, it should have a reasonable chance of success. Finally, only the minimum amount of force should be employed, commensurate with meeting the objectives.[17] This UN Report sought to balance, on the one hand, the reluctance of States to intervene in the domestic affairs of other countries and, on the other, the growing sense within the international community that countries had a moral obligation towards humanitarian intervention when there was a self-evident and massive abuse of human rights. Following on from the horrors of the Rwandan genocide and ethnic cleansing in the Balkans, it was unsatisfactory for countries to stand by and say they were helpless because the principle of state sovereignty precluded their intervention.

The US-led 'War on Terror', resulting from the 9/11 attacks, and the ensuing conflicts in Afghanistan and Iraq increased the pressure upon the EU to confront the evolving global security agenda. The US identified a nexus of security threats that included international terrorism, 'States of concern' and the proliferation of weapons of mass destruction (WMD).[18] The principal US fear was that highly destructive nuclear, chemical or bacteriological weapons could be provided by proliferant States to terrorist groups who might proceed to employ them. It was clear from the case of Iraq that the US was prepared to use force pre-emptively to forestall these dangers and this confronted the EU with the dilemma of whether to support or oppose US policy. In 2003 the Union demonstrated its preparedness to engage with the US agenda of issues when it published its 'EU Strategy against Proliferation of Weapons of Mass Destruction'.[19] This was complemented by the decision of the UK, France and Germany (the 'E-3'), joined by the High Representative for Foreign and Security Policy, to assume a lead role in Western efforts to contain Iran's alleged nuclear weapons programme. In order to try to wean it away from its programme, the E-3 offered Iran trade and investment, supplies of nuclear fuel and possible admission to the World Trade Organisation.[20] Failure to comply risked Iran being reported to the UN Security Council and harsher economic sanctions being applied.[21]

In addition to States of concern, the EU has responded to American calls to address the problem of weak or 'failing' States. These have been defined as either economically very poor or countries that have been undermined by domestic unrest and civil conflict. The result is a chaotic environment with the government unable to provide security for the population and the institutions of the state unable to function. The West has viewed such countries as lawless communities in which nefarious actors can seek sanctuary and conduct their activities.[22] Organised criminals, drugs and arms traffickers and potentially terrorists can exploit such 'ungoverned spaces' and export disorder to wealthy countries in the Northern hemisphere. The EU sought to align policy closer to that of the US through the 2003 European Security Strategy. It acknowledged that waiting for threats to mature before acting could be counterproductive and that the Union needed to possess the capacity for 'early and robust action'.[23]

The EU finds itself part of the peaceful and developed world facing a turbulent and conflict-prone, less developed world. Singer and Wildavsky characterised this as the juxtaposition of zones of peace and conflict.[24] Because of increasing interdependence, the problems of the less developed world risk spilling over into the peaceful half; in the form of refugees fleeing violent conflict and persecution or ethnic conflict that presents Western countries with dilemmas over intervention. The

EU has to face up to these pressures and decide whether it wants to become involved. Its interventions in Congo and Darfur in 2003 and 2005 suggest that it has ambitions in this regard. Yet the fulfilment thus far of tasks at only the lower end of the Petersberg spectrum[25] reinforces an important sense of perspective about the modest capabilities that are available to the EU.

Re-ordering the security agenda

The diminished focus on military issues following the end of the Cold War facilitated a re-ordering of the security agenda. Security issues, other than of a military nature, that had been relegated in importance in the past were now accorded greater significance. This adjusting of the hierarchy of issues also reflected wider changes going on within the international system. These included the effects of globalisation, increasing interdependence between different regions of the world and the diffusion of power to various types of transnational actors.

The contemporary phenomenon of globalisation has revolutionised the degree of interconnectedness among Western democracies. The movement of goods and services between continents, the spread of telecommunications and the world-wide web, cross-border flows of people for work and leisure and the ubiquity of air travel have effectively shrunk the world. This has reduced the significance of borders as obstacles to all forms of human interchange. As part of these processes, the traditional divide between internal and external security has become blurred because there is no longer a clear delineation of state boundaries. The state is penetrated at a variety of levels, its external borders have become highly porous and it finds it difficult to monitor activity that can pass across its frontiers. In the case of the EU, globalisation has been embraced by the abolition of borders between most of its Members and their replacement with a common external frontier.

The dark side of the globalisation process means that illicit commodities and actors can move around with increasing ease, especially within the borderless space of the Union. Some of these challenges are only indirectly security in nature. For example, illegal migrants, asylum seekers and refugees have no malevolent intent towards the countries they seek to enter: their only objective is to obtain safety, a better life and improved economic prospects. Other types of sub-state actors represent a different case. Transnational organised crime groups, people traffickers and drug trafficking organisations pursue their trades across frontiers with the aim of securing huge profits. They conduct a variety of clandestine activities ranging from the smuggling of commodities such as cigarettes, narcotics and small arms, to people who are sold into a form of modern-day slavery. Another category of actors are international terrorist movements. These have become the most high profile examples of transnational security challenges.[26]

EU Member States have, to varying degrees, come to recognise that these new sorts of security challenges lie beyond the capacity of individual States to solve. Unless there is a recognition of their shared vulnerability and a desire to combat these challenges collectively, they will not be effective. Within the Treaty on European Union, the Member States created a third, intergovernmental pillar in the field of Justice and Home Affairs (JHA).[27] This pillar was aimed at addressing these sorts of challenges and accorded the Union novel competences in relation to judicial cooperation, immigration, asylum and border matters that no other international organisation in Europe enjoyed. These powers were shared with Member States as there was a marked reluctance to hand over substantial new areas of responsibility entirely to the EU.

Through the course of the 1990s the EU has come to accept that transnational security challenges cannot be kept out by a hard external border. Instead threats need to be tackled and eradicated in those areas in which they originate if their importation into the Union is to be avoided. The EU realised that it would have to help to shape its external neighbourhood, rather than withdraw behind the walls of a twenty-first century fortress.[28] This thinking has been built into external relations by linking trade, cooperation and association agreements to each third-country's willingness to work with the EU on issues such as illegal migration and transnational crime.

The prospect of organisational enlargement has sharpened the EU's thinking and put pressure on Member States to formulate strategies. The accession of CEECs would move the borders of the Union further to the East and introduced the prospect of organised crime groups from Russia, Ukraine and Chechnya being able to penetrate the Union. A further stimulus arose as a result of EU action in the Balkans and the prospect of States from that region being offered accession to the EU. The conflicts in Bosnia and Kosovo increased the instability and chaos within those territories and made it possible for criminal groups to establish networks from which to perpetrate their activities into the EU. A major example of this was the increase in people and drugs trafficking via the so-called 'Balkan route'.

With regard to States in the Mediterranean, the Union has recognised the dangers of importing insecurity from them in the form of economic migrants, refugees from civil conflicts, people trafficked by criminal gangs and narcotics. The Union has been forced to confront the reality that it must contribute to the economic stability of these countries on its periphery, if it is to avoid dealing with the consequences of their problems. The EU has used its economic power to offer access to the European Single Market and encouraged them to develop patterns of regional economic cooperation amongst themselves. It has complemented these measures with financial and technical assistance on issues such as border security. Furthermore, the EU has extolled the importance of good governance, placing emphasis on the inclusion of human rights provisions, the building of the rule of law and efforts to stamp out corruption.

Jihadist terrorism has presented a very particular form of problem over the last decade. This terrorism has been perpetrated on a global, rather than national, scale and has been targeted against both Western and Arab governments.[29] It is networked in structure, employing the internet to spread its message and it has tried to inflict the maximum number of casualties as a form of communication to its target audience. The threat to the Union derives not only from *jihadis* in places such as Pakistan, Saudi Arabia and Yemen, but home-grown Muslims that have adopted extreme views too.[30] Radicalisation amongst the 13 million Muslims in Europe has been perceived as the foremost danger.[31] Second- or third-generation immigrants have proved to be fertile soil for the violent propaganda disseminated on the internet by al-Qaeda or preaching by extremist clerics in city mosques.

The response adopted by the EU has concentrated upon creating appropriate frameworks for cooperation, based on the belief that only the widest pattern of collaboration can serve to thwart this campaign. The EU has mobilised the judicial and law enforcement agencies of its Member States to work together. It has also taken steps to enhance the security of its external borders and assist its less advanced Members in technologies to police frontiers. Unlike the United States, that has created a new Department of Homeland Security to oversee its domestic counter-terrorism efforts,[32] the EU has pursued its efforts in more of an *ad hoc* fashion in cooperation with the national efforts of its Members.

A broader security agenda

The end of the Cold War marked a broadening of the security agenda to encapsulate issues that had not previously been regarded as security concerns. This approach owed much to a tradition of security thinking that saw violence and under-development as structural processes, integral to patterns of inequality between Western and poorer Southern States. These broader security challenges were largely non-malevolent and indirect in nature, and not the result of hostile state or non-state actors seeking to inflict harm. Such concepts provide an alternative security paradigm that can be discursively constructed to represent the Union as providing added value to contemporaneous national security discourses.

The EU has regarded itself as well-equipped to respond to broader non-military security problems. The EU has been drawn to concepts that side-step the traditional attention paid to state security because of its own nature as a non-state actor and because such ideas appeal to the consensual values of the Union. In the words of Cottey, 'The EU's unique combination of ... competences means that it operates across the entire spectrum of issues that constitute the wider security agenda'.[33] It has been able to draw upon its own strengths in soft security instruments rather than expose its limitations and constraints in relation to hard security.[34] Whilst the Union's powers of compellence have been difficult to mobilise, it has been able to harness its soft power. Prior to the Treaty of Lisbon its soft power instruments were dispersed across its three pillar structure, making it necessary to conduct cross-pillar coordination in order to act effectively.

The EU has striven to integrate its non-military instruments into a wider strategy aimed at conflict management. Kirchner and Sperling characterise this as security policies of 'prevention' and 'assurance'.[35] These include diplomatic, trade and aid instruments that the Union is prepared to employ in an active way to try to arrest the development of regional conflicts, promote cooperation between States amidst periods of tension and target the sources of poverty that could lead to political and economic instability. The European Security Strategy described preventive engagement in regional conflicts as one of the principal security objectives of the Union.[36]

The former EU High Representative, Javier Solana, commissioned a study on the relevance of human security chaired by Professor Mary Kaldor of the London School of Economics that attempted to delineate a role for the EU in this debate. The resulting report was entitled 'A Human Security Doctrine for Europe'.[37] It attempted to sketch out how the use of force could be made compatible with concepts of human security thinking. It argued that EU action should be conditional upon UN authority, multilateral action by as large a group of States as possible and the use of legal instruments. The Report advocated that the Union create a 'Human Security Response Force' of divisional size involving an integration of civilian and military staff capable of rapid deployment to a crisis zone. This force was envisaged as having a role somewhere between the concepts of peacekeeping and military intervention.[38]

There has been no consensus within the EU on adopting human security as the primary referent for security. While the positivism inherent in this approach is a welcome addition to security thinking and foregrounds important issues for a globalizing world, its claims to offer Europe an enduring and dynamic organizing frame for security action are overstated.[39] Human security is too nebulous and too far removed from first order national interests to serve as an overarching organisational frame for EU policy and capability development. Moreover, if overtly streamed throughout the EU's external relations it risks exposing the EU on at least three counts. First, joining universal values to the protection of the individual as the referent of security dramatically expands the expectations placed upon EU action. Second, human security risks appropriation by Member States within their discourses of (de)legitimation for national security (in)actions. It could easily become a political leitmotif akin to the ubiquitous 'force for good' and the increasingly evident 'responsibility' in EU parlance,[40] and a justification for a wide range of divergent positions and views.[41] Furthermore, the strong normative base of human security might sit comfortably with European publics and serve the interests of the EU as a supranational entity. But whenever not complementary, EU national security interests will tend to trump those of human security. Human security studies also thus far offer too little practical guidance about what to do when regimes do not share 'Western' views of the balance between national and human security.

Acknowledging that insecurity can be intimately related to poverty and disease has been a major factor in the EU's conception of a broadening security agenda.[42] The European Security Strategy notes that extreme economic deprivation can lead people to leave their native countries in search of better economic prospects and can foment radicalism that results in recruitment to terrorist organisations. Boatloads of economic migrants arriving in Southern Italy, Malta and the Canary Islands has brought home to Brussels the need to try to tackle some of these problems at source, as well as coordinate Europe-wide action. Problems of poverty are compounded by the spread of infectious diseases such as HIV/AIDS, malaria and tuberculosis.[43] They represent threats to the health of European countries because of the speed of modern communications. This threat was exemplified by the spread of the swine flu pandemic from Mexico in 2009. It is further compounded by the fear that terrorist groups may seek to cultivate and release pathogens as a form of 'bio-violence'.[44]

Responding to that agenda by attempting to alleviate mass poverty and disease, the EU has become the world's largest provider of aid. It has accepted that security and development are mutually interdependent: the latter cannot proceed without the former. The EU has focused its assistance programmes and favourable terms of trade on a group of African, Caribbean and Pacific States (ACP). It has sought to stimulate their exports by providing them with duty-free access to the internal market.[45] However, critics have argued that the EU's relative generosity in aid is undermined by other aspects of its protectionist policies on trade and particularly in relation to agricultural imports and the Common Agricultural Policy.[46]

Another feature of the broader security agenda is the action of the EU in relation to the environmental problem of global warming through the burning of fossil fuels. The resulting build up in the atmosphere of carbon dioxide and methane presents major concerns in terms of its impact on global weather patterns, the prospect of wide-scale flooding and potential desertification. Thomas Homer-Dixon played a leading role in identifying the possible linkage between environmental decline and political conflict[47] and the European Security Strategy picked up on this theme of climate change as a security threat. According to Paterson, the EU 'is at the forefront of driving forward a multilateral process within the UN system'.[48] The EU adopted ambitious reduction targets in carbon dioxide emissions under the Kyoto Protocol, despite the US treating it as a flawed agreement, and led efforts to ensure its implementation. The EU has proceeded to press for world-wide binding cuts under the December 1999 Copenhagen negotiations and took a major role in ensuring that the US was fully involved.

Energy and resource insecurity are the last of the major issues that involve significant non-military challenges. The oil crisis of 1973–74 first focused attention on the problem of fossil fuels as a finite resource, and increasing demand and competition for raw materials and fresh water have raised these matters into strategic concerns. Much of the world's reserves of oil reside in unstable parts of the Middle East, whilst increasing population is resulting in disputes over drawing rights in rivers and lakes. As well as being at risk of spill-over from conflicts over resource scarcities among neighbouring States, West European countries have increased their own dependency on supplies of Russian natural gas. This energy source has also proved to be vulnerable to disruption due to political disagreements between Russia and Soviet successor States over pipe supply lines. Since 2006, disputes between Ukraine and Russia have resulted in periodic interference in supplies of gas to EU States and this escalated to a new level in January 2009 when Moscow ordered the cutting off of gas supplies that transited through Ukrainian pipelines to the West. Analysts have warned that the dependency of EU States on Russian supplies, currently 25% of their total gas, accords the latter highly significant political leverage.[49]

The broadening of the security agenda in this way has helped the EU to capture, in its thinking, the variety of threats to human well-being and the implications that these can have for its Member States. The risk from the Union's point of view is overburdening itself with ambitions that it cannot fulfil. In the words of Terriff *et al* 'Broadening the concept of security … especially to include threats to individuals, permits inclusion of virtually anything that affects individuals adversely'.[50] Poverty and disease are fundamental threats to individuals throughout the less developed world, but alleviating these problems is likely to be beyond the capacity of the EU to deliver. This re-emphasises questions of resources and political will that already prove deeply problematic within less expansive concepts and puts Union credibility on the line in the likely event that rhetorical promises outstrip deliverables.

The approach of this book

It is in this context of geo-strategic change and reconceptualisations of security that the following chapters of this book seek to trace out how the EU has pursued its security interests within Europe and slowly become one of the region's key security actors. The book does not seek to theorise the EU as a security actor or to offer prescriptions for its development. There is an already more than ample literature that questions what type of power the EU is, seeks to characterise its actions within international relations and debates what it should or should not do in the future. For the same reason this book neither confines itself to a single external relations policy area such as CFSP (Common Foreign and Security Policy) nor examines in detail key questions internal to the EU, such as its organisational structure and questions of legitimacy and accountability. Rather, the book offers an empirical examination of what the EU has done within European security since the Cold War and the security challenges it currently faces.

The book begins with chapters on the Union's approaches to external and internal security. Though these are presented separately, the objective is to demonstrate how the changing nature of security and the Union's own security ambitions have together necessitated increasing coordination across different policy domains, legal competencies and procedures. Deepening 'intermesticity' has meant that internal security measures have become a key element of external security.

The chapter on external security surveys the instruments that the Union has at its disposal. It argues that the EU has developed as only a modest military power and that important constraints still exist, principally because its Member States are unwilling for it to do more. Nonetheless, the EU uses an array of other instruments to exert influence, ranging from trade and aid to democracy promotion. These other factors must be taken into account when assessing the influence that the Union is capable of exerting within European security. The complementing chapter on internal security charts how the EU has developed a substantive and increasingly important set of security competences. It focuses on how the key security challenges have shaped the evolution of EU policies within the 'Third Pillar'. These challenges of illegal immigration, organised crime and international terrorism have led the Member States to seek new ways of cooperating and have given birth to an array of important new EU internal security agencies.

The next two chapters focus on the US and Russia within European security and their respective security relations with the EU. The underlying premise is that these two countries have been dominant in creating a regional framework within which

EU security policy towards Europe has been developed. They remain pivotal in helping determine EU security policies and their relative effectiveness. The chapter on the US elaborates how post-Cold War American administrations have progressively de-prioritised the security commitment to the European continent, while concurrently calling upon EU allies to contribute more globally. This has destabilised the traditional transatlantic bargain and led to increasing frictions in the US–EU relationship. Transatlantic tensions reached their nadir during the 2003 War against Iraq. Though the two sides still have important interests in common, their different priorities have created significant difficulties for the EU between its Member States and within European security, especially vis-à-vis Russia and the Eastern European periphery.

The chapter on Russia argues that its relationship with the EU is vital within European security but is also one over which the Union seems less and less able to exert decisive influence. The Union has pledged a strategic partnership with Russia but the two parties have very different interpretations of what this entails. Moscow prioritises Washington in the security domain and has been both scornful of the EU's preoccupation with ethical issues and relatively disinterested in the soft security instruments that it has sought to wield. Moreover, Russia's resurgence since 2000 has created new divisions. A key normative fault line has emerged between the EU as a post-Westphalian power and Russia as the region's leading endogenous traditional sovereign state. Traditional geo-politics and geo-economics have also created tensions between Russia and the EU, and within the EU, over spheres of influence and resources, especially energy.

The next three chapters examine in detail the EU's security engagement with its European near abroad, itself a shifting constellation of States as the Union has undergone successive enlargements and has committed itself to still more. The chapter on EU enlargement contrasts markedly with that on Russia. Here the EU is shown to have exerted a powerful influence over neighbouring States despite its not being able to offer the hard security guarantees that have been the preserve of NATO. The EU's success in modelling its immediate near abroad in the aftermath of the Cold War owes much to a combination of the incentivisation for reform provided by the lure of accession and the positive desire of would-be EU Members to adopt the norms and regulations of the Union as a way of achieving economic and political renewal in the wake of communist rule. However, enlargements to the CEECs also brought problems and controversies. The process of enlargement has led the EU to consider reforms to its decision-making and institutional structures in order to avoid damage to its own internal processes. The 2007 enlargement was clearly premature and has contributed both to enlargement fatigue and to wider fears about the solidarity of an increasingly diverse Union, concerns heightened still further by the Greek-induced euro crisis in 2009–10.

The chapter on EU relations with the Balkans and Eastern Europe illustrates how the Union has emerged from a baptism of fire, as Yugoslavia collapsed, to a point where it has become a key actor within European security. At the same time immense challenges still remain in these regions and the EU seems both unsure of itself and of its key potential partners, the US and Russia. The Union's enlargement fatigue and failure to define the outer limits of what it regards as Europe – and therefore potential membership of the EU – is a key problem in setting the expectational and practical environments not only of Balkan countries but also of strategically important States such as Ukraine. Concomitantly, as the Union expands its European influence and Russia reasserts its own, so there emerges a highly sensitive zone between Europe's two leading endogenous powers. The US adds a further complicating factor. On the one hand America antagonises Moscow through measures such as missile defence, albeit soft-pedalled by the Obama administration, and by seeking to bring the European periphery into Euro-Atlantic fora. On the other, Obama's anxiety to reset US–Russia relations and his nuclear arms reduction treaty with President Medvedev illustrate Washington's continuing interest in Russia as a security partner and its willingness to make bilateral security arrangements with the Kremlin that, reminiscent of the Cold War, affect but do not include the EU.

Finally, the chapter on the Mediterranean argues that this region receives relatively little popular attention but actually presents some of the foremost security challenges to the EU. These include nuclear proliferation, radicalisation, human migration and energy supply. The EU has responded with a variety of tools and programmes but there is very limited evidence of real progress. This is in part attributable to spillback from the US-led military intervention in Iraq, the Palestine issue and Iran's regional ambitions. However, it is also the case that the dialogue across the North–South divide between the EU and the Mediterranean rim States has been a dialogue of the deaf, with the EU approaching these countries increasingly as security problems. Moreover, the EU has struggled to find both an effective policy mix in dealing with such a diverse collection of States and security challenges and to maintain sustained political commitment behind its Mediterranean policies.

The conclusion pulls together the detailed empirical work within the chapters in the form of three main arguments. The first of these is that the importance of the EU as a security actor within Europe is growing. The EU's Member States have come to recognise that the changed military agenda, the broadened nature of security and an ongoing global redistribution of power demand that they take more coordinated action at the Union level. Acting individually, even the larger States cannot hope to address effectively the plethora of issues that they confront. Many of the instruments, such as military forces, remain under national control – there is no prospect, for example, of a 'European Army' coming into existence. Yet the policies that involve the deployment of these instruments are increasingly being hammered out and coordinated at the EU level. Though CFSP and ESDP (now CSDP) often attract most attention in the context of EU security development, it is arguably the Justice, Liberty and Security portfolio that has witnessed the greatest growth over the past decade and has come to feature increasingly in the EU's external security efforts.

The second argument is that the Union's holistic view of security has meant that it has sought to use its full traditional range of security instruments, including trade and aid. However, because the relationship between the military and non-military security agendas has become more difficult to separate, this holistic view of security has also necessitated that the EU embrace hard security provision. Such commitments were made by assuming responsibility for the Petersberg tasks in the Amsterdam Treaty and the subsequent creation of the European Security and Defence Policy has seen the EU begin to develop the necessary military capabilities to match them. The EU has now become a leader in hybrid forms of conflict prevention and post-conflict reconstruction where it is able to draw upon the full spectrum of capabilities. In the recent past, this has elicited criticism from countries such as the United States that has negatively compared EU actions to America's more muscular military interventions. Yet experiences in the post-war insurgency in Iraq and subsequently in Afghanistan illustrate that this sort of hybrid approach can be extremely relevant.

The final argument is that the EU is entering a new and more difficult phase as a security actor within Europe, and beyond. Europe's place in the world is being re-conceptualised. The US and Russia significantly affect the security framework of Europe and the EU in terms both of its development and its effectiveness. The US now views Europe as a base for power projection into the Middle Eastern and Asian theatres, not as a security priority in its own right beyond preserving NATO. Russia views it as a key element of its wider resurgence and has staked a claim to a European sphere of influence that the EU explicitly rejects. The result is cross-cutting pressures and influences affecting European security and the Union. Within the EU itself there is agreement neither on the external borders of Europe, nor on the level and range of security commitment outside of the continent necessary to safeguard its internal security. In the meantime, enlargements, complete and promised, have delivered to the EU a near abroad infinitely more difficult and challenging than that which it faced in 1989 – one that the Union may be underpowered to deal with regardless of its economic weight and security capability development. The Union's primary transformative tool, enlargement, is of fading utility. Many of the States now bordering, or set to border, the Union do not harbour membership ambitions and have values and political systems very different from the EU's. Working across normative divides in a deeply troubled neighbourhood demands a range of policies, tools and resources and sustained political will. The empirical work in this book suggests that an EU comprising so many sovereign Member States, preoccupied with internal reform and still lacking a strong strategic culture, will find these assets difficult to provide and will struggle to develop new foundations for security cooperation in its new near abroad with the US and Russia.

2

THE EU AND INTERNAL SECURITY

Introduction

The end of the Cold War heralded a changed international security environment. The military security challenges that had dominated East–West relations faded, although they left a variety of residual issues in their wake. As a 'civilian power' during the Cold War, the European Community had played only a supporting role to NATO and the United States. With the collapse of the Warsaw Pact, the newly created EU was eager to ensure its relevance to the sorts of security issues that were emerging in Europe. These issues were largely non-military in nature and included threats from organised crime and drug trafficking, transnational terrorism and illegal immigration. In the face of such threats, the Union's unique character and breadth of competences meant that it would likely have a special role to play. In the Maastricht Treaty the EU developed a third pillar of intergovernmental co-operation in Justice and Home Affairs (JHA, later re-named Justice, Liberty and Security, JLS) which focused on internal security issues.

Although these emerging security challenges did not present an existing threat to the survival of European countries, they represented complex problems for two reasons. First, some threats were derived externally whilst others were indigenous in nature. For example, organised criminal activity already existed in the territories of EU Members but was likely to be exacerbated by criminal activity penetrating from outside as countries in Central Europe undertook the disorientating process of transiting to market economies and democratic control. Similarly, terrorism could be perpetrated by groups within Member States or could occur from outside. This served to blur the traditional distinction between internal and external security. In the Treaty of Amsterdam (ToA) the EU established an 'Area of Freedom, Security and Justice' (AFSJ) on the assumption that it could keep transnational security challenges outside the territory of the Union. But the process of EU enlargement and the

increasing porosity of borders led to the realisation that the Union would be vulnerable to importing the domestic security problems of its neighbours. In other
words, there was recognition of an external dimension to internal security matters.
The EU came to accept that it would have to play a role in tackling and eradicating
sources of insecurity amongst those countries that were seeking to gain accession, as
well as among States in its wider neighbourhood. This could be most efficiently
achieved if the EU were able to export its internal security norms and values to
surrounding countries. This became one of the Union's key objectives.

Second, these threats required a multilevel response, drawing upon the competences of both the Member States and the EU. It would be necessary for national and
EU-level instruments to be coordinated together. In practice, however, whilst
countries have acknowledged a role for the Union in addressing internal security
problems, they have contested the extent of its involvement. This ambivalence has
been reflected in the degree of sovereign powers that have been ceded to the EU.
For example, operational powers to arrest and prosecute criminals, policing and
intelligence agencies remain in the hands of national authorities. In order for the
EU to be granted competences in internal security matters, it has needed to demonstrate that it can 'add value' above and beyond the activities of its Members. This it
has sought to do by helping to generate a collective effort and drawing upon its full
range of legal, financial and developmental instruments. The EU has argued that its
Members share vulnerabilities to security threats and that only by acting together can
they tackle these problems effectively.

This chapter will investigate the pressures that have driven the development of the
EU's internal security agenda. It will examine initially how the internal security
portfolio became institutionalised within the EU, paying particular attention to
achievements that resulted from treaty agreements. It proceeds to investigate how the
principal security challenges of illegal immigration and asylum, organised crime and
drug trafficking, and international terrorism have shaped JHA policies and turned this
into one of the most dynamic policy fields within the Union. It seeks to demonstrate
how a delicate balance has been struck between enhancing the range of activities of
the EU while preserving many of the powers of national governments.

The institutionalisation of EU internal security

Co-operation in internal security matters amongst West European countries prior to
1991 was modest. There was the fundamental obstacle that European States had
evolved with separate civil and common law traditions, different judicial systems and
categories of crimes as well as contrasting policing systems.[1] Examples include the
English common law versus the Roman civil law traditions; the adversarial versus the
inquisitorial judicial systems and the decentralised, federal and *gendamerie* structures of
policing among various European countries. These barriers to co-operation were
exacerbated by contrasting experiences of internal security problems. For example,
organised crime was traditionally a much bigger problem in Central and Southern Italy
than in most North European countries. Illegal immigration has impacted unevenly

across the continent with countries in the South more vulnerable to the problem than States in the North. Terrorism was also, historically, a national phenomenon with countries like the United Kingdom and Spain struggling against terrorist movements that had little impact upon other European States.

An early attempt at internal security co-operation led to the creation of the TREVI (*Terrorisme, Radicalisme et Violence Internationale*) forum in 1975. It arose principally as a result of the Arab–Israeli conflict, with Palestinian terrorism occurring across international borders. TREVI provided European Interior Ministers with a framework in which to share information on terrorism issues and it comprised two working groups, one on terrorism and the other on public order issues. TREVI remained a strictly intergovernmental arrangement, outside the framework of the European Community, and as such illustrated the limited incentive for European countries to collaborate on internal security matters. Nevertheless, its utility was recognised and in 1985 its remit was extended by the addition of a third working group focused on organised crime and drug trafficking. TREVI became the forerunner for much of the EU's subsequent internal security co-operation.[2]

The other building block that helped to facilitate internal security co-operation was the 1985 Schengen Agreement, between France, Germany, the Netherlands, Belgium and Luxembourg. Schengen dismantled the internal borders between these countries whilst simultaneously erecting a common external border. Like TREVI it was undertaken outside the ambit of the European Community, but it was later folded into the EU as part of the ToA.[3] Not only did Schengen foster a sense of shared vulnerability to internal threats, but it created a series of compensatory measures that incentivised future co-operation on border security and related issues. Measures relating to immigration, border controls and illegal drugs reflected the fear that illicit goods, services and migrants would be able to circulate freely within the EU space once the common external frontier was breached.

In the 1993 Treaty on European Union (TEU/Maastricht), the territory of the Member States was declared a common internal security space and the JHA pillar was formed. A working group dealing with international organised crime and drug trafficking was established within the powerful K-4 coordinating committee framework.[4] Despite this important symbolic step forward, the Member States were only prepared to countenance the provision of weak, non-legally binding instruments – namely, 'Common Positions', 'Conventions' and 'Joint Actions'. An additional source of constraint was that the European Commission was accorded only a limited right of initiative. These limitations reflected the fact that there was little appetite among States, such as the UK and Denmark, for ambitious EU competences over internal security. While this policy field had been drawn within the ambit of the integration process, it represented more of a potential, rather than a well developed, policy domain.

A lack of political will combined with the weak instruments embodied within the Maastricht Treaty helps to explain the slow development of the JHA portfolio in the early 1990s. This contrasted with the perception of growing security threats facing all EU Members. For example, ethnic cleansing in the conflict in former Yugoslavia resulted in large-scale refugee movements into Western Europe with Germany in particular experiencing an enormous increase in asylum applications from people fleeing the war. Amid the dislocation that accompanied the violence in the Balkans, organised crime groups in Albania, Serbia and Montenegro seized upon the opportunity to expand their activities. Added to this, the EU was considering enlarging its membership to Central and East European countries (CEECs). This raised the prospect that criminal organisations kept at bay by the hard external border of Schengen might gain access to the territory of the Union. Events both inside and outside the Union were encouraging the deepening of its internal security competences.

In order to ensure a coherent policy response to this range of challenges, the EU needed to coordinate the use of its instruments across all three Pillars, in what one European Commission insider has described as a 'Machiavellian institutional game'.[5] For instance, whilst EU drug policy resided within the Third Pillar, many of the counter drug-trafficking instruments – such as trade competences over precursor chemicals – existed within the First Pillar. Similarly, counter-terrorism was divided between the Second and Third Pillars with some areas of EU competence, such as over air transport policy, in the First Pillar. This presented very real difficulties due to the fact that decision-making processes and financing arrangements were different in all three Pillars. Problems were compounded by the slow pace at which the capacity for cross-pillar coordination developed.[6] Marrying up the machinery for external affairs and internal security was especially difficult due to the innovative nature of the Third Pillar domain.

The ToA signalled a step level change in the EU's internal security competences. The Treaty brought to an end the purely intergovernmental nature of JHA by 'communitarising' the fields of asylum, border and immigration policy. Henceforth the Member States were committed to developing collective policies, based on a recognition of shared interests. Asylum, border and immigration matters were removed from former Title VI, TEU and placed in the First Pillar, under a new Title IV, with the result that Community instruments as well as processes for decision-making could be applied after a transitional period. Certain intergovernmental features were retained in Title IV, such as a shared right of initiative between the European Commission and the Member States as well as limited powers for the European Parliament.

But this move towards communitarisation did not extend to all issues in the JHA domain. Policing and criminal justice co-operation were regarded by some countries as too sensitive to be included in the First Pillar because they impacted directly on national sovereignty. These issues were preserved in the intergovernmental Title VI, TEU, in which decisions had to be taken by unanimity. A new committee was given oversight of policing and judicial co-operation, the Article 36 Committee, and replaced the K-4 Committee.

The Treaty of Amsterdam heralded the creation of a single security space, the AFSJ, and asserted the aim of, 'provid(ing) citizens with a high level of safety'.[7] A Multidisciplinary Group on Organised Crime was created to drive forward this important policy area. The Schengen Convention was incorporated within the treaty, and the UK, Ireland and Denmark were given leave to opt out. The incorporation of the Schengen *acquis* endorsed the connection between the principle of freedom of movement and the need for additional security measures. The unlawful entry of migrants into the AFSJ was thereby linked with the threat of activities perpetrated by cross-border criminal gangs and the smuggling of illegal drugs.

A special European Council meeting in 1999 at Tampere, sought to translate the newfound momentum in JHA matters into a workable programme of action.[8] It acknowledged the importance of the external dimension of internal security and stated as one of its goals the creation of 'stronger external relations in the field of JHA'.[9] This was seen to have two facets. The first was getting neighbouring countries to assist in achieving the EU's internal security objectives. An integral part of this was the Union's willingness to help countries improve their domestic security situations by drawing up legislation, providing technical assistance and seconding staff. Rather than trying to harmonize criminal law across all countries, the Union agreed to a process of mutual recognition and the approximation of legal codes. Transposing JHA norms and practices to other countries was seen as having a direct benefit for the EU in terms of stiffening the internal security measures of its neighbours and drawing them closer to its model of security.

The second facet was recognising a JHA agenda within EU external action. Experience drawn from the conflicts in Bosnia and Kosovo, and subsequently in European Security and Defence Policy (ESDP) operations after 1999, illustrated that JHA issues were often some of the biggest challenges in post-conflict situations. Upholding the rule of law, creating viable police and judicial agencies and combating organised criminal activity, were prerequisites to promoting good governance in war-torn societies. Failure to address these problems could result in them festering and growing to the point where they spilled over and impacted on the security of EU Members. The Union went on to develop dedicated tools for this purpose. In its Civilian Crisis Management capacity, a European Gendarmerie Force was established for rapid intervention into crisis zones, as well as judicial and administrative personnel that can contribute towards the restoration of a functioning society.[10]

The Tampere European Council began a four-year policy framework whose principal focus was the development of asylum and migration policy. It envisaged common rules on the entry of immigrants into EU countries, standardised methods for assessing rights of residence and the granting of asylum status, as well as common procedures for the removal and return of those with no right to remain.[11] Tampere also initiated steps towards the goal of a genuine area of justice for the EU, based on the acknowledgement that the Union has tended to be preoccupied with enhancing security to the detriment of the rights and freedoms of its citizens. According to the Presidency Conclusions, 'The enjoyment of freedom requires a genuine area of justice, where people can approach courts and authorities in any Member State as easily as in their own. Criminals must find no ways of exploiting differences in the judicial systems of Member States'.[12] To this end there were efforts to achieve the mutual recognition of judicial decisions among EU Members.

The Hague programme of 2004 superseded the Tampere policy framework.[13] The Dutch Presidency played a central role in shaping the Hague programme and concentrated on implementing the policies that had been agreed, such as in immigration and asylum, rather than initiating new ones. The Hague programme was also targeted at counter-terrorism, in light of the attacks that took place in Madrid in March 2004 and subsequently in London in July 2005. One of the objectives became to improve the sharing of law enforcement information between the police forces of the Member States. Instead of a whole series of bilateral agreements between European countries, the 'principle of availability' created the expectation that information would be shared where possible between the police forces of Member States.[14] This principle was embodied in the 2005 Treaty of Prum that was subsequently absorbed into the Union.

The Lisbon Treaty, which came into force in December 2009 after a long and convoluted process, took forward many of the ideas formulated in the failed Constitutional Treaty. Of particular importance was the ending of the traditional Pillar structure of the Union that had artificially separated EU competences. It also extended Qualified Majority Voting to JLS, including police co-operation and criminal policy, which had previously remained intergovernmental in nature. Furthermore, the Lisbon Treaty accorded a right of initiative to the European Commission, co-decision powers to the European Parliament and widened the scope of the European Court of Justice.[15] Internal security provisions were made one of the priority areas of the Lisbon Treaty with the objective of creating a single internal security strategy for the whole Union.[16]

Illegal immigration and asylum

Migration is sometimes regarded as one of the unfortunate by-products of globalisation: increased economic connectedness and a greater ease of travel has led people to seek better prospects in other countries. Its significance has been increased by the fact that it has become linked to a number of ills. The influx of immigrants is believed to put at risk perceptions of identity and a sense of safety within the host society.[17] Economically disadvantaged sections of the population in European States fear for the loss of social housing and employment opportunities. This has stimulated a powerful debate in many EU countries and contributed to the rise of fiercely anti-immigrant political parties in the UK, France, the Netherlands and Italy.

Some authors have resisted attempts to 'securitise' the issue of migration. Kirchner and Sperling argue that, 'While uncontrolled or illegal migration may pose a vexing social problem, it only presents a security challenge to the extent that either side aids the operation or consolidation of criminal organisations.'[18] This linkage of the problem to crime may occur in a number of ways. Because illegal migrants do not possess the right to work, they are often forced to work in the illicit economy. Those individuals who have been transported to the West by human traffickers may be forced to pay off their debts by criminal activities. Furthermore, migration has even been linked in the security discourse to terrorism out of fear that would-be *jihadists* could infiltrate European countries prior to conducting attacks.

The pressures resulting from the movement of people into Europe have impacted unevenly across the territories of the Member States and the EU has been at the heart of efforts to share the burdens of immigration and asylum more equitably. This led the European Commission to argue for the creation of a Common European Asylum System with agreed standards and mechanisms for processing asylum applications and a European Refugee Fund for use in crises.[19] In the aftermath of the Cold War, the expected influx of people from Central and East European countries did not materialise. Instead, legal migration followed the accession of ten new countries in May 2004. Most EU countries imposed a minimum period before they would allow labour market migration but the UK and Ireland offered the right to work in their countries immediately. Illegal immigration has tended to weigh most heavily on Southern EU States, such as Spain and Italy, who have been particularly badly affected from two migration routes: one that comes from North Africa across the Straits of Gibraltar and the other from the Balkans into Southern Italy. Asylum and immigration pressures have tended to feed upon the weakest link in the Union's external border and in recent years, the biggest stress has arisen from migrants entering territories such as Malta, the Canary Islands and Greece.[20] Once inside the Union, migrants can move relatively easily between the territories of the Member States.

Many of the EU's efforts have been invested in trying to deal with the illegal migration and asylum problems before migrants arrive at its borders. The EU has attempted to get States, of both origin and transit, to adopt remedial action within their own domestic contexts. Boswell has described this as illustrative of the Union's 'externalization of control'.[21] The Union has sought to promote democracy, human rights and economic development among its neighbours in order to lessen the push factors that can lead people to seek a better life in Europe. It has also pressured third countries to tighten their border controls, providing them with financial and technological assistance, so that they can prevent potential migrants from transiting their territory *en route* to the EU.

In the case of the CEECs and States in the Western Balkans, the EU has enjoyed considerable leverage over their policies.[22] Conditionality in relation to the JHA *acquis* was imposed upon the accession States from the time of the Copenhagen European Council in 1993.[23] This amounted to a significant burden because it complicated their border arrangements with adjacent countries and because JHA policy itself was in a process of dynamic evolution. Two evaluation mechanisms were initiated to monitor the adherence by accession States to the strictures of JHA: one was a 'collective evaluation' process by the Council and the other was carried out by the Commission. Even after accession, the EU imposed transition arrangements on the new Members so that they were not granted all of the benefits of the existing Members immediately. For example, the new entrants in 2004 had to wait for a period of three years before they were admitted to the Schengen open borders arrangements.[24]

The 2002 Seville European Council led to a 'Comprehensive Plan to Combat Illegal Immigration and Trafficking of Human Beings in the European Union'. It asserted that co-operation in the area of illegal immigration should henceforth be at the centre of EU relations with third countries.[25] All agreements with such countries had to stipulate that failed asylum seekers could be returned to the state of origin or transit. Those States negotiating 'Stabilisation and Association Agreements', such as the Former Yugoslav Republic of Macedonia (FYROM), Croatia and Albania, were all expected to sign readmission agreements with the EU. Similarly, Community Assistance to Reconstruction, Development and Stabilisation (CARDS) funding for countries in the Balkans was gradually focused on Justice and Home Affairs issues.

The bigger challenge for the Union, however, has been to obtain compliance with its policies on illegal immigration and asylum from countries with no accession perspective. Russia has had no chance of membership in the short to medium term, while European Neighbourhood Policy (ENP) countries have been offered an enhanced relationship with the Union that falls short of membership.[26] The EU has possessed relatively little to offer these countries in return for their implementing measures that would improve the Union's security. North African countries have tended to view the Union as pursuing policies at their expense. Countries with their own demographic and economic problems have been reluctant to accede to EU demands which they regard as motivated by European self-interest, unless they are accompanied by substantial developmental assistance.

The EU has found it necessary to mix incentives with threats of punishment in order to obtain a satisfactory degree of co-operation. On the negative side of the equation, it has embedded readmission agreements in its trade policies with third countries. These require countries to accept the return of their own illegal migrants as well as individuals who have transited across their territory.[27] Readmission agreements have been concluded with countries ranging from Bosnia-Herzegovina, Russia and Ukraine to Macao and Sri Lanka. The Union has also designated certain States as 'Safe Third Countries' from whom all asylum applications will be considered unfounded. Safe Third Countries are those whose human rights records are considered to be free from large-scale abuse, thereby facilitating the swift repatriation of their own nationals.

On the positive side, the EU has adopted a 'Global Approach to Migration' that accepts the need for a comprehensive strategy.[28] It has drawn up Action Plans with ENP countries and has 'recognise(d) that partnerships with third countries are necessary to assist them in their efforts to improve their capacity for migration management and refugee protection'.[29] Trade agreements, technical assistance with border management, the secondment of officials and advice on legislative programmes have all been put forward. In addition, the European Commission has approved the liberalisation of European travel visas for nationals from States that cooperate actively with Union policies.[30]

The EU has mobilised many of its own internal instruments to crack down on illegal immigration. It has enhanced the databases that it makes available to border protection authorities and law enforcement officials and sought to build interoperability between them. For example, the original Schengen Information System (SIS) of 1995 stored criminal records and the applications of asylum seekers. It has been upgraded by the introduction of SIS II, to incorporate the States that joined in 2004 and represents an improvement in the capacity of the system to incorporate digital images and biometric data.[31] SIS II is being linked to both the Visa

Information System (VIS) and the Eurodac computerised database of finger prints of asylum seekers.

Frontex, or the 'European Agency for the Management of Operational Co-operation at the External Borders of the Member States of the European Union', is also relevant in this regard. It became operational in October 2005 with the aim of promoting coordination amongst its Member States on border security issues, conducting risk assessments and carrying out monitoring.[32] It cooperates with third countries to ensure the implementation of Union objectives. Frontex has developed patterns of relationships with countries through the sharing of information, technology transfer and the secondment of personnel. It has conducted a monitoring mission on the Ukrainian-Moldovan border and it has undertaken patrols in the Mediterranean and the Atlantic. A joint co-operation plan between Frontex and the Russian Border Guard Service was reached for the period 2007–10. Sea patrols have been designed to assist countries that have been suffering an influx of illegal migrants, both to manage the flow of human beings and to assist with their welfare.[33]

Organised crime and drug trafficking

Following the end of the Cold War, the challenge to EU internal security from organised crime and drug trafficking was accorded the highest priority, providing the backbone of the internal security agenda for most of the 1990s. Progress towards a Single Market, the attendant abolition of internal border controls amongst Member States and the transition of Central and East European States to capitalist economies, presented criminal organisations with attractive opportunities for exploitation. This applied both to pre-existing groups within the EU as well as to those within neighbouring countries that were intent upon accessing lucrative Western markets. The events of 9/11 diverted attention from transnational crime and less effort has been dedicated to it ever since.

One of the principal drivers of the effort to counter organised crime was the fear that the process of EU enlargement would lead to a large-scale influx of criminal groups. Enlargement would result in the borders of the Union being pushed out and former Western adversaries becoming the new frontiers of the EU. The CEECs would no longer serve as a buffer zone; instead EU borders would come into contact with Russia, Belarus and Ukraine whose internal security problems were significant. The Russian enclave of Kaliningrad was a particular source of concerns for the EU because it was known to be the base for organised criminal gangs conducting illegal trade in goods, such as cigarettes and stolen cars, as well as people trafficking and prostitution.[34] Consequently, the EU had a vested interest, in the period leading up to 2007, in improving the security capabilities of the CEECs prior to their absorption into Schengen. There were proposals for the creation of a European body of border guards but,[35] when this was abandoned, attention switched to maximising the efficiency of border guards from countries such as Poland. The Union committed resources, including sensors and night vision equipment, to ensure that its external frontiers were policed as effectively as possible.

Nevertheless, there remained a tension at the heart of EU policy towards these problems. While there were fears that organised crime presented a growing threat to EU Members, there continued to be a reluctance to increase the powers of the Union. Certain States, such as the UK, were opposed to endowing the EU with additional competences in policing and criminal justice. The desire to preserve sovereign powers persisted as an obstacle to tackling the challenges on a collective basis.

Conditionality became the vital instrument by which the EU was able to shape the policies of accession States in conformity with its own model of internal security.[36] Under the 'Agenda 2000' programme, accession States were expected to conform to the JHA *acquis* as well as the Union's institutional structures, despite the fact that they had been denied any part in fashioning the measures. The CEECs had to implement the Union's 'Pre-Accession Pact on Organised Crime',[37] that was agreed in May 1998, despite the lack of conceptual clarity regarding what activities justified the description of 'organised' crime.[38] The Pre-Accession Pact required the drafting of laws against criminal organisations and corrupt practices and the drawing up of anti-money laundering measures. It also mandated co-operation with Europol as one of the frontline agencies of the Union in countering transnational crime.[39] States were subject to regular monitoring by the European Commission. The same logic of policy transfer that was imposed on the CEECs was subsequently applied to accession States in the Western Balkans.

The 1997 Action Plan to Combat Organised Crime was aimed at developing co-operation between EU Member States in matters of criminal justice as well as establishing national contact points to facilitate the transmission of information.[40] It recommended the creation of legal instruments for countering various forms of organised criminal activity and set out mechanisms by which criminal assets could be seized. Some of these same priorities were taken forward within the Tampere agenda. These included plans to establish joint investigative teams that would be capable of conducting cross-border investigations: a European police chief's operational task force that could assist in setting priority action across the territories of all Member States and the creation of a European Police College (CEPOL) to disseminate best practice amongst national police forces.[41]

In the case of the Russian Federation, the EU was especially concerned by the threat from organised crime, money laundering through the proliferation of new banks, commodity crime and human trafficking. The EU drew up a Common Strategy for Russia and created a Common Space on 'Freedom, Security and Justice'.[42] This Common Space envisaged co-operation on border issues, asylum and migration policy, counter-terrorism, combating transnational organised crime, document security, anti-money laundering, tackling the narcotics problem, human trafficking, anti-corruption, increasing the efficiency of the judicial system and developing mechanisms for collaboration on criminal and civil matters. Europol offered assistance in the training of judicial and law enforcement personnel as well as the drafting of appropriate legislation.[43] A Europol liaison office was situated in Moscow in order to facilitate a closer working relationship with the EU. But the Russian government made no secret of the fact that it had little interest in following policy prescriptions laid down in Brussels. Although the EU and Russia agreed an Action Plan on Organised Crime (2000) and implemented a Readmission and Visa Facilitation Agreements (1 June 2007), internal security co-operation has lacked substance.

Drug trafficking

Countering drug trafficking has represented an important sub-section of the overall organised crime phenomenon. The scale of the problem has been impossible to determine: the traditional practice has been to assume that drug seizures represent a fraction of the trade and then to extrapolate the estimated level of activity. European Commissioner for Home Affairs, Cecilia Malmstrom, estimated in May 2010 that the sale of illicit drugs amounted to 100 billion euros per year.[44] Drug trafficking has continued to be the issue that accounts for the majority of Member State enquiries to Europol. Indeed, Europol itself was originally established as the European Drugs Unit and only later was its remit extended to people smuggling and the trade in illegal commodities.

Whilst the scale of the drugs problem remains opaque, the regions from which the narcotics originate and the smuggling routes that bring them into the EU space are better understood. Heroin comes into the EU either from Afghanistan and Pakistan, or from Laos, Thailand and Myanmar. It is trafficked via Russia, the Balkans or through Turkey. Cocaine derives from the Andean States of Colombia, Bolivia and Peru and is either shipped from there or through the Caribbean, or it is transported to West Africa and from there flown into Europe. Cannabis comes principally from North Africa and is smuggled across the borders of Southern European countries. Synthetic drugs, such as amphetamines, can be produced anywhere: large amounts are produced within EU countries such as the Netherlands and Poland, while others enter the Union from countries such as Russia.[45]

EU Member States assume different priorities towards illegal drugs and this has complicated efforts to achieve a uniform policy framework. Some countries have chosen to focus on the problem as a crime while others have emphasised the socio-economic causes of drug misuse and responded with medical and social strategies. Broadly, the EU has steered towards the latter model and adopted a harm reduction strategy. The European Monitoring Centre for Drugs and Drug Addiction (EMCDDA), established in Lisbon in 2003, provides drug information to the Member States and plays a role in outreach to third countries.[46] The EU has drawn up Action Plans on counter-drug trafficking that reflect the policy priorities outlined by the United Nations Drug Control Programme (UNDCP) (There were Action Plans in the periods 2000–2004, 2005–8 and 2009–12). Accession States have been expected to conform to both EU and UN provisions against drug trafficking and to create the necessary institutional infrastructure and national laws to implement these measures. Working relations must be established with the EMCDDA and with Europol in order to facilitate the sharing of information.

Drug trafficking is linked to a range of harms other than just drug addiction. One of the most notable harms is money laundering, resulting from the huge criminal profits that are generated. Even in developed economies, this money can fuel corruption, pollute the financial system and provide unfair competition for legitimate businesses. The EU has enacted a series of Directives designed to tackle money laundering and implemented the recommendations of the Financial Action Task Force that was created under the auspices of the Group of Eight leading industrial countries. Efforts undertaken by the EU in this field have been adapted to counter terrorist fundraising as well as to freezing the assets of organisations suspected of supporting terrorism.

The EU has provided assistance to less developed countries to reduce the supply of drugs, through aid and alternative cash crop cultivation policies. In the case of cocaine, it has eschewed the American prioritisation of supply reduction that has led to US interventions and the provision of military assistance. The EU has engaged in customs-exempted trade with some less developed countries, on the assumption that eliminating poverty provides the most effective way of countering drug production. The difference of approach between the US and the EU was most sharply exemplified in the case of Colombia where the US requested EU participation in 'Plan Colombia'.[47] The Clinton administration authorised the selling of arms to the government of Colombia to address the problem of links between the insurgents and coca cultivation. It also undertook large-scale crop eradication. The EU refused to support the American approach and chose to provide development assistance and crop substitution instead.

A similar sort of disagreement arose contemporaneously between Europe and the US in relation to poppy growing in Afghanistan. With the International Security Assistance Forces (ISAF) trying to combat a Taliban insurgency, European countries have wanted to preserve good civil–military relations in regions such as Helmand and avoid antagonising local people. To this end they were willing to ignore opium production for fear that this could bring them into direct conflict with tribal leaders. In contrast, the US chose to confront the growers and has championed a policy of poppy eradication, even at the risk of antagonising local warlords.[48]

Transnational terrorism

While organised crime and drug trafficking were the security threats that were accorded priority in the decade following the end of the Cold War, they were eclipsed by the threat from international terrorism after the 9/11 attacks on the US. The 'new terrorism' of Al-Qaeda, identified by analysts such as Hoffman, represents a novel type of challenge that is truly transnational in nature.[49] It is perceived to be a global insurgency driven by politico-religious motivations that perpetrates acts of violence around the world. The Al-Qaeda ideology has become a sort of franchise under which a range of disparate groups shelter and it is disseminated via the internet. The European Security Strategy identified the particular danger that a terrorist group might gain access to a nuclear weapon.[50] In the light of such a threat, it was envisaged that the EU could complement national counter-terrorism capacities, assist in developing new capabilities amongst Member States and help to stimulate international co-operation among the Union's allies.

Bobbitt argues that 'market States' are particularly vulnerable to this new form of terrorism.[51] Western liberal democracies derive their legitimacy from their ability to deliver economic prosperity to their citizens; from their openness and the freedoms that they guarantee as well as the technological sophistication that they embody. Many of the facets of the modern state are preyed upon by this form of terrorism. The very strengths of the society are targeted with the aim of depriving the state of its legitimacy and undermining the will and cohesion of its people.[52] The challenge for the modern state is to achieve a balance between improving security while at the same time preserving the values and liberties of its citizens.

The EU's response to 9/11 has reflected the complex, multilevel relationship it has with its Member States. The operational powers of police forces, judiciaries and intelligence agencies have remained under national jurisdiction. To a greater extent even than in combating organised crime, States have proved unwilling to relinquish their powers, not least because they see the national security implications of politically motivated terrorist attacks. Hence its Members have scrutinised carefully what additional contribution the EU can provide. The Union has been employed as a support, rather than as an alternative, to national counter-terrorism efforts. It has focused its principal efforts within the JHA domain rather than the Common Foreign and Security Policy (CFSP). Interior ministers have taken lead responsibility and they have included foreign ministries on those occasions when there have been external dimensions to the issue, such as third country involvement.[53]

The immediate response of the EU after 9/11 was the declaration of an EU Action Plan, prompted by a desire to demonstrate solidarity with the US.[54] The Action Plan contained over 200 counter-terrorism measures including enhanced judicial co-operation, freezing the assets of those suspected of supporting terrorism and tighter document and border security.[55] The Union was able to adapt measures that it had developed to counter the problems of organised crime and drug trafficking. The EU agreed a common definition of terrorism that had previously been elusive, and stipulated minimum sentences for two categories of terrorist crimes.

The Madrid and London attacks marked an intensification of the Union's counter-terrorism efforts. Foiled plots in Germany and the Netherlands also contributed to this change in emphasis. Greater budgetary resources were allocated to Europol and its personnel were increased. Eurojust, a body of magistrates and judges specialising in cross-border terrorism prosecutions, which had been established at Tampere, also received additional support. A Situation Centre was created to process intelligence and a counter-terrorism coordinator was appointed to drive forward the EU's efforts and galvanise support from among its Members. The former Dutch interior minister, Gijs de Vries, was the first incumbent but he expressed a sense of frustration with the limitations of the role. The coordinator possessed no budgetary authority, few staff and was dependent on the priority attached to counter-terrorism by the EU presidency of the day. De Vries resigned and was replaced by Gilles de Kerchove, a senior official from within the Council Secretariat.

The London bombs served to highlight one of the foremost vulnerabilities of the Union – the threat of attacks carried out by the EU's own citizens. This re-emphasised the blurring of distinctions between internal and external security. The attacks were carried out by Muslims who had been born and grown up in the UK, but had subsequently been radicalised by internet propaganda and trained in camps overseas. With millions of Muslims living in European countries, especially France, the UK and Germany, this presented a dilemma for governments. Radicalisation meant that individuals of varying socio-economic backgrounds, hitherto unknown to the security services, could suddenly decide to stage suicidal attacks.[56] It led to the EU developing a 'Strategy for Combating Radicalisation and Recruitment to Terrorism' and making this one of the priority areas in its 2005 Counter-Terrorism Strategy.[57] European Commissioner Malmstrom contended that, 'We need to do much more to address the situations of individuals on the margins of our society and to reduce their susceptibility to radicalisation'.[58]

As well as countering radicalisation, the Counter-Terrorism Strategy focused on disrupting terrorist networks and minimising the damage from terrorist attacks.[59] It sought to maximise the protection of citizens, an ambitious yet vital task. It has established the goal of protecting key infrastructures that are shared by more than one European state. Thus the EU has devoted attention to strategic transport systems, power generation and chemical refineries, government buildings, food distribution and health care systems.[60]

There remain, however, weaknesses in EU counter-terrorism efforts. Countries have varied in the priority that they have attached to this issue. Whilst States such as Spain, the UK and France have readily enacted EU counter-terrorism agreements, other countries have been much more lackadaisical. In the case of the European Arrest Warrant, that built upon the principle of mutual recognition of legal decisions and was designed to overhaul extradition procedures between EU countries, Member States such as Italy resisted its implementation.[61] Similarly, transposing EU agreements into national legislation has sometimes taken inordinate periods of time. Some countries have proved reluctant to provide information to Europol, thereby reducing its effectiveness, because they have not shared the threat perceptions of the majority of their European allies.

A second source of weakness has been the creation of intergovernmental frameworks that rival the Union's capabilities. Leading Member States have regarded the initiation of *ad hoc* counter-terrorism fora as more effective than facilitating action inside the EU. This attitude has been particularly evident in relation to intelligence co-operation where key States have preferred to share information only with close allies and resisted the creation of an EU-wide intelligence agency. The 'Group of 6' (formerly G-5), comprising France, Germany, the UK, Italy, Spain and Poland share intelligence information among themselves that is not made available to the rest of the EU.[62]

Lastly, the external dimension of combating terrorism has proved to be a tricky issue for the EU to navigate due to the multiplicity of interests amongst its Members. In multilateral frameworks, such as the United Nations, the EU has spoken with one voice. It played an important role in September 2001 in securing UN Security Council Resolution 1373 that declared terrorism to be a threat to international peace and security, and helped to establish a dedicated Counter Terrorism Committee (CTC).[63] Since the Seville European Council the EU has mandated counter-terrorism clauses into the trade agreements that it signs with third countries. For instance, the EU champions the ratification and implementation of the International Convention Against Acts of Nuclear Terrorism as well as 12 UN counter-terrorism conventions and protocols.

But amidst a turbulent international environment structured by the so-called 'War on Terror', the EU has been unable to find consensus. Over the 2003 War against Iraq, EU Member States splintered and as a result the Union was paralysed from playing any meaningful role. In the context of the war in Afghanistan, once more differences of view have consigned the EU to a minor role in the shadow of NATO. The EU took over from Germany the mission of training the Afghan police but the presence of only 200 EU police indicates the different visions among key States. In no small part this has reflected the difficulty for the EU, composed of 27 different Members, of defining its relationship with a global political, military and economic power such as the US.

Counter-terrorism co-operation with the US

Working with the US became one of the four principal components of the EU's counter-terrorism programme, alongside mutual recognition of legal measures, the approximation of criminal law and the development of bodies like Europol and Eurojust. The EU had long cooperated with the US against threats such as international crime and drug trafficking but the post-9/11 situation transformed the internal security relationship between the two sides. The administration of George W. Bush regarded Europe as its foremost potential partner and it exerted irresistible pressure on its allies to enhance co-operation. Yet the manner in which the US chose to pursue its War on Terror placed significant strains on the transatlantic relationship.

By regarding itself as at war, the Bush administration signalled that it disagreed with Europe over the nature of the threat from terrorism and the appropriate ways to deal with the problem.[64] It designated individuals caught in conflict zones as 'enemy combatants' and incarcerated them in the Guantanamo Bay facility on Cuba, beyond the jurisdiction of US civilian courts. This generated friction with EU governments, who were committed to pursuing a criminal law approach to terrorism, and these were critical when they found their nationals detained in a legal limbo. Furthermore, in 2005 it became apparent that the US had been engaged in the extra-judicial transfer of prisoners to the territories of allied countries where they could be interrogated using torture. This issue of 'extraordinary rendition' caused outrage in the EU because the airspace of Member States had been involved in conveying prisoners around the world. It appeared to confirm that America was willing to fight terrorism using instruments that contravened the rule of law.

The 9/11 tragedy also prompted the US to re-order its domestic security arrangements with enormous implications for Europe as America's closest allies. The Bush administration created a whole new arm of government, the 'Department of

Homeland Security', and put within its remit such bureaucracies as the Immigration and Naturalisation Service and the Coastguard. The US proceeded to overhaul its border security arrangements, its airline security, the powers of its law enforcement agencies and its intelligence services. All of these changes had relevance for the EU.

The US has been in the driving seat of counter-terrorism co-operation with the EU and has been accorded a special status by the Union unlike any other country. US officials have been provided with access to all of the Union's main counter-terrorism institutions. For example, an FBI liaison officer sits in Europol and an experienced attorney from the Department of Justice attends Eurojust. The US has also been provided with privileged access to some of the EU's databases, such as within Europol. This has been achieved despite the differences in powers that America and Europe invest in their respective law enforcement and intelligence agencies.

In border security, the EU found itself reacting to a series of US initiatives. The American government inaugurated the 'Visitor and Immigrant Status Indicator Technology' (VISIT) after 9/11 in order to increase the screening of people entering its territory. Europe allowed biometric information to be gathered from its citizens in order to preserve the visa-waiver arrangements that had long been enjoyed with the US. In relation to container security, the US began a programme to screen cargoes before they are put onto ships in foreign ports and dispatched to America. The EU agreed in April 2004 to be part of the Container Security Initiative and allowed US customs officials to sit in key European ports.[65] Such experiences as these demonstrated to both sides that a dedicated forum was needed to discuss future policy initiatives. The result was the 'High Level Policy Dialogue on Borders and Transport Security', that led to a smoother dialogue between Brussels and Washington.[66]

The US and the EU have also recognised the importance of sharing data. This has proved to be a highly controversial area because of the different standards of data protection adhered to by the two sides. The 'Passenger Name Records' agreement was a powerful illustration of this as it led to a re-negotiation of a May 2004 US–EU accord. The US Department of Homeland Security insisted upon receiving passenger details of European citizens flying to America on European airlines but the European Parliament (EP) challenged the agreement on the grounds that US data handling procedures were unsatisfactory. The European Commission was forced to negotiate a revised agreement under Third Pillar provisions that excluded the involvement of the European Parliament.[67]

The US has been eager to secure the maximum co-operation from the EU and has recognised the efficiency gains it can achieve by interacting with the Union at the level of the '27', rather than conducting so many bilateral relationships. For example, the Mutual Legal Assistance Treaty, negotiated between the US and the EU in June 2003, secured terms for the provision of evidence and extradition arrangements with all EU Members at once. What is less clear is the degree of reciprocity that the EU enjoys from the US. America has to be careful that its tactics do not backfire and cause resentment within the EU that could undermine the prospects for future agreements. If the US gives the impression that it is willing to bully its allies, it may find that the door to future co-operation is closed.

Conclusion

The drift of internal security powers to the EU level has demonstrated that Member States appreciate the added value that the Union can offer. In the face of complex and growing threats that impact in different ways, Members of the Union have recognised the necessity of working together. The blurring of boundaries between internal and external security has made it more important that security responses are not limited to one or other field of action. Acknowledgement of this fact was first made in the Tampere Conclusions and was subsequently endorsed in the Hague Programme. The latter noted that: 'in the field of security, the coordination and coherence between the internal and the external dimension has been growing in importance'.[68]

This is not to say that progress has been uniform across all policy areas. With regard to asylum, for example, the Union has moved towards the development of a Common European Asylum System, and away from a patchwork of national approaches. By contrast, in counter-terrorism where the post-9/11 environment has stimulated a considerable range of responses, individual governments remain the principal actors, and national agencies provide the instruments for combating these security challenges. In the latter circumstances, the EU acts in more of a coordinating capacity, agreeing overall priorities that are then enacted by Member States. Tensions continue to persist between the desires of Member States to preserve their sovereignty and the nature of security challenges that cross legal jurisdictions.

Nevertheless, internal security has grown to become an important aspect of EU activity. The threats have become mutually reinforcing: illegal immigration and organised crime preoccupied attention during the 1990s, but since 9/11 terrorism has eclipsed them. The measures that were conceived to combat immigration and crime were adapted and developed to deal with terrorism. The EU now has an evolving policy domain that, within a relatively short space of time, has become a major aspect of its relations with other countries. As such, the EU's internal security system is increasingly representing a distinctive regime with which many countries have to interact and some are coming to emulate.

3

THE EU AND EXTERNAL SECURITY RELATIONS

Introduction

The EU's external relations are of a different order to national foreign policies; some prefer the term 'international public policy' as a descriptor of its action in world politics.[1] The Union's principal external policies are the Common Commercial Policy (CCP), Development Policy and CFSP, but these form just part of its security toolbox and it draws frequently on other policy elements. In the context of European security these include enlargement, strategic partnership (NATO, Russia), the Eastern Partnership and the Union for the Mediterranean (within the European Neighbourhood Policy) and Development Policy (Mauritania), which also has to be coordinated with EU Africa strategy.

The Union's character and external relations' intergovernmental/Community duality owes much to its development within the Cold War security environment. History bears strongly on contemporary EU objectives, preferred *modus operandi* and its distinctive external security relations narrative. Also, the EU has had to carve out space from within an existing architecture, undergo a steep learning curve, provide new capabilities and find ideological and institutional means by which it can export security in a collective, coordinated and effective manner. Its post-Cold War reforms have prompted much debate, ranging from whether limited military capabilities end the EU's traditional civilian power status, through to the extent to which the process of constructing security 'actorness' is eclipsing its actual provision of security.

This chapter begins with an outline of the importance of history in shaping the EU as a security actor. It then considers the Union's key external relations policies and what it has done to develop institutional capacity, accommodate issues of legal competency and improve decision-making and implementation since the Cold War. Particular attention is paid to the challenges of developing military capabilities, which has caused much debate and demonstrates starkly Member States' determination to retain sovereignty. Also, the European Security Strategy (ESS) of December 2003 is examined for what it reveals of the EU as a security actor. Finally, an examination is undertaken of how the EU fits into the continent's security architecture.

History and the shaping of EU external relations

The EU's character, policy preferences and favoured *modus operandi* owe much to its unique history. European integration, in conjunction with Marshall Aid, helped revive Europe's war-torn economies, avert fears of a return to 1930s-style depression, guard against communist subversion and underwrite West European rearmament. There were hopes that a federal system might tame volatile nationalisms without destroying Europe's cultural, political and historical diversity, integration potentially offered political reconstruction and psychological reconciliation. The early potential of integration in this respect was demonstrated by the importance of the European Coal and Steel Community (ECSC) in rehabilitating West Germany through supranational controls, which offered a compromise between greater German autonomy and the restoration of full national sovereignty.

Western European States developed intergovernmental co-operation in foreign policy, as demonstrated by the Fouchet Plan and European Political Co-operation (EPC). Neither were US and NATO leadership unquestioned. In the 1960s French President De Gaulle touted European integration and its independent nuclear force, the *Force de Frappe,* as the basis for a 'third force' between the superpowers. In the 1980s concern about Reagan's second Cold War encouraged France to try to resurrect the Western European Union (WEU). Nevertheless, concerns over national sovereignty and the Cold War fatally compromised the European Defence Community in 1954 and ensured European integration and Western defence became mutually supportive but largely separate enterprises.[2] US nuclear guarantees and the development of mutual assured destruction (MAD) provided Europe with an uneasy strategic balance.

The Treaty of Rome contained little explicitly related to foreign, security and defence policies and created both a dual external relations character for the EU and an enduring battle for competencies between the EC institutions and between the EC and its Member States. For example, the Treaty maintained Member States' foreign policy sovereignty but provided for Community application of economic sanctions as part of trade policy. The Community was also charged with responsibility for association agreements with third countries that involved a raft of special measures and reciprocal rights and obligations. By 1975 the EC was linked to over 40 per cent of the UN membership through association, co-operation or trade agreements.[3] Treaty base also served subsequently to provide a basis for the expansion of Community competencies into a wider range of external relations. The European Court of Justice's establishment of the doctrine of 'parallelism' in the 1970 European Road Transport Agreement and subsequent ruling in favour of 'potential competence' allowed the European Commission to acquire competencies in external environmental issues. Potentially more far-reaching was the Court's judgment in the 1976

Kramer case that the Community's authority to enter into international commitments arose 'not only from an express conferment by the Treaty but may equally flow implicitly from other provisions of the Treaty, from the Act of Accession and from measures adopted, within the framework of those provisions, by the Community institutions.'[4]

This shaped the functioning of the Community in external relations, defined tools and policies therein and helped establish particular patterns of behaviour and expectation. EU external relations became associated with multilateralism, soft power, positive rather than negative conditionality, and conflict prevention. They also reflect the combination of the Union's unique experience of integration, its status as a post-Westphalian model of governance and its shared values. Liberty, human rights, democracy and regional co-operation are consistent and strong themes in EU external relations; some contend that EU policies are as much, if not more, about developing milieu rather than possession goals. In other words, the EU seeks to shape the international environment in ways reflective of its own experience. Hence there is much focus on norms such as justice, equality and tolerance, on 'domesticising' international relations and on promoting international solidarity, multilateralism and the rule of law.

An abundant literature seeks to characterise and theorise the EU as a *sui generis* actor. The intricacies – and contradictions – of these debates are not a focus of this book but reviewing some of their basic contours helps contextualise later chapters. How should the EU be characterised as an international actor? Civilian power Europe was an early idea developed from Duchene's work and applied by Maull also to Germany and Japan.[5] The EU's absence of military tools at the end of the Cold War appeared to signify it as a civilian power, though the concept itself was unclear and emphasised also the ends to which power is used, persuasion rather than coercion and civilian control over foreign and defence policymaking.[6] Later work, especially within the liberal and constructivist traditions, spoke of the EU variously as a normative, ethical or civilising power. A common thread running through these characterisations is that the EU is normatively different from other actors, that the way it diffuses its norms through a communicative process is unique and that it seeks to change the international environment within which it operates in ways reflective of its own polity. In coining the term 'normative power Europe', for instance, Manners argued the ideational impact of the EU's international identity/role as representing normative power.[7]

However, valuable as such characterisations are, they are also fraught with conceptual inexactitude and vulnerable to events. The EU's development of putative military power especially has re-ignited debates about the sustainability of civilian and normative power in Europe. In 2006 Manners conceded that the EU's apparent progressive militarisation jeopardised its normative power and that the latter would certainly be lost unless military tasks be strictly delimited to a UN mandate for genocide. As for the relationship between Civilian Power Europe and military instruments, a spectrum of opinion has developed ranging from these capabilities assuring its final denouement through to their ensuring its viability, the latter contention being premised on the need of military instruments to enable civilian ends.[8]

Straddling these different opinions are wider debates about EU intent and international relations. Hedley Bull famously dismissed the civilian power of the EC as being conditional upon the military power of States. Similar arguments have been reprised since 9/11 especially by the likes of Robert Kagan, who argued that the EU existed in a type of Kantian sub-system but that its ability to do so rested in part on the international security provided by others, especially the US.[9] However, such (neo-)realist views are premised on an international system characterised by state sovereignty and international anarchy and critics argue this situation is being transformed by globalisation, transnationalism and the disaggregation of power within a mixed actor system. In its stead is an emerging order based on international law, regimes, institutions that constrain state sovereignty, mitigate international anarchy and make normative power more important.

The EU's development of military tools suggests that the Hobbesian world is reluctant to relinquish its mantle. This, in turn, raises the question of EU intent – and perception of its intent – which is, of course, immediately problematic because it demands consideration of (currently) 27 national foreign policies plus the EC institutions. Norms and values are a common denominator of and for these actors, and values are inherent in interests. Nevertheless, values are not a substitute for interests and when the latter are vitally and publicly at stake the EU often finds policy more difficult to develop. Lerch and Schwellnus have thus suggested that the EU is not necessarily 'normative by nature' and that its normative power varies between issue areas dependent upon interaction between, and consistency within, policy objectives, means and justificatory discourse.[10] However, this raises more questions. If the EU is not normative by nature then is it a civilian power actor by choice or default? In other words, did the particular circumstances of the Cold War that denied the EC access to and the use of military tools determine its nature? If so, then is that nature transitory and conditional upon a particular international environment? In respect of the former, as constraints upon its military power continue to diminish will the EU increasingly resemble a traditional state? Conversely, will the EU 'compromise' itself if it takes the advice of those such as Cooper who argue that spreading its postmodern values depends upon the Union playing by the rules of the Hobbesian jungle beyond its borders? After all, Duchene cautioned long ago that 'the European Community will only make the most of its opportunities if it remains true to its inner characteristics.'[11]

Finally, even if EU external relations continue their strong normative thrust, is the EU really *as* different from other major powers as the European institutions especially contend? This comparative approach is often adopted in respect of the US and, even allowing for the EU not being a state, it throws up some awkward issues. For instance, it is difficult to argue that US external relations are less informed by norms, moral argumentation and ideals than are the EU's. They each also have milieu objectives and seek to replicate their norms and 'models' of governance beyond their borders. As for military power, if its exercise is justified for Civilian Power Europe in the context of achieving civilian ends, just how different is this from the US? One might argue that the answer lies in the degree of coercion, but that then raises questions of the dividing line between persuasion and coercion (not to mention whether the EU would use military force to achieve 'civilian ends' as readily as the US if it had that capability). As Smith points out, 'persuasion may be the intention, but may not be perceived as such', especially where there is an obvious asymmetry of power.[12] Given this, and that command power is not confined to the military domain, concepts of the EU as, especially, a civilising power become (too) readily associated with neo-colonialism.

In fact, a growing literature takes a much less benign perspective on the EU. Normative power is implicitly linked with notions of legitimacy, but what makes EU norms particularly legitimate? Sjursen, for instance, argues that EU normative power could be simply (mis)construed as an expression of Eurocentric cultural imperialism.[13] Also, EU self-presentation as a moral or ethical power may be construed as a discursive shield that deflects criticism from what in reality is an interest-driven policy implemented through conditionality, military missions, and (ab)use of asymmetric interdependencies. Cast in this light the EU is little different from other global powers that routinely redefine particular interests as universal goods. Indeed, an emerging research trend is to apply the theoretical concept of a hegemonic or imperial power to the EU on the premise that in an era where military power has diminished in its relative utility, hegemonic powers increasingly extend their influence and interests by promising peace and economic development.

EU external relations: policies and competencies

EU external relations draw upon a range of internal and external assets but the key policies are the CCP, Development Policy and CFSP. Only EPC/CFSP was designed explicitly with external security in mind but CCP and Development policies impact upon, and contribute to, EU objectives. The CCP is the most integrated and potent expression of the EU as a coherent actor.[14] Its effects on security objectives range from control of dual use goods, including software and technology, through to terms of market access. The CCP consists of two sub-sets, namely an autonomous and a contractual trade policy. The former can promote directly political and security objectives. For instance, trade embargoes and economic sanctions can be invoked to convey disapproval and encourage States to change policies. The autonomous trade policy can also have indirect security effects, especially in terms of third party economic development. For example, the Union can take anti-dumping and countervailing duty actions and implement safeguard measures, which involve imposing quantitative restrictions.[15]

Contractual commercial policy enables EC agreements with third countries and its participation in multilateral agreements. This has become very important because the scope of agreements has progressively broadened and their terms amended to better empower the EU vis-à-vis third parties. First generation trade agreements developed during the 1970s were sectorally based and either preferential or non-preferential. Second generation agreements added to this basic trade relationship financial and technical co-operation. From the 1990s co-operation agreements became much more expansive, especially so-called 'mixed' association agreements. These added dialogue on CFSP and JHA to the issues covered by third generation agreements. Examples include the Europe Agreements, Development Association Agreements with the Maghreb and Mashreq States and agreements within the Stabilisation and Association Process.

The progressive politicisation and securitisation of these agreements has given EU external relations teeth, principally via conditionality (see Chapters 6–8). Clauses set minimum expectations of the third party and provide for suspension of agreements in the event of non-compliance. Trading preferences, aid, association and co-operation agreements and prospective EU membership have all been made conditional upon partners' respect for democracy and human rights and willingness to develop 'good governance'.[16] The EU prefers positive conditionality, which is essentially the carrot of progressively deeper integration with and more substantive support from the Union as the third party fulfils normative and practical criteria. This is argued to reinforce local ownership and avoid a sense of imposition and an image of an 'imperial' EU. However, negative conditionality exists through target-setting, rigorous monitoring procedures and often phased programming, thereby tying successive tranches of support to satisfactory progress. The EU can suspend, reduce or re-route aid, and, in the case of its enlargement policy, threaten or actually suspend the candidate state's membership perspective.

The Treaty of European Union (TEU) set Development Policy objectives as being to foster the economic and social development of developing countries, assist their integration into the world economy and contribute to the campaign against poverty. It was also to contribute to the promotion of good governance, respect for human rights and the rule of law and democratisation. Unlike CCP, Development Policy is an area of parallel competence whereby EC and Member State activities run alongside one another and on the proviso that Community initiatives should be complementary to Member States' initiatives. The EC leads on trade issues. It also co-ordinates, especially through the EuropeAid Co-operation Office, most Commission external aid instruments funded by the Community budget and the European Development Fund (EDF). Member States' concerns for national sovereignty and specific historical ties mean that they provide the vast majority of Development funding through the EDF and the European Investment Bank (EIB).

Development Policy was in the Treaty of Rome primarily to accommodate Member States' interests in their overseas countries and territories. Subsequent EU involvement in Development Policy has traditionally been explained in terms of moral obligation, historical legacy and economic imperative.[17] The former arises from a general belief in solidarity and the consequent need to help combat world poverty and hunger. The historical aspect stems from some Member States' colonial pasts. And the economic rationale derives from the EU's need of raw materials, export markets and investment opportunities. The EU has thus long been interested in the political and economic governance of Developing Countries and their role in international security. Indeed, EC Member States used the Community as a mechanism to manage decolonisation and re-bind former dependencies to the West during the

Cold War. In 1963 the Yaoundé Convention linked Member States and seventeen associate States and Madagascar; the first of the Lomé Conventions in 1975 established a much larger framework with ACP countries.

EU linkages between development and security have become more explicit. Article 130u of the TEU formally linked Development Policy to EU foreign policy, stating that it 'shall contribute to the general objective of developing and consolidating democracy and the rule of law, and to that of respecting human rights and fundamental freedoms'. Also, the shift in concern from territorial security to transnational threats encouraged the entwining of discourses of poverty and (in)security, especially as focus turned to the so-called dark side of globalisation and to root causes of state failure, radicalisation and terrorism. Thus when the Cotonou Agreement was signed in June 2000 as replacement for the Lomé Conventions, it included dialogue across a range of issues far beyond traditional development co-operation, such as peace and security, the arms trade and migration.[18] It also placed strong obligations upon ACP States to respect human rights and democracy, fight corruption and provide for sustainable development, something EU officials have linked overtly to the European Security Strategy (ESS). 9/11 and subsequent terrorist attacks sharpened the articulation of poverty as a security issue. For example, the 2003 ESS argued that 'poverty and disease ... give rise to pressing security concerns', 'A number of countries and regions are caught in a cycle of conflict, insecurity and poverty', and 'Security is a precondition of development'.[19]

Development Policy is now a key element of the EU's preventive engagement. This is consistent with aims set out in the TEU in that poverty reduction, economic and social development and integration into the world economy all contribute to breaking the perceived cycle of poverty, insecurity and conflict. The Commission emphasises that article 177 TEC 'underlines the fact that the political dimension of external relations is overarching and pivotal' and contends that the European Consensus on Development 'provides a strategic foundation for EU development co-operation ... particularly in relation to security, migration and the social dimension of globalisation.'[20] This strengthening of the EU emphasis on good governance has, though, prompted suggestions of Development Policy's priorities being subtly changed and securitised by stealth.[21]

The third and most important external security relations policy is CFSP. European ambitions in foreign and security policy co-operation are longstanding. The particular progeny of EPC dates back to the Davignon report and an attempt to re-invigorate the EC in the wake of the Empty Chair Crisis. EPC's creation in 1973 was further inspired by a variety of factors, especially European disarray in the face of the international oil crisis and concerns about *Ostpolitik* and American leadership. EPC thus reflected and encouraged common EC security appreciations and responses, promoted the Community's international profile, provided an alternative forum to NATO for multilateral European security consultation, and strengthened the Community's ability to act collectively. EPC secured a symbolically significant treaty base in the 1986 Single European Act (SEA) and Member States agreed to work with the European Commission in intensifying, through mutual assistance and information, co-operation between their Representatives accredited to third countries and to international organisations. They also undertook to 'endeavour jointly to formulate and implement a European Foreign Policy', which included prior consultation with, and consideration of the views of, fellow Member States in deciding policy, and seeking common positions within EPC.[22]

EPC's post-Cold War up-grade to CFSP demonstrated that Member States remained determined to safeguard their sovereignty but recognised the benefits of collective action and improved coordination with the EC pillar. CFSP provides general orientation for other EC policies with external influence as well as for specific acts of foreign and security policy co-operation. The policy as set out in the TEU was to help safeguard the common values, fundamental interests and independence of the EU. Demonstrating strong normative and *modus operandi* preferences, CFSP would support a post-Cold War international order that was multipolar, rule-based and geared to securing and maintaining peace. To this end the EU would develop and consolidate democracy and the rule of law, and respect for human rights and fundamental freedoms. The Union's commitment to multilateralism was evident in its undertaking to strengthen international co-operation, peace and security in accordance with the principles of the UN Charter and the Helsinki Final Act and the objectives of the Paris Charter.

The EU emphasises within CFSP the mainstreaming of human rights and often presents its use of sanctions in milieu terms: 'Sanctions are an instrument … which seek to bring about a change in activities or policies such as violations of international law or human rights, or policies that do not respect the rule of law or democratic principles.'[23] Such measures can be targeted at governments, non-state entities and individuals and range from arms embargoes and other specific or general trade restrictions through to financial restrictions and restrictions on admission to the EU. The EU's CFSP agenda is unsurprisingly full. The ESS gave some shape to the pressing security dimensions of CFSP, highlighting threats posed by terrorism, WMD proliferation, regional conflicts, state failure and organised crime. The EU has stressed as central to four of these challenges the consequences of the illicit manufacture, transfer and circulation of small arms and light weapons (SALW). It consequently supported from 2005 a UK-led initiative to promote the adoption of an Arms Trade Treaty. The EU also adopted in December of that year a Strategy to combat illicit accumulation and trafficking of SALW and their ammunition. In respect of WMD the European Council resolved in November 2003 to focus on non-proliferation policies in the EU's wider relations with third countries. It agreed that a MD clause should be inserted into the EU's mixed or specifically tailored agreements. In December 2003 it also adopted a Strategy against the proliferation of WMD.[24] Key priorities are strengthening the international system of non-proliferation; pursuing the universalisation of multilateral agreements; reinforcing strict implementation of and compliance with these agreements; co-operating closely with key partners; and assistance to third countries. In August 2009 the EU also established in force Community regimes for the control of exports, transfer, brokering and transit of dual-use items.

CFSP and its integral component ESDP have developed rapidly. A brief summary suffices here given numerous accounts elsewhere. CFSP continues EPC practice of non-binding declaratory diplomacy, issuing common statements, declarations and *demarches* but has added potentially stronger instruments. The TEU introduced Common Positions and Joint Actions designed to enable better co-ordination, impose an element of discipline in the implementation stage, and raise the Union's profile. The Amsterdam Treaty introduced Common Strategies that set overall policy guidelines and stipulated objectives, resource requirements and expected duration of actions. However, the single most important innovation in that treaty was EU assumption from the WEU of responsibility for the Petersberg Tasks. The Union thus had to develop military instruments and became committed to a seemingly ever-expanding set of tasks. The Lisbon Treaty details these as including 'joint disarmament operations, humanitarian and rescue tasks, military advice and assistance tasks, conflict prevention and peace-keeping tasks, tasks of combat forces in crisis management, including peace-making and post-conflict stabilisation. All these tasks may contribute to the fight against terrorism, including by supporting third countries in combating terrorism in their territories.'[25]

The EU has done reasonably well in terms of developing institutional infrastructure to support a meaningful foreign and security policy, especially in view of the awkward pillar structure that it first tried unsuccessfully to jettison in the Constitutional Treaty. The Amsterdam Treaty gave CFSP a higher profile, a coordinating influence in the shape of a High Representative for CFSP, and a Policy Planning and Early Warning Unit. The Nice Treaty provided for a Political and Security Committee, a Military Committee and a Military Staff, with a politico-military working group and a committee for civilian aspects of crisis management in support. There is also a limited Planning Cell and Joint Situation Centre, together with the General Affairs and External Relations Council, Committee of the Permanent Representatives and the European Commission in its 'fully affiliated' guise. Furthermore, the EU has created a European Defence Agency (EDA) charged with developing military capabilities, promoting cooperative defence research and technology across Europe, encouraging armaments collaborations, and strengthening the European Defence Technology and Industrial Base (EDTIB).

Within ESDP, which the Lisbon Treaty symbolically upgrades from a 'European' to a 'Common' Security and Defence Policy, military capabilities were central. The 1999 Helsinki Headline Goal aimed by the end of 2003 to deploy within 60 days a 60,000 strong force capable of meeting the Petersberg Tasks and being sustainable in the field for at least one year. Evident shortfalls meant that the December 2001 Laeken Summit launched the European Capabilities Action Plan, which focused initially on 19 priority areas. In 2004 a new Headline Goal 2010 was approved, which placed renewed emphasis on interoperability, deployability and sustainability, and the battlegroups concept. Officially launched at the November 2004 Brussels Military Capabilities Commitment Conference, these battlegroups comprise 1,500 troops, deployable to theatre within 15 days, and sustainable for 30 days (120 with rotation). This was followed two years later by the drafting of a 'Long Term Vision' (LTV) for capability needs.

The EU has already deployed a number of both civilian and military missions under ESDP. These began on 1 January 2003 with a Police Mission in Bosnia. In March *Operation Concordia* in the Former Yugoslav Republic of Macedonia (FYROM) became its first military peace support mission, and *Operation Artemis* was its first military operation beyond Europe and without NATO assets. The EU's level of ambition has increased. The position as summarised by the Council in December 2008 was that the EU should, within the range of operations envisaged in Headline Goal 2010 and Civilian Headline Goal 2010, be capable of: 'planning and conducting simultaneously a series of operations and missions, of varying scope: two major stabilisation and reconstruction operations, with a suitable civilian component, supported by up to 10,000 troops for at least two years; two rapid-response operations of limited duration using inter alia EU battlegroups; an emergency operation for the evacuation of European nationals (in less than ten days) ... a maritime or air surveillance/interdiction mission; a civilian-military humanitarian assistance operation lasting up to 90 days ... '[26]

Matching military resources to commitments is proving a major challenge. The EDA's LTV argued ESDP operations would be 'expeditionary, multinational and multi-instrument, directed at achieving security and stability more than "victory"', and force would typically be applied in opaque circumstances against an obscure enemy and under tight rules of engagement and intense media scrutiny.[27] Particular emphasis was thus placed on technology, synergy between military and non-military actors, an expansive toolbox from which to select appropriately, sustainability and agility, ability to reconfigure for optimum force size and balance, and capacity to move quickly at the tactical level.[28] The EDA's 26 participating Member States (pMS) accepted in July 2008 a Capability Development Plan (CDP) and reached agreement in November 2008 on a European Defence Research and Technology Strategy.[29]

A single defence equipment market could save the EU approximately 6 billion euros per year[30] and some progress has been made in this direction. Most EDA pMS agreed a code of conduct on defence procurement on 21 November 2005 and a Code of Best Practice in the Supply Chain on 15 May 2006.[31] On 1 July 2006 a new European defence equipment market came into operation.[32] And the EDA is charged with monitoring instances where pMS elect to invoke Article 296 provisions to avoid Single Market rules.[33] The European Commission is also slowly developing competencies impinging upon defence activity. It is trying to channel industry towards transformational defence capabilities through its FP7 Thematic Priority on Security and Space. From 2007 this included space and homeland security research and development, and some commentators argued that creation of specific budgets for earth observation and detection of chemical and biological agents marked a first step in the development of a European-wide security capability.[34] The Commission has also sought to promote European capabilities and the EDTIB through its Single Market competencies.[35] For example, in 2007 it developed a defence package comprising a Communication with recommendations for improving the competitiveness of the defence sector, a Directive on intra-Community transfers of defence products and a Directive to enhance openness and intra-European competition in the award of some public works contracts.[36] The EP approved the two proposed directives in December 2008 and January 2009.

Nevertheless, EU capability drives encounter a myriad of problems. The EDA's pMS nominally increased overall defence expenditure in the period 2006–7 but as a percentage of GDP their spending actually fell from an average 1.78 per cent to 1.69 per cent GDP.[37] Ongoing tight constraints on national defence budgets were demonstrated in the Anglo-French Declaration on Defence and Security Co-operation in November 2010, which is particularly significant given that these countries provided nearly 48 per cent of all defence expenditure among European Members of NATO in 2008 and, together with Germany, Italy and Sweden account for almost 90 per cent of EU defence equipment production.[38] Impressive EU Member State defence expenditure in 2008 of $254 billion (20.74 per cent of global military expenditure)[39] is compromised by duplication, difficulties in prioritising procurement, and lingering commitment to legacy platforms, unnecessary bases and expensive staffing policies. In an era of expeditionary warfare European countries still maintained in 2005 some 10,000 main battle tanks, 3,000 combat aircraft and considerable conscript forces.[40] National military spending mixes also vary widely and often draw American criticism of 'defence spending for social welfare'.[41] Eight EDA pMS allocated over 65 per cent of their defence expenditure to personnel costs in 2007.[42]

EU Member States recognise the need for a strong EDTIB but divide over procurement philosophies, industrial strategies and the relationship between an EDTIB and a transatlantic DTIB.[43] Also, though engaged in some pooling of resources and collaborative projects[44] they remain deeply cautious. Collaborative projects are vulnerable to partners' decisions and have a history of over-runs and over-budgets: an example being Germany's indecision about how many Eurofighters and A400Ms it was willing to procure.[45] More importantly, clashes of bureaucratic interests and traditions become increasingly pronounced the closer one gets to decisions over autonomy and sovereignty in armaments policy co-operation, and Commission activism foregrounds legal competency battles within the EU and the centrality of security and defence to national sovereignty.[46] Leading Member States have thus promoted national defence champions and all EDA pMS have carefully preserved their autonomy. The 2005 Code of Conduct on Defence Procurement and 2006 Code of Best Practice in the Supply Chain are not legally binding. The EDA can only name and shame pMS that invoke Article 296[47] and pMS have stressed that open competition in the defence sector is subject to national security qualifications.[48]

These specific sensitivities reflect wider problems that all EU external relations security policies run up against, captured in divisions between the *acquis communautaire* and the *acquis politique* and epitomised by the TEU pillar system. In terms of the EU security framework they delimit a policy space marked by intense institutional competition for control between the Council, the Commission and to a lesser extent the EP.[49] Moreover, the EU Member States compete for external relations influence among themselves and over the EC institutions, seeking to steer them in particular directions and/or prevent institutional dynamics overly compromising national interests. As the EU progressively moves into more and more sensitive areas of foreign, security and even defence policy, so some Member State resistance to communitaurisation and/or surrender of veto powers increases.

This dual character of EU external relations has become increasingly problematic. 'Intermesticity' is developing rapidly and the Union's export of the *acquis communautaire* in the enlargement process especially 'domesticises' external relations. Challenges to a state's internal security were traditionally understood 'in terms of criminal or otherwise disturbing activities within the boundaries of the state, threats to external security were seen as arising first and foremost from the aggressive behaviour of other States.'[50] Post-Cold War emphasis on transnational security, though, has spawned a predominant Western discourse of de-territorialised security that de-differentiates internal and external realms.[51] Furthermore, internal EC policies such as fisheries, energy, immigration and asylum and the CAP impinge, sometimes negatively, on external relations/security objectives. For instance, the EU emphasises poverty reduction as a security objective as well as a moral imperative but reportedly provides under the CAP a typical cow in the Union with a daily subsidy of $2.20 – above what 1.2 billion of the world's poorest people subsist on.[52]

Efforts have been made to complement greater institutional resources with improved decision-making procedures and moving beyond the need for unanimity in many aspects of foreign and security policy. Constructive abstention introduced in the Amsterdam Treaty effectively provided a conditional opt-out option, thereby allowing national interests to be respected whilst still allowing the EU to proceed subject to gaining a minimum of two-thirds of weighted Council votes. The Nice Treaty introduced enhanced co-operation to CFSP for the implementation of joint actions and common positions provided there were no military or defence implications. No Member State objected or applied the so-called 'emergency brake' and there existed a threshold of eight supportive Member States. The Lisbon Treaty introduces Permanent Structured Co-operation to allow military capability development between 'those Member States whose military capabilities fulfil higher criteria and which have made more binding commitments to one another in this area with a view to the most demanding missions'.

The Lisbon Treaty also offers some improvements in terms of external representation and longstanding problems of policy (dis)continuity within the European Council and between the Council and the European Commission. The EU gains legal personality, the European Council has an elected President with a minimum mandate of 30 months, and a High Representative of the Union for Foreign Affairs and Security Policy is created by merging the posts of High Representative for CFSP and the European Commissioner for External Relations. Also, a new European External Action Service (EEAS) aims at streamlining EU external services.

However, all of this promises to have limited effect. The EU is engaged increasingly in external security activities that span areas of competence, including dual-use goods, election monitoring, conflict prevention and civilian crisis management. Scrapping the pillar system does not remove the dual character of the EU's external relations. CFSP remains distinct and as set out in the TEU while the first and third pillar merge in the Treaty on the Functioning of the European Union. The position of High Representative embodies rather than overcomes the intergovernmental/ community duality. And innovations such as the EEAS could become the focus of competency struggles. Its scope and staffing are ill-defined and numerous contentious questions remain, such as whether it will include the Situation Centre. Moreover, even after the Lisbon Treaty is fully implemented the Council and the Commission will still each be theoretically able to claim competence over all aspects of the Union's external activities as they are charged jointly with ensuring consistency.[53]

Most important of all, though, the effectiveness of Lisbon Treaty reforms depends upon Member States' implementation. Here the tortuous process of finally ratifying the Treaty and the outcome of intense negotiation about who should fill key new appointments do not inspire confidence. Moreover, the determination of EU Member States to preserve their influence in foreign and security affairs was indicated by their refusal to endorse any high profile personality as either EU President or foreign affairs 'supremo'. Former Belgian Prime Minister Herman van Rompuy and former EU Trade Commissioner, Baroness Ashton may fill these respective roles efficiently but neither generates the popular and professional excitement and interest that more ambitious selections could have done.

The European Security Strategy (ESS)

EU High Representative for CFSP Javier Solana emphasised in 2002 that without real political will to act, efficient structures, access to suitable resources, and institutional clarity 'count for little'.[54] This, and efficient capability development, depends upon there being agreed interpretations of the security landscape and appropriate responses.[55] The ESS is the EU's principal conceptual response to these challenges.

The ESS is frequently invoked by the Union in articulating and justifying external policies and capability development. It has also been, and remains, keenly debated. Solana argued that its approval signalled the 'the arrival of strategy in our security thinking'.[56] So enthusiastically was it welcomed in some quarters that more was arguably read into the document than was actually there.[57] The ESS has also been castigated as 'a recipe for masterly inactivity', dismissed as fantasy and criticised for being dangerous for transatlantic relations.[58]

Set against a background of optimism prompted by conclusion of the Convention and desperation to avoid division after the Iraq debacle, the ESS was adopted with relative ease.[59] Three further factors contributed to its smooth passage. First, it was not a revolutionary document by nature, but built upon and codified what had gone before. And while it has been justifiably noted that the exposition of threats in the ESS was new,[60] those identified were not. Second, the ESS is not legally binding, which enabled Member States to endorse it as good Europeans without committing to specific new obligations. Finally, the ESS was not a security strategy in any recognisable meaning of the term.

Strategy as traditionally conceived concerns war and its conduct, albeit it has recently 'acquired a universality which has robbed it of meaning, and left it only with banalities.'[61] As Colin Gray explains, the noun 'strategy' and the adjective 'strategic' have been 'purloined by the unscrupulous or misapplied by those who are careless or ignorant.'[62] While the drafters of the ESS were not ignorant of terminological exactitude, they used the term 'security strategy' to send signals of intent, at the same time ensuring the document contained nothing resembling strategy that might cause dissent. Hence the ESS eschews naming countries that it says 'have placed themselves outside the bounds of international society'.[63] It makes no prioritisation of the key threats identified, and its very few references to military instruments are invariably presented as part of a wider toolbox and hedged.[64] This, together with an emphasis on preventive engagement, encouraged a view that the ESS was largely about avoiding military action rather than preparing the EU to exercise coercive instruments.[65]

Those who bemoan the ESS for offering little guideline as to how to apply economic and military tools in order to exert influence are correct.[66] Some have sought to defend use of the term 'strategy'. But even they have had to embed it in public management terms and concede that it might have been more appropriate to use the term 'foreign policy strategy' rather than 'security strategy'.[67] To call this a failing of the ESS depends on whether its drafters are held to the (mis)use of the term 'strategy' or it is accepted that it was never intended to be one. Yet even accepting the ESS was not a strategy at all does not explain the many different interpretations made of it.

Probably the best way of doing so is to view the ESS as a political document written for multiple audiences. The principal audience was the EU Member States for which the ESS served as a reassertion of common interests after Iraq and a reminder that 'The point of the Common Foreign and Security Policy and European Security and Defence Policy is that we are stronger when we act together.'[68] The document also addressed the Member States and the EC institutions together for two purposes. It performed an immediate inspirational function, designed 'not so much to embody good policy decisions as to create the environment and mood for taking them.'[69] And in the longer term it served, in the words of the June 2004 European Council, as a 'key framework for policy formulation'.[70]

The ESS also addressed EC institutions, the Member States and European publics in a collective identity-building exercise. It sought to define the EU as a distinctive and coherent actor in world affairs and to mobilise support for capability development. In doing so it reassured European publics and governments by emphasising multilateralism, the UN and soft power and toning down the ESS by removing the term 'pre-emptive engagement' that appeared in its June 2003 draft form in favour of 'preventive engagement'. These also distinguished the EU from other international actors. This identity construction dimension is further evident in the valedictory trumpeting of the distinctive European experience,[71] the impression-building of an active Europe through a list of EU responses already made to key threats, and the implicit 'othering' of the US. Bailes, for instance, argues that the EU exploited the controversial US 2002 NSS by using 'concomitant language to signal subtle differences as well as togetherness'.[72] Furthermore, the ESS appeals directly for development of a European strategic culture 'that fosters early, rapid and when necessary, robust intervention' and has itself been seen as constitutive of that process.[73]

The ESS also aimed at a variety of audiences beyond the EU, so much so that in parts inclusivity seems more important than substance. For instance, in its support of an effective international multilateral order the ESS includes reference to a miscellany of international institutions and regimes. It also talks vaguely about connections with countries in the Middle East, Africa, Latin America and Asia and the importance of developing strategic partnerships with an odd collection of specified countries: Russia, India, China, Japan and Canada. However, two audiences are particularly defined and important: Washington and the EU's neighbourhood. While implicitly criticising US tactics and unilateralism, the ESS sought common ground by largely accepting US threat assessments and declaring the transatlantic relationship alone to be 'irreplaceable'. NATO was also reaffirmed as 'an important expression of this [transatlantic] relationship.' As for the neighbourhood, it received disproportionately lengthy treatment in a document that made much ado about its global focus. In terms of substance, considerable effort was invested in emphasising inclusive rather than exclusive security and continued EU commitment to a Europe 'whole and free'. For instance, the Barcelona Process was foregrounded in the context of the Mediterranean, and EU credibility was mortgaged to success in the Balkans.[74]

The ESS presents the EU as a value-orientated actor that prioritises conflict prevention and the construction of an international order built upon effective multilateralism. The fundamental framework of this order is stated to be the UN Charter and primary responsibility for international peace and security is accorded to the Security Council. The range of threats and challenges identified by the ESS and the causal claims it makes suggest a holistic conceptualisation of security. Furthermore, the ESS explicitly connects internal and external dimensions of security in terms of threat and response: 'the first line of defence will often be abroad', and that 'better coordination between external and Justice and Home Affairs policies is crucial in the fight both against terrorism and organised crime.'[75]

However, the closer the ESS is scrutinised, the more unresolved issues emerge. It uses the term 'security' in almost as elastic a fashion as it does 'strategy'. As Wyllie notes, 'The concept of security adopted is so wide as to be of marginal utility in the construction of a doctrine or the identification of strategic theories on which to build doctrine'.[76] This is important because without clearly defined and agreed strategic priorities ongoing capability drives risk wasting resources. The battlegroups have been described as a capability in 'search of a strategy' and the demands placed upon the military, and the instruments needed, in a conventional Peace Support Operation could be quite different were it conducted under a human security paradigm.[77] Even were it attainable, increased European defence spending in the face of fundamental disagreement about where and when to deploy troops could be 'a waste of resources' and threaten European credibility.[78]

Here the ambiguity of the ESS is revealing. While its approach towards security is holistic, it is far from clear what the referent point of security is. Whitman suggests three possible interpretations. If the ESS is treated as a piece of public diplomacy seeking to convert aspirations into implemented policy, then the referent is the EU. A humanist perspective, though, would allow the ESS to be read as putting the individual at the centre of security policy and hence the referent. A realist standpoint would see the structure of international relations as the referent.[79]

It may be argued that there is an element of constructive ambiguity here that will enable learning and consensus-building to be developed through doing. The ambiguity as to the referent of security might also be linked to identity building and objectives for developing a European strategic culture. On both counts the EU must be seen to add value rather than compete with nation States. This encourages emphasis on, and linkages between, common values and de-territorialised security, with the former seemingly substituting for interests, to an extent, at EU level. Matlary, for instance, has argued that 'A strategic culture for Europe must necessarily depend on notions of human security and human rights more than on traditional territorial defence of nationals.'[80] Indeed, the allure of human security as a 'strategic narrative' for Europe is strong. It appeals to the consensual values of the Union, its prescriptions foreground EU soft security strengths rather than hard security limitations, and it provides an alternative security paradigm that can represent the Union as providing added value to contemporaneous national security discourses. A human security agenda could potentially also improve policy-making coherence and 'facilitate the ESS's goal of "effective multilateralism" since it opens doors to co-operation, with the UN in particular.'[81] Moreover, there is a synergetic relationship between EU and national foreign policy discourses insofar as the latter have increasingly emphasised their ideological components since the Cold War.[82]

Nevertheless, the ESS suggests no consensus on human security as the primary referent, which is unsurprising given the limitations discussed in Chapter 1. It similarly suggests in its vagueness and terminological ambiguity unresolved strategic tensions between EU Member States. Some phrases can be read to produce almost opposite meanings. Consider, for instance, 'Our aim should be an effective and balanced partnership with the USA. This is an additional reason for the EU to build up further its capabilities and increase its coherence.'[83] It could be read in the British mode whereby the EU needs to better share the burdens of international security to persuade the US to remain engaged with Europe and the Union. Alternatively, it could be read in the traditional French mode whereby an increasingly powerful EU would be more autonomous of Washington and engage in 'soft balancing'.[84] The following extract is similarly opaque: 'EU–NATO permanent arrangements, in particular Berlin Plus, enhance the operational capacity of the EU and provide the framework for the strategic partnership between the two organisations in crisis management.' This can be read as reaffirming the importance of NATO, accepting that the EU will remain dependent on NATO for some assets and that EU capability development therefore complements NATO. Alternatively, it can be read 'more like a retirement tribute than a consensus on future utility' because NATO is portrayed as a toolbox for EU missions and/or a bridge in transatlantic relations rather than as a security actor in its own right.[85]

This Atlanticist–Europeanist division is not the only one evident in the ESS. Writing of ESDP, Meyer suggests three normative cleavages between EU Member States, namely NATO Members and the non-aligned/neutral; those prepared to militarise the EU and those that want it to remain purely or largely civilian; and those that can take action largely on executive authority and those that need/desire explicit domestic, European and international authorization.[86] Martinsen suggests a slightly different set of divisions: an Anglo-French led group that would see the EU undertake a wide range of missions globally; a neutrality-inclined group headed by Austria and Sweden that favours ESDP remaining regionally based and focused upon UN-mandated crisis management missions; and a third group led by Germany that is disinclined to project power abroad in favour of deepening integration 'at home'.[87] Vrettos uses the Petersberg tasks to identify another three-way division: Member States only prepared to participate at the least demanding end in humanitarian, peacekeeping and rescue tasks; a group favouring permanent structured co-operation that consists of States ready and able to participate in even the most demanding tasks; and a group that is prepared to make a mutual defence commitment.[88]

These cleavages overlap but the ESS embraces them all to one degree or another. It emphasises the potential need for robust intervention but implicitly ties this to a UN-based approach. It mentions the possible need of military instruments and the importance of capability building but also stresses good governance and the importance of soft power tools. References to the importance of the US and transatlantic relations are matched by those stressing the desirability of a multi-polar world and an independent EU global security role. And emphasis on the global is counterpoised by equal if not greater focus on the neighbourhood and the Union itself.

Tactical drafting eased acceptance of the ESS but neither in its original nor updated form in 2008 does this inspire confidence that the EU has sufficient strategic cohesion and common purpose to become a consistent strategic actor in the foreseeable future. It is true that the Union 'has over time been building on sets of values, while developing common expectations about pooled sovereignty, the role of intervention, peace-keeping, "protectorates", state-building, and relations with the UN and Organisation for Security and Co-operation in Europe'.[89] It is also the case that the EDA, European Security and Defence College, the ESS and even the St Malo agreement aim at the development of a shared European strategic culture and that consociationalisation between the Committee of Permanent Representatives (COR-EPER), the Political and Security Committee, EU Military Staff and the Policy Unit formerly attached to the High Representative for CFSP is likely to encourage a 'collective ethos of their own', 'trans-European perspectives on CFSP and ESDP' and possible tensions with European capitals.[90]

National strategic cultures are also to an extent 'mutually constitutive and reinforcing' and some argue the EU already has an embryonic strategic culture (especially when defined narrowly).[91] However, while a putative European strategic culture is encouraging especially for supporters of a continuing European political project, there are inherent potential dangers that the ESS either implicitly recognises or embodies. A genuine European strategic culture could profoundly affect the transatlantic relationship, the cohesion of which has thus far been facilitated by Atlanticism in key European States and the dominance of US norms through NATO. The ESS recognises that a genuine European strategic culture is a long way off in that it was written originally with a view to accommodating fifteen different national strategic cultures. Subsequent accessions added to this diversity and underscore Cederman's observation that enlargement may be a balance between widening and deepening *and* between exclusion and dilution.[92] A consequent problem that is further strengthened by the ESS's need to reassure and to appeal to common values is that the strategic culture it largely reflects is that of the post-World War Two Western European experience, with an emphasis on soft power, containment, deterrence, confidence-building, accommodation, multilateralism, Eurocentrism and an abhorrence of war. This can impede conceptual and policy innovation in a radically changed strategic environment,[93] hold back the seemingly few Member States that are seeking to adapt to it, and exacerbate difficulties with the US, for which 9/11 was a traumatic moment that reshaped its strategic assumptions and culture.

The EU and the European security architecture

Since the Cold War the EU has carved institutional space from an established European security architecture. The velvet revolutions suggested greater interaction opportunities through which to develop mutual confidence, shared norms and common values.[94] Hopes flourished for a pan-European security system rooted in an inclusive architecture of interlocking institutions, possibly even a collective security system.[95] The EC quickly laid claim in December 1989 to being 'the corner-stone of a new European architecture'.[96]

The EC would ideally have worked smoothly alongside the Council of Europe, NATO, C/OSCE, UN, WEU and financially based institutions that channelled reconstruction funds. These institutions included the International Bank for Construction and Development (IBRD), the European Investment Bank (EIB), in which the EU was the majority shareholder, and a new EU-sponsored European Bank for Reconstruction and Development (EBRD). Working together, a sense of inclusiveness could potentially be exported to the strategically homeless, normative congruence established and maintained, and concerns met regarding coherence within and complementarity between the economic and military security domains.[97]

However, the EU establishing itself as a security actor and a Darwinian struggle among existing security institutions effectively squandered this early opportunity. As the EU developed more systematic political co-operation it 'inevitably started to move into security-related areas such as Organisation for Security and Co-operation in Europe policy and disarmament'.[98] Its growing involvement in election monitoring caused significant overlap with OSCE and UN competencies. Its democracy promotion strategies, provision of technical and legal assistance within its Europe Agreements and JHA initiatives, such as increased border guard co-operation, led to increasing overlap with the Council of Europe. And commitment in the TEU to the eventual framing of a common defence policy, EU take-over of the Petersberg Tasks and French-led aspirations for greater European autonomy threatened overlap with NATO and friction with the US.

The post-Cold War re-inventions of other institutions exacerbated overlap and duplication. The WEU sought a niche role between the EU and NATO and devised outreach programmes to the CEECs.[99] The CSCE became a permanent regional organisation and began extending its competencies beyond norm setting. Its 1992 Helsinki document *The Challenges of Change* laid claim to peacekeeping operations. Furthermore, the Yugoslav crisis dragged the UN into European security affairs to an unprecedented degree and NATO confounded predictions of its demise by embarking upon a dramatic re-invention.[100] Its New Strategic Doctrine laid claim in November 1991 to responsibilities far beyond collective defence.[101] Though NATO Secretary-General Manfred Wörner signalled support for the CSCE,[102] the New Strategic Doctrine nevertheless marked an incursion into its soft security competencies. NATO later nullified the WEU's advantage of potential geographic deployment by abandoning the restrictions of Article 5 and undertook a series of outreach programmes that began tentatively with the North Atlantic Co-operation Council and Partnership for Peace[103] but eventually included formal enlargements.

EU difficulties were compounded by questions of institutional scope, enlargement, alternative architectures and EU Member States exploiting *directoires* and institutional polyphony. The UN was global, NATO transatlantic and the OSCE, Council of Europe, WEU and EU all predominantly or exclusively regional. A post-1990 '"ideology" in favour of membership',[104] driven by CEEC fears of exclusion and deteriorating security conditions, ensured differentiated memberships and inter-institutional tensions. Leading States also favoured different security architectures. Germany favoured a pan-European collective security arrangement orchestrated through an augmented C/OSCE.[105] Britain's special relationship with the US encouraged it to promote NATO primacy, which successive American administrations also insisted upon as they pressed Europeans to undertake greater burden-sharing. Russia wanted some type of European Security Council, prioritised existing institutions in which it enjoyed full Member status, and opposed NATO. At the December 1994 Budapest OSCE Summit Russia proposed that NATO and the CIS be placed under OSCE control and run through a directorate of major powers.[106] Finally France favoured a re-invigorated WEU to promote greater European autonomy and develop the EU as a counterpoise to the US and NATO.

The absence of an agreed architecture encouraged European States to act outside of it and to exploit the multiplicity of security institutions. For example, during the dissolution of Yugoslavia Germany unilaterally extended recognition to Croatia and Slovenia, and Greece imposed sanctions on FYROM in 1994. Formation of the Contact Group symbolised the apparent failure in the Balkans of established institutions and a *de facto* resort to continued Great Power politics. The EU-3 and the so-called Quint conveyed a similar message, the latter seemingly influencing heavily the outcome of EU discussions on the Balkans.[107] Furthermore, States actively exploited their memberships of multiple security institutions. The Bosnia crisis provides a case in point. European States acquiesced to US pressure within NATO to increased air strikes designed to relieve pressure on the UN 'safe haven' of Bihac. However, they tied their agreement to UN authorisation, which was predictably withheld given a Security Council where Britain and France held potential vetoes and Russia and China were known to oppose NATO action.[108]

The EU and its Member States thus helped create during the 1990s an inter-blocking[109] European security architecture. Responsibilities, roles and purposes became increasingly blurred and resources were wasted. That said, the miserable Balkan experience especially also prompted some rationalisation of the architecture.[110] Within the gaggle of financial institutions charged with providing for CEEC and Balkan reconstruction and political transformation, the EBRD struggled to deliver and became somewhat eclipsed by the EIB.[111] The Nice Treaty portended WEU obscurity as the EU assumed responsibility for all but its collective defence provisions and 'cherry-picked' its assets.[112] And though the OSCE still harboured significant ambitions,[113] the progressive loss of Russian support and its limited resources pushed it increasingly to the margins.

The EU and NATO have consequently emerged as the primary institutions within the European security architecture. The two are a potentially formidable combination, their memberships overlap considerably and both institutions face some common challenges, including funding and capabilities. NATO traditionally operates a 'costs lay as they fall' system. The EU operates the Athena mechanism whereby it administers the financing of the common costs of military operations. National sovereignty concerns, though, mean the majority of costs are still borne where they fall. Both of these systems are ever less appropriate in an expeditionary era where coalitions of the willing are an increasingly frequent *modus operandi*. They encourage free-riders, potentially weaken cohesion and deter Member States from committing to institutionally sanctioned operations. This is particularly problematic given that extensive overlap in NATO-EU memberships and a very uneven distribution of military capabilities result in a high probability of the same countries being called upon repeatedly to lead the more demanding and risky higher-end operations. US officials have urged reconsideration of NATO's system, as has the NATO Parliamentary Assembly. Similarly, the European Commission recommended in March 2003 that some central financial mechanism be developed to ensure that States with small defence budgets nevertheless contributed their fair share to EU capabilities.[114]

The issue of funding operations would be best addressed through close EU–NATO coordination, as would capabilities. National forces are often double-hatted and the same equipment made available for NATO and EU use. Also, NATO is engaged in a sustained capability drive. In 1999 NATO's Defence Capabilities Initiative identified 59 key capability shortfalls.[115] Three years later the Prague Capabilities Commitment secured Member state pledges to improve capabilities in more than 400 specific areas[116] and Allied Command Transformation (ACT) was created to oversee the transformation of NATO structures, forces, capabilities and doctrines. In June 2004 at NATO's Istanbul Summit Member States undertook to make 40 per cent of their land forces deployable to operations under NATO or other auspices and to maintain 8 per cent of these forces either deployed to, or earmarked for, sustained operations.[117] And in 2006, NATO's Comprehensive Political Guidance set out the framework and priorities for Alliance capability issues, planning disciplines and intelligence for the next ten to fifteen years.

Common problems, shared memberships, limited resources and potentially complementary security toolboxes make close EU–NATO collaboration essential. The

2003 Berlin Plus agreement formalised arrangements for the EU–NATO partnership, including EU access to NATO assets. The EU–NATO Capability Group created in March 2003 was to be the linchpin of coordination between the two organisations in an effort to realise the commitment made in December 2002 to ensure 'effective mutual consultation, dialogue, co-operation and transparency'.[118] And in December 2003, the crisis sparked by the 'chocolate summit' the preceding April[119] was resolved through a threefold agreement on enhancing the EU's military planning capabilities and NATO-EU links. First, an EU planning cell would be established at NATO headquarters (SHAPE) to help coordinate any EU missions using NATO assets. Second, a new, small cell with the capacity for operational planning would be added to the EU Military Staff to conduct possible EU missions without recourse to NATO assets. Finally, NATO liaison officers would be invited to the EU Military Staff to help improve EU–NATO transparency and coordination.

However, the reality of EU–NATO relations is far less positive. Berlin Plus failed to prevent NATO and the EU organising simultaneous missions in support of the African Union in Sudan in 2005. The EU–NATO Capability Group has been seriously hampered by political differences, and capability drives lack coordination and reconciliation of priorities. In October 2005 Sir Peter Ricketts, Permanent Representative of the UK to NATO, observed that EU–NATO debate was non-existent at the strategic level.[120]

There are a number of reasons for this situation, three of the most important being problems accruing from overlapping but differentiated memberships, transatlantic relations, and lack of strategic consensus about the roles and purpose of both organisations. NATO has five non-EU Members, the EU has 6 non-NATO Members, and one Member of the EU and NATO (Denmark) opted out of all EU defence-related aspects in the TEU. Differentiated memberships demand mutually acceptable arrangements for non-Members of each organisation to cooperate with the others. These are yet to be satisfactorily developed, Turkey's relationship with ESDP being a case in point. Even more problematically, States have used differentiated memberships for political purposes. For a long time France used them to limit EU–NATO discussion and collaboration, especially in the context of the Turkish–Cypriot dispute. This tactic was particularly pronounced under Chirac's presidency, which viewed EU–NATO relations in almost zero-sum terms.[121] Hence France regularly blocked debates on fundamental political issues such as energy security and a direct relationship between the EDA and ACT, thereby forcing discussions to go through the rather sterile EU–NATO Capability Group where it had greater influence. Although France's return to NATO's military command in 2009 signalled a more cooperative approach, problems relating to Turkey and Turkey–Cyprus relations remain.

Transatlantic relations are the second factor affecting EU–NATO co-operation. Former US Ambassador John Kornblum argues that without a vision of transatlantic strategic partnership the EU's security and defence policy would be inoperable.[122] Even under the Obama administration there is no disguising major differences in strategic priorities, primary threat perception and appropriate responses. America is formally a nation engaged in a war on terrorism, has global military predominance and the will to use it, and has a primary strategic focus on an arc of crisis spanning from West Africa through the Mediterranean to the Gulf and on to South and Central Asia. The EU is on a peacetime footing, its primary strategic focus remains Europe, and it is frequently internally divided on where, when and how to apply force. These differing threat perceptions affect EU–NATO relations across a range of capability issues, including defence market access, technology transfer and interoperability. As Michael Ryan of the US Mission to the EU stressed in 2006, disagreement over threats has resulted in US fears about technology-sharing with its allies falling into the wrong hands and causing the loss of combat advantage. More broadly, the US insists on NATO primacy and has blown hot and cold over ESDP depending on whether administrations have seen it as complementary to or competitive with NATO.[123] Furthermore, US willingness to work through NATO has progressively weakened, especially during the George W. Bush era.

This leads on to the third major problem for EU–NATO co-operation, namely the lack of transatlantic and intra-European consensus about the roles and purposes of both organisations. American global interests, the war on terrorism and difficulties in developing transatlantic consensus have encouraged the US to view Europe as a base for power projection and NATO as both a repository of coalitions of the willing and a key element in the construction of a global security community. There is consequently an intense debate within NATO about whether it should 'go global'. Within the EU, too, there is limited consensus on the use of force generally and, specifically, on how far to commit ESDP to a global rather than primarily European neighbourhood function.

At a strategic level the EU's principal goal of deepening political union is different from NATO's goals.[124] However, NATO's post-Cold War transformation and the EU's continuing and ill-defined development as a security actor lead increasingly to potential role and capability duplication. Both organisations would benefit from closer co-operation between ACT and the EDA and from coordination as the EU refines the ESS and looks beyond Headline Goal 2010 and as NATO takes forward its Strategic Concept following the Lisbon Summit in November 2010. Formal lines of communication, though, are likely to remain blocked. Also, while the EU's solidarity clause in the Lisbon Treaty falls far short of a NATO-style collective defence commitment, potential for future duplication remains. According to Article 27, 'The common security and defence policy shall include the progressive framing of a common Union defence policy. This will lead to a common defence, when the European Council, acting unanimously, so decides.'

More immediately, NATO and EU political agendas increasingly overlap and both have mandates covering Petersberg-style tasks. This situation encourages bureaucratic competition and capability duplication and potentially endangers the lives of deployed personnel. For instance, Turkish opposition meant it was not possible to conclude an agreement enabling NATO to guarantee protection of police forces participating in the EUPOL mission in Afghanistan. Also, Berlin Plus arrangements were based in part on an assumption that the EU and NATO would operate in different theatres. This is ever less the case. In consequence Berlin Plus is under pressure and, in the view of the former NATO Secretary General Jaap de Hoop Scheffer, 'has become too often a straitjacket rather than a facilitator.'[125]

Conclusion

The EU has significantly developed its external security relations, institutional infra-structure and capabilities since the Cold War. This process has both helped establish the EU as a leading security actor in Europe and been a source of contention. Russia continues to call for a new European security architecture and especially resists NATO and EU influence in the shared neighbourhood. The EU has moved away from being a purely civilian power, but there is little consensus about how far it should go in developing military capabilities and applying force. This is reflected in the ESS's failure to develop a clear strategic vision for the EU and match capabilities to objectives. It is also reflected in the very limited progress made by the EDA, the highly selective and low-end ESDP missions undertaken to date, ongoing contention about and deleterious implications of funding mechanisms for ESDP missions, and in basic differences between Member States' security postures, relative willingness to develop military capabilities and conditions under which they are prepared to use force.

The EU's putative security culture has a very long way to go before genuine, sustained strategic cohesion is a realistic expectation. Meanwhile there is no foreseeable prospect of the EU's dual EC/intergovernmental character being resolved. Its exter-nal security relations will remain contested between the EC institutions, the Member States and between the institutions and the Member States. National governments will also have to balance capability commitments to the EU with others elsewhere (including NATO and the UN) and will remain stubbornly protective of sovereignty in the security and defence realms, thereby perpetuating the debilitating 'combination of dissension and requirement for consensus'.[126] With further enlargements scheduled, pressure is obvious for more creative solutions to acute problems in decision-making, implementation, capability development and funding. Yet though the Lisbon Treaty makes nods in this direction, its provisions are neither radical nor especially detailed in parts, leaving their implementation open to contestation between the Member States and creating positions that could serve as a new focus for competency battles.

Though the EU has become more capable and ambitious (at least rhetorically) as a security actor, challenges in matching resources and political will to potential com-mitments remain enormous, especially in the military domain. The circle needs to be squared between increasingly expansive objectives, tight defence budgets, escalating costs of developing and maintaining global expeditionary capabilities, and the importance of ensuring sufficient technological sophistication to reassure casualty-shy European publics about their military personnel being exposed to minimum possible risk. However, military expenditure in Western and Central Europe remains flat, whereas all other regions and sub regions of the world have seen significant increases since 1999.[127] EU–NATO relations remain largely blocked despite French reintegration into NATO's military command. And national sovereignty concerns, differing strategic alignments and low, often inefficient defence expenditure impede efforts by the European Commission and the EDA to promote collaborative military projects, pooling, specialisation and a more competitive EDTIB. Moreover, the EU's effectiveness, its development of ESDP and the sustainability of the Anglo-French compromise all depend in part on US policies and whether the opportunity provided by the Obama administration for a revitalised transatlantic relationship is, or can, be seized.

4

THE US, EUROPEAN SECURITY AND EU–US RELATIONS

'The indispensable nation'?[1]

The US is the world's last superpower and the EU's single most important ally. During the Cold War it sponsored European integration, provided hegemonic leadership for the West and underwrote European security through NATO and its extended nuclear deterrent. Its subsequent importance to European security and to the EU has remained of the highest order. US commitment to NATO has helped extend the transatlantic security community to Russian borders. Its hard power retrieved desperate European positions in the Balkans during the 1990s and still underwrites global security in ways indispensable to the EU.

The EU is entwined with the US through shared values, historical experiences, mutual utility and complex webs of interaction at all levels of EU and Member State governance. Yet since the Cold War the EU has sometimes found working with the US to be as awkward as it is indispensable. The US frequently sets the agenda of security relations. Different US and EU security priorities and proximity considerations encourage different degrees of sensitivity to, for instance, Moscow's attitudes towards European security, which in turn feed back into EU–US relations. And the US is a key factor in determining the EU's own development and its relations with NATO on account of American importance to European security, Atlanticist sentiment within a number of European countries and Washington's ability to (sometimes actively) divide EU Member States on key issues.

The US also has foreign policy traditions, strategic culture, capabilities and global interests that set it apart from the EU and afford it security options very different from the Union. The George W. Bush administration's Global War on Terrorism (GWOT) put the US nation alone amongst its allies on a war footing. Obama's discursive preference for 'overseas contingency operations' rather than the GWOT scarcely disguises that American reaction to 9/11 has foregrounded security priorities and methods very differently from the EU's. American strategic focus has progressively shifted from Europe to the Middle East and Asia; in November 2009 Obama declared himself the first Pacific President. This de-prioritisation of European security and pursuit of the GWOT have simultaneously encouraged transatlantic strategic dissonance and increased US demands that the EU contribute better to providing security.

Understanding EU–US security relations therefore requires as much if not more of an understanding of American foreign policy and its objectives as it does the infrastructure of their relations and the plethora of activities within which they are engaged. This chapter is consequently developed in four parts. The first addresses the post-Cold War architecture of EU–US relations. The second part examines the broad contours of US foreign policy on the premise that America has undergone major transitions as a consequence of the collapse of bipolarity and 9/11 and these have had significant implications for European security and transatlantic relations. The next part examines US attitudes towards European security and argues that therein the EU is just one of three, not necessarily complementary, key relationships that Washington looks to, the other two being NATO Europe and Russia. The final part examines from the EU perspective the importance of its security relationship with the US and some of the difficulties it experiences in managing this.

Managing the EU–US security relationship

Attention has focused in recent years on potential challenges to the established international order – everything from US overextension and radical Islam through to control over energy resources, the implications of the emergent BRIC countries (Brazil, Russia, China and India) and the consequences of global recession. Yet Russian railing, for instance, against the Anglo-Saxon order underscores that the US, EU and the latter's Member States remain collectively preponderant in most facets of power. They are militarily dominant in terms of technology, arms production, nuclear weaponry and spending. They form the bedrock of global governance and have tremendous global cultural influence and diplomatic representation. Americans and Europeans largely devised the world's principal institutions and organisations, still enjoy arguably disproportionate influence in a number of them and have unrivalled connections with most of the world's countries, organisations and NGOs. Even in the economic domain they remain dominant players, possessing two of the world's leading currencies and accounting for approximately 40 per cent of world trade and over 60 per cent of global GDP.

Yet, as US Principal Deputy Assistant Secretary of State for European and Eurasian Affairs Kurt Volker observed in May 2008, the US–EU relationship is still 'in its infancy ... the sense of being a single "U.S.–EU community" is not a phrase that usually rolls off the tongue.'[2] This is especially the case in security affairs where it was primarily NATO and bilateral relations between national capitals that delivered European security during the Cold War. It was thus not just a rebalancing of transatlantic relations that was needed in the aftermath of the Soviet Union's collapse; a framework for EU–US relations needed to be constructed.

The George H. Bush administration took the initial lead in reinforcing the transatlantic relationship, not least to ease European fears for NATO and about reunifying

Germany. In May 1989 Bush suggested closer EU–US consultative links and accorded the EC increasing recognition as a potential full partner. The European Commission's Delegation to Washington was given full diplomatic status and the G7 charged the Commission with responsibility for co-ordinating aid to Poland and Hungary. US Secretary of State James Baker subsequently called for a 'New Atlanticism'.[3] In February 1990 the Irish EC Presidency and the Bush administration agreed biannual meetings between the US President and the Presidents of the European Council and of the Commission. Biannual meetings were also provided for between the US Secretary of State, EC Foreign Ministers and Commission Representatives. In addition, there would be biannual Cabinet level meetings between the Secretary of State and the Presidency Foreign Minister/or the troika, and ad hoc consultations.

The Italian EC Presidency adopted the Declaration on EC–US Relations on 20 November 1990. This has been criticised for being 'long on rhetoric and short on substance'.[4] Nevertheless, it reaffirmed the salience of shared values, developed common objectives similar to those adopted for CFSP in the TEU, and formalised earlier contacts between the European Parliament and Congress. The Declaration also heralded the potential for a genuine EC–US security relationship by formally recognising 'the accelerating process by which the European Community is acquiring its own identity in economic and monetary matters, in foreign policy and in the domain of security'.[5]

The procedural limitations of the Declaration, such as a lack of co-ordination between different bureaucratic levels of dialogue and insufficient follow-through from EC/EU–US summits, were quickly exposed during the first Gulf War and the early years of the Balkan conflicts. Redressing them became increasingly urgent and in November 1992 Germany's Chancellor, Helmut Kohl, advocated a more comprehensive transatlantic structure to improve continuity between summits, deepen the level of consultation and provide for greater practical collaboration. The EU–US Summit in July 1994 approved three working groups, comprising representatives of the US, the Commission and the EU Presidency, to examine the stabilisation of Central and Eastern Europe, CFSP and international crime, including nuclear smuggling and drugs trafficking. The eventual product was a new, comprehensive framework for EU–US cooperaton – a New Transatlantic Agenda (NTA) and an accompanying Joint Action Plan (JAP) that were adopted at the EU–US Madrid Summit on 3 December 1995.

The NTA placed EU–US relations firmly within a global framework and signalled the launch of 'an era of unprecedented cooperaton on a wide range of political, economic and civil society issues'.[6] Improved dialogue and continuity were provided for through a Senior Level Group of sub-cabinet level officials and an NTA Task Force. The latter comprised numerous working level officials and was charged with monitoring and co-ordinating progress in designated areas. These areas were clustered around four themes: 'Promoting peace and stability, democracy and development around the world; Responding to global challenges; Contributing to the expansion of world trade and closer economic relations; and building bridges across the Atlantic'. The JAP developed numerous specific short and medium term EU–US actions designed to fulfil objectives contained within the four themes.[7]

Four aspects of the NTA and JAP were particularly important for EU–US security relations. First, it renewed the American invitation to the EU to become a global security partner, which was particularly timely given the fraught transatlantic experience in the Balkans. Areas designated for joint leadership included consolidation of democracy in Russia and Central Europe, reconstruction of Bosnia and Herzegovina, and efforts to combat transnational threats including international crime and narcotics. Crucially, the NTA also emphasised EU strengths by adopting a broad conceptualisation of security that explicitly recognised links between security and economic transformation and liberalisation. Herein the EU and US were to act jointly in preventative diplomacy, provision of humanitarian assistance and promotion of multilateral free trade. The NTA acknowledged, too, that effective security cooperaton and the achievement of shared objectives needed to involve other actors, including international regimes, NGOs, lobbyists and interest groups. Similarly, recognition was given to the relationship between public opinion and sustainable security cooperaton, especially given the so-called CNN factor and blurring of the foreign and domestic realms of policy.[8] Hence the People-to-People Chapter sought to 'educate' American and European parliamentarians in support of EU–US cooperaton and to counter any weakening of transatlantic identification that demographic and generational change might encourage.[9] Perhaps most important, though, was that the NTA effectively developed a joint transatlantic security agenda, with the JAP delineating specific measures to address this.

The NTA marked the first time the US dealt comprehensively with the EU as a partner in a whole array of foreign policy and diplomatic initiatives rather than simply as a trade and economic organization.[10] At the Gothenburg Summit in June 2001 the NTA was developed into six strategic themes that were said to mark 'a new chapter in the EU–US relationship, characterised by clear and sustainable political priorities and more streamlined, political and results-orientated methods of cooperaton.'[11] As the British Presidency of the EU rightly noted in December 2005, 9/11 caused the strategic partnership with the US and the wider Transatlantic Dialogue to break new ground and sponsored 'a substantial growing agenda of security co-operation which is well set to continue.'[12]

The Obama administration was warmly welcomed in Europe in the wake of the more unilateralist inclined Bush administrations. Prior to the EU–US summit in November 2009 Commissioner for External Relations and European Neighbourhood Policy, Benita Ferrero-Waldner, spoke of the 'new energy [in] our strategic relationship ... thanks to even more intense co-operation with the new US Administration.'[13] Yet Obama's decision not to attend a planned EU–US summit in spring 2010 caused its cancellation and renewed speculation about the extent of his relative commitment to Europe. One EU diplomat noted, 'He does not always seem as interested in Europe as Europe is in the United States'.[14] Moreover, the fact remains that 9/11 and reactions to it sharpened EU–US differences, brought into tight focus warnings of post-Cold War transatlantic malaise and sponsored critiques of the EU and US occupying different social worlds that, while often being populist polemics, also contained insights difficult to refute.[15] Thus, though the EU and US have developed a much improved institutional and programme framework within which to advance security co-operation and resolve inevitable differences, its effectiveness has varied depending upon the willingness of all parties to operate through it, the temper of broader transatlantic relations and revisions of strategic priorities.

American foreign policy and the emergence of transatlantic strategic dissonance

Post-Cold War America emerged into the putative dawn of a New World Order and the teeth of fierce debate. Were Paul Kennedy and the 'declinists' right that US relative power had so waned that its global interests and obligations now outstripped the country's power to defend them?[16] Also, was the international system now in a unipolar, multipolar or hybrid uni-multipolar configuration?[17] If it were unipolar around America, was this desirable and/or sustainable?[18] And should America exercise (benign) unilateralism or constructive multilateralism in its defence?[19] Alternatively, if the system were some variant of multipolarity, would American interests be best advanced through neo-isolationist unilateralism that would allegedly allow America to offload many of its overseas commitments or through multilateralism that could preserve American interests, accommodate difference and provide for peace?[20]

Successive post-Cold War presidencies were clear on what America's world role should not be, namely, as Condoleezza Rice put it in 2000, 'the world's 911.'[21] Also, though often overlooked amidst the George W. Bush administration's poor public diplomacy and the controversy surrounding the legality of military intervention in Iraq in 2003, there has been considerable continuity in basic premises of American foreign policy.[22] American primacy has been a largely unspoken objective since the Second World War.[23] Unilateralism has a long progeny in US history, often being closely entwined with isolationism,[24] and unilateral-multilateral leanings within American policy have further fluctuated in tune with debates between America and the rest of the world over the purpose and definition of multilateralism. Even preventative military action has long been entertained, and sometimes exercised.[25] Furthermore, all post-Cold War administrations have exported the American model consistent with US political traditions of exceptionalism and manifest destiny.

However, new constraints were undeniably experienced by the Executive when adjusting US foreign policy to a post-Cold War era. The US public demanded a peace dividend and Clinton was elected in 1992 on a domestic platform. Also, isolationist sentiment waxed and waned and once freed of the Cold War consensus Congress interjected more often in American foreign policy. Congress is frequently an incoherent actor and its relationship with the Executive is unpredictable. It temporarily abdicated responsibility in the 2001 Patriot Act and the 2002 Joint Resolution to Authorize the Use of United States Armed Forces Against Iraq. Yet George H. Bush indicated just what a constraint it can be in his quip that 'I myself have sometimes thought the ageing process could be delayed if it had to make its way through Congress.'[26]

Re-defining American strategic interests was also a major challenge and one that saw US interest in Europe wane progressively. Few conventional state-based threats to the US remained. Russia was the initial focus but American attention soon moved to the Middle East and the Pacific. When in 2006 US strategy papers cited 'shaping the choices of countries at strategic crossroads' as one of four priorities[27] and argued that America must 'hedge' lest States choose 'unwisely',[28] policymakers were referring to China especially. In 1991 the Bush administration developed some now familiar themes – regional 'hotspots' such as the Korean Peninsula, non-proliferation, arms control, combating international terrorism, preventing the 'transfer of military critical technologies and resources to hostile countries or groups', countering States that had made themselves 'champions of regional radicalism', and ameliorating the conditions of human existence that made citizens 'ripe for radicalization'.[29] Clinton proceeded to call for a global effort to combat terrorism, and propounded the linkage between rogue States, WMD proliferation and terrorism whilst 9/11 enabled George W. Bush to establish this nexus as the most dangerous immediate threat to the US and to initiate the GWOT.[30]

These re-orientations and the rapid succession of George H. Bush's '*status quo* plus' foreign policy strategy, Clinton's democratic enlargement, and Bush's GWOT, reflect the flux in post-Cold War American foreign policy. Often likened to Pearl Harbor as a defining moment in American history,[31] the 9/11 attacks introduced new and enduring psychological and strategic considerations for the US that had major implications for American foreign policy and transatlantic relations. As George W. Bush put it, before September 11 'we were a country which was able to sit back in our – kind of in our geographical posture and pick and choose where a threat might emerge and say, we may have to deal with that or we may not deal with it; we were pretty confident that we were protected ourselves by oceans. That changed.'[32] America's newly demonstrated vulnerability profoundly changed both the balance between security and individual freedoms within America and the resources – physical and attitudinal – that the Executive could draw upon to discharge foreign policy abroad.

After 9/11 the US ceased to be a stalwart supporter of the *status quo*, something that constitutes a significant break with almost 60 years of American foreign policy. This is reflected in the military interventions in Afghanistan and Iraq, the aggressive promotion of democracy and free markets and the State Department's reorientation toward transformational diplomacy. It is reflected, too, in US qualification of its support of the Westphalian system and questioning of the definition of immanency in international law. The Clinton administration embraced the idea of sovereignty as responsibility in its 1996 National Security Strategy (NSS) and arguably acted militarily on that basis in Bosnia and in Kosovo. Condoleezza Rice went further in arguing that 'The fundamental character of regimes now matters more than the international distribution of power.'[33]

The GWOT accelerated the shift in American strategic focus away from Europe. Even Africa was hailed in the 2006 NSS as holding growing strategic importance and being a high priority – a radical change on Bush's view in February 2000 that it did not fit into US strategic interests.[34] Also, the Bush administrations temporarily at least laid to rest the Vietnam and Mogadishu syndromes and re-engaged America in nation-building. Admittedly, Obama encountered renewed post-Iraq sensitivity about combat deployments when committing more US troops to Afghanistan. Nevertheless, the Bush administrations sent clear messages about US willingness to use all available resources to achieve its ends, Richard Perle, famously summing these up in the two words 'You're next'.[35]

Finally, the George W. Bush administrations appeared determined to re-model the world in ways analogous in some respects to the aftermath of World War Two. Intervention in Iraq was conventional and far less dramatic than the atomic attacks on Hiroshima and Nagasaki but there were resonances of 1945 in the signals sent by the devastating exercise of military superiority and the ambition for Iraq to become a democratic catalyst for the wider Middle East. Condoleezza Rice explicitly reminded the world in January 2006 that 'America has done this kind of thing before'.[36] Controversial appointments to international institutions such as John Bolton to the UN and Paul Wolfowitz as President of the World Bank arguably indicated less a disregard for institutions than a desire to make them vehicles of 'effective' multilateralism – at least by American definition. And the 2006 NSS declared that 'Where existing institutions can be reformed to meet new challenges, we, along with our partners, must reform them. Where appropriate institutions do not exist, we, along with our partners, must create them.'[37] This referred not only to NATO's enlargement and ongoing role revision (explored further later in this chapter) but also to promoting liberalisation and free markets via the WTO, regional trade arrangements and Free Trade Agreements as antidotes to insecurity and societal unrest and as vehicles through which to institutionalise American values and policy preferences.

Obama has similarly refuted 'the cynics who say that this new century cannot be another when, in the words of President Franklin Roosevelt, we lead the world in battling immediate evils and promoting the ultimate good.'[38] Moreover, whereas the George H. Bush and the Clinton administrations tended to associate US interests with the existing order, the Obama administration has embraced its predecessor's move away from the *status quo* and its interest in social and institutional engineering in ways that are different from pre-9/11. Speaking in the aftermath of the G-20 summit in April 2009, Obama conceded that negotiations had become more complex than when Roosevelt and Churchill sat in a room with a brandy to re-make the international architecture.[39] But his re-investment in multilateralism is inconsistent neither with re-casting institutions to make them more effective for American interests nor with commitment to American primacy.[40]

America, European security and the EU

The George H. Bush administration prioritised a 'Europe whole and free'.[41] Successive administrations maintained that mantra but adopted progressively more expansive definitions of Europe as democracy and the free market marched eastwards, and as energy resources, the GWOT and the need for staging posts from which to project

American power focused attention on its outer periphery. Nowadays the US is less interested in, and less committed to, security in Europe than at any time since World War Two. Resource allocations reflect this. The George H. Bush administration battled Congress to maintain 150,000 American troops in Europe. Clinton pledged in 1994 to maintain roughly 100,000 troops in Europe.[42] George W. Bush was determined to withdraw one third of remaining US troops based in Europe within ten years. America's diplomatic resources are also being redistributed. Condoleezza Rice noted the obsolescence of having almost as many State Department officials in Germany as in India, and several hundred diplomatic positions were quickly slated for redeployment to new priority regions – beginning with the removal of 100 positions from Europe.[43]

Europe is no longer a significant focus of US strategic concern or resources, regardless of the fragility of the Balkans and Russia's reassertion. What attention Washington does pay is dedicated to consolidating democracy in Georgia, Moldova and Ukraine and ensuring a place in the Euro-Atlantic community for the countries of the Southern Caucasus. However, this does not mean Europe is unimportant to Washington. American officials readily acknowledge, for example, that 'Europe is a vital partner in the war on terrorism'.[44] Rather, the big difference is that Washington now looks to Europe to export security and to provide vital physical and moral resources that the US can tap in pursuit of global and extra-European regional priorities. The US Strategic Plan Fiscal Years 2007–12 makes clear this American inversion of the Cold War era equation. The 'top priority is to realize the President's and Secretary's transformational goals beyond Europe. In Western and Central Europe, about 75 percent of our work focuses on engaging allies to support U.S. priorities beyond Europe.'[45]

It is important to recognise, too, that for Washington the EU is just one of three key European relationships, the other two being NATO Europe and Russia. Thus far it has been relatively consistent in its post-Cold War approach towards these relationships: persuading NATO Europe and the EU to accept greater responsibilities in providing for European and international security; instrumental recruitment of Russian co-operation; retaining American freedom of manoeuvre; and ensuring that European initiatives remain embedded within the wider Atlantic security framework. At the same time, Washington has experienced plenty of frustration in tending these relationships and often found its three European 'horses' tend to ride in different directions to Washington and/or to each other.

For Washington the EU offers significant soft power resources; allies that can add legitimacy to US operations; sufficient military capabilities to at least maintain the post-Dayton peace in the Balkans; expertise in peacekeeping and reconstruction; and sometimes useful political connections with countries in American-designated 'hot spots'. For example, former British Prime Minister Blair played a leading part in developing the international coalition in support of US intervention in Afghanistan. EU co-operation is also important in America's drive to reform international institutions and forge new partnerships in the GWOT. EU countries have significant collective voting power in the IMF and World Bank. The EU is America's principal partner in the WTO. It is also committed to improving military capabilities at least to deal with the Petersberg tasks, which in turn is vital to the success of NATO and its Response Force given the sharing of assets. Furthermore, counter-terrorism has become a mainstay of US–EU relations, spanning closer coordination on multilateral export control regimes, extradition and mutual legal assistance treaties, intelligence sharing, transportation security, membership of several EU countries of the US Pro-liferation Security Initiative to interdict the illicit transfer of nuclear equipment, and co-operation against terrorist assets in the UN Counterterrorism Committee, the G-8 Counterterrorism Action Group, and the Financial Action Task Force.

The US relationship with NATO Europe has focused on outreach programmes, formal enlargement, capability drives and progressive revision of its role to embrace non-traditional and out-of-area missions. Elizabeth Jones, Assistant Secretary for European and Eurasian Affairs, indicated new US priorities in March 2004 when she stressed the significance of refocusing the Partnership for Peace (PFP) programme, which provides a mechanism to export NATO civil-military norms and procedures, on the Caucasus and Central Asia as 'front-line regions in the War on Terrorism.'[46] NATO commitments to ISAF and the training of Iraqi troops and police reflect American emphasis on improved capabilities and revised mission if NATO is to remain a 'forward looking' institution. Furthermore, though enlargement has been primarily politically motivated, it has provided some marginal additional military contributions and geographic advantages for forward deployment and Ballistic Missile Defence (BMD) facilities. The US has also looked to NATO enlargement in terms of hedging against Russian reassertion and to bolster Atlanticism within European countries. The latter especially strengthens America's influence in European security and over the development of security initiatives, including the European Security and Defence Policy given the large overlap between NATO and EU memberships.

The US argues that NATO could catalyse improved transatlantic and intra-European interoperability and coordination between war fighting and crisis response operations. However, to do so NATO Europe needs to spend more on defence, allocate resources more effectively, reduce duplication, re-orientate military planning and assets to contemporary threats and improve procurement co-operation. American determination to drive these reforms is reflected in the 2002 NATO Prague Cap-ability Commitments, Allied Command Transformation (ACT) and unrelenting pressure upon European countries to better 'pull their weight' in military matters. The US has also sought NATO's transformation from a vehicle of collective defence to one of power projection and to develop its emergence 'at the center of our global democratic security community.'[47] Hence the 2006 NSS called for NATO to 'deepen working relationships between and across institutions' and Kurt Volker sug-gested that same year that 'maybe we should create some kind of relationship, whatever you would call it – partnership, liaison, communication, something, with countries with which we are likely to be operating in various spots in the world in the future as we deal with crises or peacekeeping or humanitarian support.'[48]

The US–Russia relationship has changed considerably. It was initially dominated by concern about Russia's instability, strategic nuclear weapons and the security of

WMD stockpiles. The mainstay of the relationship was arms control and non-proliferation; by the time George H. Bush left office in January 1993 five major nuclear arms control initiatives had been accomplished, providing for a 66 per cent reduction on 1990 levels of US strategic nuclear forces and a 75 per cent reduction in the overall American nuclear arsenal.[49] The Clinton administration subsequently pledged strategic partnership with Russia. WMD remained paramount. Clinton and Russian President Yeltsin agreed provisions in January 1994 for de-targeting strategic weapons away from each other's homelands and US incentives were offered to encourage Russian nuclear co-operation and prevent the haemorrhage of Russian WMD expertise.[50] The Clinton administration also sought to mollify Russian opposition to NATO enlargement, develop co-operaton over Middle Eastern issues through the Quartet, and engage Russia in stabilising the Balkans through the Contact Group and KFOR (the NATO- led Kosovo Force).

George W. Bush's agenda was different but arguably more important to the US. First, the administration ideally wanted Russian acquiescence to its withdrawal from the anti-ballistic missile treaty (ABM) in readiness for development of BMD. In May 2002 it gave Russian President Putin political cover for this move by agreeing the Strategic Offensive Reductions Treaty.[51] Second, nuclear co-operation continued. For instance, in August 2002 they collaborated to remove enriched uranium from Serbia's Vinca reactor, and in January 2003 the Bush administration authorised $450 million within the Nunn-Lugar Programme to facilitate work on a chemical weapons destruction facility at Shchuch'ye in Russia.[52] Third, and most important, the GWOT provided new coincidences of interest. Russia could help to arrange forward bases, offer valuable intelligence and bring influence to bear on States over which the US had limited purchase, including Iran.

Europe broadly conceived is thus now an indispensable ally, as opposed to strategic theatre, for the US. However, Washington has found securing American objectives increasingly difficult and frustrating. Europe's greater geostrategic independence, EU security actor ambitions and reservations about the foreign policies of the George W. Bush administrations especially generated greater questions of US leadership. US–Russia relations deteriorated badly as a result of US 'light-switch' rather than sustained engagement diplomacy, the Kremlin's increasingly strident criticism of American policies, and re-emerging strategic competition as the US pushes into post-Soviet space. An energy-fuelled Russia has reasserted itself in its neighbourhood and actively promotes its rival development model and multipolarity as alternatives to US-style liberal democratic capitalism and unipolarity. Russia now seeks to weaken US influence in Europe – something epitomised by President Medvedev's call in June 2008 for an all-European security pact[53]– and has repeatedly challenged the US in the UN Security Council, including over US-led military interventions in the Balkans and its controversial sponsorship of Kosovo's independence. Moscow has repeatedly opposed NATO enlargement and its approach to conflict with Georgia in August 2008 was undoubtedly informed by hostility to US penetration of post-Soviet space and support for Tblisi's prospective membership of NATO. The EU, too, has opposed American policy across a well-rehearsed range of security issues, and its ESDP still has potential to weaken American ability to work with key European allies, squander scarce resources through duplication, damage interoperability and encourage strategic competition with NATO.

US frustration with European partners and suspicion of their pursuing instrumental soft balancing has encouraged American criticism of European 'muddling through' and exposed transatlantic differences over multilateralism, justice and legitimacy.[54] US security discourse is undoubtedly different from Europe's, the EU's especially. The US talks in terms of strategic threat, confrontation and isolation; the EU speaks more of security challenges and of engagement, socialisation and multilateralism. But important though these differences are, they are not what really irritates US officials. One burning grievance is 'something of a European campaign, heavily associated in the U.S. view with some Member state governments and the European Commission, to de-legitimate U.S. policy through reckless and indiscriminate wielding of the "unilateralism" charge.'[55] US officials have also 'long been irritated by what they see as the tendency of the EU, assisted by some allies outside Europe, to define, unilaterally as it were, what constitutes true multilateralism and to label all dissenting views as unilateralist.'[56] Kissinger, for example, observed that Americans discern in EU attitudes a merging of multilateralism 'with new forms of self-righteous moralistic nationalism', and US officials complain that in international negotiations the EU often confronts them with ultimatum positions: 'Europeans ask us for real consultations, but, too often we are also told by Europeans that they cannot tell us their views on an issue with us because there is no common position. And then, once a common position is forged, we are told it cannot be adapted or changed because it is based on a fragile set of compromises. Hence it is the EU that often presents us with a unilateral, take-it-or-leave-it position that cannot be negotiated.'[57]

American policymakers also suspect ulterior motives when European multilateralism seemingly elevates process above policy. In such circumstances multilateralism may be less a European value than a strategy, or rather, strategies. It may be used to avoid responsibilities – evidence of this perception includes US interest in reviewing NATO's funding practices for missions. Multilateralism might also be used to protect vested interests in the *status quo* or to constrain a dominant power, i.e. the US. For instance, US representative to the Conference on Disarmament, Rademaker, observed in February 2003 that 'if multilateralism of the type we have witnessed here were to persist within the CD and spread to other multilateral institutions, we would all soon be unilateralists, or at least something other than multilateralists.'[58]

Yet ultimately the US needs the transatlantic security relationship almost as much as the Europeans do, albeit for different reasons. A secure Europe is a vital springboard for America's wider priorities, and to have this it needs the EU to consolidate the Western Balkans and, together with NATO, support transition processes in Eastern Europe and the Southern Caucasus. Indeed, Obama and Secretary of State Hillary Clinton reportedly praised the EU's new Eastern Partnership (see Chapter 7) during an informal EU–US summit in April 2009, and Deputy Assistant Secretary of State Bryza welcomed it as 'a positive sign that things are moving finally in the right direction'.[59] Deeper US–EU–Russia co-operation would also be advantageous, especially in Central Asia, the Middle East and the Caucasus, albeit that the prospects of this remain in the balance.

The Bush administration's second term reflected these calculations. Crude disaggregation policies and belittling of alliances and allies characteristic of the Rumsfeld years were replaced with greater investment in persuasion, presentation and tone. Bush visited Europe three times in the first six months of his second term. In February 2005, Condoleezza Rice made Europe her first overseas destination as Secretary of State, as did US Secretary for Homeland Security Michael Chertoff in a visit to Brussels to meet Solana. Furthermore, Obama's pre-presidential Berlin speech in July 2008 and charm offensive during his first visit as president to Europe in spring 2009 suggested that this more diplomatic American approach would continue, and with more credibility.

High level representations were complemented by a major investment in public diplomacy and acknowledgement at the highest levels of mistakes made in policy presentation.[60] In November 2007 Colleen Graffy, Deputy Assistant Secretary of State for Public Diplomacy for Europe and Eurasia, observed that 'Communicating is tough – we used to be good at it, at least to one part of Europe, and then we became less good.'[61] Bush hailed the importance of allies in his second term inaugural speech, called for a 'new era of transatlantic unity' and sought to relativise differences within the context of the maturity of the transatlantic relationship and as being nothing more than 'fleeting disagreements between friends.'[62] His second administration also made gestures and concessions to European concerns. The 2006 NSS downplayed preventative action and unilateralism and foregrounded a Clintonesque focus on addressing globalisation, promoting democratisation, and searching for diplomatic solutions with allies. Its 'two pillars' – promoting freedom, justice and human dignity and leading a growing community of democracies – might have been taken from almost any postwar American administration.[63] Furthermore, following NATO's endorsement of BMD the Bush administration made efforts to reassure Russia, and by extension Poland, about the missile shield and to develop an agenda for security co-operation with the Kremlin. It suggested several transparency measures for BMD, including access for Russian liaison officers, agreed to engage in discussions about Russian ideas for building a jointly managed regional defence system, committed to further mutual cuts in nuclear arsenals, and signed a Strategic Framework Declaration in April 2008 setting out areas for further US–Russia co-operation.

US officials also endeavoured to draw a line under the crisis years surrounding the intervention in Iraq. In an obvious riposte to Rumsfeld's dictum that the mission should determine the coalition, US Ambassador to NATO Victoria Nuland argued in February 2008 that 'coalitions of the willing have their limitations' and that, while the US would always 'consult early' with EU Member state capitals, 'increasingly we are also turning to European institutions as well.'[64] Particularly interesting in the latter context were two revised messages sent about ESDP. The first was of newfound encouragement. In its dying days the Bush administration seemingly accepted the conclusion drawn by the Clinton administration as it left office that whatever the Europeans did to meet US burden-sharing demands would have to be supported provided it was compatible with what NATO does.[65] The second, related message was one of interest in much closer coordination between NATO and ESDP, and between the US and the EU, especially in crisis management. In 2005, NATO's Allied Command Transformation (ACT) emphasised the need for effects-based operations that encompass the military, political, economic and civil power of alliance Members 'and potentially beyond, in partnership with other international organisations and agencies'.[66] A recurring phrase in speeches by American officials to European audiences became 'seamless co-operation'.[67] And action accompanied rhetoric. For instance, on 17 March 2008 *notes verbales* were exchanged confirming intent to implement initiatives outlined in December 2007 in a work plan on EU–US Technical Dialogue and Increased Co-operation in Crisis Management and Conflict Prevention.

The Bush administration thus made a conscious effort to re-engage Europe in its second term: resolving security challenges requires soft as well as hard power, 'No country can be isolationist, no country can be unilateralist', and 'most of the time diplomacy, coalitions and international institutions are the way that problems are resolved.'[68] Nevertheless, the US agenda in and for Europe actually changed little. Daniel Fried, US Assistant Secretary of State for European and Eurasian Affairs, reasserted the changing place of Europe in American calculations: 'For most of the twentieth century, and especially between 1914 and 1999, U.S. policy toward Europe was about Europe … U.S. policy today is about what we can do together with Europe in the rest of the world.'[69] At the institutional level the Bush administration reaffirmed NATO as the place where transatlantic power 'including political, economic and moral power – is translated into action',[70] and re-iterated its dictum that ESDP must become 'a supportive part of an effective NATO and a transatlantic link'.[71] It also continued to promote the Atlanticist caucus within the EU – actual and potential. This included securing NATO membership for Croatia, Albania and (potentially) FYROM, and pressing for Turkey's accession to the EU – something that Obama, much to Franco-German chagrin, has done too.[72]

Meantime, American focus on Europe's periphery and half-hearted acknowledgement of Russian concerns continued. In the Balkans the US worked to expand NATO's influence and cooperated closely with EU countries over the Ahtisaari Plan, Kosovo's independence and EULEX (see Chapter 7).[73] It then generally allowed the EU to lead the agreed 'supervision' of Kosovo[74] and the stabilisation of the wider Balkan region and (re)turned its attention to the Ukraine, the Southern Caucasus and Central Asia. Hence the Bush administration pushed for greater NATO and European involvement in Afghanistan, hailed the contributions of Azerbaijan and Georgia especially to the GWOT, strongly opposed Russia in its conflict with Georgia and campaigned, to the alarm of a number of European countries, for Georgia and Ukraine to be given NATO membership perspectives in 2008. In April 2008 Putin reportedly threatened Ukraine's existence as a sovereign state if it were to join NATO[75] and the Georgia conflict brought deteriorating US–Russia relations to arguably their 'lowest point since before the Reykjavik summit between Ronald Reagan and Mikhail Gorbachev in 1986.'[76] The Obama administration subsequently softened the tone and concluded a deal with Medvedev in April 2009 to develop a new arms-control treaty but there has been little evident change to date in America's policies towards the European periphery.

The EU, European security and the US

The EU remains heavily indebted to the US for its own security and that of wider Europe. US security, especially nuclear, guarantees allowed the EU to establish and consolidate integration within a type of geostrategic vacuum during the Cold War. Afterwards, the US took the lead in addressing Russia's residual WMD threat, helped consolidate Central, Eastern and South Eastern Europe, especially through NATO's Partnership for Peace (PFP) programme, Membership Action Plan (MAP) and successive enlargements, and intervened twice militarily in the Balkans. The majority of EU countries still base territorial defence on NATO guarantees and, as the Balkans conflicts demonstrated, NATO is credible primarily because of US commitment and leadership. Even where the EU takes the lead in its European neighbourhood, its constituent countries often view their relations with the US and the American security commitment to Europe as the principal guarantee of peace and stability. Furthermore, the US has a global foreign policy strategy and genuine global reach to back it up whereas the EU often talks global but in terms of delivery and focus is still a predominantly regional power in security terms. The combination of EU recognition that 'in an era of globalisation distant threats may be as much a concern as those that are near at hand'[77] and the reality of limited EU security influence beyond its neighbourhood has three significant consequences for EU–US relations and European security. First, it encourages European dependency upon US security provision. Second this dependency reaffirms the US as the Union's most important, and senior, security partner. Finally, the EU and European security are potentially newly vulnerable to the contours of American foreign policy. Given that US priorities no longer lie in Europe and that Europe is viewed by Washington within a truly global strategy framework, the White House might be tempted to threaten to or actually trade interests in Europe (or with parts of Europe) for wider gains in its global priorities.

America's commitment to European security *per se* is now more important to the EU and its Member States than to the US. However, the EU often disagrees with how America provides that security and finds that European–American policies, even when geared to similar ends, are not necessarily fully complementary. This concern is not confined to aforementioned differences over hard and soft power, varieties and relative importance of multilateralism and sensitivities about meaningful consultation. Rather, it also reflects competition for influence in Europe and the different political sensitivities of Washington, Brussels and European capitals that stem from geography, distribution of resources and world-views. America and the EU are close allies but Washington is interested foremost in extending American and transatlantic influence into Eastern Europe and the Southern Caucasus rather than the Union's. This reflects US interest in energy resources, economic opportunities, forward projection and continued suspicion that some EU Member States would still like the Union to balance America. The EU has thus found, for example, that US assistance programmes that spread American influence also raise the possibility of US conditionality and socialisation weakening EU conditionality and Europeanisation.

The EU has also found that relations with Russia complicate EU–US relations. The George W. Bush administrations' combination of instrumental engagement of Russia with strident criticism of Moscow's sovereign democracy and of its policies wherever they ran up against American objectives was encouraged by the US being the world's most powerful nation, being situated on a different continent from Russia, and obtaining much of its energy needs from Middle Eastern, African and domestic sources. The EU has to balance its conflicting values and interests with Russia against its dependence on Russian energy supplies, the Kremlin's importance in their shared neighbourhood, the implications of shared borders and the evident reality that EU Member States are divided on how to handle Russia's contemporary reassertion. These EU–US differences help explain why the US was more vociferous than Brussels and most European capitals in its support of the Orange and Rose revolutions, in its encouragement of Ukraine and Georgia entering NATO, and in its advocacy of BMD. It also helps explain Washington's greater willingness to support opposition movements against authoritarian regimes in Eastern Europe and to use negative conditionality.

There is potential currently for the EU and US to close the gap in their appreciations of Russia and how to deal with Moscow. The Obama administration's early engagement of Moscow contrasts favourably with its predecessor's almost routine neglect and/or chastisement. Concomitantly, the Georgia crisis in August 2008 and the gas supply crisis in January 2009 hardened many EU attitudes towards Moscow and demonstrated a need for a new approach given the evident failure of an EU–Russia strategic partnership premised on shared values (see Chapter 5). Yet EU–US interests and calculations vis-à-vis Russia will not automatically better align and they will continue to affect, and be affected by, EU–Russia and US–Russia relations. For instance, US support for further NATO expansion into Eastern Europe and the Southern Caucasus contrasts sharply with the EU's Eastern Partnership/European Security Strategy/European Neighborhood Policy long-term approach and emphasis on reform from within. Also, the EU is relatively more concerned about security co-operation with Russia within Europe than is Washington, the latter prioritising instead Russian co-operation in addressing global threats, such as terrorism and proliferation, and extra-European regional issues such as the nuclear programmes of Iran and North Korea and stabilising Iraq, Afghanistan and Pakistan. There is a consequent danger for the EU that US–Russia tensions impact negatively on the Union's strategic partnership with Russia and/or that Washington cuts deals with Moscow in the interests of advancing US–Russia co-operation on America's big strategic priorities at the expense of EU interests. The latter danger is exacerbated by Russia's longstanding view of the US as the most important security interlocutor and by its prioritisation of hard security issues, where the EU is a weak player next to its leading Member States and NATO.

The EU also finds the US to be very influential in how, and how well, it develops its own security capabilities and under what conditions it uses them. The most obvious cause of this is the fault line running through the EU between Atlanticists and Europeanists and the sensitivity of both sides to American rhetoric and policies. British, Czech and Polish willingness to provide facilities for BMD reflects their anxiety to strengthen ties with the US. The military intervention in Iraq in 2003 provided a disastrous demonstration of how badly, with active US encouragement on this occasion, this fault line could rupture the EU. More generally, the tension between Atlanticism and Europeanism has framed the EU's development of hard power security tools. British determination to preserve NATO and prevent the EU moving into the military domain without American approval contributed to European inability in the early 1990s to back their diplomacy towards the Socialist Federal Republic of Yugoslavia with a credible threat of force. The subsequent development of ESDP relied upon constructive ambiguity between the Atlanticist and Europeanist concerns of Britain and France respectively. Even after the Berlin Plus arrangements there have been numerous examples of Atlanticist–Europeanist disputes and of lack of NATO–EU coordination – including parallel missions in support of the African Union Mission in Sudan in 2005. In October 2005 Sir Peter Ricketts, Permanent Representative of the UK to NATO, observed that EU–NATO debate was non-existent at the strategic level. Two years later, NATO Secretary General de Hoop Scheffer likened the EU–NATO relationship to a 'frozen conflict'.[78]

US priorities, inconsistency and determination to develop co-operation on its own terms compound problems caused by competing Atlanticist–Europeanist preferences for the EU, EU–US relations and European security. A case in point, and one of such importance that it is worth expanding on in some detail, concerns interoperability and capability development in the context of consistent American demands that Europeans contribute more to international security, especially militarily. There are strong reasons to favour closer transatlantic defence procurement and defence industry collaboration. The US is leading a Revolution in Military Affairs (RMA), whereby innovative incorporation of new technologies into military systems is being combined with changes in operational and organizational concepts to alter fundamentally the character and conduct of military operations. However, the RMA technological package of sophisticated C4ISR, data links and precision-guided munitions that enables net-centric operations[79] is extremely expensive. Within Europe even the UK and France accept that they cannot realistically pursue wholesale transformation. They are instead concentrating on policies of net-enabled capability that selectively and incrementally transform the capabilities of their militaries in those areas most likely to improve their effectiveness in the context of coalition warfare.[80]

The US also has significant political and technological reasons to participate. Europe can offer niche technologies in which it has advantages, such as Swedish Ultra High Frequency (UHF) mobile communications systems and British anti-Improvised Explosive Device Technology. This importance is liable to grow as traditional military contractors remain systems integrators but draw increasingly for the sources of cutting-edge RMA technology upon newer, smaller firms – often on an international basis – for which defence is a small, even invisible, share of total business.[81] Second, the US needs help in controlling access to the most sensitive dual use technologies that are integral to RMA, especially given their commercial availability and global access to information. Third, the US needs co-operation in key aspects of defence critical technologies to safeguard the technological supremacy of its military and intelligence gathering services, which is threatened by the globalisation of technology information and commercial off-the-shelf technology (COTS).[82] Finally, technology sharing and closer transatlantic defence company collaboration could boost European military capabilities, strengthen NATO and invigorate the American defence industry, which has suffered from over-consolidation.[83] A transatlantic rather than bipolar Defence Technology Industrial Base (DTIB), which has widely been seen as contributing to the capability gap among NATO Members,[84] could restore competition, promote innovation and encourage weapons programme collaborations that enhance interoperability, share costs and conserve scarce materials.

US administrations recognise these considerations and have sought to facilitate co-operation. The Joint Strike Fighter project helps lock-in transatlantic security commitment and at a bilateral level Anglo-American interoperability is being promoted by securing compatibility between military voice and digital communications systems, respectively Bowman and the Joint Tactical Radio System.[85] The George W. Bush administration commissioned NSPD-19, a comprehensive review of defence trade export policy and national security, and its predecessor launched the Defense Trade Security Initiative (DTSI). Designed to support NATO interoperability and the organisation's DCI, this initiative was hailed as enabling American defence industries to work in collaborative cross-border arrangements with allied industries, helping maintain a strong and robust transatlantic DTIB and providing innovative and affordable products needed by NATO governments to transform their militaries to the demands of twenty-first century war-fighting. It also contributed to strengthening technology controls among American allies by offering potential exemption of favoured allies from some US arms export license requirements in exchange for modifications to their export licensing systems.[86]

Yet the logic of transatlantic defence collaboration is being confounded by inter-related internal EU tensions and American equivocation. French industrial activism and concern about American influence inclines France to promote a European DTIB. Paris has long favoured some equivalent of the Buy America Act, and partial ownership by the state and trusted shareholders (*noyau dur*) of French defence companies makes their acquisition by, for instance, US firms, almost impossible.[87] Also, in January 2006 Alain Picq, Armaments Counsellor in the Delegation of France to NATO, argued that the European Defence Agency (EDA) should focus on a consolidated marketplace via the establishment of a European defence equipment market.[88] In this view the EDA might institutionalise a bipolar DTIB by advocating on the supply side rationalisation and restructuring of European defence industries and on the demand side more open procurement processes within Europe (e.g. Code of Practice) and more frequent collaboration in project development to provide the rationalised defence industry with sustainable, reliable and sufficient income. However, EU non-arms-producing countries often buy US weapons systems and have little investment in a European armaments policy. The 2004 enlargement brought in countries such as Poland, which are highly aligned with the US and often favour purchasing American defence products and services.[89] Also, Britain favours neither French industrial activism nor the intervention of the European Commission in defence markets[90] and seeks preferential market access and collaborative arrangements with the US, such as the US–UK Defence Trade Co-operation Treaty approved by the US Senate in September 2010.

Neither is the 'American factor' merely passive. Unless the EU adopts NATO standards, then US-led RMA risks making constructive ambiguity in ESDP increasingly difficult. Experience of working alongside US forces in Iraq convinced the British MOD that potential partners would need to adjust their force structures and be close to US policy-making and planning if they were to maintain congruence and contact with accelerating American technological and doctrinal pre-eminence.[91] These calculations, in turn, set parameters for multinational defence co-operation[92] and make it difficult for some countries to avoid choosing between American and European futures through their procurement policies. Sceptics of British claims to bridge the transatlantic DTIB argue that Britain will likely face a choice between purchasing limited amounts of equipment in order to allow its armed forces to remain compatible with the US and building equipment in conjunction with European partners.[93]

The US often exacerbates problems by distinguishing between 'good' and 'better' allies.[94] In 1998 US Deputy Defense Secretary John Hamre infamously classified trading partners of the US into A, B, and C categories – A included Britain and Norway; B included France and Germany, C was reserved for Russia and China. This approach can be seen in intelligence relationships, technology sharing and defence market access. The UK is a Member of the Echelon network and has privileged access to the Secret Internet Protocol Router Network, the primary secret-level computer network. America shares some stealth technology with Britain on the express proviso that this should not be passed on to the French, who are suspected of leaking information, industrial espionage and lax export controls, which Americans fear might allow sensitive technology to get into the wrong hands.[95] Furthermore, Britain's 'A' rating has a direct bearing on transatlantic defence company collaboration. The majority of transatlantic defence investment flows begin or end in Britain, and British companies are more successful than their European counterparts in accessing the lucrative US defence market: in 2005 the US Department of Defense became BAE's biggest customer.[96]

US export licensing and technology transfer regimes, coupled with protectionist initiatives such as the Buy American Act and the Committee on Foreign Investment in the United States, further obstruct interoperability and standardisation. EADS Senior Advisor Pierre Sabatié-Garat observed that in January 2006 there were approximately 60 cooperative programmes being blocked by ITAR.[97] US willingness or otherwise to share technology is wrapped up in national concerns for defence technology supremacy and perceptions of both threat and transatlantic relations. The DTSI, for example, was seriously weakened by its applying only to unclassified technology and equipment, and some observers doubt whether even BAE Systems' acquisition of Lockheed Martin's Control and Aerospace Electronic Systems business would have been sanctioned had George W. Bush been in office at the time.[98] The attack of 9/11 increased American resistance to technology sharing and made it ever harder for non-American companies – even subcontractors – to gain the necessary security clearances to access the US market. NSPD-19 sparked a turf war between the US State and Defence Departments, the former tending to support strict controls as a part of wider US foreign policy, while the latter favoured limited relaxation for reasons of competition, economy and interoperability. Moreover, Congress has tended to relegate political and strategic considerations of transatlantic defence co-operation to national security, protecting the US DTIB, and preserving associated jobs.

This debate about market access and technology transfer is also about interoperability. It is about the technology gap and the prospects of ever closing it. And, above all, it is about the extent of American influence in Europe and the degree of European military dependence upon the US. Transatlantic sensitivities about command and control structures and about the potential of a Galileo-enabled ESDP indicate that unresolved competition and mistrust underlie the EU–NATO relationship. Some observers even fear that key Atlanticist countries might become drawn inexorably into a Galileo dominated network at the expense of interoperability with the US.[99] It is clear, too, that the American defence industry and market are significantly greater levers of US influence than are their European counterparts. The US government has a large array of incentives and rewards to encourage foreign co-operation – military credits, offset arrangements, technology transfers, loans, economic aid, joint ventures, various forms of military assistance, and the removal of penalties – such as arms embargoes, technology transfer restrictions, onerous export regulations and high trans-action costs.[100] So pervasive are American controls and so dominant are the American armed forces and defence industry as principal technology drivers in defence that third parties are keen to collaborate with the US. But the 'price of entering the US market is increasing US influence over the direction of their technological develop-ment, the stability of their military industries, and the autonomy of their foreign policy decisions.'[101]

The EU is a more capable security actor than at any time in its history. Yet it still finds that the US is an indispensable partner in providing European security and a key, sometimes unpredictable, variable, that influences the effectiveness of EU security policies towards Europe. It also finds that the US is a deeply complicating factor for its own development as a security actor because of American policies and inconsistencies and because of the Atlanticist–Europeanist fault line that runs through the Union. President Sarkozy has eased Franco-American relations since he came to office and Washington seems prepared to accept an implicit trade of French re-integration into NATO in return for a more tolerant approach towards ESDP. However, it will take more than words and gestures to convince the White House either that there has been a fundamental change of French ambitions or to arrest NATO's hollowing out as a collective defence organisation. And it is difficult to see what will overcome the miscellany of concerns that encourages Congress's restrictive approach to sharing with the Union as a whole technology, intelligence and defence market access.

Conclusion

America remains the 'indispensable nation' in helping the EU to address security threats in Europe and, especially, to Europe from beyond its borders. Conversely, the EU can offer America moral, political, economic and military resources that Washington urgently needs as the global security agenda becomes more complex, power becomes more dispersed and US constraints grow at home in the face of Obama's ambitious domestic programme, massive US deficits, public weariness with commitments to Afghanistan and Iraq, and Congress's unpredictable influence in foreign affairs. The Obama administration is actively seeking to rebuild America's image and re-gather some of the soft power squandered by the Bush administrations. And optimism about a new window of opportunity for EU–US relations has been raised by Obama's more multilateral tone, weak inheritance in terms of America's global standing and onerous commitments, and substantive early policy changes – including on climate change, the Comprehensive Test Ban Treaty, closure of Guantanamo Bay and tentative re-engagement of Russia.

However, America's post-Cold War and post-9/11 reassessments of the global threat landscape, of American interests and of foreign policy options have introduced strategic dissonance and some value differences more squarely into the EU–US relationship. 9/11 changed the psychology of America, and in embarking upon the Global War on Terror and moving America generally away from support of the *status quo* the George W. Bush administrations most likely determined the primary focus of US global strategy for years to come. European security has become marginalised in Washington to the point that the US is little concerned about it *per se* beyond drawing Europe's Eastern periphery into Euro-Atlantic structures and striking an elusive balance between engagement and containment of Russia. Instead, Washington looks to Europe to contribute more to extra-European security, to help re-shape the architecture of international relations and to provide moral and practical support sufficient to confer greater legitimacy upon US actions and maintain domestic support for its continued global engagement.

There is potential to strike a new grand transatlantic bargain and end twenty years of post-Cold War drift and periodic acrimony. There was certainly much talk at the November 2009 EU–US summit about reinvigorating dialogue and setting 'a course for enhanced co-operation'[102] and relations will likely continue to improve from the low ebb of the George W. Bush years. However, this does not mean the US will abandon the American primacy that many Europeans find so irksome, that there will necessarily be greater agreement on how to make multilateralism effective, or that there will be better alignment of strategic priorities. Washington's promotion of Atlanticism will continue to sensitise the Atlanticist–Europeanist fault line within the EU, encourage 'cross-conditionality' and 'cross-socialization' to the possible detriment of EU long-term approaches in its neighbourhood, and potentially produce effects contrary even to American desires of the EU, such as encouraging a bipolar rather than transatlantic defence market and DTIB. Most important of all, the basic fact remains that since the Cold War the EU has, and remains, focused on security *in* Europe, whilst the US has focused increasingly on projecting security *from* Europe. And even within Europe Obama has limited room for manoeuvre. NATO remains America's principal institutional lever in European affairs and though the US may hollow out the organisation's collective defence function as it seeks to develop its global security vocation, Washington still regards NATO primacy in Europe as non-negotiable. Furthermore, the Obama administration shows little sign of retreating on a series of inherited stances controversial within Europe, including NATO enlargement, Turkey's accession to the EU and securing greater European commitment to international security in Afghanistan and beyond.

5

RUSSIA, EUROPEAN SECURITY AND RELATIONS WITH THE EU

The underprivileged strategic partnership?

In 1999 the EU offered the Kremlin a strategic partnership. In 2003 the European Security Strategy gave Russia a seemingly privileged status in EU external relations as one of just five States accorded strategic partnership status.[1] Numerous EU and Russian statements, documents and speeches have since re-affirmed an ever-deepening relationship. All of this reflects Russia's importance to the EU and European security. It is a critical player in WMD non-proliferation, environmental security, combating international terrorism and organised crime as well as in regional (in)security, especially in its immediate neighbourhood, the Balkans and the Middle East. Russia's UN Security Council membership, possession of the world's second most powerful nuclear arsenal, regional influence and triple status as a leading Eurasian state, a direct EU neighbour and a bridge between Europe and Asia make Moscow an indispensable security interlocutor for the Union.

Yet from 2000 EU–Russia security relations have become progressively more difficult, reaching a low point in the Russo-Georgian conflict in August 2008. Russia is dissatisfied with the extant European and international order. A Member of the BRIC's grouping it sits astride some of the world's key fault lines, including radical Islam and Christianity, energy exporters and importers, and Western liberal and authoritarian capitalism.[2] Fuelled by its hydrocarbon wealth and influence Russia has steadily reasserted itself under the Presidencies of Putin and Medvedev. Handling Russia has become the EU's single most important and challenging problem.

Russia is in a different category of power, status and foreign policy tradition from any other state in the EU's neighbourhood. It has unique foreign policy options, has no desire to join the Union and is an inveterate Westphalian power with a strong autocratic political tradition and still formidable hard power capabilities. It is also undergoing an enormous post-Soviet transition that, though far from complete, is sufficiently advanced to establish that Russia is embracing a very different form of democracy, capitalism and development model from those of the EU.

This chapter is based on the premise that understanding EU–Russia security relations requires an understanding of Russian foreign policy objectives as well as of the infrastructure of EU–Russia relations and the plethora of activities within which the two powers are engaged. The chapter is developed in four parts. The first addresses an architecture of EU–Russia relations that suggests ever deepening security interdependence and co-operation. The following three sections explain why such appearances are at least in part deceptive. The first of these examines the (still developing) contours of post-Cold War Russian foreign policy. Here it is argued that Russia is still modernising and this has important ramifications for European security and the EU. Russia is revisionist, increasingly assertive and increasingly distinct from the EU in terms of norms and preferred *modus operandi*. The next section examines how Russia's wider foreign and security policy objectives inform its approach to European security and the EU. Amongst the key implications that emerge are that Europe is just one – and not consistently dominant – aspect of Russian concern, that Russia looks more to the US than the EU in hard security domains especially and that Russia is seeking increasingly to counter what it perceives to be Euro-Atlantic penetration of former Soviet space. The final section examines from the EU perspective the implications of Russian reassertion and why the Union is finding it difficult to drive security co-operation with Moscow.

From agreement on trade and economic and commercial co-operation to common spaces: the architecture of a strategic partnership

The EU's approach towards Russia in the 1990s was marked by reactivism and incoherence.[3] In December 1989 it concluded with the Soviet Union an Agreement on Trade and Economic and Commercial Co-operation, and in 1994 a Partnership and Co-operation Agreement (PCA) provided the legal basis of EU–Russia relations. However, physical distance from each other's borders and Moscow's view of the EU as an economic actor meant little perceived imperative to drive a closer security partnership. Though the PCA included all sorts of references to common values, political and economic liberties and promotion of international security, it was largely about economics.[4]

Both powers were preoccupied. Politically, they were absorbed in internal transformations. The EU was focused on Germany and the Maastricht Treaty. It subsequently had to manage the 1995 enlargement, a wave of applicants from Central and Eastern Europe, successive Treaty revisions at Amsterdam and Nice and a shift away from being an exclusively soft power actor. Moscow's challenges were more daunting still and its experience considerably more troubled. It had to cope with the loss of an internal and external empire and with radical political, strategic, economic and social transitions.[5] There was genuine risk of radical elements seizing power, severe economic dislocation, basic governance deficits, *de facto* nuclear proliferation and concern for the security of WMD materials, and an urgent need to redefine Russia's place in the world. And beyond their borders, Russia and the EU differed over humanitarian interventionism and national sovereignty and focused on different crises. Russia became embroiled in a long and controversial military campaign in Chechnya as part of its effort to hold the Federation together. The EU experienced humiliation in, and became preoccupied with, the Balkans.

However, the 1995 enlargement brought the EU close to Russian borders and together with the Europe Agreements presaged greater (security) interdependence and common challenges. The European Commission duly called that year for: greater dialogue with Moscow and Russia's integration into the European security architecture; Russia's liberalization and establishment of a market economy; the consolidation there of democratic norms, institutions and practices; respect of human rights, individual liberties and the rule of law; and an intensification of bilateral and multi-lateral co-operation in other fields, *inter alia* justice, home affairs and crime prevention, and crisis prevention and management.[6] It took four more years, the fallout from the Kosovo war and a more imminent sense of EU enlargement for the EU to heed the Commission. When it did so, Russia became the first object of its new common strategy instrument. This was significant symbolically and the commitment to 'strengthen the strategic partnership between the Union and Russia at the dawn of a new century'[7] seemingly heralded a qualitative step change in the relationship.

Moscow still viewed the EU as primarily an economic actor. The 'Medium-term Strategy for Development of Relations between the Russian Federation and the European Union (2000–2010)' (Medium-term Strategy) stressed the importance of 'mobilizing the economic potential and managerial experience of the European Union. ... '. Russian knowledge of the EU was very limited, even among its foreign policy elite.[8] Nevertheless, Russia embraced the idea of having a special type of relationship with the EU, including the specific terminology of a strategic partnership. It was an invitation to practical co-operation and, as an international 'prestige token', was something valued by the Kremlin.

Putin's assumption of the Russian Presidency from Yeltsin in 2000 and subsequent offer of practical steps to 'create new, higher forms, of co-operation between Russia and the EU'[9] signalled the onset of the infrastructural development of their strategic partnership. The EU–Russia Summit in October 2000 in Paris announced the opening of consultations on security and defence matters and of bilateral cooperation in crisis management. Bilateral security networks developed rapidly thereafter to include six-monthly EU–Russia summits, annual Co-operation Councils, co-operation committees and numerous sub-committees. Russia became the first non-EU state to have regular monthly meetings with the EU's Political and Security Committee and, prompted by the development of ESDP, it was decided at the May 2002 EU–Russia Summit in Moscow to establish military contacts and develop a common approach to crisis management. At the St Petersburg summit in May 2003 it was agreed to upgrade the Co-operation Council to the status of Permanent Partnership Council, the first of its kind in EU external relations and a status mirror of the NATO–Russia Council (which had replaced the Permanent Joint Council). The EU and Russia also agreed to develop four Common Spaces, two of which dealt directly with security issues, namely the Common Space on Freedom, Security and Justice, and the Common Space on Co-operation in the Field of External Security.

The Common Space on Freedom, Security and Justice was presented in the May 2003 St Petersburg statement as a key component in building a new Europe without dividing lines. This was complemented by the Common Space on External Security, which focused on anti-terrorism; strengthening dialogue and co-operation on the international scene; non-proliferation of WMD and their means of delivery, strengthening export control regimes and disarmament; co-operation in crisis management; and co-operation in the field of civil protection, especially responses to disasters and emergencies. These objectives were to be progressed through EU–Russia co-operation to promote an international order based on effective multi-lateralism and through extensive bilateral political dialogue on common regional and sectoral concerns.[10]

The Common Spaces have been developed through the creation of Road Maps and monitoring mechanisms to assess and hone co-operation within a list of agreed objectives. The extensive nature of this list demonstrates recognition of EU–Russia security interdependence across a spectrum of issues ranging from nuclear safety and environmental concerns through to effective border controls and judicial co-operation. This security interdependence and the status of Russia and the EU as the two key indigenous European powers is now reflected in a highly developed institutional infrastructure that provides for more meetings at ministerial, administrative and parliamentary levels than even that between the EU and the US.[11] After a period of suspension following the Georgia conflict, negotiations resumed in search of a replacement for the PCA as the legal basis of EU–Russia relations, which nominally expired in December 2007.

All of this indicates greater mutual appreciation of the importance of the EU–Russia relationship to European security and suggests a future of ever-closer relations. Indeed, the European Commission set out unambiguously in its 2007–13 country strategy paper that 'EU co-operation with Russia is conceived in terms of, and is designed to strengthen, a strategic partnership'.[12] However, all is not as it seems. There remain major obstacles to filling the Common Spaces with substantive security co-operation. Some of the problems rest with limited EU–Russia institutional experience of dealing with one another. But much more important are how Russia and the EU view themselves and each other.

Russian foreign policy contours

Understanding EU security relations with Russia requires an appreciation of the evolving contours of Russian foreign policy and of Moscow's priorities and preferred *modus operandi* within and beyond European security. On the one hand, greater Russian assertiveness from Putin's second term onwards sparked renewed international speculation about Russian imperialism, an anti-American posture and even a new Cold War.[13] On the other hand, Russia still faces major challenges in sustaining its resurgent international status, and internal debates continue about the domestic reform process and the country's place in, and relationships with, the rest of the world.

Russia has suffered policy inconsistency on account of events and unresolved internal debates. 'Westernisers' were briefly ascendant in Russia after the Cold War. However, in the late 1990s Prime Minister Primakov de-prioritised integration with the West and flirted with a balancing 'strategic triangle' of Russia, India and China. President Putin subsequently 'pragmatised' and 'economised' Russian foreign policy in the interests of rebuilding the State as the basis of Russia's return to the international mainstream. Medvedev has continued the emphasis on economic modernisation and the importance of a strong state at home and pragmatism abroad.[14] Even so, Medvedev still has to build his power base. Part of Russian support for sovereign democracy remains tied up now in Prime Minister Putin's personal popularity, and Russian foreign policy continues to be driven by potentially irreconcilable tensions.[15]

Numerous labels have been used to identify different positions within this Russian debate. In 1999 Dzyaloshinsky and Dzyaloshinskaya divided Russian elite opinion into 'Isolationists', 'Convergents' and 'Unionists'. Six years later Zimmerman reprised nineteenth century debates and reduced the position to 'Westernisers' and 'Slavophiles', with the latter seeking to counterbalance US hegemony and develop an autonomous developmental path. That same year Ambrosio and Sergunin each suggested an expanded number of groupings. The former emphasised 'Atlanticists', 'Imperialists', and 'neo-Slavophiles'; the latter included 'Atlanticists/Westernisers', 'Eurasians', 'Realists', 'Liberals', 'Neomarxists' and 'Postmodernists'. Tsygankov subsequently identified four groupings: 'integrationists', 'balancers', 'neoimperialists' and 'great power normalisers'. And in 2007 White promoted 'Liberal Westernisers', 'Pragmatic Nationalists', and 'Fundamentalist Nationalists'.[16]

Similar difficulties arise in characterising official Russian foreign policy. In March 2007 Foreign Minister Sergey Lavrov asserted that in 2000 Russia had decided 'in favour of pragmatism, multivectorness and our firm, but unconfrontational upholding of national interests in foreign affairs'.[17] But what did this mean in practice? Flenley argues that Putin's foreign policy constituted 'pragmatic nationalism'; Tsygankov viewed his first four years in power as conforming to a course of 'great power normalization, or great power realism'. Sakwa likewise emphasised normalisation under Putin but suggested a 'new realism' that combined traditional Russian *realpolitik* with integration into the world community.[18] There is an added complication, too, in that terminology is often inexact or conceptually weak. Former Foreign Minister Kozyrev spoke of and envisaged Russia as a 'normal great power', for instance, very differently from Putin. Kozyrev was a Westernizer; Putin's integrationism was tempered by neo-Slavophile tendencies.[19] Similarly, the impact of Eurasianism in Russian foreign policy is much debated. Yet there are so many strands of Eurasianism – including 'pragmatic Eurasianism', 'neo-Eurasianism', 'civilisational Eurasianism' and 'intercivilisationism' – that the concept has limited intellectual coherence.[20]

Aside from indicating the complexity of interpreting Russian foreign policy, the above suggests three important things. First, the different significant positions within

Russia on foreign policy are difficult to characterise, fluid and evolving. Second, despite the broadly supported foreign policy established by Putin and largely continued by Medvedev, Russia's foreign policy discourse remains contested and policy volatility can be expected in response to events and changes of leadership. It may not always be possible to ensure the managed transition that characterised the formal handover of the Presidency from Putin to Medvedev in May 2008. Third, there is no singular Russian position on European security and the EU. Rather, official positions have evolved over time and contending perspectives are inextricably entwined with the ongoing attempt to identify modernist Russia and to articulate its international role.

However, major themes and currently ascendant discourses in Russian foreign policy are discernable from Russia's key published foreign and security policy documents.[21] In 2000, after almost 10 years of a largely 'domesticated'[22] foreign policy, Russia developed its security vision in three documents: The National Security Concept, the Foreign Policy Concept of the Russian Federation (FPC) and the Military Doctrine. In March 2007 it presented an updated vision in the Survey of Russian Federation Foreign Policy (Survey) and in July 2008 Medvedev approved an updated Foreign Policy Concept (2008 FPC).

Comparing the Survey and the 2008 FPC with the earlier documents reveals consistent elements of Russia's official world view. Russia is presented as a Great Power: 'Being a permanent Member of the UN Security Council, possessing a substantial potential and resources in all fields of vital activity and maintaining intensive relations with the leading States of the world. ... '.[23] The documents emphasise repeatedly the importance of multilateralism, the rule of law, the centrality of the UN to global security, a multipolar order and Russia being treated as an equal. Consistently opposed are: 'destabilising unilateralism', the weakening of the UN and international law, and the vesting of solutions to international security in 'Western institutions and forums of limited composition'.[24] The latter reflects Russia's exclusion from key decision-making fora in European security and beyond. A thread of disillusionment runs through the different documents. In 2000 the FPC noted that 'Certain plans related to establishing new, equitable and mutually advantageous partnership relations of Russia with the rest of the world ... have not been justified.' The 2007 Survey and the 2008 FPC were more direct; both advocate a new global security architecture that better balances the interests of all participants in international intercourse.[25]

A further consistent element is an appreciation of sovereign democracy being a project in the making and of the consequent importance of matching resources to key national interests and of shaping the external environment to create favourable 'conditions for steady development of Russia'.[26] The 2008 FPC notes explicitly that foreign policy is 'one of [the] major instruments of the steady national development and of ensuring its competitiveness in a globalising world'[27] – an emphasis on foreign policy serving the interests of domestic reform that is far from new. Kozyrev stressed in the early 1990s the importance of a benign international environment to Russia's political and economic reconstruction. The 2000 FPC echoed his emphasis on the importance of Russia securing participation in the IMF, World Bank and GATT / WTO, together with close relations with the G7.[28]

The priority of foreign policy serving the domestic in 2000 also reflected Putin's particular inheritance. Time was needed to address widespread corruption, weak governance structures and economic turmoil in the wake of the 1998 financial meltdown. Foreign policy also needed to be emancipated from a decade of Russian dependence on Western credit. Indeed, the 2000 FPC noted explicitly that 'limited resource support for the foreign policy of the Russian Federation' made difficult the attaining of objectives abroad.[29] Growing Russia internally would eventually re-empower foreign policy and foster a mutually supportive symbiosis.

Putin's emphasis on economics led some to speak of the 'commercialisation' of Russian foreign policy.[30] Certainly the 2007 Survey noted assistance to Russian business abroad to be 'an ever more noticeable direction of our foreign policy efforts.'[31] This was also, though, part of (re-)building Russia's soft power resources, and focusing overly on the economic thrust of Putin's foreign policies impoverishes his pragmatic reconstruction of Russia and aspiration for its 'greatness renewed'. Defence Minister Sergei Ivanov in 2006 identified a 'new triad of Russian national values', namely 'sovereign democracy, robust economy, and military power'. Baev points out that while 'robust economy' is hardly a value, Ivanov's intention was probably that military power and robust economy be seen as prerequisite to sovereign democracy, and that sovereignty is synonymous with 'greatness'.[32]

The development of the third element of this triad has encouraged a symbolic, rhetorical and practical Russian emphasis on hard security that sets it at odds with the EU. In August 2007 Russia announced the resumption, after 15 years, of long-range patrols by its strategic bombers. At the Shanghai Co-operation Organisation (SCO) summit in Kyrgyzstan in August 2007, Putin stressed that though Russia was not looking to build a Cold-War style military bloc it nevertheless envisaged the SCO expanding its remit to include a greater military role. Also, fuelled by substantial revenues developed from oil and gas exports especially, Moscow committed to a $200 billion military modernisation programme that includes new nuclear submarines, aircraft carriers, a fleet of Tu-160 supersonic strategic bombers, development of a fifth-generation fighter jet and the re-starting of the Black Shark attack helicopter. In September 2008 Medvdev issued five principles of his defence doctrine: the armed forces were to be permanently combat-ready, more efficient, better trained, equipped with sophisticated weapons and better rewarded to improve retention and morale. He also spoke of acquiring air superiority in conducting high-precision strikes on land and sea targets and the creation of an air-space defence system.[33] Furthermore, there has been greater Russian emphasis placed on the strategic arsenal. Russia has combined a decision in 1993 to allow first use of nuclear weapons with an expanded mission of deterrence and a lower threshold for the use of these weapons.[34] It repeatedly threatened to deploy SS-26 ("Iskander") missiles in the Kaliningrad exclave, to target Ukraine with nuclear weapons were it to become a Member of NATO, and, in response to US-led BMD, both to re-arm its Baltic Fleet with nuclear weapons and to target Poland and the Czech Republic with nuclear weapons.[35]

In terms of Russia's contemporary perspective on international relations, the 2007 Survey and 2008 FPC signal three key contemporaneous developments. First, they assert renewed optimism about Russia's 'newly acquired foreign policy independence'. Indeed, one declared purpose of the Survey was to get Russians 'intellectually and psychologically accustomed' to Russia's re-entry to 'the mainstream of international life'.[36] At the same time, they communicate an increasing sense of security threat. For instance, the 2000 FPC noted that military power 'still retains significance among States' but that economic, political, scientific and technological, ecological, and information factors were assuming an ever greater role.[37] Seven years later the Survey noted an increased danger of outside interference in domestic affairs of sovereign States 'under the pretext of tackling WMD non-proliferation tasks' and implicitly accused the US and its allies of imposing 'a hypertrophied significance of the factor of force in international relations.'[38] The 2008 FPC also criticised unilateral coercive actions and noted explicitly 'the continued political and psychological policy of "containing" Russia'.[39]

US-led military intervention in Iraq led the Kremlin to perceive a Western strategy of neo-containment. Enlargements have brought NATO and the EU to Russia's borders and encroached upon its traditional spheres of interest. Their emphasis on a friendly neighbourhood /circle of friends could easily be interpreted as the construction of a *cordon sanitaire*.[40] And both NATO and the EU have offered support for regime change from within and the geopolitical reorientation of Russia's borderlands towards the Euro-Atlantic space – Ukrainian elections in 2004 being a good example. Moreover, NATO military bases are being established in Central and Eastern Europe, and the Czech Republic and Poland did agree to host elements of US BMD. Medvedev has dismissed as a 'fairy tale' Western protestation that BMD is intended to deter and deflect missile threats from the Middle East[41] and during the Bush administrations Russia's sense of vulnerability was magnified by possible imminent and purposeful US nuclear supremacy.[42]

The third significant development signalled in the Survey and the 2008 FPC is a Russian emphasis on civilisation, inter-civilisational discourse and the threat posed to both by globalisation and alleged attempts by the US especially to impose its own political systems and development models. Medvedev has asserted Russia as one of three branches of European civilisation, the other two being the EU and the US.[43] This keeps open Russia's European identity but emphasises its uniqueness. Moscow's reconstitution of a Russian civilisation revolves broadly around a combination of state centrism, ethno-nationalism and Orthodoxy. Though sometimes dismissed as adding a dash of legitimacy and grandeur to authoritarianism,[44] the Russian civilisation concept has enabled the State to consolidate sovereign democracy by serving as guardian of its independence and distinctive character and by 'othering' the US in particular – a process to which some argue the West has contributed handsomely by reducing complex Russian internal reforms 'to a single narrative of authoritarian restoration'.[45] Hence, when asserting in set piece speeches Russia's democratic vocation, Medvedev and Putin have repeatedly rejected the imposition of imported value systems and defended Russia's right to determine its own interpretations of freedom and democracy and the means by which to develop and protect them.[46]

Looking outwards the 2008 FPC argues that 'global competition is acquiring a civilisational dimension'.[47] With Russia positioned as a distinctive civilisation, it is thus constitutive of, and a key contributor to, this civilisational dimension, the principal aspect of which is perceived to be 'competition between different value systems and development models within the framework of universal democratic and market economy principles.'[48] As part of Russia's claim to renewed international leadership Russian officials have portrayed inter-civilisational dialogue as the 'big idea' and coordinating theme of Russian diplomacy for the foreseeable future. Within this, 'intercivilisational harmony' is presented as an 'unconfrontational' means of taking up 'a whole series of principled issues reflecting our vision of a new world pattern.'[49] '[N]ew world pattern' is shorthand for Russia's desire to revise the rules of international security and economics devised during the 1990s when it was too weak to contribute.[50]

Russian leaders recognise that sustaining its energy-fuelled resurgence depends upon stability and economic modernisation at home and their ability to combine hard power with being seen to offer something distinctive and attractive abroad. Moscow is seemingly seeking to substitute sovereign democracy and Russia's development model for the leadership potential previously afforded the USSR by communist ideology. Of course, parallels are limited, not least because this represents a clash within rather than between ideologies and Russia is in a much weaker position to promote its alternative model. Nevertheless, inter-civilisational discourse provides a pulpit for Russia to pronounce upon world events and a vehicle by which to consolidate the impression of its return as a powerful international actor. It also calls to a potentially considerable constituency that either rejects US-style political systems and development models, or resents the abuse of US hard power, or sees political advantage in closer relations with the Kremlin. It is particularly interesting in this context that the Survey emphasised that 'the eastern civilisations ... have yet to play a positive role in the formation of global development trends.'[51] Furthermore, sovereign democracy, Russia's development model and notions of a distinctive Russian civilisation all have a potential power of attraction in Russia's neighbourhood and/or a legitimizing discourse for the re-consolidation of Russian power. Putin talked in 2005 of 'the civilising mission of the Russian Federation on the Eurasian continent';[52] the 2007 Survey contended that 'a guarantee of Russia's leadership in the CIS space could be the design of an attractive realistic model of evolutionary transition to a full-fledged market and democracy for partners.'[53]

Russia, European security and the EU

What does all of this mean for Russia's view of European security and of security co-operation with the EU? In terms of the security architecture, Russia is strongly revisionist. The 2008 FPC set out Russia's main European objective as the creation of 'a truly open, democratic system of regional collective security and co-operation ensuring the unity of the Euro-Atlantic region, from Vancouver to Vladivostok, in such a way as not to allow its new fragmentation and the reproduction of bloc-based approaches which still persist in the European architecture that took shape during the Cold War period.'[54] Medvedev outlined proposals for a new pan-European Security Treaty on 5 June 2008 in Berlin and subsequently reiterated them in a variety of high-level formats, including at the G-8 summit and bi-laterally with German Chancellor Merkel and French President Sarkozy.

Meantime, Russia attacks rhetorically and undermines practically the existing architecture. Russian officials consistently bemoan the exclusive nature of Europe's security 'clubs' and consequent asymmetric security conditions. In July 2007 Putin suspended Russia's participation in the Conventional Forces in Europe Treaty (CFE) and in related agreements. And in August 2008 Medvedev recognised the independence of the Georgian enclaves of South Ossetia and Abkhazia, citing the contentious recognition of Kosovo's independence as precedent. Russian relations with NATO especially suffer from Cold War perceptual hangovers, the failure, in Medevdev's view, of Russia and the George W. Bush administrations to 'find a common language in many areas',[55] and from the consequences of NATO's ongoing evolution, especially support for BMD, potential membership of Ukraine and Georgia (deferred in December 2008), the creation of forward bases in Romania and Bulgaria, and the non-ratification of the Agreement on Adaptation of the CFE Treaty. Even the OSCE, once favoured by Moscow as a potential pan-European security organisation, is considered to have been hijacked by the US and a number of other Western countries as a 'unilateral instrument' to influence CIS processes, reconstruct the 'European periphery' according to 'externally imposed patterns', to 'pressure States which are not Members of NATO and the EU to alter their vector of political orientation, even as far as a change of ruling regimes, and to oust Russia from negotiation and peacekeeping formats for the settlement of frozen conflicts'.[56] Soon after Putin assumed the Presidency in 2000, Russia began hollowing out the OSCE, especially in its neighbourhood. For instance, it set up parallel election monitoring organisations within the Collective Security Organisation, the Collective Security Treaty Organisation and the CIS. CIS observers delivered opposite views to those of the OSCE on the regularity of the Russian Duma elections in December 2007 and the parliamentary elections in Belarus in September 2008.[57]

Moscow's determination to draw 'red lines' in its neighbourhood is increasingly apparent. The conflict in Georgia and nuclear targeting threats over NATO enlargement and BMD are obvious examples. More subtle, and arguably more important, is a *de facto* claim to a US-style Monroe Doctrine in Russia's neighbourhood. Such ideas are not new and there has long been concern in Russia about the penetration by outside powers of post-Soviet geo-political space.[58] However, Russia has demonstrated a newfound willingness to claim privileged spheres of influence. The 2000 FPC set the development of 'good neighbourly relations and strategic partnership with all CIS Member States' as a regional priority. The 2007 Survey upgraded relations with the CIS countries to 'the chief priority of Russian foreign policy.' And in August 2008 Medvedev declared that 'as is the case of other countries, there are regions in which Russia has privileged interests. These regions are home to countries with which we share special historical relations and are bound together as friends and good neighbours.' Furthermore, this sphere of influence claim was set alongside another principle, namely that 'protecting the lives and dignity of our citizens, wherever they may be, is an unquestionable priority for our country. ... It should be clear to all that we will respond to any aggressive acts committed against us.'[59] This self-proclaimed right potentially opens a Pandora's box of possible interventions in neighbouring States with Russian or Russian-speaking minorities, especially as it is left to the Russian government to define what 'dignity' is.[60]

Russia recognises that EU technical assistance, investment and markets are essential to secure sovereign democracy and to escape potential petro-state status. Also, the EU and Russia do enjoy a greater degree of convergence on some international security issues than either does with the US. The litany of well rehearsed examples includes Iran, the Kyoto Protocol, the Middle East Peace Process and a general commitment to multilateralism (albeit for different reasons). Furthermore, the Common Spaces and their associated Roadmaps do not deceive. Moscow perceives an extensive list of shared security challenges within Europe and now, officially at least, recognises the EU as being a 'powerful geopolitical factor' and 'our chief partner in Europe'.[61]

Russia's domestic agenda and revisionist ambitions sensitise Moscow to the potential of co-operation with the EU. Yet they also threaten to drain energy and resources from developing technicalities of soft security provision with the EU. Moscow's threat perception and tendency to focus on aspects of the security agenda where it enjoys comparative advantage incline it to emphasise hard security issues. In contrast, the EU emphasises soft security, where it is better equipped and more cohesive, and depoliticises security co-operation.[62] Also, Medvedev's proposal for a new pan-European security treaty suggests that Russia is most interested in re-organising the European security architecture or, failing that, disrupting the existing arrangements. Even setting aside likely EU resistance to radical change in the architecture, this objective encourages Russia's traditional disposition to downgrade the Union (in the security field) relative to other actors for a number of reasons. First, the US has long assumed centre stage in Russian grand strategy; some commentators suggest reasonably that Moscow selectively engages the EU over borders and trade and the US over global security problems.[63] This was evident in the Obama–Medvedev nuclear arms reduction agreement in March 2010 within the wider drive to 're-set' US–Russia relations. Second, Russia's permanent seat on the Security Council has been regarded as the best institutional vehicle for safeguarding its interests. Third, Moscow seems increasingly dismissive of the EU's utility in shaping a regional, let alone global, security environment conducive to its interests. The 2007 Survey contained none of the optimism about EU–Russia partnership of the 2000 FPC and the Medium Term Strategy. It declared that 'the fulcrum of Russian policy on the European continent' was bilateral relations, that these were 'of key significance for the construction of a European security architecture corresponding to our interests', and that their development would 'help us decide on the scale of priorities regarding the multilateral organizations.'[64]

Russia's greater confidence and consolidation of sovereign democracy especially expose that its security commonalities with the EU result from coincidences of interest rather than converging approaches to international relations. In April 2005 Putin called the USSR's collapse 'the greatest geopolitical catastrophe of the 20th century'. Largely lost in the ensuing outcry was that Russian attachment to, as opposed to ability to promote, balance of power had never disappeared. Putin underscored this message in February 2007, arguing that 'from the point of view of stability in this or that region of the world in general, the balance of power is the main achievement of these past decades and indeed of the whole history of humanity'.[65] Medvedev has continued in this vein. He committed in the five principles of Russian foreign policy to spheres of influence and to a multipolar world order, and has argued that 'the world is still searching for a new equilibrium'[66] in an era in which 'Atlanticism has already had its day.'[67] Moscow openly advocates turning 'to the positive elements of the Cold War experience', including containment by deterrence and the pursuit of peaceful coexistence.[68]

This sharpened philosophical contrast between Russian and EU security management manifests itself in practical ways. Russian withdrawal from the CFE Treaty and strident criticism of the OSCE reflects dissatisfaction with the order developed during the 1990s. Conversely, EU officials have rejected any 'big need to put down the structures of security in Europe'[69] and cautioned that the CFE Treaty 'remains a cornerstone of European security'.[70] Similarly, Russia's methods in strengthening its international position and its encouragement of regional balances of power are very different from, and a source of grave concern to, the EU. In October 2008 EU Commissioner for External Relations, Benita Ferrero-Walder, declared bluntly that 'we cannot share the principles of foreign policy recently articulated in Moscow, including the resurgence of spheres of influence.'[71]

Cohen draws analogies between Russia's current use of weapons and nuclear reactor sales and imperial Germany's use of railroads before World War I to attract allies, bolster influence, and undermine the dominant power in the Middle East.[72] Though an exaggeration, there is some substance to this. Whereas the EU advocates arms control and confidence building measures, Russia views military technology co-operation as an important component of Russian foreign policy, especially given the perceived strengthening of the role of military force in recent years. A declared objective is 'raising the threshold for using force in relations between States'[73] by assisting them to strengthen their self-defence capability consistent with Article 51 of the UN Charter. Some commentators view Russian arms sales as 'promiscuous';[74] Moscow certainly exhibits few of the EU's ethical concerns. For example, in the aftermath of a $1 billion arms deal in September 2007, Indonesian Defence Minister Juwono Sudarsano confirmed that the Russian deal came with none of the human rights, accountability and licensing preconditions that 'encumber' US and West European arms deals.[75]

Finally, and perhaps most problematically for the EU, the Kremlin seems determined that Russia become a second pole of power within Europe. Russia negatively contrasts Western models against the distinctiveness of Russian civilisation, sovereign democracy and its authoritarian semi-democratic capitalism development model.[76]

This encourages the foregrounding of Russia–EU differences and competition, rather than commonalities and co-operation. It also contributes to EU and Russian officials talking past one another because, while they may use a similar language of values, they have different interpretations of them.

The impact of the overlay of contending value systems over Russia's reassertion and the traditional political and strategic concerns that accompany two major powers bordering each other is most evident in the shared neighbourhood. It is understandable that Moscow perceives the EU as a vehicle of 'soft imperialism' and an agent of Euro-Atlantic penetration. The EU may formally eschew balance of power politics and spheres of influence but the reality is that enlargements, ENP and the power of the Single Market extend the Union's influence into former Soviet space. Also, its admission of Poland and the Baltic States in particular has created an anti-Russian caucus within the Union, and the Union's membership overlaps extensively with that of NATO.[77] Moreover, Moscow is undoubtedly disappointed by the failure to realise the hope expressed in the 1999 Medium Strategy that partnership with the EU 'should contribute to consolidating Russia's role as a leading power in shaping up a new system of interstate political and economic relations in the CIS area'.[78]

Today Moscow is drawing red lines in its neighbourhood, pushing back against the EU's influence and seeking to promote abroad its rival development model. Its sensitisation to the EU's power of attraction and use of cross border activities for norm diffusion is demonstrated by Moscow's curtailment of non-governmental organisations within Russia[79] and soft-pedalling of its involvement in EU cross-border co-operation, neighbourhood and regional programmes under the ENP.[80] Moscow is also actively developing soft power resources, ranging from manipulation of energy resources, attempts to dominate integrative agents in the CIS[81] and the possibility of the rouble becoming a regional currency[82] through to sponsorship of NGOs and the creation of new agencies such as the Kremlin department for Interregional and Cultural Relations with Foreign Countries[83] and the Federal Agency for CIS Affairs.[84] And then, of course, there was Russia's dramatic response to Georgian President Mikhail Saakashvili's disastrously misjudged military action in the breakaway region of South Ossetia. The Russian military operation weakened the EU's leading ally in the Caucasus and underscored Russia's possession of, and willingness to use, considerable hard power in defence of its interests. Two particularly important outcomes of the conflict concern the signals sent through it by Moscow. First, the military action helped President Medvedev establish himself as a strong leader within Russia and suggested that Russian foreign policy under the Medvedev-Putin tandem would emphasise continuity. Second, the Kremlin used the Georgia conflict to alert outsiders that its 'red lines' were being drawn and that the 'rules of the game' developed during the 1990s were being revised.

The EU, European security and Russia

The EU has an increasingly difficult hand to play with Moscow. Its growing security interdependence with Russia cannot be addressed as it was with the CEEC's through enlargement. Common EU policies towards Russia are also hard to evolve and maintain. On the one hand, the Member States harbour different attitudes towards and have different degrees of interest in Russia. Over time the spectrum of opinion has widened as a result of enlargement, with countries like Poland and the Baltic States generally driving a harder line on account of their broadly pro-Atlanticist orientations, proximity to Russia and their Cold War experiences of Moscow. On the other hand, Moscow actively exploits EU Member state differences through a variety of disaggregation tactics. Furthermore, the EU struggles to hold Moscow's attention as a security interlocutor given its prioritisation of hard security. Russia–US relations add further difficulties for the EU, leading some Members to fear 'Yalta-style' agreements that neglect their interests as President Obama seeks to reset US–Russian relations and prioritises the Middle East and Asia.

The EU's approach towards Russia has been to expand its regulatory regimes beyond its borders, to target assistance at key areas of concern and to develop co-operation at the international, national and sub-national levels within both its own projects and collaborative endeavours with other international actors. For example, on 21 May 2003 international agreement was reached on a Multilateral Nuclear Environmental Programme in Russia (MNEPR), to which the EC budget contribution of €40 million was designed to help clear up radioactive waste in Northwest Russia and to facilitate co-operation regarding the safety of spent nuclear fuel, radioactive waste management and the decommissioning of nuclear submarines and icebreakers.[85] Similarly, the EU contributes help to Russia through the G8 Global Partnership against the Proliferation of WMD, and a number of the objectives set out in the Common Spaces are linked to acceptance of, and abidance by, international norms, laws and conventions.

The EU and Russia have agreed a series of bilateral measures within the realm of justice and home affairs and work together within the Black Sea Synergy and the Northern Dimension project, which the European Commission regards 'as a regional expression of the Common Spaces'[86] and forms part of a proximity policy that seeks to slowly integrate Russia into trans-border security governance. Good-governance programmes designed to encourage democratisation and the development of civil society grounded in the rule of law include the European Initiative for Democracy and Human Rights in Russia, which can finance human rights, democratisation and conflict prevention activities in partnership with NGOs and other international organisations. ECHO (European Commission Humanitarian Aid and Civil Protection) has channeled humanitarian aid since the mid-1990s into the Caucasus and Chechnya especially, and emergency food aid was provided to Russia between March 1999 and April 2000 to alleviate the crisis caused by its economic collapse. And several CFSP Joint Actions have sought to assist non-proliferation and disarmament in the Russian Federation, including support for Russia's commitment in 1997 under the Chemical Weapons Convention to destroy a stockpile of 40,000 tons of such weapons.[87]

Despite, and sometimes because of this plethora of initiatives, the EU has been accused of the 'triumph of process over policy' in relation to Russia.[88] Today practical outcomes remain limited and there has been a surge of EU–Russia disputes. Six EU countries either lost or experienced reduced levels of Russian energy supplies in January 2009 as part of a bitter Russia–Ukraine dispute.[89] Russia's bilateral relations with some EU Member States have also experienced tension. Relations with Britain declined sharply as a result of the Iraq war, disputes over BP and Shell investments, the refusal of British courts to extradite Russian oligarch Boris Berezovsky and Chechen leader Akhmed Zakaev and the murder in London in 2006 of Russian émigré Alexandr Litvinenko. Polish–Russia relations have been even worse. In April 2007 Poland's Deputy Prime Minister, Roman Giertych, spoke of entering a period of 'icy' relations.[90] The Baltic States are especially sensitive to Moscow's newfound power. Kremlin manipulation of energy supplies is the most obvious example of this, but more pervasive are its financing of media, local politicians and economic development, identity policy towards its border regions,[91] and renewed focus on protecting the interests of compatriots abroad – one third of the Baltic population is of Russian heritage.[92] Growing tension was demonstrated starkly in April 2007 by riots sparked by Tallinn's removal of the Bronze Soldier Soviet war memorial and a subsequent cyber-attack on Estonia was widely attributed to Moscow.[93]

These specific disputes contribute to, and are symptomatic of, a general decline in the temper of EU–Russia relations. The EU–Russia Common Spaces Report (2007) concluded that although day-to-day business was conducted efficiently under all the common spaces, 'there were no major breakthroughs' and much remained to be done, including addressing implementation deficits.[94] The European Commission's review of EU–Russia relations in November 2008 concluded that 'a serious shadow' had been cast over them by the Georgian conflict and Russia's unilateral recognition of Abkhazia and South Ossetia.[95] As if to underline the perilous state of affairs, Putin threatened in March 2009 that 'If Russia's interests are ignored, we will also have to start reviewing the fundamentals of our relations' with the EU.[96]

Sir Roderic Lyne, former British Ambassador to Moscow spoke in February 2009 of EU–Russia relations being in 'a mess'.[97] Analysts speak of 'Russia's inability to establish systematic relations with the EU bureaucracy in Brussels'.[98] Russian officials likewise attribute some difficulties to 'the internal restructuring of the EU after the last two waves of expansion'.[99] However, three far more important factors are EU ambivalence in its relations with Russia, a lack of internal cohesion that Russia's increasingly assertive policies have badly exposed, and the unsustainable assumptions that underpin EU interpretations of the strategic partnership.

EU ambivalence in its relations with Russia reflects difficulties in securing Moscow's co-operation and a strengthening tension between co-operation and guarding against Russian re-assertion. Restricted Russian collaboration in ESDP suggests a lack of EU confidence in Moscow's reliability as a security partner and suspicion about its motives for wanting to cooperate.[100] The EU evidently wants to avoid creating dependencies on Russia for key assets such as transport aircraft, equipment and spares.[101] The EU also prioritises the transatlantic security relationship and is anxious lest closer co-operation with Russia antagonise already sensitive relations with Washington over the ESDP–NATO relationship. Likewise, the October 2008

European Council noted the regional impact of the Georgia crisis and concluded that it was 'more necessary than ever' to support regional co-operation and step up relations with Eastern neighbours, in particular through the neighbourhood policy, Black Sea Synergy initiative and an Eastern Partnership.[102] The consolidation of relations with the Eastern countries aims to combat Russia's sphere of influence claims and to weaken Moscow's 'energy weapon'. One of the European Commission's five proposed flagship initiatives in the Eastern Partnership is the development of a Southern energy corridor as 'a key infrastructure initiative serving to diversify transit routes and sources of supply for the EU and its partners.'[103]

More generally, the nomenclature strategic partnership erroneously suggests bilateral relations that are qualitatively 'better' than those the partners have in many of their other external relations. The EU has numerous relationships in its neighbourhood that have become far more privileged than that with Russia in terms of political association, market access and even security co-operation. Western neglect of Russia during the 1990s, in which the EU played a part, is seen as constituting a lost opportunity to acculturate and reassure the Kremlin.[104] The EU's relations with Russia in this period contrasted sharply with its development of privileged Europe Agreements with the CEECs and with special arrangements made for countries within the Barcelona Process. Following the EU's declaration of strategic partnership with Russia it established the more generous Stabilisation and Association Process for countries of the former Yugoslavia. And alongside the development of the Common Spaces with Russia, Brussels created equally if not potentially more privileged relationships with a host of countries within the ENP.[105] Similarly, remaining EFTA and EEA Members have preferred access to the EU's Single Market while Russia has only MFN status, and the continuing absence of a much talked about EU–Russia visa-free regime contrasts markedly with EU relations with all Members of EFTA and the Schengen *acquis* and over 30 other countries.

This pattern of an 'un-privileged' EU–Russia strategic partnership is mirrored in Russia's external relations. The EU is its most important trade partner, but Russia has more preferential and integrated economic ties with a number of the CIS countries. This is owing to the historical legacy whereby 'many Soviet technological chains that were broken along the borders of the newly independent States have tenaciously maintained their connections',[106] also to the relative weight of Russia's economy in the region, its ability to manipulate energy supplies and its active promotion of various multi-speed integration projects – including the Single Economic Space and the Eurasian Economic Community. In the security domain Russia prefers to work with the CIS in its neighbourhood[107] and has far closer formal relations within, for instance, the Collective Security Treaty Organisation than it does with the EU. It has integrated army units with Belarus and Armenia and has full treaties of friendship, co-operation and mutual assistance with these countries. It also has comprehensive military co-operation agreements with Kyrgyzstan and Kazakhstan. Furthermore, there is an embarrassing and revealing mismatch between meagre Russian involvement in ESDP operations and Russia's military exercises with SCO partner China in the summers of 2005 and 2007. Even Russia's so-called 'enemy of choice', NATO, is viewed in Moscow by comparison with the EU as more credible and important to develop security co-operation with.[108]

The EU's second major problem is the growing divergence between its values and those of Russia. The EU formally regards shared values as the basis of a strategic partnership with Russia and these are critical in promoting normative convergence. The 1999 Common Strategy talked to 'the foundations of shared values enshrined in the common heritage of European Civilisation.'[109] Similarly, the declared underlying principles of the Common Space on Freedom, Security and Justice are 'democracy, the rule of law, respect for human rights and fundamental freedoms, including free and independent media and the effective application of common values by independent judicial systems.'[110] However, the prospects of achieving its underlying normative goals – and hence greater convergence on how to promote European security with Russia – have faded. In December 2001 the European Commission concluded that longstanding EU objectives of facilitating Russia's transition to a fully fledged market economy, founded on the core principles of democracy, respect for human rights and the rule of law, were 'still valid'[111] and that on balance extant reforms and Russia's international opening and exposure especially to Europe, would have 'enough momentum to maintain and develop a democratic state governed by the rule of law.'[112] By the time of its Country Strategy paper 2007–13 the Commission felt the tide had turned. It was now 'far from being the case that everyone in Russia shares the European view of what a stable, secure and prosperous Federation will involve'.[113]

The strategic partnership is increasingly driven by two key philosophical divides, namely between democracy and authoritarianism and between post-modern entities and traditional States. For the EU, progressive normative divergence caused by Russia's international reassertion and establishment of sovereign democracy undermines its own conception of the strategic partnership. In 1995 the European Commission argued that without the demonstration of mutual responsiveness and respect for human rights EU–Russia 'co-operation will remain unfulfilled and void of substance.'[114] Today the EU's democratisation programme is in serious trouble; some argue that it is 'officially dead.'[115] Even more importantly, the EU and Russia do not agree on what constitutes a strategic partnership and their *modus operandi* militates against closer security co-operation. Close relations with the EU generally depend on the willingness of the third party to approximate to the Union's standards and norms. Moscow rejects the imposition of norms and seeks to make co-operation interest- rather than value-based. In July 2008 Medvedev argued that 'a strategic partnership between Russia and the EU could act as the so-called cornerstone of a Greater Europe without dividing lines. … But I repeat that first we must conduct our relations in a business-like fashion and without being influenced by ideology.'[116] This suggests that from the EU's perspective shared values and norms are central to the strategic partnership, whereas to Moscow its success depends upon its becoming more pragmatic and 'post-ideological'.

The now obvious EU–Russia value gap feeds into the EU's third major problem – how to deal with Russia – insofar as it helps to 'unglue' the Member States' relations with

Russia and opens them up to Moscow's 'divide-and-rule' tactics. Russia's breaking of the consensus about becoming a liberal democracy based on the rule of law and a market economy, through the development of sovereign democracy and its international reassertion, has caused fragmentation within the EU. Studies disagree about how many intra-EU groups exist according to different interests and desired general approach towards Russia. Bordachev identifies three: a Franco-German-Italian bloc, a bloc of Member States, and a central Brussels line. Kempe also identifies three groups: a group of Russia sceptics; a group that does not care much about Moscow, such as Portugal and Greece; and a group of proponents of fruitful relations with Russia, such as Finland and Germany.[117] Leonard and Popescu suggest five groupings (and evidently disagree with Kempe over Greek loyalties):

> "Trojan horses" (Cyprus and Greece) who often defend Russian interests in the EU system, and are willing to veto common EU positions; "strategic partners" (France, Germany, Italy and Spain) who enjoy a "special relationship" with Russia which occasionally undermines common EU policies; "Friendly Pragmatists (Austria, Belgium, Bulgaria, Finland, Hungary, Luxembourg, Malta, Portugal, Slovakia and Slovenia) who maintain a close relationship with Russia and tend to put their business interest above political goals; "Frosty Pragmatist" (Czech Republic, Denmark, Estonia, Ireland, Latvia, the Netherlands, Romania, Sweden and the United Kingdom) who also focus on business interests but are less afraid to speak out against Russian behaviour on human rights or other issues; and "New Cold Warriors" (Lithuania and Poland) who have an overtly hostile relationship with Moscow and are willing to use the veto to block EU negotiations with Russia.[118]

No matter how many groups there are, though, one thing is certain: the EC institutions and Member States are divided along a policy continuum between what Leonard and Popescu call 'creeping engagement'– involving Russia in as many international institutions as possible and encouraging Russian investment in the EU energy sector – and 'soft containment' – excluding Russia from the G8 and Russian investment in the EU energy sector, developing an 'Energy NATO', building missile defence shields, supporting anti-Russian regimes in its Neighbourhood, and expanding NATO to include Georgia. Moreover, problems stemming from these differences are exacerbated by Russia and by the EU Member States themselves.

Some analysts argue that Russia's long-term interests are better served by a united EU.[119] However, in the short-term, Russia's active bilateralism and relative downgrading of relations with Brussels allow it to promote differences between EU States and to exploit their lack of unity. Consider for instance, Russo-German agreement on the Northern European Gas pipeline between Vyborg and Germany in the Baltic Sea. This enables Moscow to have a direct energy dialogue with the major European powers and draw Berlin closer, while also denying the Baltic States influence as transit States and increasing Polish vulnerability by potentially allowing the Kremlin to cut gas supplies to Poland (and the Baltic States) without affecting supply to

Western Europe. Former Polish Defence Minister, Radek Sikorski, likened the deal to the Molotov-Ribbentrop pact.[120]

The EU recognises the desirability of an agreed line towards Russia. In February 2008 the Polish Prime Minister advised that 'The faster all EU countries understand that a common voice in the EU's foreign policy is important, the better the relations of respective Member States and the EU as a whole with our largest Eastern neighbour will be.' In the aftermath of the Georgia conflict the Commission stressed that 'the will and the capacity of the EU to act as one' were *sine qua non* for dealing with Moscow successfully.[121] Similarly, pressure has grown for EU energy solidarity given that the January 2009 gas crisis exposed the Union's failure to respond adequately after the interruption of gas supplies through Ukraine in 2006, and that market integration could weaken significantly the impact of Russian energy supplies in EU–Russia and EU Member state–Russia relations.[122] Indeed, in March 2009 Benita Ferrero-Waldner called explicitly for the EU to decide whether or not 'it is ready to pool sovereignty in the delicate area of energy security – we must react with solidarity, and with the weight appropriate to our value as a consumer.'[123]

In many ways, though, Ferrero-Waldner's call merely underlines that EU States lack discipline and disagree over how, and to what extent, to engage Russia beyond purely defensive mechanisms – such as legal protection of the Union's Eastern border.[124] EU unity vis-à-vis Russia is hampered by indecision beyond the declaratory about how much energy and resources the Union wants to commit to the Caucasus and the CIS. A strong push into these regions will upset Moscow and risk the relative weakness of the ENP being exposed and its being unable to hold off further demands for full EU membership.[125] The European Commission recognises that Moscow is 'sensitive to any suggestion that the EU might be meddling in outlying regions of the Federation' and Russia's military confrontation with Georgia signalled both red lines in its Neighbourhood and determination to protect its energy leverage within the battle of pipeline politics. Bringing Georgia into the West would potentially allow Western powers to put pipelines across the Black Sea through to the Mediterranean. Yet a weak EU approach risks 'losing' Westward leaning States such as Georgia and Ukraine, facilitating Moscow's reassertion in its Neighbourhood and tensions with the US given Washington's unequivocal commitment to 'completing transformational work at Europe's and Eurasia's "frontiers of freedom"'.[126] There is, in short, a Catch 22 situation. Until the EU decides how far to commit to the Caucasus and the CIS, it will be fearful of alienating Moscow. Yet until it decides whether or not to take a firm stance vis-à-vis Moscow's reassertion, it will most probably defer a decision on the former.

These problems are compounded by Member States often prioritising national over collective interests and their tendency to pursue bilateral relations with Moscow when things are going well and Europeanise matters when things go badly.[127] EU States favouring a close relationship with Moscow habitually block potential EU actions of which Moscow disapproves. Those favouring a tougher line towards Moscow repeatedly undermine the 'creeping integration' favoured in other European capitals. Indeed, in April 2009 Foreign Minister Lavrov bemoaned that 'the European Union sometimes becomes hostage to the so-called principle of "Euro-solidarity," when in dispute situations between an EU Member and a third state the EU presents a united front in support of the selfish interests of its "own" country.'[128]

EU handling of the Georgia crisis was indicative of this lack of unity. The EU was Russia's mediator of choice, and it quickly agreed a one-year Monitoring Mission in Georgia. Sarkozy, as holder of the EU presidency at the time, did reasonably well in negotiating a ceasefire and sponsoring the Geneva talks for resolution of the conflict – no doubt helped by Moscow's view of France as one of its more reliable European partners. Yet the immediate reactions of EU Member States to the Georgia conflict revealed that the façade of EU unity was paper thin. France refused to condemn either side and Germany sought to position the EU as 'an honest broker'. Meanwhile, Polish, Latvian, Lithuanian and Estonian leaders flew to Tbilisi on August 12th to demonstrate support for Saakashvili. Poland's government also offered Tbilisi the use of its internet servers as Georgia's had been attacked by hackers, presumably from Russia, and British Prime Minister Gordon Brown subsequently called for a 'root and branch' review of the EU's relationship with Russia.[129] EU rhetoric has since toughened, with much talk of EU–Russia relations being 'at a crossroads',[130] but there is little as yet to suggest sufficient internal consensus to enable policy adjustments commensurate with the 'entirely new' agenda in the Southern Caucasus[131] and the wider Russian reassertion in its neighbourhood.

Conclusion

The EU's claim to a strategic partnership with Russia based on common values has lost credibility. Russia dislikes EU tutelage,[132] refuses its conditionality-laden ENP, and has priorities and preferred *modus operandi* very different from those of the Union. EU and Russian officials have spoken openly of lack of trust, 'double standards', a 'tendency to zero sum thinking' and 'an inclination to see much of the relationship between Western Europe and Russia as power manoeuvring based on mutually exclusive interests'.[133] And the EU is feeling Russia's reassertion in the Mediterranean, Middle East and Central Asia. Russian pressure upon the Baltic States is increasing, Ukraine has become a key fault line within Europe and Russia has re-written the strategic environment of the Caucasus by dint of its Georgian adventure. Syria is potentially emerging as a Russian strategic bridgehead in the Mediterranean littoral[134] and Moscow is central to addressing Iran's potential nuclear threat and the stability of Iraq, Pakistan and Afghanistan. Moreover, the shared neighbourhood is becoming an area of contest between rival political and development models, the Commission conceding in November 2008 that here, where theoretically security co-operation should be most intense, the two powers were 'farther apart' than on broader international issues.[135]

The EU's difficulties reflect its status as a major energy importer and its inability to develop and hold an agreed policy stance. They also reflect Russia's chosen path towards reasserting itself within and beyond Europe and the Union's difficulties when confronted by actors that reject its norms. Russia is revisionist and determined to establish itself as a second pole of power in Europe. This is reflected in its consolidation of sovereign democracy, the newly proclaimed Monroe Doctrine, willingness to use hard power, emphasis on inter-civilisational dialogue and in its discursive construction of foreign policy in terms of value differences rather than commonalities with the West. The contrast with the EU is particularly sharp: liberal democracy versus sovereign/authoritarian democracy; post-modern entity versus traditional modern state; and soft versus hard power actor. Crucially, too, Moscow has very different security concerns and priorities. Its emphasis on hard security and Russia's self-image as a great power foreground Washington as Moscow's single most important security interlocutor. Russia's vast landmass and relations with some of its neighbours mean that Moscow is less Eurocentric in its priorities than Brussels. And when Moscow does look at Europe, need and opportunity for co-operation with the EU sit alongside fear of and resentment at Euro-Atlantic penetration of former Soviet space.

Solana conceded in February 2008 that 'little of value can be achieved without Russia, and almost nothing against it.'[136] There is little cause for optimism. Neither Russia nor the EU is likely to change significantly in the near future and negotiations on a replacement for the PCA will likely remain tortuously slow. Medvedev has a narrow range of foreign policy options and Putin's influence seems assured, given the extension of powers of foreign policy implementation to the Prime Minister's office.[137] Also, Moscow recognises its energy leverage, the existence of exploitable differences between European and US agendas vis-à-vis Russia, and the EU's internal divisions over how to react to Russia's reassertion, how far to commit to Eastern Europe and how far the EU and NATO should enlarge into post-Soviet space. Meantime, the EU is unlikely to achieve sustained security partnership with Russia across the spectrum of common concerns until such time that it develops an alternative to its failed common values-based approach to strategic partnership, addresses its ambiguous commitment to Eastern Europe and takes adequate steps to weaken the impact of Russian bilateralism. The Lisbon Treaty will not achieve this; it requires political will and this is currently in short supply, especially given the global financial crisis and severe Greek-led problems in the Euro-zone.

6

EU ENLARGEMENT TO CENTRAL AND EASTERN EUROPE

The 'Return to Europe'

The ending of the Cold War brought to a conclusion the military division of the European continent. With the wave of peaceful revolutions in Central Europe, countries that had experienced forty-five years of Soviet domination broke free of that suffocating embrace. They appealed to be allowed to align themselves with democratic nations in the Western half of the continent. The moral power behind this claim to join the West was hard to deny: after all, West European States had been calling for the end of Soviet control and now this had come to pass. The Central European countries made the case that their path of development had been artificially skewed by post-war history and that they now sought to revise the identity they had been forced to assume. They argued that they were owed a place among West European States and that they should be allowed to 'Return to Europe'.

A core element of this return was a desire to join those Western political, economic and security organisations that had emerged during the Cold War. Organisations such as the European Community/European Union, NATO and the Council of Europe had come to both embody and express West European identity. They had proven their vitality by outlasting the rival structures that had been created in the East and now symbolised the sense of common purpose among Western countries. Foremost among these organisations was the European Union because its membership was uniquely European and because its supranational character epitomised a continental identity. Its extensive range of competences made it a central actor in the political and economic affairs of Europe and ensured that it would be considered amongst the greatest prizes for States from the East asserting their place in the European mainstream.

The desire of Central and East European countries to join the West offered a corresponding moment of opportunity to the EU. It led to a range of opinions being expressed among and within West European States over the desirability of rapid Eastern enlargement. For advocates of enlargement, this was the chance to overcome the historic division of the continent and to complement the processes of economic and political integration. For those wary of enlargement, there was the risk of undermining the momentum of closer integration by diluting the Union. Deciding between these contending perspectives was vital because the EU could not proceed without unanimous support amongst its Members.

The Federal Republic of Germany was an example of a country that had long been an enthusiastic supporter of better relations with the Eastern half of the continent. It had been the frontline of the Cold War and now sought to transcend the East–West divide. West Germany's pursuit of 'Ostpolitik' during the 1970s had been designed to maximise trade with the East. It had resulted in the disputed border between Germany and Poland being recognised as the Oder-Neisse line.[2] When the Reagan administration had returned to a Cold War stance with the USSR in the 1980s, Germany had been reluctant to follow because it had experienced important benefits from the process of European détente. The end of the Cold War offered an historic opportunity both to re-unite the two halves of Germany and to place it at the forefront of efforts to reach out to Central Europe.

At the other end of the spectrum was France. Its President, François Mitterand, was wary that Germany's attention could shift to the East, and that its willingness to act alongside France as the co-promoter of European integration could be compromised. He was also alarmed at the prospect of Germany's power being enhanced by a new-found leadership role to Central Europe.[3] France was nervous that bringing new Members into the EU would weaken the organisation's homogeneity and diminish its wider influence.[4]

The drafting of the Copenhagen Criteria, in June 1993, was an attempt to crystallise EU values as well as the obligations that new Members would have to assume for the purposes of accession.[5] It celebrated the superiority of the Western model of political and economic development and affirmed the goal of exporting these values to the rest of the continent. The Copenhagen Criteria laid out that the maintenance of a democratic form of government; the principles of a market economy; civilian control over armed forces and adherence to the rule of law, were all central requirements of EU membership. States were expected to uphold civil and political rights and to protect the interests of minorities within their own populations. It was also made clear that aspirants would have to adopt the goals that the EU was seeking to achieve, such as economic and monetary union.

This chapter analyses the issues that have confronted the EU in its enlargement process to the CEECs. It argues that the EU was not in a position to offer Central and East European States military security guarantees because its own defence identity was still at an early stage of development. The EU did seek to provide new Members with soft security in terms of economic stability. The Union imposed its political and economic model upon the accession States and offered them no opportunity to influence its own path of evolution. The process of enlargement caused the EU to reflect on the implications for its own structure: forcing it to confront the need for its own reform in order to prepare for the entry of a diverse range of new Members. The EU is currently uncertain about its future prospects for expansion.

Enlargement and hard security

The EC was not a military security organisation at the time of the end of the Cold War. Unlike NATO, the Community was not a collective defence arrangement, it could not boast military forces under its command and among its Members there was no superpower present. It could not offer defence guarantees to Central and East European countries because it did not possess the means to enact them. At the same time it was asking States that sought to join the organisation to accept a constrained form of sovereignty. In addition to relinquishing some of their freedom of action, new Members were committing themselves to an uncertain goal of closer union.[6] This was an important issue for countries that had suffered under the concept of 'limited sovereignty' imposed during the Soviet era. Joining the EU involved convincing new Members that they would have more to gain from the practice of pooling sovereignty.

The challenge after 1989 was to find ways to project Eastward the economic and political stability that had been built up in the West. There was a potential for a vacuum to develop amongst the CEECs, following the collapse of both the Warsaw Treaty Organisation and the Council on Mutual Economic Assistance. If the Eastern half of the continent was not provided with an anchor, there was a risk that the rise of nationalism could lead to tension and conflict both between and within countries in the region. The worst case scenario was a return to balance-of-power politics in which the CEECs entered into conflict with one another, with all the risks of spill-over into Western Europe. Accession to the EU, by contrast, offered a way to regularise patterns of interaction, ensure democratic government, promote prosperity and improve relations between individual countries. In the words of German Foreign Minister Joschka Fisher, if the future of the East was not resolved, 'this would make Europe a continent of uncertainty, and in the medium term these traditional lines of conflict would shift from Eastern Europe into the EU again'.[7]

This policy was not without geopolitical risks for the EU's Members. Many of the EU's prospective Members were located in unstable parts of Europe and there was the danger of importing their own particular external and internal security problems into the Union. Foremost amongst the security concerns of many of the aspirants was the potential resurgence of Russian power and its capacity to exert military or economic pressure upon its neighbours. The Baltic States, formerly annexed within the USSR, had declared full independence in 1990 but continued to experience tensions with the Kremlin over the citizenship rights of Russian minorities. Estonia and Latvia had over 35 per cent and 44 per cent Russian-speaking populations respectively.[8] This was a prickly issue that had led to bloodshed in 1991 and the EU was wary of entering into a confrontation with Russia.[9]

The EU was fortunate in that the Moscow did not view EU enlargement as an inherent threat. Whilst Russia has given no more than fleeting consideration to its own membership of the Union, it has tended to treat enlargement as a non-strategic issue. Rather, it has looked upon the EU as a trading partner and one with whom it has been willing to designate four 'common spaces' (see Chapter 5).[10] NATO, instead of the EU, has drawn the post-Cold War ire of Russia. Moscow looked upon the enlargement of the Alliance as a core threat to its security interests and reacted with alarm to its advance to the borders of Russia.

There were other vulnerabilities for the EU, however, beyond that of Russia. Enlargement raised the possibility of the Union becoming neighbours with such countries as Belarus and Ukraine. In the Balkans the constituent Republics of former-Yugoslavia, such as Slovenia and Croatia, were preparing to secede and trigger a major internal conflict that would draw in Western Europe.[11] The accession of Cyprus threatened to involve the EU in the long-standing tensions between Greece and Turkey, while Hungary and Romania had experienced their own protracted border disputes. Nor were these problems confined to the potential for external aggression. There were internal security challenges that were of a lower profile than inter-state confrontations, but were still important from the perspective of assuring the safety of EU citizens. Some States were likely to import problems of organised crime and drug trafficking into the Union (see Chapter 2), while its external borders would become the responsibility of new Members. There were fears about the ability of accession countries to police these borders effectively, as well as to deal with structural issues such as corruption in their police and judicial agencies.[12]

A pressing concern was over how EU enlargement would interface with the enlargement of NATO.[13] Article V of the Washington Treaty provided a collective defence guarantee that if a state was attacked, it could look to its allies, and more importantly, the United States, to come to its assistance. There was the potential for complementary enlargement processes to unfold between the two organisations, with the Union having responsibility for political and economic stability and NATO complementing this with defence guarantees. The expectation arose of a so-called 'Royal Road' of enlargement in which detailed consultation and coordination could occur between both organisations.[14] There was reassuring talk of the creation of a security 'architecture' that would be interlocking and mutually reinforcing. It was envisaged that there might be trade-offs between the two organisations, for example, the EU offering membership to reassure States that did not receive early NATO membership.

This vision of mutually compatible and reinforcing enlargement processes was given additional impetus by the TEU. Apart from creating the CFSP intergovernmental pillar structure, the EU was endowed with a security identity and with ambitions in defence. For the time being, the Union's defence ambitions were expressed through the WEU, which represented a compromise between those States that wanted a defence identity to be created within the EU and those that feared undermining the centrality of NATO. The WEU was placed equidistant between the EU and NATO and was meant to serve simultaneously as the defence expression of the Union and as the European identity within the Alliance.[15] The WEU seemed to offer a potential bridge between the EU and NATO and thereby served to reconcile the enlargement processes of both. The WEU's defence guarantees were already operationalised by NATO and this was an obvious source of attraction to CEECs trying to secure membership in either the EU or the Alliance.[16] The WEU even went so far as to create a special category of 'Associate Partner' status for ten Central and East European countries that was viewed by them as a sort of waiting chamber for EU and NATO membership.

Yet such a vision of complementary EU and NATO enlargements overlooked the differences between the organisations and the rivalries that marred their relationship. NATO's enlargement was more of a political process in which the organisation extended defence guarantees to new Members.[17] It was driven to a considerable extent by post-Cold War questions about the Alliance's *raison d'être* in the absence of the Soviet military threat and the desire of the United States to preserve its influence in Europe. In contrast, the enlargement of the EU was more of a technical process requiring States to fulfil a range of responsibilities conferred by membership. The enlargement of the EU did not carry the same negative connotations as enlarging NATO, because the former was not associated with Europe's East–West military divide. The EU had stringent criteria that aspirant States needed to attain: something that could not be resolved with a political declaration.

Rivalry between the EU and NATO, particularly among the elites in both organisations, further undermined the possibility of a coordinated enlargement process. There was surprisingly little consultation between the two despite their overlapping memberships and the locations of both their headquarters in Brussels. In the words of Sperling, 'At the outset, the interdependence of the two enlargements was recognised … (but) parallelism was eventually abandoned, more a consequence of practical politics than a strategic decision to disengage the two processes'.[18] The announcement of the Partnership for Peace (PfP) policy at its Brussels summit in 1994 marked a turning point for the Alliance in which the US seized the initiative and drove forward a 'NATO First' enlargement policy.[19] President Clinton and his National Security Adviser, Tony Lake, saw in enlargement a vehicle for reinvigorating an American vision for European security and reasserting a leadership role. This chimed with the President's domestic agenda as it garnered votes for Clinton's re-election amongst Polish and other émigré communities within the US.[20] It culminated in the invitation at the 1997 Madrid Summit to Poland, Hungary and the Czech Republic to join the Alliance. Their accession to NATO in 1999 was to be five years before the first CEE States entered the EU.

Unlike the role the US plays within the Alliance, there is no country within the EU with overarching power capable of providing leadership. A small group of countries within the Union are key players in defence policy decisions. France and the UK, in particular, must be in agreement for an initiative to prosper as they are the foremost military actors. The development of policy inside the EU relies upon the building of coalitions and the creation of a consensus. Where different bodies of opinion exist, the European Council plays an important role in brokering compromises and trade-offs while the European Commission has a part to play in ensuring that the voice of smaller States is not overlooked.

The CEECs have been circumspect about the extent of the reliance they have placed upon the Union to protect their security interests. Even after the UK and France took the lead role in forging the ESDP, replacing the role assigned to the WEU, this was treated by aspirant States with caution.[21] The CEECs were initially doubtful of the 'value added' offered by a European defence capacity. They feared that it could detract from the central role of NATO and have the effect of alienating Washington. This fear had been borne out by the hostile reaction of the Clinton administration to ESDP: Secretary of State, Madeleine Albright, warned that it risked duplicating NATO, de-coupling the transatlantic bond and discriminating against States in the Alliance that were not Members of the EU.[22] Under both Presidents Bill Clinton and George W. Bush, the US saw ESDP, with its stated aim of European autonomy, as a potential threat to American interests. CEE States were unwilling to sacrifice proven defence guarantees orchestrated by the US for unproven security arrangements under the auspices of the EU. American power was regarded as the foremost guarantee against the rise of any Russian attempt to pressure or coerce these countries.

The subsequent policy positions of the CEECs attested to this concern. As relations between France, Germany and America deteriorated over the 'War on Terror', the CEECs made no secret of the fact that they sympathised broadly with Washington's stance. At the Prague Summit of NATO in November 2002, seven central European States were invited to join the Alliance and this was seen as recompense for their support for US policies. In January 2003, an open letter, including signatories from several countries in Central and Eastern Europe, expressed support for the American confrontation with Iraq.[23] The next month, the 'Vilnius Ten' – comprising Albania, Bulgaria, Croatia, the Baltic States, Macedonia, Slovakia, Slovenia and Romania – argued in favour of American actions, in sharp contrast to the critical stance adopted by France's President Chirac and Germany's Chancellor Schroeder. This behaviour led Chirac to accuse these States of missing a good opportunity to keep silent. In contrast, American Defense Secretary Donald Rumsfeld praised the attitudes of what he called 'new Europe', while making derogatory comments about 'Old Europe'.[24] Countries such as Poland and the Czech Republic also proved willing to be part of the US National Missile Defense programme by agreeing to host radar and interceptor missiles on their home territories, despite the opposition this excited from Russia.

The CEECs were also aware of the persistence of diversity among EU Members over strategic issues. The 1995 enlargement had brought into the EU States with a tradition of neutralism; Austria, Sweden and Finland.[25] With the prospect of new Members from Central and Eastern Europe, the range of attitudes to security issues would be broadened still further. The existence of differing strategic cultures rendered it difficult to obtain consensus over the use of force and tended to result in the Union fracturing when a major foreign policy crisis arose.[26] Differing security priorities, significant differences in military capabilities and contrasting perceptions of legitimacy gave the CEECs grounds for scepticism when choosing between US and EU security leadership on the continent.

Yet by the time of the second term of the George W. Bush administration, the strategic value of ESDP was more apparent to CEE States. In the first place, American suspicion of European defence efforts had been mitigated and concern re-doubled that European contributions to defence burden-sharing were inadequate. In the words of Kupchan: 'The main threat to the Atlantic link stems from too little Europe, *not too much*' (emphasis added).[27] Second, the period of the first Bush administration had illustrated how US and European security interests could diverge, especially when the issues were no longer focused on the defence of the continent. Having joined the EU in May 2004, States in Central Europe had more of a stake in the security aspirations of the organisation and were less inclined to privilege NATO interests. Third, the EU demonstrated its capacity to undertake a range of security tasks, both inside and outside of the continent. In the case of Operation *Artemis* in June 2003, EU forces had been deployed many thousands of miles away to the Congo. In sum, ESDP had become an important part of EU membership.

The costs of enlargement for the EU

If the EU could not offer convincing hard security guarantees to the CEECs then it could offer a softer security relationship founded upon economic considerations. As the biggest market in the world, the EU was in a position to offer new Members preferential terms of trade on which to build their economic growth. It tendered membership of a common currency that would enable relatively small countries to keep inflation and interest rates low and withstand the turmoil of global financial shocks. These economic factors would provide foreign investors with the confidence to help guarantee the inflow of foreign direct investment (FDI). For example, between 1985 to 1995, FDI in Poland amounted to only about $1billion whereas in 1995 alone this had jumped to $7.5billion.[28]

During the Cold War the EC had created trade links with countries in Eastern Europe: for example, trade and cooperation agreements were signed with Hungary in September 1988, with Czechoslovakia in December 1988 and with Poland in September of the following year. But with the end of the Cold War, the EU signalled its intention to transform the economies of aspirant States by initiating the PHARE programme of assistance (*Pologne et Hongrie assistance à la reconstruction economique*).[29] This was complemented by the signing of 'Europe Agreements' that detailed the relationship between prospective new Members and the EU. The very choice of the name signalled a sense of belonging on the part of the aspirant States. By this mechanism the EU initiated or developed further extant trading links with the CEECs and began to give them access to the all-important single market. The Union signed its first Europe Agreements with the Visegrad countries of Hungary, Poland and Czechoslovakia in 1992: a first step on a long road of conducting a structured dialogue that would lead ultimately to membership. In April 1994, Poland and Hungary were the first CEE States to apply formally for EU membership.

The extent of the economic challenge confronting the Union was impossible to ignore. Whilst the CEECs represented a potential 30 per cent increase in population for the fifteen Members of the Union, they were only about a third of the size of the average gross domestic product (GDP).[30] The Union could be expected to provide aid to facilitate the new Members to catch up with their Western neighbours but the Union was reluctant to undertake the task of reconstructing their economies from scratch. While aspirants looked admiringly at the experiences of countries like Spain and Ireland, EU States were wary of major new commitments and the European Commission was determined to avoid imposing too great a strain on the Union's budget. Germany, the traditional source of EU funds, was already committed to the re-building of its Eastern counterpart.[31] The Union faced the task of trying to converge the economies of the CEECs and the Commission had the responsibility of ensuring that the CEECs could withstand the economic competition inherent in membership.

Those countries trying to join the EU were dependent to a disproportionate extent on their agricultural sectors, with a higher proportion of their populations still engaged in working the land. Many of their farms were small and would struggle to compete against the mechanised farming of their Western counterparts. The implication for the existing Member States was that they could face a diminution in Common Agricultural Policy (CAP) spending – amounting to some 45% of total EU spending – as funds were stretched to include new Members. Resources would be distributed more thinly and less productive farms in the East would be likely to require greater subsidy. While advocates of CAP reform feared the reinforcement of protectionism from amongst the CEECs,[32] others such as France harboured concerns that enlargement would lead to cuts to the CAP in expectation of preparing the Union for the influx of new States. In the event a deal was done between France and Germany that minimised the prospect of substantive CAP reform. Germany was one of the staunchest supporters of the enlargement process as part of its strategy of promoting European integration and developing its own strategy towards the East. France secured German support for limited cuts in CAP spending in return for French support for Germany's enlargement project.

A similar set of concerns existed in relation to structural funds. The European Regional Development Fund, the European Social Fund and the Cohesion Fund were disbursed to countries lagging in economic development or suffering with declining industrial regions. Structural funds were seen as a means to bring countries up to a common level of development in an attempt to promote 'economic and social cohesion'.[33] By the late 1990s this had come to account for some 35% of EU spending.[34] Countries such as Spain, Portugal and Ireland had used this money to stimulate and underpin their own economic growth. Yet with CEECs vying to enter the Union it was likely that traditional beneficiaries would see a downturn in funding as the needs of poorer economies took precedence. This generated a powerful set of interests inside the Union that were sceptical of enlargement.

New Member States were also likely to bring other sorts of economic problems. In addition to access to medical treatment and education in the West, their populations would have the right to move into Western countries once the right of free movement was granted. One fear was the migration of large numbers of Roma peoples. Labour migration was another major issue as workers in the East were expected to seek higher paid jobs in Western countries – the UK, Ireland and Sweden were the only countries amongst the 15 to open their labour markets from the outset.[35] The loss of jobs from West to East was a possible manifestation of the problem as Western firms would seek cheaper manufacturing opportunities by re-locating to Central and East European countries.

One option for addressing this problem would have been to increase substantially the Union's budget: thereby enabling new obligations to be assumed whilst fulfilling the existing commitments. However, it was clear at the time that there was no appetite amongst the fifteen Members for significant growth in the EU budget. Enlargement was to be pursued within tight financial constraints that would effectively foreclose the possibility of a major transfer of resources from West to East. This generated considerable resentment amongst EU countries that were net contributors to the EU budget, especially from Germany.[36] The costs it had to shoulder in relation to EU enlargement led to a more sceptical German attitude to the process.

Thus the financial costs of enlargement were likely to be very significant for the EU as it sought to absorb relatively poor new Members. This could impact upon the economic growth rates of Member States before the benefits of enlargement, such as expanded trade, began to be experienced. But more important were the other security risks to the EU that could result from the process. Societal instability could result from greater competition and from the influx of immigrants. It was possible that higher levels of unemployment would result from the outsourcing of jobs whilst social and cultural frictions could be generated by foreign workers re-locating to poor neighbourhoods in West European towns and cities.

Diversity and reform within the EU

In addition to the prospective cost, the enlargement of the EU was an inherently complex project. It was complex because the Union was seeking simultaneously to expand its functions as well as its membership. As a result of the Treaty of European Union, the organisation was taking on a range of new competencies such as in the fields of Justice and Home Affairs, Foreign policy and Social policy. Changing the organisation in these ways raised a tension with the perspective of allowing in new Members. This became characterised as the debate between 'deepening versus widening'. Advocates of a deeper, more integrated Union, were anxious that granting accession to new States would undermine their goal. They were concerned that bringing in States with different socio-economic and cultural heritages would serve to dilute the EU and make it more diverse. This risked paralysing the advance of political and economic integration and, at worst, threatened to break the Union apart. Conversely, the advocates of widening emphasised that this was a historic opportunity to bring the two halves of the continent together and overcome nearly five decades of division.

The debate over deepening versus widening exposed the spectrum of opinion within the EU over the organisation's long-term goals. States that were reluctant to relinquish more sovereign powers to Brussels tended to view enlargement as a way to slow down the momentum of integration. The United Kingdom, for example, was a champion of enlargement partly because it viewed the process of assimilating the CEECs as a means to arrest the federal-vision of some of its allies. Its former Prime Minister Margaret Thatcher described having CEECs lining up to join the EU as 'ma(king) my vision of a looser, more open Community seem timely rather than backward'.[37] On the other hand, those countries that were sympathetic to the aim of 'ever closer union' were determined to deepen integration as a precursor to accommodating new Members. The process of preparing the EU for enlargement was portrayed by some of its States as a commonsensical adaptation of structures to cope with new Members: and by others as a closet attempt to push ahead with a far-reaching economic and political integration project. The European Commission made clear its view that deepening could not be sacrificed in the cause of widening, arguing that the two processes were mutually complementary.[38]

The EU had to navigate between these contending approaches and the process of enlargement proved to be a difficult balancing act. The Essen European Council, in December 1994, envisaged that a series of inter-governmental conferences (IGCs) would provide the vehicle for reforms to the Union prior to enlargement.[39] The IGCs at Amsterdam in 1997, and at Nice in 2000, were dominated by debates over how far to push forward with the internal reform process. Some argued that the Union should not be empowered to take in new Members until far-reaching changes had been agreed. Yet this perspective ignored the considerable political momentum that had built up behind enlargement. The moral imperative to welcome the CEECs back into the European mainstream – and the fear that excluding them could lead to them turning away from democracy – proved irresistible. Despite only limited reform of the TEU, the Union moved inexorably towards enlargement.[40]

Three issue areas were symptomatic of the underlying debate. The first was over how to avoid a larger Union becoming paralysed in its decision-making ability. The question of the appropriate voting weights in the European Council of Ministers had always been a matter of sensitivity, as disproportionate influence had been accorded to smaller States to ensure their voice was heard. But enlargement threatened to exacerbate the problem of voting weights as the addition of more small countries would tip the scales further against those countries with large populations. With the 1995 enlargement, the share of the EU's population residing in small States rose to 21% whilst their voting strength in the Council increased to 45%.[41] Countries such as France, Germany and the UK became nervous that they would be outvoted in the Council by coalitions of smaller States and that their overall influence within the Union would diminish.

Second, was the range of issues subject to decision by Qualified Majority Voting (QMV). The assumption here was that new accession States would have the effect of making the Union more heterogenous. Therefore, in order to prevent increasing conflicts due to unanimity, the Council should bring more of its policy decisions under QMV. For example, in the Treaty of Amsterdam, aspects of JHA policy were 'communitarised'. Yet this approach was a source of concern to countries resistant to an extension of the competences of the Union as it reduced the number of issues over which national vetoes could be wielded. The voting weights were re-negotiated in the Treaty of Nice: France, Germany, Italy and the UK were allocated 29 votes; Spain and Poland received the next largest allocation with 27 votes and countries like Estonia and Latvia were only accorded 4 votes.[42]

Third were attempts to increase the efficiency with which the EU transacted its business. This focused on efforts to limit the number of European Parliamentarians and reduce the portfolios within the European Commission. Controlling the size of the Parliament to prevent it from becoming unwieldy proved to be much less controversial than attempting to reduce the representation of small countries on the European Commission. There had been an agreement that by the time the EU expanded to 20 Member States, the number of Commissioners would be reduced to one per country, irrespective of the size of the country. Yet with the prospect of additional enlargement, it was feared that the system would become unworkable if all new States were accorded an area of responsibility. The argument was put forward that the European Commission needed to be of a limited size if it was to serve as an efficient decision-making structure and if the Commissioners were to control significant policy domains.[43] Nevertheless, smaller EU States were wary of losing their national voice at the table and suspected an attempt by the larger countries to carve up the major portfolios amongst themselves. When the ten States acceded in May 2004, they each had only one Commissioner.

An alternative option for those States determined to deepen the Union prior to enlargement was to seek a pathway that would enable them to progress at the speed of their choice. There was much discussion of the concept of creating an *avant garde* within the Union, where those States committed to faster integration were allowed to proceed. Instead of accepting lowest common denominator solutions to which all States could subscribe, an *avant garde* would move forward alone. This might include different groups of States depending on the issue; for example, there could be core groups in areas such as monetary union or defence. It might then be possible for other States to join these groups at a later stage, or for new Members to link up with these groupings once they had attained the necessary criteria. Advocates of a multi-speed Europe, such as France, could argue that this was already developing in practice. Issues such as border security were already being taken forward by groups of States. An initiative relating to CFSP had been agreed in the Treaty of Amsterdam and was labelled 'Constructive Abstention'. Under new Article 23 of the TEU, a Member state could abstain on a vote in the Council without blocking a unanimous decision.

Whilst the concept of a multi-speed Europe has been seen in some quarters as a potential solution to the tensions induced by enlargement, it has been viewed with distaste in others. Amongst States suspicious of the objective of political union, a multi-speed Europe has been seen as divisive, risking the creation of levels of membership and perceptions of second-class status. Countries such as France and Germany have been viewed as attempting to preserve their special influence within the EU by the creation of core groupings. Amongst the CEECs it has tended to be treated warily, not least because they could find themselves outside some of the inner circles of the organisation.

Reform of the new Members

As well as seeking to reform the EU prior to enlargement, the Members were clear in their view that they expected applicant States to reform in preparation for joining. There was a huge body of laws and regulation with which to conform – the 80,000 page *acquis communitaire*. The *acquis* ranged across all manner of issues, from environmental policies and regulations to judicial actions. The breadth of issues was a source of concern for the CEECs because it meant altering almost all aspects of national life. What was well appreciated amongst the existing Members was that their ability to influence and reform aspirants existed during the period leading up to accession.[44] Those countries seeking to join could be expected to promise much in order to qualify, but the delivery on those promises once the incentive of membership had been removed, would be limited.

Conditionality was therefore a powerful instrument in the hands of the Commissioners responsible for enlargement, namely Hans van den Broek, Gunter Verheugen and Olli Rehn. The power of attraction of the Union was significant but its shelf life was limited.[45] The EU was capable of exercising considerable influence over accession States whilst they resided in the 'waiting room' of membership. In addition to explaining what comprised the *acquis*, the Commission offered a range of other services. It provided advice to accession States on the legislation that needed to be drafted to comply with Union requirements; technical assistance on the implementation of measures; twinning arrangements with Member countries and the secondment of Commission officials to provide practical guidance. After 1998 the Commission drew up 'Regular Reports' on the candidates' compliance with the *acquis* and published an annual scoreboard to monitor the progress of each country.

The CEECs could be forgiven for feeling hard done by during the enlargement process. They were expected to conform to the entire *acquis* and were offered no potential opt outs on issues with which they disagreed. This carried the risk that States could accept measures in order to obtain entry, but might then oppose implementation once inside the Union. There was also a risk of a backlash amongst the populations of CEE countries when the glow of accession became a distant memory and the true costs of membership were apparent. This view is borne out by contemporary Eurobarometer data that demonstrates high levels of dissatisfaction amongst the general population in Central European countries. For example, in survey results in 2009, 46% of Czechs that were interviewed regarded EU membership as neither a good nor a bad thing, while in Poland, only 53% of people questioned were enthusiastic about their country's membership of the Union.[46]

The treatment of the CEECs contrasted unfavourably with the experience of existing Members that had been allowed to opt out of certain portfolios. For example, the UK had opted out of the European Social Chapter whilst Denmark and the UK had remained outside of monetary union. The accession countries were offered no opportunity to influence the organisation that they were aspiring to join. Furthermore, the organisation itself was evolving and taking on new areas of responsibility. In effect the CEECs were joining a dynamic and evolving policy framework and they were expected to sign something akin to a blank cheque because they were not fully cogniscent of the EU's final destination.

Little notice was taken of the pain incurred by the CEECs as a result of the membership process. Some States experienced significant disruption to the rights of freedom of movement of their citizens as well as to informal cross-border trade, particularly with their own neighbours. Poland, for example, had a long-standing trading relationship with both the Ukraine and Belarus, that fell victim to the common external tariff and to visa regulations on the movement of people.[47] Approximately 6 million Ukrainians and 4 million Belarussians crossed the border with Poland in the year prior to its accession to the EU and many were small traders carrying out lucrative business.[48] Poland subsequently championed the cause of Ukrainian membership of the EU in recognition of the important economic and historic links it has enjoyed with that country. Other minority groups were affected such as Hungarians in Ukraine and Romania and the Slovak minority in Romania. This served to reinforce 'the growing socio-economic and psychological gap between the two parts of Europe',[49] and even to challenge the proper implementation of Council of Europe conventions on minority protection.[50]

These experiences contributed to a perception amongst the CEECs that they were viewed as lesser Members within the EU 'club'. This arose from the fact that they had played no part in determining the structures or policies of the Union. It was driven by certain conditions that were placed on those States acceding to the EU in 2004. They were not accorded the right of free movement for their citizens under Schengen arrangements for a three year period until 2007. Furthermore, they were not granted full CAP and structural funding from the time of accession. These transition arrangements helped to foster a sense of resentment on behalf of the new Members that risked sowing the seeds of long-term tensions.

The risk of exclusion

The question of which States to include in the enlargement process, and over what period of time, was debated intensely. Whether to pursue a phased process in which there would be successive waves of membership, or whether to embrace a simultaneous enlargement, divided opinion across the continent during the 1990s. Accepting a phased process would render it more digestible for the EU. On the other hand, it was evident that the 'new' Europe was being defined by organisational membership and those States left outside institutional frameworks, whilst others were admitted, for however long a period of time, might suffer a sense of alienation. The EU had to weigh up what new lines of division and exclusion it would be creating by admitting a new group of countries. It found itself trying to determine an appropriate balance between the progress individual States had achieved in implementing the EU *acquis* and the political pressures to lock in States to a Western model of development.

By 1996 ten States had applied for membership. In July of the following year the European Commission published *Agenda 2000: For a Stronger and Wider Union*,[51] that explained the enlargement strategy and expressed opinions on the eligibility of the applicants. In *Agenda 2000* the Commission initially identified six States as being in the first round of enlargement, reflecting the progress that they had made in relation to the *acquis*.[52] This was in spite of contrary opinions that argued that all States should be invited and it be left open to see who progressed most quickly.[53] The six States chosen by the Commission were the Czech Republic, Estonia, Poland, Hungary, Cyprus and Slovenia. What was envisaged by Brussels was that the six would be able to enter at their own pace through a so-called 'accession partnership' in which a set of measures were agreed between the Commission and each individual country and underpinned with PHARE funding.[54] The Commission wanted aspirants to differentiate amongst themselves by determining their own speed of accession.

The applications of Bulgaria, Romania, Slovakia, Latvia and Lithuania were deferred into a second wave of the process. The application from Malta was delayed by the election of a government on the island that suspended its application. But over time, the decision to designate a second wave was increasingly questioned as concerns grew about the potential negative implications of leaving countries to languish outside.[55] It was feared that differentiating between first and second wave countries could undermine the reformist momentum amongst some of the CEECs in which populations had been experiencing real pain in order to bring their country into compliance with EU regulations. In security terms, there were anxieties that reformist leaders could be replaced by nationalists and that States could become politically and economically de-stabilised. Disillusionment might have led to a counter-action and a turning back of the clock to patterns of government in the East that would be detrimental to the long-term interests of the EU and its Members.

These warnings helped to sway opinions amongst EU governments and the decision was taken to begin accession negotiations with second wave States in February 2000. It quickly became clear that the Union was heading towards a 'Big Bang' enlargement in which most of the States would accede. This was endorsed at the Copenhagen Summit in December 2002 when all the applicants except for Romania and Bulgaria were given a date to become Members.[56] Cyprus was allowed to go forward even though its future status between Greece and Turkey had not been resolved. In May 2004 ten countries joined and thereby increased EU membership to 25 countries.

The path towards enlargement was far from a technical process devoid of political considerations. Although considerable variations could be detected amongst the ten in their suitability to accede, the need to keep these States travelling in the same direction had overridden other concerns. The same was to prove to be the case for the candidacies of Romania and Bulgaria. Although they had been excluded from the tranche of States admitted in 2004, due to the nascent stage of their reform processes, it became difficult to deny them membership for too long. Fears that the progression of reform could be reversed resulted in a firm date being set and Romania and Bulgaria being granted EU membership in January 2007.[57] Arguably, Bulgaria was let in too soon as it had not addressed adequately the problem of domestic organised crime and corruption. This was borne out by the fact that certain EU funds to Bulgaria were suspended on the grounds that corrupt practices in its government and judicial sectors were still prevalent.

Future enlargements

The absorption of the countries of Central and Eastern Europe into the EU and the prospect of accession for countries in South Eastern Europe, such as Croatia and Serbia, has raised the question of what future enlargements it might undertake. The 'return to Europe' of the CEECs was seen as fitting because those countries had been part of a common civilisation. But the prospect of future enlargements has led to much soul searching about the nature of 'what is Europe' and where its natural limits might lie. Should issues of geography, culture and identity play a part in determining the boundaries of the continent? Is it justified, for example, to specify that countries entering the EU must share a common Judeo-Christian heritage, when there are millions of Muslims already living in West European countries? Or should the EU just apply the criteria that it agreed at Copenhagen in 1993: that countries should be functioning democracies with market economies, they should adhere to human rights and they should maintain civilian control over their armed forces?

The answers to these questions have considerable import because they will shape the decision whether the EU continues to enlarge to the East and South. The prospect of future enlargement will determine which new lines of division are imposed on the continent and which countries find themselves permanently excluded from the club. The implications for the Union itself are equally significant. If it were to enlarge further the EU could find itself neighbouring countries such as Syria and Iran as well as States in Central Asia. This would have the effect of drawing the Union into a series of new security debates to which it has not hitherto been exposed.

Decisions about where next to enlarge presuppose a rational calculation of interests that may not be available to EU decision-makers. Fatigue with the process of enlargement has set in and this may prove to be a powerful source of constraint. In the words of *The Economist*, 'It is something of an irony ... that while enlargement has become the most popular and successful instrument of regime change in Europe's history, the European Union is losing the will to enlarge any more'.[58] Even amongst countries that were ardent supporters of new Members, a sense of scepticism has set in, driven by a range of concerns. These include worries about European identity, as the borders of the Union stretch farther to the East and about the financial cost. This was compounded by the economic pessimism that accompanied the recession in 2008–9, resulting in a perception that Europe was in crisis and that it would be best to focus on its own problems rather than on admitting new entrants.

Growing disillusion with the EU amongst some of its most fervent Members has been partly blamed on dissatisfaction with the enlargement process. When the French and Dutch people rejected the Constitutional Treaty, prior to the Lisbon Treaty, the cause was ascribed partly to fears of immigration and to the loss of job opportunities.

It highlighted perceptions that European citizens feel divorced from the policies advocated by their elites. This forced some national leaders to express misgivings about future rounds of enlargement. President Sarkozy, for example, called for a freeze in the process in 2006, and went on to promise in April 2008 that he would instigate a referendum on Turkish accession.[59] In the autumn of 2008 significant majorities in Germany and France perceived the 2004 and 2007 enlargements to have weakened the Union overall.[60]

The potential candidatures of Georgia and Ukraine highlighted the risks that the EU faced in relation to enlargement. In 2007–8, the Union was considering the terms of an association agreement with Ukraine and was undertaking a rule of law mission in Georgia. It had come under pressure from the US, at the NATO Bucharest summit, to begin accession negotiations with the two States. The US has been a consistent supporter of EU enlargement because it has viewed this as a way for European powers to share an increasing portion of the global security burden. The US promoted membership for Ukraine and Georgia as a way of locking them into the Western orbit and out of the Russian embrace and EU reluctance towards these States risked stimulating American ire. The conflict between Russia and Georgia in August 2008, however, vindicated the EU's caution. As the holder of the EU Presidency at the time, France helped to broker a ceasefire between the parties. The EU was then drawn even deeper into the situation when, at the end of September, an EU civilian monitoring mission of 200 personnel was despatched to oversee the agreement.[61]

Turkey remains the most intractable problem for the EU's expansion debate. In its favour stand an array of geopolitical, economic and strategic arguments. Turkey has long expressed a desire to join: it was made an Associate Member of the European Community as early as 1963. Over 50 per cent of Turkey's exports go to the EU and it sits at the crossroads of East and West. It is a Muslim country but with a secular tradition and many commentators have pointed to the excellent role model it would present if it entered the European Union. America has offered strong support for Turkey's candidature, although this has sometimes been seen as meddling in Brussels.[62] The country's strategic importance has increased following its two command roles of the International Security Assistance Force in Afghanistan.

But despite these positive points, Turkey embodies all the questions about what sort of club the EU seeks to be. Its size of 65 million means that Turkey would be second only to Germany within the Union; it sits on the edges of Europe with a relatively poor population and with limited cultural ties to Europe. Its candidature languished and in the 1990s it watched as a variety of States leap-frogged over its prospects for accession. It was held in limbo on the grounds that it was not ready due to its human rights record in relation to its Kurdish minority and the historical interventions of its Army in domestic politics. Not until the Helsinki European Council in October 1999 was the country accorded candidate status. In October 2005 accession talks were begun but delays in Turkey's programme of reforms led to the suspension of the negotiations in the area of key portfolios. Turkey has formally been told that its membership is in prospect but some way off in the future.

The question of Turkish accession has caused wider security problems for the EU: one being the tension with Cyprus. Cyprus was admitted to the Union before the division between the Greek half of the island and the so-called 'Turkish Republic of Northern Cyprus' had been resolved. The government in Athens had hinted that it would veto the enlargement of all ten CEECs if Cyprus was not admitted to the EU in 2004. The Greek-Cypriots went on to reject the plan that was put forward by former UN Secretary General Kofi Annan to reunite the two halves of the island. Cyprus now wields a potential veto over Turkish accession to the EU and, along with Greece, has blocked Turkish participation in the European Defence Agency (see chapter 3). In turn, as a NATO Member, Turkey wields a potential veto over a security relationship between Cyprus and NATO and has refused to allow it to attend EU-NATO meetings on grounds that it is not a Member of the Alliance's Partnership for Peace arrangement. It has insisted that meetings between the North Atlantic Council and the EU's Permanent Security Committee exclude Cyprus, which some EU Members have opposed.[63] Intelligence sharing of classified information has also been severely limited, with NATO classified information only being made available to the EU Military Staff on the proviso that Cypriot officers cannot access it.[64]

Turkey has demonstrated its dissatisfaction with how it has been treated by the EU by acting against the European Security and Defence Policy. It has used its membership of NATO to block EU access to Alliance military assets under the 'Berlin Plus' arrangements. Its obduracy was a salutary lesson to the EU and Ankara only changed its stance after considerable pressure from Washington and London. The underlying concern remains that by alienating Turkey the cause of fundamentalism could be promoted. The US has warned the Union that its procrastination could spark an anti-European backlash in Turkey that could lead its reform process to falter. Nevertheless, there remain powerful voices within the EU opposed to Turkey's accession. Germany, and France have both expressed opposition to full membership and President Sarkozy has offered only a special type of partnership to Turkey on the grounds that it is a country in 'Asia Minor'.[65] Amongst EU Members there are those that fear the damage that could be done by Turkish accession outweighs the risks of alienating the government in Ankara.

Conclusion

The importance of EU enlargement to Central and Eastern Europe cannot be over-emphasised because it has changed the face of Europe. It has transformed the States of Western and Eastern Europe from an adversarial relationship into a close-knit grouping in which sovereignty is pooled. The process has drawn States that were in a security vacuum into a security community. Enlargement has provided a framework in two other sorts of ways. First, in economic terms so that new Members can prosper and levels of trade between old and new accession States can grow. Second, as a means for promoting the pro-Western identity of the CEECs. In addition, enlargement has had the effect of altering the path of development of the Union and has injected new dynamism into its structures and policies.

Whilst enlargement to the CEECs has been the EU's biggest success, it has not been an unqualified success. On the negative side, the Union has been castigated, both by the accession States and by allies such as the US, for being slow to enlarge. Second, it has not been able to avoid creating new dividing lines in Europe as it admits some States but resists the applications of others. Third, enlargement has made the EU a broader and more diverse organisation than it would otherwise have been, full of competing voices and perspectives. Fourth, enlargement has occurred in the absence of a master plan and has proceeded, instead, in more of an *ad hoc* fashion. Like the EU itself, the enlargement process has emerged from the bargaining and competing visions of its membership and it remains, even today, a work in progress. The conundrum it now faces is if its Members, and more importantly their electorates, perceive that the Union is reaching saturation, what alternatives to enlargement does the Union have to offer?

To a large extent the EU has already taken steps to confront this dilemma and the challenges thrown up by the Union's expanded boundaries bringing it into contact with a range of new countries and security concerns. It has acknowledged that membership is not a viable option for all States and it has defined new forms of relationship with countries in its vicinity. Partnership and Cooperation Agreements (PCAs) have been formed with countries such as Ukraine, Belarus and Georgia, while in March 2004 the Commission published its document 'Wider Europe – Neighbourhood'.[66] This was to form the basis for the 2004 European Neighbourhood Programme that was introduced to offer a level of cooperation and trading relationship to States that were never likely to become Members.[67] The EU has thus developed a wider range of options in its inventory. At the same time, though, enlargement has moved its borders into much more difficult territory that severely tests alternatives to the highly interventionist and successful enlargement formula.

7

THE EU AND THE EASTERN ARC OF INSTABILITY

The Western Balkans, Eastern Europe and Southern Caucasus

The EU has to its East and South East an arc of instability that poses an ongoing and multifaceted security challenge. Managing and resolving security threats originating from these areas has tested both the EU's external relations competence and the re-balancing of the transatlantic relationship, especially given their proximity to the Union and America's strategic re-orientation towards Asia and the Middle East. Addressing these security challenges has also become intimately entwined in the EU enlargement debate. EU borders are now effectively delimited to the North, South and West by the seas of the Arctic, the Mediterranean and the Atlantic. This makes where exactly Europe meets Asia the focal point of discussion about the Union's final geographical framework.

Security challenges emanating from this arc of instability range from civil war in Bosnia, armed conflict between Russia and Georgia and frozen conflicts in Transnistria and Nagorno-Karabakh through to trafficking, illegal immigration and environmental degradation. Their relative salience has also changed in line with successive EU enlargements and geo-strategic shifts, especially that occasioned by 9/11. In responding to these challenges the EU has had to develop constantly its own capabilities and muscle its way into a crowded security space.

The EU had a 'baptisim of fire' in the Balkans and is still redeeming lost credibility.[1] Questions remain, too, about the Union's transformative power in the Balkans, even though it is applying its most powerful external relations tool, namely enlargement. The impact of a membership perspective risks dilution due to limited interim incentivisation for and the slow pace of reform in many Balkan States and ambiguity about the prospects of EU membership for some of these States. The latter is encouraged by the EU's tightening accession criteria, foregrounding of absorption capacity and internal focus on Treaty reform. The position to the East is arguably still more challenging insofar as European Neighbourhood Policy (ENP) has less trans-formative capability than enlargement, Eastern States demonstrate different degrees of willingness to engage and Russian influence is re-emerging. Moreover, the Union's failure to determine the Eastern borders of what might be 'European' breeds discontent amongst those States ambitious of eventual full EU membership.

A decade of disaster

The Union had ample reason to act decisively in the crisis in Yugoslavia. It bordered several Member States and weakness could damage the ambitions of the Union as a security actor, its preparations for the Maastricht treaty and transatlantic relations. There was also a high potential for security spillover and an opportunity to redeem the EU's relative impotence in the Middle East peace process and poor collective performance in the first Gulf War.[2] The EU duly claimed responsibility for dealing with the crisis and in fulfilling this Commission President Delors emphasised three key tools: economic sanctions, public opinion and potential recognition of breakaway republics.[3] It did have some limited success, including setting up the European Community Monitoring Mission (ECMM),[4] delivering aid, sponsoring initiatives such as the Brioni Accords, and supporting wider international efforts, including a UN arms embargo on Yugoslavia. It also targeted sanctions on Serbia and Montenegro and its Member States collectively withdrew their ambassadors from Belgrade and orchestrated Serbia's expulsion from the Conference on Security and Co-operation in Europe.

However, the Yugoslav crises proved too politically divisive, too demanding and too early in the EU's development as a security actor. The litany of EU problems spanned expectation-raising hubris through to intra-institutional wrangling, from budget lines to Member state discord, and from weak coordination with other security actors through to profound disagreement within the Union and the transatlantic relationship, particularly over military intervention. The EU arguably precipitated Yugoslavia's descent into civil war[5] and its rapid marginalisation magnified the embarrassing contrast between Jacques Poos' 'hour of Europe' and WEU Secretary-General Van Eekelen's public acceptance in February 1993 that 'our credibility has fallen very low in the Balkans ... We are looking for the US to take the lead again.'[6] The Carrington Commission was rapidly superseded by a jointly run EC–UN international conference, the Vance-Owen Peace Plan, and, especially, by the Contact Group. The EU's subsequent security development became framed negatively in the capability-expectation gap paradigm articulated by Christopher Hill in respect of its early Balkan performance.[7]

The depressing history of the EU's initial involvement in the Balkans is well known.[8] Indeed, one of the more interesting retrospective debates is just how early the EU ceased to function as a single entity in the Yugoslav crisis.[9] It is thus sufficient here to tease out from the detail three key lessons that help contextualise the EU's current approach to the region,[10] namely its immaturity as a security actor, Member state discord and the lack of political will and capability to intervene militarily. The Union's rotating presidency was debilitating, EU mediators lacked experience, and the complex Maastricht pillar structure caused severe coordination problems.[11] The

ECMM was undermined by wrangling over how it should be funded and whether it should be armed. A joint action in autumn 1993 regarding increased humanitarian food supplies to Bosnia and Herzegovina before the winter similarly fell foul of a six month internal argument, nominally over whether the appropriated 48 million ecu should be serviced from the Community budget or by the Member States, but in practice over what influence the European Parliament should have in EU external relations.[12]

The EU Member States engaged in frequent fratricidal conduct. Britain castigated French President Mitterand in June 1992 for 'playing "cavalier seul"' and undermining EU unity by unexpectedly appearing in Sarajevo in an effort to break a siege.[13] Covert German, US and allied military aid and materials were funneled to Croatia and Muslim Bosnia irrespective of the EU and UN arms embargo.[14] Greece imposed in February 1994 a unilateral trade embargo on the FYROM, which effectively sealed it off from all EU trade by closing its Northern port of Thessaloniki, and successfully defended this blockade in a bruising battle against the European Commission before the European Court of Justice.[15] And the longer the Yugoslav crisis went on, the more leading EU Member States marginalised the Union in preference for the UN, NATO and, especially, the Contact Group.

The debate about recognition of the breakaway republics demonstrates how one of Delors' key identified strengths of the Union was squandered. The EU initially pledged political and economic support for the continuance of a single Yugoslav state but the brittleness of this position was exposed once Slovenia and Croatia declared independence in June 1991. The EU publicly shifted from insistence on a single Yugoslav state to a single entity; behind the scenes its Member States were divided. Germany sympathised with calls for independence, influenced not least by its large Croatian émigré community, German reunification, Bavaria's particularly close ties through the Alpe-Adria association with Croatia and Slovenia, and over 50 per cent of German investments in Yugoslavia being vested in these two countries. France preferred to work with the Serbs to effect a peaceful resolution based on a single Yugoslav state, a stance underpinned by fears of provoking further separatist demands elsewhere and encouraging a *Mitteleuropa* under German influence.[16] Britain agreed with maintaining the territorial integrity of Yugoslavia, an approach that some critics have since argued reflected the Conservative government's 'unprincipled pragmatism' and 'Serbophilia'.[17] Moreover, these two rival camps sought legitimisation in international law. Britain, France, Greece and Spain supported maintenance of the Yugoslav federation in line with Principles III (inviolability of borders), IV (territorial integrity) and VI (non-intervention in the internal affairs of a sovereign state) of the Helsinki Final Act. Germany headed a group more sympathetic to the aspirations of Croatia and Slovenia in line with Principle VIII, the guarantee to self-determination.[18]

Germany unilaterally recognised Croatia and Slovenia on 23 December, irrespective of commitments just made in the Maastricht Treaty to a CFSP. Further disarray ensued. The EU sought to cover its embarrassment by making collective recognition of breakaway republics conditional upon their meeting certain criteria, including that borders be altered only by peaceful means, protection be afforded to refugees and ethnic minorities, human rights be observed and adherence to the nuclear non-proliferation treaty be ensured. The Badinter Committee was charged with assessing compliance but the EU subsequently compromised its own procedures. The Committee concluded that Croatia did not have in place the necessary constitutional safeguards for minority rights. Yet Germany's unilateral recognition of Croatia on 23 December rendered academic the Committee's decision not to make this explicitly a reason against extending recognition.[19] Bosnia and Herzegovina failed to satisfy the EU's guidelines but was granted recognition regardless.[20] Macedonia (FYROM) met the criteria but recognition was prevented by a Greek veto imposed nominally on grounds of FYROM's potential territorial claims upon Greek Macedonia.[21] As one observer damningly concluded, EU recognitions 'were startling in that they contravened most of the recognizing countries' own rules for recognition'.[22]

Whether early military intervention by the EU and the wider international community could have prevented Yugoslavia's slide into civil war is debatable.[23] However, Britain and France were at loggerheads and this meant the EU could not deploy force, despite the potential inherent in the WEU.[24] London and Paris were divided over the merits of deploying an inter-positionary force and Britain did not want to give any encouragement to either French ambitions to weaken NATO or to the possibility of the EU developing a military component.[25] Once Britain and France did commit peacekeeping troops under UNPROFOR, the mandate proved too restrictive. Furthermore, a combination of Anglo-French troops on the ground, the Clinton administration's refusal to commit American ground troops while also favouring 'lift and strike', and disagreement about the likely decisiveness of air strikes[26] severely strained transatlantic relations.

Ultimately Chirac forced Clinton's hand by threatening to invoke NATO's OpPlan 40–104 in the absence of stronger action. This was a contingency plan for an extraction of UNPROFOR to which the US had previously promised 20,000 ground troops.[27] Decisive American military intervention, the Dayton Accords and their subsequent management underscored the EU's lost credibility. Clinton marginalized the EU in the negotiations that led to the Dayton settlement. Overall responsibility for Bosnia was given to a High Representative, the OSCE was tasked with arms control and confidence building in the Balkans, and NATO was charged with providing security on the ground. The EU was confined to coordinating and assisting Bosnia's economic reconstruction. Subsequent crises in Albania and Kosovo re-emphasised EU weakness and European dependence upon NATO and the US.

When civil war threatened in Albania as its government and economy collapsed amid fraudulent pyramid schemes the European Commission quickly organised international aid and Italy, under UN Security Council Resolution 1101 of 28 March 1997, led Operation Alba – a 7,000 strong multinational protection force designed to safeguard aid supplies and to re-establish a viable police force. However, it was actually the OSCE that took the lead in Albania and Operation Alba was executed by a coalition of the willing that included non-EU States. In Kosovo military intervention by the international community came quicker thanks to fears of the Dayton Accords unravelling, extant military deployments in the Balkans, an easier consensus on identifying Serb President Milosevic as the principal aggressor, and the massacre of 25 Kosovo civilians at Raczek in October 1998 that served as a trigger for action. The Union, though, was palpably eclipsed during NATO's 78-day air assault that eventually helped ease Milosevic into another peace settlement,[28] its leading Member States preferred the Quint,[29] and the limited European military contribution once more demonstrated the emptiness of EU responsibility for the Petersberg Tasks. Kosovo subsequently became a *de facto* UN protectorate with UNMIK entrusted with establishing an interim administration, NATO responsible for on ground security in the guise of KFOR, the OSCE charged with leading institution and democracy building, the rule of law and human rights, and the UNHCR heading up the humanitarian component. The EU was again confined to coordinating economic reconstruction.

Taking stock, re-dividing Europe

Taking stock of the situation in the aftermath of the Kosovo War, EU officials had evidently learnt to tone down their rhetoric. Successive crises had exposed the shortcomings of the European security architecture generally and the Union's pretensions to being a coherent and capable security actor specifically. Also, EU Member States had failed to develop and maintain cohesion at key junctures, been all too willing to circumvent the EU and other organisations in favour of informal directoires, and struggled to contribute meaningfully to NATO's two major air campaigns. US aircraft flew 65.9 per cent of the 3,515 sorties during Operation Deliberate Force; four years later in Operation Allied Force this proportion increased to almost 79 per cent of the 38,004 sorties flown. European dependence on the US was even more pronounced in key functions, such as airlift and tactical jamming, and from a potential 2 million military personnel European NATO Members struggled to provide just 40,000 troops for Kosovo and to maintain thereafter 50,000 peacekeepers in the wider Balkans.[30] Indeed, Kosovo was another sore test of transatlantic relations, especially over targeting, the potential deployment of ground troops and the relative poverty of European contributions. There was predictable criticism of European military capabilities and much talk that the US would never again wage 'war by committee'. As one senior Pentagon official put it: 'If anyone thinks that the US is ever going to use the North Atlantic Council … to run another major military campaign, they must be smoking pot'.[31]

These Balkan experiences galvanised EU efforts to improve progressively the quantity, quality and deployability of its security capabilities and to refine its relationship with NATO. However, the immediate future focused EU attention also upon its immediate neighbourhood. The conflict in Kosovo, the crisis in Albania, ethnic tensions in Macedonia, and Montenegro's aspirations for independence all demonstrated the region's continued volatility. Kosovo's status was also unresolved, being under interim UN administration but recognised under UN Security Council Resolution 1244 as part of a sovereign Federal Republic of Yugoslavia. The EU consequently still faced spillover security threats ranging from uncontrollable migratory flows and human trafficking through to increased drug flows into the Union from the Golden Crescent and even renewed conflict.

Balkan problems also spilled over into the EU's wider external relations. First, the region was a significant complication in EU efforts at this time to inject substance into its declared strategic partnership with Russia. Moscow's sensitivity about the erosion of Russia's sphere of influence was demonstrated graphically by its deployment from Bosnia and Herzegovina of a military unit in 1999 to take control of Pristina airport before NATO could get there. Also Russia had opposed military strikes against Serbia, and its broader sympathy for Belgrade ensured Moscow's importance in the future regional dynamics of the Western Balkans and the status of Kosovo. Second, the EU's continuing role in Bosnia and newly accorded responsibility for economic reconstruction in Kosovo offered it yet another opportunity in the Balkans to develop its credentials as Europe's leading security provider. Aside from being of paramount importance for its own ambitions and the redemption of its severely damaged credentials within its own backyard, this was vital to rebalancing the transatlantic relationship. Quarrels over the Kosovo war, renewed debate about burden-sharing, and indications in the 2000 US election campaign that a George W. Bush administration would favour withdrawing US troops from the Balkans were all symptomatic of a wider malaise into which the relationship had slipped. Finally, international handling of the Balkans was becoming viewed increasingly in part through the prism of the wider relationship between Islam and Christianity. The Clinton administration's sympathy for the Bosnian Muslims had been encouraged by anxiety to counteract Iranian influence in the Western Balkans and to calm fears amongst moderate Muslims of a 'clash of civilizations'. 9/11 and the consequent war on terrorism accentuated these considerations. As Lord Ashdown, former High Representative in Bosnia, argued, 'We have an asset in the Western Balkans that we do not sufficiently value and that is European Islam … In the dialogue of the deaf we have between ancient Christendom and modern Islam, they are a uniquely valuable asset to us, acting as a bridge.'[32]

Yet the EU could not focus solely on the Balkans within its neighbourhood because concomitantly the implications of its prospective enlargement to the CEECs were becoming increasingly pressing. The Union classified Slovenia as a CEEC, not least because the European Commission favoured an expansive definition to minimise perceptions of an exclusionary dynamic.[33] Nevertheless, Slovenia's location meant that its eventual membership would *de facto* expand the Union into the Balkans. Accelerating preparations for enlargement also raised the importance of the neighbours of those countries earmarked for full membership. Russia's Kaliningrad oblast would become completely surrounded by EU territory and the Union would share borders with Russia, Belarus, Ukraine, Moldova, Turkey and the Black Sea. In addition, Turkey's candidate status meant that the Union had to consider its borders with Bulgaria and other very problematic neighbours, including Iran, Iraq and Syria.

The EU thus had plenty of motivation to think more strategically about Eastern and South Eastern Europe as a whole and to devise policies better equipped to deal with the multiple and diverse security challenges emanating from these regions. The results have been profoundly important for Europe in at least two key respects. First, the Union has thus far formally resisted French President Sarkozy's call to fix its geographical framework and to 'say who is European and who is not'.[34] However, the principal contested dividing line is where Europe meets Asia. The EU has *de facto* drawn a dividing line by splitting the CIS into Eastern European and Central Asian States and adopting different policy frameworks towards each grouping. The Eastern European group comprises Azerbaijan, Armenia, Belarus, Georgia, Moldova, Russia and Ukraine and, with the exception of Russia, is now part of the ENP; the Central Asian States of the CIS are Kazakhstan, Kyrgyzstan, Tajikistan, Turkmenistan and Uzbekistan and these are addressed under Development and Economic co-operation. Also, despite the Commission's repeated rhetoric about 'determination to avoid drawing new dividing lines in Europe',[35] the Union has divided Europe further into an inner and an outer circle by addressing the issues and countries of Eastern and South Eastern Europe in different policy frameworks and within consequently different expectational regimes. While Eastern Europe is dealt with through ENP, the Western Balkans countries have been given an EU membership perspective and are therefore dealt with through the Stabilisation and Association Process (SAP) and enlargement framework.

The division of Europe: inner Europe

After Dayton the EU made an initially modest contribution to the international protectorate in Bosnia and Herzegovina and continued in the wider region to deliver humanitarian aid and reconstruction assistance. In 1995 the European Commission initiated the Regional Approach. This involved financial assistance and contractual relations through first generation co-operation agreements conditional upon recipients' willingness to re-establish economic co-operation with one another, abide by the Dayton Accords, and respect human rights, the rights of minorities and democratic principles.[36] In July 1996 the Council adopted the OBNOVA programme for assistance to Bosnia and Herzegovina, Croatia, FYROM, and Serbia and Montenegro.[37] This was specifically in support of the Dayton Accords and tied in part to the reconstruction of civil society in Bosnia and Herzegovina and to the development of regional co-operation in the Western Balkans. The PHARE programme was also used to supplement OBNOVA and provided Bosnia and Herzegovina with $1 billion from 1996–99. Also reflecting the EU's emphasis on regional co-operation as an essential component of reconciliation and reconstruction was the French-initiated Royaumont Process for Stability and Good Neighbourliness in South East Europe. This brought together the Balkan countries, the EU, the Council of Europe, OSCE, Russia, US, Bulgaria, Hungary, Romania, Slovenia and Turkey.

However, the conflict in Kosovo and the lack of progress in Bosnia and Herzegovina suggested that the combination of expensive international stewardship and the EU's regional approach had insufficient transformational influence to pull the region out of its political, ethnic, cultural and religious rivalries. Something more was needed if the international community were ever to have an effective exit strategy from the

Balkans. As part of the response the Royaumont Process was incorporated within a new Stability Pact for South Eastern Europe, which was adopted in Cologne in June 1999. Security matters were prominent, explicit goals including enhanced regional co-operation, prevention of further violent conflicts and the creation of proper foundations for democratisation. Work was divided into three tables, one of which was dedicated to security issues. This was in turn divided into two sub-tables, one on JHA matters, which included asylum, organised crime and security institutions, and the other on security and defence, which included military and defence reform, arms control and de-mining.[38]

The most important EU initiative, though, came in May 1999 when the Commission initiated the SAP. The single most important element of this was its conferral upon the Balkan countries of an EU membership perspective, the Union's support of which was developed further at the 2003 Thessaloniki European Council.[39] This allowed the EU to apply its most powerful external policy framework to its troubled immediate neighbouring region and changed radically the expectational environment of the Balkan countries, which began to see prospective membership as a 'guarantee not only of the irreversibility of reforms, but also of peace and regional stability.'[40] The SAP offers the Balkan countries a structured path towards EU accession and substantial assistance for the promotion of democracy, institutional capacity and political dialogue. During the first phase the EU helps to implement a free trade area and supports States' development of institutions and convergence to EU standards. Once political and economic stability and institutional capacity are demonstrated to a level satisfactory to the EU, Balkan countries enter a Stabilisation and Association Agreement (SAA), which is a *sui generis* type of agreement similar to the Europe Agreements. The reform process then continues with more detailed obligations and commitments set out in a European Partnership Agreement, comprising short and medium term priorities for reform.

The EU's financial investment in the Balkans has been restructured several times and increased significantly. In December 2000 CARDS replaced OBNOVA and PHARE assistance to the Balkans and established a single legal framework for assistance to the region. A special European Agency for Reconstruction was charged with local administration of EC assistance to FYROM, Kosovo, and Serbia and Montenegro. From 2000–2006 the EU allotted 4.65 billion euros to the Balkans under CARDS. Since 2007 all EU financial assistance to the region has been provided through a single framework via the new Instrument for Pre-accession Assistance (IPA). According to the European Commission the IPA 'places more focus on ownership of implementation by the beneficiary countries, on support for cross-border co-operation, and on "learning by doing"'.[41] As for funding, the 2007–11 indicative amount of EU financial assistance to Balkan countries plus Turkey is 7.58 billion euros. Delivery comes in the form of country-specific financial assistance and a multi-beneficiary programme, the latter including regional co-operation, infrastructure, justice and home affairs, internal market and trade, market economy, supporting civil society, education, youth and research.[42]

The SAP is, of course, highly conditional. The Commission stresses that 'negotiations may be suspended in the event of a serious and persistent breach of the principles of liberty, democracy, respect for human rights and fundamental freedoms and the rule of law on which the Union is founded … '[43] The product is, like the CEECs' experience, another highly asymmetric, intrusive and interventionist regime of scrutiny in which the Union sets priorities, measures progress regularly against benchmarks of its setting, and monopolises the granting of incentives and imposition of punitive measures for non-compliance. The Commission emphasises the importance of tangible interim rewards and maintaining a credible and visible prospect of eventual integration into the Union.[44] Though it charges the EU Member States and accession partners to better communicate the benefits and challenges of enlargement,[45] the Commission has pushed for more visible dimensions of the process and increased contact with Western Balkan publics. For example, the EU signed visa facilitation agreements with Western Balkan countries in September 2007 and these entered into force on 1 January 2008. Funding for civil society promotion is scheduled to triple between 2008 and 2010 over the 27 million euros provided from 2005–7.[46] And the Commission aims to complete a 'Transport Community Treaty' with the Western Balkans, something Jacques Barrot, former Commission Vice-President in charge of transport, presented as 'a concrete way of fostering regional co-operation, stability and peace.'[47]

In addition to the SAP, the Balkans has seen the Commission assume an increasingly important role and has been the principal testing ground of developing ESDP capabilities. In Bosnia ESDP instruments have included an EU Special Representative, EUFOR Althea (which took over from SFOR in 2004) and the EU Police Mission, launched in January 2003. In Montenegro the EU High Representative for CFSP, Solana, helped broker a deal whereby in 2002 the Yugoslav federation became a loose Union of Serbia and Montenegro. This avoided temporarily granting Montenegro independence which could have destabilised the region again.[48] By the time that Montenegro activated its right of opt-out after three years, its independence from Serbia in June 2006 was much less controversial. In Kosovo the Commission headed the department of the UN mission charged with reconstruction and development and provided political guidance to the European Agency for Reconstruction. And in the FYROM intense EU and US pressure, helped substantially by the government's prospective EU membership, prevented full-scale war by bringing ethnic Macedonian and Albanian communities together under the Ohrid Framework Agreement, signed on 13 August 2001.[49] Following on from NATO's 4,000 man, UK-led Operation Essential Harvest the EU utilised CARDS funding and, together with the OSCE, provided monitors under the protection of NATO's Task Force Fox to oversee the process of peace and constitutional reform. The EU then launched Operation Concordia upon expiry of the NATO operation in March 2003.[50]

More recently the Commission has progressively assumed responsibility for aid implementation from the European Agency for Reconstruction and stepped up co-operation with international financial institutions and bilateral donors for modernisation and development in the Balkans. In December 2009 the Western Balkans Investment Framework was launched.[51] Following its unilateral declaration of independence in February 2008, Kosovo has become effectively an EU rather than UN protectorate. The European Commission has estimated that the Union's financial commitment there will exceed 1 billion euros 2007–10,[52] with specific assistance for the micro-state including through the TAIEX instrument (Technical Assistance and Information Exchange Instrument), an ESDP rule of law mission (EULEX Kosovo – adopted by joint action on 4 February 2008 and operational on 9 December 2008), an international Civilian mission headed by an EU Special Representative, and a European Commission Liaison Office.[53] Perhaps most significant, though, is that the EU has affirmed that under UN Security Council Resolution 1244 Kosovo has a membership perspective.

Security sector reform in the Balkans has become an increasing focus of EU SAAs and ESDP operations, including judicial and police reform. The Commission emphasises that co-operation and reforms in the field of internal security, 'notably in combating organised crime and corruption, reforming the judiciary and police, as well as strengthening border management, are … a core priority of their European agenda.'[54] FRONTEX coordinates work on border security, and the Western Balkans is a 'priority area' of Europol.[55] The latter has strategic agreements in place that allow exchange of non-personal data with Albania, Bosnia and Herzegovina, FYROM, Montenegro and Serbia. Croatia has a more advanced operational agreement with Europol that enables exchange of personal data and in November 2007 it also signed a co-operation agreement with Eurojust.[56]

The SAP is a bilateral process but the size of constituent Balkan countries, their economic fragmentation and particular security problems, such as refugees and displaced persons, all require regional co-operation. Also, the establishment of new sovereign borders could potentially hinder reconciliation and reconstruction because, as Mungui-Pippidi argues, once a border is established it starts to generate differences across it and homogeneity within.[57] This is not least because it cuts down the number of crossings and economic, political and civil interaction. By making regional co-operation a pre-requisite for integration the EU has been much more prescriptive with the Balkan States than with the CEECs, for which such co-operation was simply encouraged.[58]

Embedding the Western Balkans within its enlargement framework, together with its associated policies and security capability reforms, has finally made the EU the region's principal guarantor of security. There are now grounds for some optimism. The South East European Cooperation Process set up in 2000 indicated a genuine Balkan co-operation forum across a range of issues, including security, justice and home affairs.[59] In 2008 the Western Balkan countries assumed responsibility from the Stability Pact for promoting regional co-operation through the Regional Cooperation Council, which it is hoped will encourage a greater sense of ownership and provide a forum for bilateral and multilateral issues to be addressed. Croatia and the FYROM have achieved candidate status and the European Commission is hopeful that the former's progress especially 'sends a signal to the other Western Balkan countries on their own membership prospects, once they fulfil the necessary conditions.'[60] Some observers argue that even in Bosnia and Herzegovina, long held back by indigenous problems, EU conditionality backed by a multi-dimensional ESDP presence has increasingly become a viable alternative to international trusteeship and that the potential exists to transform the country into a sustainable multi-ethnic democracy.[61] The EU has improved security governance coordination with NATO and demonstrated some flexibility in using the granting of SAAs to influence political processes within the Balkan States.

The EU tackles internal and border security issues while NATO's Partnership for Peace promotes the reform of armed forces in the Balkans and interoperability with the Alliance, and its Membership Action Plan prepares selected countries for possible future NATO membership. Croatia and Albania joined NATO through this route in April 2009 and FYROM has been invited to upgrade its MAP status to full membership subject to its reaching a mutually acceptable solution to the country's name with Greece. As for strategic use of SAAs, the initialling by the EU of agreements with Serbia and Bosnia and Herzegovina in late 2007, despite their progress falling short in some areas, was probably informed by a desire to bind them closer to the EU before Kosovo's status was decided. Similarly, the presentation of a roadmap towards lifting visa restrictions on Serbians wishing to travel to the EU on 7 May 2008 was evidently an attempt to influence the early parliamentary elections in Serbia on 11 May.

There remain, however, immense challenges in the Balkans and the potential fragility of many reform processes is evident in Commission reports. In its annual review of enlargement strategy the Commission concluded in November 2007 that none of the Western Balkan countries were taking measures to enforce the rule of law 'commensurate with the magnitude of the problem' and in a number of them the overall reform process had slowed down.[62] Also, civil society remained 'weak', democratic forces in Serbia were rated as 'fragile', the political climate in Albania was 'highly confrontational', relations in Kosovo between ethnic Albanians and Serbs remained 'strained', and Bosnia and Herzegovina was 'yet to assume full ownership of its governance'.[63] In March 2008 the European Commission re-iterated that Western Balkan societies 'remain divided on a number of key issues related to the co-existence and integration of different communities and, in some cases, constitutional reform.'[64] And in its 2008 annual report on enlargement strategy the Commission identified a dangerous combination whereby reform and reconciliation were 'yet to become entrenched' while economic conditions especially were deteriorating as a result of global recession. In addition, elections in FYROM were marred by violence and serious irregularities, progress with Serbia remained complicated by questions over its compliance with the International Criminal Tribunal for the former Yugoslavia, and in Bosnia and Herzegovina EU reforms had 'stagnated' as a result of weak consensus on reform priorities and both entities challenging elements of the constitutional arrangements set by the Dayton Accords. More generally, judicial reform and the fight against corruption and organised crime remained major issues throughout the region, as did serious deficits in state-building, consolidation of institutions and governance.

The EU has effectively given the international community an exit strategy from the Western Balkans by internalising within itself the region and all its problems. This has been predictably welcomed by the UN and US but has also caused much consternation about the Union's capacity to absorb these States and deal with their problems. One critical challenge is that the expectations of the Western Balkan countries and the effectiveness of conditionality are influenced heavily by perceptions regarding achieving membership. These perceptions are shaped in part by EU debates about enlargement, which in recent years have become more critical of both the process and the prospect of enlarging the Union further. In March 2008 Olli Rehn, EU Commissioner for Enlargement, argued that the EU's reaffirmation of the Balkan's enlargement perspective in 2006 'gave us political peace and quiet, and we could get on with our work.'[65] But this was a superficial consensus and resolved few underlying equivocations. The protracted process of securing the eventual passage of the Lisbon Treaty directed EU attention inwards, and the imposition of post-accession benchmarking and monitoring of crime and corruption in Bulgaria and Romania brought into question the robustness of enlargement strategy.

Doubt has thus grown in Western Balkan countries about the seriousness of the EU's commitment to them.[66] EU membership was originally in the gift of the Balkan States insofar as the pace towards accession depended on their own commitment to, and successful undertaking of, reform. The EU subsequently backtracked, emphasising not only the readiness of candidate States but also the consolidation and absorption capacity of the Union. The bar to accession is effectively being raised as a consequence of lessons learned from the CEEC enlargements and weakening popular support for enlargement. In November 2006 the Commission argued that 'Further improvement in the quality of preparations has become crucial as the scope of EU activities has developed. This warrants the strict application of conditionality during the pre-accession phase, and thorough fulfilment of the requirements at each stage of the accession process.'[67] Evident failings during the accession of Bulgaria and Romania ratcheted up the pressure still further for even tighter criteria and enforcement of them. In November 2007 the Commission promised 'tighter focus on reform priorities' in programming IPA assistance, further improvement in 'the quality of the enlargement process' and more emphasis on 'fundamental issues of state-building, good governance, administrative and judicial reform, rule of law, reconciliation, compliance with the International Criminal Court for the Former Yugoslavia (ICTY), and civil society.'[68]

Perceived wavering of EU commitment to the Balkans is also attracting increasing criticism from beyond the region. Alexandros Mallias, Greek Ambassador to the US, warned in autumn 2007 that the initial impact of EU engagement in the Balkans was fading and called for the urgent development of reassuring measures.[69] The following spring Wolfgang Petritsch, the EU's former Special Envoy to Kosovo, rated the Union's work with the Balkan States to prepare them for accession as 'piecemeal' and accused it of failing to follow through in line with the Thessaloniki promise of 2003.[70] Matters have been further complicated by internal disagreement over Kosovo's independence. Often seen as the least worst option, given the unsustainability of the *status quo* under UN Resolution 1244, independence nevertheless leaves Kosovo in international limbo and *de facto* partitioned between Kosovo Albanians and Kosovo Serbs.[71] On 18 February 2008 the Council confirmed that EU Member States would 'decide on their relations with Kosovo, in accordance with national practice and international law',[72] thereby effectively ignoring the Commission's call in November 2007 for EU unity on the possible status of Kosovo.[73] In February 2009 the European Parliament called for all EU States to extend recognition to Kosovo but at the time of writing five States had refused to do so either out of solidarity with Serbia or for fear of setting a separatist precedent.

Critics also argue that pre-accession aid to the Western Balkans compares unfavourably with the levels of assistance given to the CEECs and Romania and Bulgaria[74] and that without very careful management the EU's multi-speed, bilateral approach to the accession of Balkan countries risks dividing the region rather than modernising it. In 2006 *The Economist* warned that for Bosnians and Serbs there was 'a danger of EU membership becoming like an old Soviet joke: we pretend to prepare for membership, they pretend to be ready to give it to us.'[75] The reality, of course, is that the EU faces two almost impossible balancing acts. First, it cannot disincentivise the most rapidly reforming Balkan countries by making their progress towards membership contingent upon that of others. For instance, Croatia's fear of being stigmatised as a Balkan country and of a regional 'drag' effect on its progress was reflected in its early efforts to emulate Slovenia's re-branding as Central European.[76] Yet phased integration risks undermining regional cohesion by exacerbating differences between already very heterogeneous national transition processes and by encouraging perceptions of a re-divided Balkans. Second, an overly-long preparatory period for enlargement could seriously disincentivise reform in the Balkans, particularly in the most problematic countries where membership is most distant. Already in March 2008 the European Commission was forced to develop a Communication entitled 'The Western Balkans: Enhancing the European Perspective'.

The division of Europe: outer Europe

Granting the Western Balkans a membership perspective, together with impending enlargement to the CEECs, put considerable pressure upon the Union to identify and devise coherent and comprehensive policies towards the countries of Eastern Europe and the Balkan periphery. In 2002 the European Commission called for a policy towards 'all our neighbours'.[77] In 2003 it released its Communication on 'Wider Europe', which was designed to set out a strengthened framework for the Union's relations 'with those neighbouring countries that do not currently have the perspective of membership of the EU.'[78] It seemed in this document that the key identifier of the EU's Eastern European was prospective shared borders. Hence the Eastern perspective of what would become the ENP included only Belarus, Ukraine and Moldova. Russia rejected participation in favour of its strategic partnership framework and the Southern Caucasus were dismissed on account of their location.

However, the following year Armenia, Azerbaijan and Georgia were raised from a footnote in the 'Wider Europe' communication to full partners in ENP. This set new operational limits at least of what the EU regarded as Eastern Europe. The border rationale for including the Southern Caucasus, though, was less obvious and consistent.

Georgia shares a border with the EU only by dint of the Black Sea. Armenia's shared border status is contingent upon Turkey becoming a full Member of the EU. And Azerbaijan's claim is still more tenuous, being based potentially on its land-locked exclave of Nakhchivan having a 9 km border with Turkey. Moreover, not all of Turkey's other neighbours were included in ENP.

Evidently more than geography ultimately defined the EU's revised conception of Eastern Europe, and for that matter membership of ENP. Politics played an important, if inconsistent, part. Political sanction helps explain the exclusion of Turkey's neighbours Iraq and Iran from ENP, though this was muddied by the inclusion of Syria and Belarus from which the EU currently withholds active ENP membership for political reasons. The shaping of the EU's Eastern Europe has also been influenced by EU Member States championing different countries in the Caucasus and by external pressure. For instance, Georgia's case for inclusion undoubtedly benefited from American support, its aspirations to be part of Euro-Atlantic structures and from the Rose Revolution which increased pressure upon the EU to do something to assist Tbilisi's consolidation of democracy.

However, security considerations perhaps most influenced the inclusion of the Southern Caucasus in ENP. The ESS foregrounded security concerns in the region in 2003 and recommended more active EU involvement in addressing them. Frozen conflicts in South Ossetia, Nagorno-Karabakh and Abkhazia, as the Commission prophetically noted in December 2006, demonstrated 'that the conditions for peaceful coexistence remain to be established, both between some of our neighbours and with other key countries.'[79] The following year, elaborating upon why the EU 'has a direct interest in working with partners to promote their resolution', the Commission emphasised that these conflicts undermined efforts to promote political reform and economic development in the neighbourhood and affected the EU's own security 'through regional escalation, unmanageable migratory flows, disruption of energy supply and trade routes, or the creation of breeding grounds for terrorist and criminal activity of all kinds.'[80]

The region's geostrategic significance has also risen. Within the US-led war on terrorism it has become a connector between NATO territory and military operations in Afghanistan and bases in Asia.[81] Georgia especially has been keen to co-operate in this endeavour, not least to boost its prospects of NATO membership. Western desire to contain Iran has increased the salience of Turkey's borders with the Caucasus and the region's potential as a geostrategic buffer, where currently Armenia is Teheran's principal regional partner. Furthermore, the Southern Caucasus has become a significant producer of hydrocarbons and a crucial transit corridor for Caspian energy sources – the importance of which has been increased by greater recent Russian assertiveness, fears about Moscow's use of energy as a political weapon, and Brussels' consequent anxiety to diversify urgently the EU's energy import base. Consider in this light the EU-Azerbaijan Memorandum of Understanding in the energy field (November 2006) and Baku's recognition as 'a strategic partner for the EU' on Caspian oil and gas resources.[82] Similarly, in April 2008 the Commission noted the importance in Georgia's 'positioning itself as a key transit country for the export of Caspian energy resources to the EU' of the full operation of the Baku–Tbilisi–Ceyhan oil pipeline and the first gas flows through the Baku–Tbilisi–Erzurum gas pipeline.[83]

Finally, the Southern Caucasus is increasingly volatile as a result of a revenue windfall from a period of generally rising energy prices and an intensifying battle for influence within the region. Azerbaijan has refused to rule out military means to resolve the Nagorno-Karabakh issue and is rearming rapidly on the back of burgeoning energy export revenue. Armenia is doing likewise, albeit at a slower rate. Another conflict could provoke serious security spillover into the EU's wider neighbourhood and potentially 'deal a fatal blow to one of Europe's energy policy options.'[84] Meantime the frozen conflicts and wider Southern Caucasus are subject increasingly to competing exogenous influences. In addition to EU interest in the region the US is being driven by a compelling nexus of energy interests, anti-terrorism and global power projection considerations to strengthen its influence there directly and through its relations with Georgia, Turkey and Azerbaijan.

Iran sees in the Southern Caucasus limited potential relief from Western pressure, opportunity to diversify exports beyond hydrocarbons, and potential both to deepen its relationship with Russia and to develop its interests in Caspian energy. Still more importantly, Russian reassertion within the CIS emphasises the importance of Armenia, along with Belarus, Kazakhstan, Kyrgyzstan and Tajikistan, to Moscow's ambitions for Russian-led integration there.[85] The Kremlin's fear of further American and NATO penetration of its borderlands contributes significantly to acute tension in Russia–Georgia relations. This undoubtedly informed Russia's disproportionate military campaign against Tbilisi in 2008, as did pipeline politics. Russia is interested in acquiring and transporting Caspian energy sources and in using energy to consolidate its regional influence. It has an energy partnership with Armenia and in April 2006 Gazprom became the sole owner of the Armenian gas transportation system. Also, Moscow is simultaneously hostile to the development of pipeline infrastructure that might loosen its grip over the energy needs of Europe in particular, and desirous of diversifying its oil and gas export structure away from its present overly-heavy Westwards orientation. The latter gives the EU counter-leverage against its current dependence on Russian energy supplies and makes Russia vulnerable should the European Commission succeed in its repeated calls for the EU to establish a balanced energy mix with diversified sources and delivery routes.[86]

A range of reasons, not always internally consistent or consistently applied, therefore encouraged the EU to delineate the 'outer Europe' of the East as comprising Belarus, Ukraine, Moldova, the Southern Caucasus and Russia. Yet identifying and politically upgrading Eastern Europe only highlighted that the EU had hitherto largely neglected these countries owing to their physical distance, the lack of a strong caucus within the Union championing closer relations with them, and the Union's preoccupation with the European project and the Balkans. The extant arrangements for dealing with these countries were unsurprisingly neither appropriate nor strategically considered for a post-CEEC enlargement context. For example, the Partnership and Cooperation Agreements with Russia, Moldova and the Ukraine granted neither preferential trade treatment nor a timetable for regulatory convergence.

The decision to include Eastern Europe within the wider ENP was therefore a qualitative improvement of the EU's relations with these countries (less Russia on account of its preference for the strategic partnership framework). EU officials have repeatedly described the ENP as a 'strategic policy' aimed at promoting the stability, security and prosperity of the common neighbourhood.[87] By encouraging political and economic reform and regional co-operation it is intended that ENP will help establish a 'circle of friends' on the Union's periphery that become locked into increasing interdependence with one another and with the Union. The Commission suggests that resolutions even to seemingly intractable frozen conflicts might be facilitated by the Union 'working around the conflict issues, promoting similar reforms on both sides of the boundary lines, to foster convergence between political, economic and legal systems, enabling greater social inclusion and contributing to confidence building.'[88]

The ENP has allowed the EU to deal with Eastern Europe within a single framework and to rationalise progressively the funding and programmes it provided until the vast majority were replaced by the European Neighbourhood and Partnership Instrument (ENPI). The normative dimension is applied universally with the EU emphasising in particular human rights, democracy and the rule of law. In practice, the ENP applies lessons learnt from EU enlargements and attempts to expand the EU's legal hegemony by exporting the *acquis* into its neighbourhood. In 2004 the Council injected greater emphasis into ENP on security issues and the Commission now stresses that all Action Plans have a 'strong focus on justice, freedom and security issues'. This is designed to provide a basis to: cooperate towards joint management of migratory flows, including combating illegal immigration; develop transparency, judicial reform and anti-corruption within partner countries; collaborate on issues of mutual concern such as organised crime, drugs, terrorism and money laundering; and share information. An integral operational objective therein is 'to move towards greater approximation between respective systems and compliance with international standards in key sectors.'[89]

The Action Plans, however, aim to provide for differentiation, ownership and tailored programmes of activity. This reflects the Commission's early recognition that the political, economic, cultural and geographic situations of the Eastern European countries were and remain very different from one another and that their political will and capacity to undertake reforms and commitments within Action Plans would vary too. The ENP's emphasis on regional co-operation is much weaker than the SAP's, despite the introduction of Cross-border Cooperation Programmes that are designed to benefit both sides of the EU's external border. As such, differentiation encourages ENP partners to progress at their own speeds and to have relatively less fear than SAP countries of being held back by others. This also reflects the Commission's hope that, together with positive conditionality, differentiation will create a virtuous circle of competition among ENP countries for EU aid and benefits.

It is one thing, though, to design a new framework for the EU's relations with Eastern Europe. It is another to deliver it and make it produce the desired effects. A quick review of EU relations with Eastern Europe since the introduction of ENP suggests ambiguous results at best. Belarus lies at one end of the spectrum. In 2003 the European Commission noted that relations with Minsk had 'progressed little since 1996.'[90] It concluded in the same document that a policy of engagement and step-by-step integration of Belarus into the ENP was preferable to leaving things 'to drift'.[91] Yet the Union has since made no substantive progress and in June 2007 Belarus became only the second country to have its generalised system of preferences (GSP) removed by the EU. The picture is not much brighter in the Southern Caucasus. Between 1991 and 2004 the EC directed over 1.2 billion euros of aid into the region[92] and then included its constituent countries in ENP. However, while the EC contribution to humanitarian and rehabilitation projects has been useful, many observers argue that the actual impact of EU policies demonstrates that the 'EU's rhetorical reach exceeds its grasp'.[93] The Commission acknowledged in 2006 that 'The ENP has achieved little in supporting the resolution of frozen or open conflicts in the region'[94] and armed conflict between Georgia and Russia in August 2008 re-cast the regional geostrategic environment in ways that re-asserted Russian influence and weakened the ability and/or willingness of some ENP partners to continue reforms.

Regarded by the EU as a 'determinant regional actor',[95] the Ukraine is second only in importance to Russia in the Eastern Neighbourhood and it might be expected that EU energies would be channelled into this relationship especially. Ukraine is a key actor in regional pipeline politics and an object of intense competition between the West and Russia. 80 per cent of Russian gas exports to the EU flow through Ukrainian pipeline infrastructure and Ukraine's transit significance will increase as oil and merchandise trade between the EU and the Black Sea and Caspian regions grows. The EU's reliance on Ukrainian infrastructure was demonstrated by the 2006 and 2009 Russia–Ukraine gas crises and even if Russia manages to skirt Ukraine and other transit countries by completing the Nord Stream and South Stream projects to deliver gas straight to Western Europe, Ukraine will still deliver significantly more gas to Europe than these two pipelines.[96]

EU energy security concerns and desire to make energy supplies less internally divisive in EU relations with Russia featured strongly in an EU–Ukraine energy deal in March 2009 that effectively provided for the export of EU energy legislation and its being made binding by Ukraine joining the European Energy Community. Coupled with major investment in Ukraine's ageing pipeline infrastructure the deal potentially improves Ukraine's reliability as a transit country and contributes to de-politicising the EU–Russia gas relationship by moving towards a single, competitive gas market. The EU has also sought to draw Ukraine into its orbit through trade and security measures. Visa facilitation and readmission agreements entered into force on 1 January 2008 and in October 2008 a visa dialogue was launched with the aim of establishing a visa-free regime as a long-term perspective. In February 2008 negotiations began on a Common Aviation Area and a comprehensive free trade area, and discussions continued on the upgrade of Ukraine's PCA to an Association Agreement and the replacement of the current Action Plan with a 'New Practical Instrument'. The EU has included Ukrainian contributions to its Police Missions in Bosnia and Macedonia and cooperates with Kiev in its Border Assistance Mission to Moldova and Ukraine (EUBAM). Furthermore, the EU's export of its JHA regime pushes up against Russian influence and objectives in Ukraine. For instance, Moscow wishes the internal borders of the former USSR to remain open and hopes to deal with consequent problems by drawing neighbours into the regional and economic and political projects that it leads. The EU, though, is pushing for increased border demarcation and security in ENP partners. Hence the Revised EU–Ukraine Action Plan of Freedom, Security and Justice emphasised supporting the process of delimiting and demarcating Ukrainian borders to international standards, strengthening the institutional and administrative framework and capacity to implement border controls and improve border surveillance, and promoting Ukrainian efforts to introduce secure and machine-readable passports and travel documents.[97] To the extent that the EU succeeds in insisting upon the demarcation of the Ukraine–Russia border and its 'informationalization' by means of databases, liaison officers and so forth, it will alter Russia–Ukraine politics in its favour and render impossible reintegration between Ukraine and Russia at the level of borders.[98]

Despite the sizeable stakes involved, progress in EU–Ukraine relations has been slow even since the Orange Revolution of 2004, which seemingly put Ukraine on a path to integration with the West. The European Commission concluded that in 2007 political instability had caused the pace of economic and structural reforms to stall somewhat and 2008 was little better, irrespective of the Verkhovna Rada's ratification of a framework for Ukrainian participation in EU crisis management operations.[99] Reforms slowed in the face of continuing domestic political instability, the deepening global financial and economic crisis and Kiev's need to tread a careful path between co-operation with Brussels and Moscow. Ukraine had also failed to either sign or ratify a number of international security-related agreements, such as the Rome Statute of the International Criminal Court and the Council of Europe Convention on Action against Trafficking in Human Beings. This non-ratification of agreements was also impinging directly on co-operation with the EU. For example, signature of a Co-operation Agreement between the Public Prosecutor's Office and Eurojust remained suspended due to non-ratification of the Council of Europe Convention for the Protection of Individuals with regard to the Automatic Processing of Personal Data.

It is tempting in defence of ENP to relativise its performance. The Commission rightly argues that 'In most ENP partner countries the need for political, social and economic reform is huge'[100] and in the Southern Caucasus other security actors have had little or no greater success than the EU in advancing resolution of the open and frozen conflicts there. Nevertheless, the ENP signalled a more ambitious and responsible EU approach towards Eastern Europe and raised expectations. In December 2007 the Commission argued that what is at stake in developing ENP is nothing less than 'the EU's ability to develop an external policy complementary to enlargement that is effective in promoting transformation and reform.'[101] Cast in this light it is important to examine what is going wrong.

One problem is that EU commitment to Eastern Europe is ambiguous. The European Commission divorces ENP from enlargement but is unable to rule it out for the Eastern European countries in the absence of an agreed Eastern frontier of the Union. This has caused countries such as Ukraine to continue to focus on potential membership.[102] In May 2008 Polish Foreign Minister Radoslaw Sikorski designated Eastern countries as 'European neighbours' and those to the South as 'neighbours of Europe'.[103] The basis and importance of this distinction, he argued, was that only the Eastern European countries could one day apply for EU membership. This situation generates potential for disappointment and alienation, encourages dissatisfaction with the 'enlargement minus' formula of ENP, and raises questions about the suitability of the single ENP framework for Eastern Europe where some countries aspire to full EU membership and others do not.

This debilitating ambiguity is compounded by an evident mis-match between the transformational challenges in the Eastern Neighbourhood and the transformative capacity of ENP. On the one hand, the Eastern European countries face challenges even greater than those encountered by the CEECs and do so now, unlike the CEECs in their transformative years, in an era of Russian reassertion. On the other, ENP has a far weaker incentive structure than the Europe Agreements and the SAP and a far inferior funding commitment.[104] Indeed, the contrast in per capita funding between the Western Balkans and Eastern Europe underscores the EU's ambiguous commitment to the latter. Moldova has the highest per capita support of any Eastern European country in the ENP programme at just below 15 euros per capita; pre-accession assistance to the Western Balkans runs at 30 euros per capita, with substantial security assistance on top of this.[105]

ENP's relatively weak incentive structure combines with particular conditions in Eastern Europe to question some of the assumptions within the EU's 'gradualist, performance-based and differentiated'[106] approach. Norm-based incentives are less compelling for the Eastern countries than they were for the CEECs. The latter feared a resurgent Russia and were wedded to political and economic transformation along Western models. That is not the case for all Eastern European countries. For example, research by Freedom House suggests that many Eastern European ENP partners have poor, even deteriorating, human rights and democracy records. In the period 1 January –31 December 2008 only Ukraine was rated as a 'free' country. Armenia and Moldova were just partly free with declining political liberties trends, Georgia was partly free with a declining performance, and Belarus and Azerbaijan were classed as not free.[107] In these circumstances elites are more resistant to socialization, EU values less familiar and attractive to Eastern European populations, and the potential for reformist elements within civil society are limited. In turn, this brings into question the effectiveness of the EU's resistance to supporting opposition movements to non-democratic governments in the hopes of promoting democracy. It also increases the potential for 'cross-conditionality' and 'cross-socialization' processes to undermine those of the EU.[108] Herein Russia is the most important player because its norms are very different, its assets in developing its neighbourhood policy arguably stronger and broader than those of the EU and its determination to establish itself as a second 'pole' in Europe increasingly evident. It has available coercive mechanisms ranging from blockades and sudden increases in energy prices through to military action, and can also offer cheap energy, a relatively open labour market as it looks to offset its declining population, a growing market, a visa-free regime, security co-operation and diplomatic protection in international fora.

The conditionality dimension of ENP also exhibits serious weaknesses in the context of Eastern Europe. The EU recognises the necessity of providing tangible and visible intermediate rewards to encourage government reforms and promote identification with progressive elements of civil society. This is a key element of the ENP's performance-based conditionality. As the UK European Presidency stressed in December 2005, 'Countries should be aware that the nature of their relationships with the EU will be positively affected by the level of their co-operation.'[109] However, the 'candy tomorrow' approach has failed to persuade Belarus to engage. Also, as Balfour argues, ENP does not allow the EU to wield a big stick if political reform falters or fails because its emphasis on ownership and partnership means reliance on positive and rewards-based conditionality.[110] For example, in explaining the EU's 'somewhat timid, if not weak'[111] reaction to the much-protested Russia-style succession between President and Prime Minister in Armenia in February 2008, one European Commission official emphasised that whereas US Millennium Development Funds to Armenia are conditional on compliance with a series of conditions, EU funds are targeted at fulfilling the conditions themselves, and so are not linked to their being achieved beforehand.[112]

The emphasis on partnership and ownership, coupled with high adaptation costs and relatively low incentives, also inclines some of the Eastern European partners to cherry pick economic integration rather than political reform.[113] This is particularly embarrassing because Action Plans were supposed to prevent this by dealing together with 'the whole range of issues ... '[114] Criticism has unsurprisingly been levied that European governments put in place insufficiently rigorous criteria to tie aid allocations to democratic progress[115] and that the EU is failing to respond to a currently more challenging environment for democracy promotion.[116] Furthermore, Eastern European resistance to democratisation exposes the assumptive linkage within ENP between stability and those countries adopting EU norms. Consider in this respect the Commission's promise in 2007 that it would 'continue to promote stability notably through the sustained promotion of democracy, human rights and the rule of law throughout the neighbourhood.'[117] Unfortunately for the EU there is an increasing number of non-democratic States demonstrating that they are capable of maintaining stability, strong economic growth and national-cultural identities. Conversely, politically 'free' Ukraine still experiences political instability and threats to its territorial integrity arising from unclear post-Soviet borders, a large minority Russian population, and potential Russian aggravation of separatism in Crimea and the breakaway Transniester region.

Finally, some analysts suggest that however well intentioned the ENP is, the Union's de-centralized policy-making structure may put beyond its capability the strategic coordination of the multifaceted foreign activities necessary to deliver it effectively.[118] Certainly there are serious problems of perceived inequity and inconsistency in its delivery. ENP is highly asymmetric and cost-benefit ratios of participation seemingly privilege the EU over the Eastern partners. For instance, tying visa facilitation agreements to readmission agreements seemingly prioritises the Union's internal security and shifts the burden of dealing with failed asylum seekers and illegal migrants to neighbours – thereby reprising arguments made in respect of the CEECs before they entered the Union.[119] Also, the incentive structure of ENP is partially dependent on EU Member States delivering promptly promised benefits at agreed points in Eastern European countries' transition processes. This is vulnerable to lack of consensus, competing priorities and political distraction. For instance, in December 2007 the Commission called explicitly for 'increased political commitment to foster economic integration and to improve market access' for ENP countries.[120] Similarly, consistent application of criteria sometimes runs up against national interests. For instance, the EU has 'punished' Belarus for its lack of democracy and respect for human rights but its criticism of political conditions within Azerbaijan has allegedly been toned down since it became the Union's leading trade partner in the Southern Caucasus and a significant exporter of hydrocarbons.[121] Likewise, pro-Western Georgia was excluded from fast track visa facilitation at the same time that the EU concluded such an agreement with Russia, where sovereign democracy was being consolidated. This reflected the priority of EU–Russia relations, missed an opportunity to signal support to nascent democracies such as Georgia and undermined Tbilisi's efforts to control the secessionist regions of Abkhazia and South Ossetia by effectively giving the many Russian passport holders there a better chance of entering the EU than Georgian citizens.[122]

The EU, recognising some of these ENP weaknesses and prompted especially by a combination of the Georgian conflict and internal trade-offs between Southern and Eastern inclined Member States, announced in 2008 an Eastern Partnership to complement a new French-driven Union of the Mediterranean initiative.[123] Details remain sketchy at the time of writing but the Commission is promoting the Eastern Partnership as a 'strategic imperative and a political investment for the EU' and a 'step change' in its relations with the Eastern European countries.[124] The Partnership maintains the ENP's differentiated bilateralism and positive conditionality but adds a new multilateral component and a series of trade, travel and aid measures designed to better incentivise reform. Increased funding for Eastern European countries from €450 million in 2008 to approximately €785 million in 2013 responds to criticism of under-investment and reflects the Commission's view that 'One of the clearest signals the EU can give of a concrete commitment to its partners is to bring funding levels in line with the Partnership's level of political ambition'.[125] The thorny issue of potential EU membership for some Eastern European countries remains unresolved. However, the Eastern Partnership does recognise their different ambitions in this respect and offers both more intensive EU accompaniment of reform efforts and the prospect for the most progressive countries of higher forms of association with the EU through new generation association agreements. Running throughout the Partnership are strong EU concerns about security and Russia's reassertion in their shared neighbourhood especially. For example, 'mobility and security pacts' are incentivised through easier travel to the EU and the long-term prospect of visa-free travel, but more immediately they advance efforts to combat corruption, organized crime and illegal migration, including upgrading asylum systems to EU standards and the establishment of integrated border management structures. Similarly, four out of five flagship initiatives proposed by the Commission are security-related. Prevention of, preparedness for, and response to natural and man-made disasters is advanced along-side an Integrated Border Management Programme designed to strengthen border security by aligning to EU standards. Energy security concerns are evident in both the Southern energy corridor and the promotion of regional electricity markets, improved energy efficiency and increased use of renewable energy sources. The Commission also signals determination to diversify energy supply and transit routes in its envisaging of third party association with the Eastern Partnership: 'the EaP should contribute towards the ongoing strengthening of the Baku Process as a genuine energy partnership, with a full participation of countries of Central Asia as a key energy producing region, and including through the development of the Southern corridor including the Transcaspian.'[126]

The Eastern Partnership signals EU determination to strengthen its security by more actively promoting its influence in and relations with its Eastern Neighbour-hood. It also raises the stakes in Eastern Europe. First, it increases expectations of the EU in the region amongst its constituent States and the wider international community. Second, much depends on whether the Eastern Partnership's formula of ENP plus but enlargement minus shifts the cost-benefit calculus sufficiently to entice the Eastern European countries into more sustained and comprehensive co-operation with the EU. Ukraine immediately cast doubts upon this when it stressed even before the Partnership was fleshed out that it 'should envisage a clear membership perspective'.[127] Since arriving in office in 2010, Ukrainian President Yanukovych has adopted a more pro-Russia stance. Third, the initiative likely heralds the onset of deepening EU–Russia competition for influence in their shared neighbourhood. The EU emphatically denies that the Eastern Partnership is anti-Russian but it is undoubtedly a response to Russia's revisionism and re-assertion generally and its conflict with Georgia especially. Moreover, the Partnership signals more purposive intent in the Union's penetration of post-Soviet space not only in Eastern Europe but also Central Asia through envi-saged third party associations and its being tied into regional initiatives such as the Black Sea synergy and Baku Process. Fourth, Moscow is bound to react with suspi-cion and resentment. This raises the stakes further because unless the EU puts decisive resources and political will behind its rhetoric, the Eastern Partnership could deliver the worst of both worlds, namely an increasingly competitive and antagonistic rela-tionship with Russia and a disillusioned Eastern Neighbourhood where pro-Western countries still hanker for full EU membership and others cherry-pick benefits of interest without assuming disproportionate political and economic risks.

Conclusion

EU achievements in exporting security to Eastern and South Eastern Europe in particular are substantial, and the financial and technical assistance and political will vested in the ongoing transition processes remain vital. At the same time, the Union still has some way to go to redeem its credibility especially in the Balkans, and it is far from clear that it has yet got the policy mix right to maximise its leverage. The EU is effectively addressing its Eastern and South-Eastern European Neighbourhood within three different frameworks, namely ENP, enlargement, and strategic partnership with Russia. This creates a problematic *de facto* division of Europe into an inner and outer circle. It sends a signal that the Western Balkans are the Union's immediate European priority and that Eastern Europe is a privileged periphery that will serve as a buffer against resurgent Russia and security threats from farther afield. The division also weakens the purchase of ENP/Eastern Partnership because unlike the case with the Balkan countries the Commission has been unable to resolve the ambiguity about whether Eastern European countries have a long-term prospect of EU membership.

Dissatisfaction with the SAP and ENP in particular is expressed increasingly by affected countries and by partisan EU States. Doubts about the ability of the SAP to maintain participating countries' commitment to painful reform processes, especially at a time of global financial and economic recession, are encouraged by the EU's struggle with the ratification and now implementation of the Lisbon Treaty, its more qualified position on enlargement, and fears that the Turkish question will spill over into the membership prospects of the Balkan countries. ENP is a far weaker trans-formational vehicle than enlargement and has evidently been insufficient to make a significant difference in Eastern Europe. No headway has been made with Belarus; little has been achieved in terms of enhancing the prospects for resolving the frozen conflicts that Russian influence appears to be spreading; and the three countries proceeding best within the ENP – Moldova, Ukraine and Georgia – were the most Western-orientated countries long before the programme's launch yet still have made only limited progress. Hopes that Action Plans would stimulate a virtuous circle of competition among ENP countries for EU aid and benefit have been compromised by the lack of easy comparability between them and the different aspirations of the Eastern partners. Furthermore, ENP has suffered inconsistent delivery in Eastern Europe, cross-cutting concerns for energy supplies and EU–Russia relations, counter-socialisation and cross-conditionality influences from Moscow especially.

Launch of the Eastern Partnership marks recognition of ENP weaknesses and a long overdue change in the EU's approach to its neighbourhood. The EU will likely maintain ENP's importance as a single policy framework for its neighbourhood but different regional conditions are now recognised in a *de facto* decoupling of the Eastern from the Southern dimension. Still, though, doubts remain about the EU's ability to guide reform processes successfully and to avoid the potential for regional fragmentation inherent in differentiation. Much will depend in South-Eastern Europe on the EU maintaining tangible rewards during the SAP reform process and a credible and visible prospect of full membership at its end. Fragmentation is even more likely in Eastern Europe where the constituent States have different aspirations vis-à-vis the Union and where the Partnership faces circumstances more challenging than at any time since the Cold War – including post-Lisbon EU reforms, global recession and Russian reassertion. Much will depend here on the increasingly doubtful prospect of constructive EU–Russia relations and on the Union's ability/willingness to define the geographical limit of enlargement to its East.

8

THE EU AND ITS SOUTHERN MEDITERRANEAN NEIGHBOURS

To the South of the Union is a zone that hosts arguably the greatest array of security challenges to the EU. As the 2003 European Security Strategy observed, 'The Mediterranean area generally continues to undergo serious problems of economic stagnation, social unrest and unresolved conflicts.'[1] Specific threats emanating from, to and via this region range from human and small arms trafficking through to energy security, radicalisation and the proliferation of WMD.

As though the challenges posed directly by the non-EU Member Southern Mediterranean States were not enough, these EU partners bring into play security challenges associated with North Africa and the wider Middle East. This raises in turn issues of co-operation with major powers, including Russia but especially the US, and co-ordination with all the different state and non-state actors involved in what is a congested policy space. It also demands that the EU synergises its internal and external security regimes and co-ordinates multiple external policy frameworks of its own making. Furthermore, the Mediterranean region is effectively fragmented into four sub-regions: Southern Europe, the Balkans, the Maghreb, and the Mashreq. Each of these has different political, security and socio-economic characteristics and different degrees of willingness and capability to engage in integration with the EU and each other.

The EU has long stood accused of according the Mediterranean too low a strategic importance compared to the Balkans and Central and Eastern Europe.[2] Since 9/11 there has been a flurry of activity owing in part to an attempt to mitigate perceptions of a Global War on Terrorism-driven 'clash of civilizations' but more especially to heightened sensitivity to security threats, particularly WMD, radicalisation and terrorism, illegal immigration, drugs and crime, and energy insecurity. The region has become enmeshed in overlapping EU and extra-EU policy frameworks and initiatives. The EU's frameworks alone include the Barcelona Process/Union for the Mediterranean, European Neighbourhood Policy (ENP), the Stabilisation and Association Process

(SAP), Africa strategy and Turkey's candidate status. Yet despite and because of this, internal tensions between EU objectives have become increasingly obvious, co-ordination difficulties more pronounced and short-term security interests of EU Member States *de facto* prioritised. At the same time, the end product is limited and Southern Mediterranean States remain at best limited stakeholders in the EU's vision of partnership. Indeed, North–South exchanges continue to exhibit characteristics of a dialogue of the deaf, the parties talking past one another as EU States focus on security threats *from* the South and Southern Mediterranean States focus on economic development and sub-regional dynamics *within* the South.

Mediterranean challenges

The Mediterranean was viewed strategically during the Cold War as the relatively unimportant Southern flank of Europe. Once released from overlay of superpower rivalry the Mediterranean gained recognition as a source of a complex mix of security challenges for Europe. Yet their diffuse nature and priorities elsewhere meant that the region failed to attract the sustained interest of the EU's non-Mediterranean States. Re-unified Germany successfully focused the EU's attention on the CEECs' transition to post-communist societies and eventual integration. Conflict in the Balkans demanded that the EU tend its backyard and consumed its political will and resources. And beyond the EU's physical land borders, energy concerns, transatlantic relations and regional political developments drew the Union into the wider Middle East rather than the littoral Mediterranean States.

Over time the EU began to take more seriously the security challenges of and interdependencies with the Southern Mediterranean littoral States. In fact, a combination of political advocacy, opportunity and the post-9/11 security environment has elevated the significance of the region's dual function as bridge and barrier between civilizations and peoples. EU enlargement, past and pending, has increased advocacy within the EU for a more sustained engagement in Mediterranean security issues. Malta and Cyprus joined the ranks of the EU's Mediterranean Members in 2004. The eventual full membership of the Balkan States raises the significance of the Adriatic. And the commitment to eventual Turkish membership foregrounds the Aegean and transit from the Black Sea. Inevitably this draws the EU further into Mediterranean and Middle Eastern security issues. The 2004 enlargement imported the Cyprus issue into the EU – and unless resolved in the meantime this will become more problematic if Turkey becomes a full Member. Also, Turkey lies in close proximity to 70 per cent of the world's proven energy resources and is a prospective regional centre for the storage and distribution of oil and natural gas.[3] Furthermore, future Turkish membership raises the prospect of direct EU borders upon the Black Sea, with 'hot spots' in the Caucasus (Armenia, Georgia and Azerbaijan) and with Members of former US President George W. Bush's infamous 'axis of evil' (Iran and Iraq).

A number of developments have increased interest in Mediterranean security. First, the importance accorded to the CEECs declined once they became full EU Members. Second, supervised peace in the Balkans and the gradual path of its constituent countries towards EU membership has reduced that region's dominance over the EU's security agenda. Third, commitment in the 2003 ESS to promoting around the EU 'a ring of well governed countries' raised the political salience of the Union's Mediterranean borders and demanded that security threats from, to and through the Mediterranean littoral States be better addressed. Finally, Southern EU States, such as France, have sought to actively promote the Mediterranean agenda. This is due partially to their being 'front-line' States in the context of security threats emanating from the area, especially illegal immigration. It is also due to strategic competition within and without the EU.[4] Southern EU Members generally seek to orientate focus and funding away from (over-) concentration on the East towards the South and South-East. France views the Mediterranean as a traditional sphere of its influence and has sought to protect its influence against the encroachment of other powers, notably the US since 9/11. President Sarkozy's Union for the Mediterranean initiative, first unveiled in 2007, can be seen very much in this light.

9/11 and subsequent events – including the London and Madrid bombings – focused attention on the Mediterranean security agenda and its entanglement with the wider Middle East. As a RAND publication warned in 1998, 'In hard security terms, the era of European sanctuary with regard to instability and conflict across the Mediterranean and beyond is rapidly drawing to a close.'[5] Though the EU is concerned about proportionately high military expenditure and small arms trafficking in a number of the Southern rim countries,[6] this is based primarily on calculations of regional (in)security and spillover consequences rather than fear of a conventional military threat to Europe. The real hard security concern is weapons of mass destruction. In 2003 the ESS warned that proliferation 'is potentially the greatest threat' and noted that in the Middle East especially there was potential for a WMD arms race.[7] Indeed, proliferation risks of WMD and of ballistic missiles potentially capable of reaching EU capitals are concentrated in the Southern rim Mediterranean States and their immediate neighbours. A number of countries are known to have used chemical weapons in past regional conflicts, including Egypt, Iran, Iraq and Libya. Israel is an undeclared nuclear power and in September 2007 Israeli jets attacked an alleged nuclear facility in Syria. Iran's nuclear programme and the successful launch in February 2009 of its first home-built satellite have raised fears that its *Safir* rocket could be used to deliver nuclear weapons. In 2008 the International Institute of Strategic Studies reported that at least thirteen countries throughout the greater Middle East had announced new or revived plans to explore civilian nuclear energy. Though this was consistent with a 'nuclear renaissance' in energy production, the underlying political motivation was thought to include competition with Iran and fear of its potential nuclear weapons capability.[8] Moreover, regional proliferation and nuclear weapon delivery capability are encouraged by overt and covert technology and weapon sales. Russia, China and North Korea are significant suppliers of technology and missiles to Middle Eastern countries and the infamous Abdul Qadeer Khan network is thought to have provided Iran (and North Korea) with atomic technology.

The US justifies its Ballistic Missile Defence programme in part in terms of Iran's alleged threat, but it is Europe that faces the most imminent consequences of proliferation in the Mediterranean and wider Middle East. The projected path of EU enlargement exacerbates proximity issues, and regional insecurity could fuel the demand for WMD and increase the likelihood of exchange. The probability of South–North conflict remains low but regional proliferation would likely heighten European perceptions of insecurity, encourage a more defensive European security posture and make dealing with security issues in the region more difficult. The physical vulnerability of EU population centres to missiles along the Southern Mediterranean rim could sap European political will, already weak in a number of countries, to engage in expeditionary operations, exacerbate differences in transatlantic threat assessments and cause further difficulties within NATO and CFSP/CSDP. Even South–South exchanges involving WMD would likely impact the Union significantly across hard and soft security domains, ranging from humanitarian disaster and refugee flows through to environmental consequences and increased fears of WMD-enabled terrorists.

The terrorist threat, conventional or otherwise, emanating from the Mediterranean region has attracted most attention in recent years. Commonly perceived sources of terrorism in the region include the Palestinian–Israeli conflict, the struggle between Arab regimes and Islamist opposition groups, Iranian-led resistance to US hegemony in the wider Middle East, fallout from the US-led intervention in Iraq and the ongoing Afghan campaign, the Turkey–PKK conflict and spiralling crisis in Pakistan. Deeper causal factors contribute too. Fertile ground for radicalisation is provided by the growing gap between the haves and the have-nots in terms of access to basic public goods,[9] large-scale unemployment resulting from a combination of weak economic growth and a demographic explosion, and the 'illegitimate' nature of the region's many authoritarian governments.

The connection between events in the Mediterranean and terrorism within Europe is not new. Between 1994 and 1995 the savagery of the Algerian war spilled over into terrorist attacks in France.[10] The London and Madrid bombings in the wake of the US-led military intervention in Iraq in 2003 reinforced this connection. However, the latter also contributed to superimposing a wider frame of reference upon this connectivity, namely the co-existence or clash of Christian and Islamic civilisations. The EU has consistently repudiated this notion. Nevertheless, border security has become increasingly sensitive politically and South–North migration and illegal immigration have become wrapped up in fears of both importing terrorism and encouraging it from within by exceeding societal capacity to integrate Muslim communities. As Javier Solana pointedly noted in his 2008 review of the ESS, within terrorism in Europe 'home-grown groups play an increasing role'.[11]

Though the potential of hard security threats is considerable, the actual EU security agenda with countries of the Southern Mediterranean rim features a range of soft security issues too. This is to be expected given the EU's proximity to the Southern littoral States and the Union's emphasis on comprehensive security. Specific issues include organized crime, migratory and environmental pressure, human rights, and maritime and energy security. Strong push and pull factors fuel migratory pressure, a problem publicised by significant media coverage of increasing numbers of boat people coming from North Africa to gain economic opportunity or escape political persecution. Indeed, the European Commission makes a linkage between the two, arguing in 2008 that in the South, where authoritarian regimes predominate, problems associated with stagnating economies were 'aggravated by three socio-political "deficits", the freedom deficit, the women's empowerment deficit and the lack of access to knowledge and education.'[12] The primary driver, though, is that the inter-regional economic differential is amongst the greatest in the world. For instance, estimated figures for 2008 suggested that Egypt had a GDP per capita of US $5,500 while the EU average was $34,000, with some Member States' average GDP per capita being considerably higher still.[13]

The problem of illegal immigration for EU States is compounded by organised crime capitalising upon migratory demand pressures and on weak governance and law enforcement structures in the South. Europol identifies inexpensive waterways connecting the Black Sea with the Mediterranean through the Bosporus, and with the heart of Western Europe via the Danube, coupled with national borders lacking sufficient protection, as reasons why the South-East region of the EU is particularly attractive for illegal shipments. It also emphasises that embarkation points for illegal entry to the Iberian Peninsula, such as Morocco, Western Sahara, Mauritania and Algeria, collect migratory flows coming by land from all over West Africa and beyond and that international human smuggling networks use Moroccan-organised crime networks to smuggle immigrants from the Middle East and Asia into the EU in the final phase of the process.[14] Organised crime also impacts on the terrorist threat and on asylum demands in the EU. The interaction of organised crime and terrorist activity ranges from money laundering through to terrorist groups using criminal organisations' transportation networks to smuggle operatives and weapons.[15] As for asylum seekers, Dutch authorities found that the percentage of asylum seekers to the EU that used a trafficker rose from 30 per cent in 1996 to 60–70 per cent by the late 1990s.[16]

The EU's growing energy import dependence, the 20-20-20 strategy and concerns over the reliability of extant energy supplies from the Gulf and Russia especially have propelled energy security up the Union's agenda. This in turn has elevated the importance of the Mediterranean region. In 2003 the Euro-Mediterranean Energy Ministerial Conferences emphasised the need for a comprehensive Euro-Mediterranean energy policy based on the security of supplies and the objective of working towards a fully interconnected and integrated energy market. In 2008 the European Commission successfully proposed in the EU Energy Security and Solidarity Action Plan: 2nd Strategic Energy Review that a number of infrastructure developments should be recognised as energy security priorities. These included the development of North–South gas and electricity interconnections within Central and South-East Europe, the development of a Southern Gas Corridor for supply from Caspian and Middle Eastern sources and possibly other countries in the longer term, and the completion of a Mediterranean energy ring designed to link Europe with the Southern Mediterranean through electricity and gas interconnections and to help develop solar and wind energy potential.[17] The Commission has also emphasised that sub-Saharan energy resources should be progressively integrated into the Southern Mediterranean energy market with a view to their possible transit to the EU.[18]

EU approaches and policies towards the Southern Mediterranean rim

The overarching EU approach towards developing Mediterranean security is broadly consistent with that adopted in its Eastern neighbourhood. The EU has, in principle at least, rejected maintenance of the status quo. Political, economic and social reforms are seen as indispensable to the pursuit of comprehensive security. The EU has also rejected the external imposition of reforms, arguing instead that reforms 'can succeed only if they are generated from within the affected societies'.[19] Closer association with the EU together with multilateral regionalism, underpinned by a series of bilateral relations, are believed to be the optimum means by which to incentivise and assist these reform processes. However, reaching this point in security approaches and policies towards the Southern Mediterranean has been and remains a difficult and sometimes haphazard process.

Early EU policies towards the Southern Mediterranean were strongly coloured by colonial legacies and economic interests, though the oil shocks of the 1970s also informed the development of the Global Mediterranean Policy and the Euro–Arab dialogue.[20] The European Commission re-examined these relations and in 1991 the Renovated Mediterranean Policy was agreed. This aimed primarily at moving EU relations with non-Member Mediterranean States away from aid in favour of assisting International Monetary Fund (IMF) and World Bank structural adjustment programmes. However, it also highlighted environmental and human rights protection and sought to encourage multilateral and cross-border activities in a new emphasis on horizontal co-operation. Some EU States sponsored other initiatives. In 1989/90 Spain and Italy sought (unsuccessfully) to replicate the CSCE experience in the Mediterranean with a proposal for a Conference on Security and Co-operation in the Mediterranean. A less comprehensive security initiative came in 1990 with final agreement of the French sponsored 5+5 Mediterranean Dialogue, which brought together five Southern European States with their Maghreb counterparts. France also sponsored, together with Egypt, the creation in 1994 of the Mediterranean Forum, a mechanism for dialogue on social, economic, cultural and security issues exclusively between Mediterranean riparian countries. In addition, established European security institutions sought to strengthen their relations with Mediterranean countries. The OSCE launched its Mediterranean Partners for Co-operation initiative, which now involves special relations between itself and Algeria, Egypt, Israel, Jordan, Morocco and Tunisia. In 1994 NATO established its Mediterranean Dialogue. Ten years later it resolved to offer a framework to the Gulf Cooperation Council through the Istanbul Co-operation Initiative and to deepen its Mediterranean dialogue, which currently involves seven non-NATO countries of the region: Algeria, Egypt, Israel, Jordan, Mauritania, Morocco and Tunisia.

This flurry of activity crowded the Mediterranean security policy space but delivered limited results and failed to hold the interest of most European States and security institutions alike. In 1995 the EU tried again with the Euro-Mediterranean

Partnership (EMP – referred to as the Barcelona Process), a more comprehensive set of arrangements that focused on three key issue 'baskets'. The political and security basket aimed to establish a common area of peace and stability; the economic and financial basket aimed at the creation of an area of shared prosperity; and the social, cultural and human basket aimed to develop human resources and promote understanding between cultures and exchanges between civil societies. In supporting this initiative the Cannes European Council emphasised that the EMP framework complemented existing bilateral relations. It also sought to distance it from the Middle East Peace Process (MEPP) especially, noting that EMP 'is not a new forum for resolving conflicts and should not be seen as the framework for this process, even if, among other objectives, it can help to promote its success.'[21]

A number of commitments were made under the political and security basket, including pursuit of a Middle East zone free of WMD, to combat terrorism and organised crime, to promote regional security and to work to prevent the proliferation of nuclear, chemical and biological weapons. Considerable emphasis was placed on international law and basic values as the underpinnings of confidence-building measures and regional co-operation. These included observation of the UN Charter, the Universal Declaration of Human Rights and other obligations under international law, respect for territorial integrity, self-determination, non-intervention in the internal affairs of another partner, and the peaceful settlement of disputes. The parties also agreed to develop the rule of law and democracy domestically, and emphasis was placed in the Barcelona Declaration on respect for human rights and fundamental freedoms (including freedom of expression, freedom of association and freedom of thought, conscience and religion).[22] It was also expected that there would be security spill-over effects from the other two baskets. The social, cultural and human basket could potentially contribute to breaking down intra-regional barriers and drawing back 'the curtain of prejudice and misperception' thought to divide the Mediterranean along a North–South axis.[23] Particular hope was invested in the economic basket. In line with the Washington consensus it was thought that economic liberalisation would spill over into political liberalization and the development of good governance. It was anticipated that fostering South–South economic interdependencies would promote co-operation and confidence-building over intra-regional fractures and state rivalries. Moreover, developing the South and its interdependencies with the EU was perceived as a vital measure given that the majority of security threats could be traced to North–South inequalities.

EMP was launched with a considerable fanfare, but the EU soon had cause to re-visit its relations with non-Member Mediterranean States. In 2000 the European Commission delivered a communication entitled 'Re-invigorating the Barcelona Process'. The tone was generally downbeat. EU human rights policy in the region 'lacked consistency', the Barcelona Process lacked visibility in 'society at large' and implementation of the MEDA programme had been so hampered by complicated procedures in the EC and partner countries that disbursements totalled just 26 per cent.[24] The negotiation and ratification of Association Agreements had also been slower than expected and South–South trade had failed to take-off.[25] The MEPP was believed to have slowed progress and limited the extent to which full regional co-operation could develop. The spirit of partnership at Barcelona had not led to a sufficiently frank and serious dialogue on issues such as human rights, prevention of terrorism and migration, and local governments were believed to be wanting. Neither would economic growth increase unless reforms were accelerated and States adapted themselves to 'the realities of the new economy.'[26]

Seeking to re-invigorate the Barcelona Process the European Council launched on 19 June 2000 a Common Strategy on the Mediterranean region. Among other things, the Strategy gave greater prominence to Justice and Home Affairs issues, emphasising refugees, crime and, especially, migration. While pledging to simplify visa procedures it also emphasised combating illegal migration networks, ensuring more effective border control, and reducing the causes of migration.[27] The Commission also pledged to develop a regional justice and home affairs programme during 2001,[28] and in 2002 the Valencia Action Plan listed plans for dialogue on political and security matters, including ESDP. The following year the Commission prioritised human rights and democratisation in its relations with third countries. The Commission noted that authoritarianism and poor economic and social performance fuelled radical movements among Mediterranean States. Some political interpretations of Islam were believed to be exploiting cultural differences to question the universality of human rights, and the development of democracy and defence of human rights were being hampered by deficits in governance, poor implementation of international human rights conventions and insufficient independence for legal and judicial systems. Furthermore, the marginalisation of women was considered to undermine political representation and hamper economic and social development, and education was unevenly dispensed, failed to overcome traditional discriminatory patterns and was ill-adapted to the requirements of a modern economy.[29]

The EU looked to combine its upgraded regional approach with improved bilateral relations with Southern Mediterranean States. The introduction of ENP and its Action Plans provided new means to shape the deeper political relationship and economic integration that are intended to foster interdependence with the Union and promote security in the Mediterranean. In return for the implementation of political, economic and institutional reforms, partner States might attain a significant degree of integration. Possibilities include conclusion of deeper free trade agreements and third country participation in key aspects of EU programmes; perspectives for lawful migration; intensified co-operation to prevent and combat common security threats; closer dialogue in the context of CFSP and ESDP; and integration into EU transport, energy, ICT and research and markets and networks. For example, in December 2008 the EU confirmed its intention to upgrade the level and intensity of relations with Israel in order to build 'a degree of trust and proximity similar to that which the Member States and Israel already enjoy in their respective bilateral relations.'[30] Israel's involvement in the EU's Research and Development Space has been seen as an example of the promised 'deep integration' rather than the shallow integration of the Barcelona Process.[31]

In 2005 Israel, Jordan, Morocco, the Palestinian Authority, and Tunisia concluded ENP Action Plans. That same year the Barcelona Process celebrated its tenth anniversary. Agreement was struck on a two-page anti-terrorism code of conduct and a five-year work programme centred around four key areas, namely advancing democracy and human rights through stronger political dialogue and co-operation, including the setting up of a 'governance facility'; opening and expanding economic and employment opportunities, particularly through the completion of a free trade area by 2010 and extending free trade to include agriculture and services; adopting a more strategic approach towards tackling immigration; and improving the quality of and access to education.[32] Nevertheless, the tenth anniversary celebrations could not disguise growing concern about the limited practical impact of the Barcelona Process. Other than the Turkish prime minister and the president of the Palestinian Authority, heads of state and government from the South were conspicuous by their absence from the Summit. Only a last-minute compromise at the Summit enabled the unanimous adoption of the work programme and code of conduct on countering terrorism. And this fell far short of the endorsement of a final declaration manifesting a shared vision of the Euro-Mediterranean region by Europeans, Arabs and Israelis, even though this had been painstakingly negotiated beforehand.[33] Within two years French President Sarkozy called for yet another scheme to breathe new life into EU (security) relations with the Mediterranean region.

Sarkozy's original ideas focused on an intergovernmental arrangement exclusively for Mediterranean States. Under great pressure, especially from Germany, this subsequently morphed into an inclusive EU initiative that the European Commission argues 'will give a new impetus to the Barcelona Process in at least three very important ways: by upgrading the political level of the EU's relationship with its Mediterranean partners; by providing more co-ownership to our multilateral relations; and by making these relations more concrete and visible through additional regional and sub-regional projects, relevant for the citizens of the region.'[34] The new Union for the Mediterranean provides for biennial Summits of Heads of State, a rotating co-presidency with one EU President and one consensually chosen President representing the Mediterranean partners, a Joint Secretariat based in Barcelona, and a Joint Permanent Committee comprised of countries' representatives in Brussels. Foreign Affairs ministerial meetings between Summits are charged with reviewing progress in the implementation of Summit conclusions and to prepare the next Summit. Particular emphasis is to be put on projects that are visible and relevant for the citizens of the region and 'have a strong potential to promote regional cohesion and economic integration, and to develop infrastructural interconnections.'[35] Identified areas include De-pollution of the Mediterranean, Maritime and Land Highways, Civil Protection, Alternative Energies: Mediterranean Solar Plan, Higher Education and Research, Euro-Mediterranean University and the Mediterranean Business Development Initiative.[36]

Problems and challenges in EU relations with the Southern Mediterranean rim

The European Commission views the EU's global and comprehensive approach as 'the only one capable of avoiding the stagnation of the past'[37] in the Mediterranean and emphasises that the Barcelona Process/Union for the Mediterranean is the only multilateral context outside the UN where all parties affected by the Middle East conflict sit together.[38] In 2008 it also affirmed that 'the formula of trade plus investment plus co-operation is as pertinent as it was in 1995.'[39] Yet this approach has delivered limited progress at best. After twenty years of encouraging economic liberalisation, the South's share of EU imports remains stuck at around 6 per cent,[40] low levels of Foreign Direct Investment demonstrate a lack of investor confidence and South–South trade remains, in the Commission's words, 'below potential'.[41] Democratisation and good governance programmes have likewise made little headway. In 2005 Youngs argued that 'democratic advance has been no greater in the Arab States included in the Barcelona process than in the Gulf States bereft of a similar EU partnership.'[42] Writing three years later of the Maghreb, Galli concluded that the Maghrebi socio-political landscape 'has undergone no significant change. The underlying characteristics of the region's political regimes remain in place and, in some cases, have even been strengthened.'[43]

The sheer number of re-launches that EU Mediterranean policies have undergone reflects the Union's difficulties in developing effective relations with its South. Similarly, the decision in 2008 to drop 'Barcelona Process' in favour of 'Union for the Mediterranean' indicates the failure of the former to establish itself as a symbol of successful EU-Mediterranean relations. Careful reading of EU documents also suggests a number of unresolved problems running through the Union's relations with its South. In June 1990 the Commission argued that EU relations with the South needed 'a qualitative and quantitative leap' because 'What is at issue is its [EC's] security in the broadest sense.'[44] Eighteen years later the Commission still felt that 'the centrality of the Mediterranean ... needs to be revisited and given greater political prominence'[45] and that the EU relationship with it 'needs a qualitative and quantitative change'.[46] In 2000 and 2008 the Commission flagged problems associated with a perceived lack of co-ownership of the Barcelona Process, as did the European Council in 2004.[47] And the Commission repeatedly criticised both the lack of visibility of the Barcelona Process[48] and the failure of Southern partner States to fully engage with the process.

So what has been going wrong? There is the usual litany of institutional and programme delivery problems often associated with the EU's external relations. The EU's Mediterranean policy has been impaired by its 'dual decision-making process',[49] by a 'guerrilla war' among its institutions over the allocation of competencies,[50] and by the different strategic priorities of Member States. Indeed, internal politics have generally meant that any major Mediterranean initiative has been accompanied or preceded by a new initiative towards the East. The Cannes European Council noted explicitly in 1995 that the launch of EMP 'forms a counterpart to the policy of openness to the East and gives the European Union's external action its geopolitical coherence.'[51] It is similarly no coincidence that the Union for the Mediterranean was launched in the same year as the new Eastern Partnership. There is also the ongoing struggle between national and EU foreign policies. For instance, Sarkozy's original Mediterranean Union plan was received in some quarters as a suspiciously French neo-colonial sounding proposal[52] and caused Germany's Chancellor Merkel to warn that the creation of a new and exclusive institution with access to the EC budget had the potential to lead to a 'a corrosion of the EU in its core area' and to unleash 'explosive forces'.[53] Furthermore, the relationship between different EU instruments is not always clear. The introduction of ENP complicated the relationship between the economic and trade-relevant stipulations in the EMAA and the provisions in the ENP Action Plans.[54] And although the EU is evidently committed to Mediterranean regionalism, its relations with Members of the Union for the Mediterranean have a hierarchy of privilege ranging from full membership candidate countries (Croatia and Turkey) through to those with Syria that rest upon a co-operation agreement concluded in 1977.[55]

Three further specific problems face the EU in its relations with the South, namely Mediterranean regionalism, relative EU leverage and the vulnerability of EU-Mediterranean relations to problems in the Greater Middle East. The first problem in the EU's determination to deal with the Mediterranean as a region is that it is difficult to delimit. Aliboni argued in 1991 that 'Unless a purely geographic approach is taken, it is pointless to consider only the littoral countries … it is necessary to include the numerous regions that skirt this frontier'.[56] These included the Maghreb and parts of the Arabised Sahel (Chad, Mauritania), the Arab Orient and the Gulf countries, and possibly the Horn of Africa too. The EU's own delimitation of the Mediterranean has, in fact, changed over time. The Southern partner States in the original EMP were Algeria, Cyprus, Egypt, Israel, Jordan, Lebanon, Malta, Morocco, the Palestinian Authority, Syria, Tunisia and Turkey. Albania and Mauritania were admitted at the beginning of November 2007. And the Union for the Mediterranean added Bosnia and Herzegovina, Croatia, Monaco, and Montenegro. The EU has thus expanded its concept of the Mediterranean to include the Balkan States bordering the Adriatic Sea. It has also aimed to complete the ring of North African States bordering upon the Mediterranean by inviting Libya to become a full Member, albeit Tripoli declined in favour of observer status. Furthermore, neither Mauritania nor Jordan border upon the Mediterranean, suggesting the importance of sub-regional dynamics in Mediterranean security that do not fully align with Mediterranean littoralism. Jordan is self-evidently a key component in the MEPP while Mauritania is a Member of the Maghreb and a transit country to the North African coastline – not to mention a former French colony.

Meantime it is no more certain that the Southern Mediterranean littoral States conceive of themselves as sharing a common regional identity, either between one another or between them and the EU Southern States.[57] The Balkans, the Maghreb, and the Mashreq face very different challenges and the 'Mediterraneanism' idea competes poorly next to other regional identities and loyalties, especially Arab and Islamic identities.[58] The South is also heavily influenced by traditional nationalist claims and regional nationalism. This is evidenced by accelerating rearmament, low levels of South–South trade, the limited degree of regional integration and the limited impact of those regional organizations that do exist, including the League of Arab States and the Arab Maghreb Union.[59] Differences are arguably even more pronounced between the Northern and Southern shores of the Mediterranean. The Mediterranean has long been divided by great antagonisms. It has experienced the East–West Byzantine versus Roman clash, suffered the competitions of three continents (Europe, Asia and Africa) and, perhaps currently most important, has been split between North and South in multiple ways. The juxtaposition of rich and developed Northern States against the poor and undeveloped Southern States draws a 'fault line' across the Mediterranean.[60] The history of colonial versus colonised States breeds suspicion. Different experiences of democracy in the North and authoritarianism in the South encourage value differences. And the Christian–Muslim dichotomy plays to a perception of a profound cleavage between cultures that some analysts argue poses deeper problems for developing security co-operation than the EU recognises.[61] The domination by Western media outlets of the information flow across the Mediterranean and global news agencies' homogenisation of international news further encourages the impression that the West is imposing economic, political and cultural models.[62]

In the absence of a common regional identity the EU is evidently seeking to develop a regional political identity as a building block in the construction of regional collective security in the Mediterranean.[63] In supporting the 1995 Barcelona Process the European Council noted explicitly that in the political and security field 'the aim here is to establish a number of common principles and interests, acceptable to all, which the partners would undertake to promote together. It involves … a reaffirmation of the importance, within each State, of respect for fundamental freedoms and the establishment of the rule of law.'[64] However, although declaratory agreement has normally been found between EMP Members on broad aims and basic principles there is in practice a limited sense of political identity and evidently significant differences in the application and interpretation of agreements. For example, debate on the Euro-Mediterranean Charter for Peace and Stability has been pending improved political circumstances since 1999. At a basic level the principal threat perceptions of North and South overlap but are far from identical. Strong sub-regional dynamics and the absence of regional peace mean that Southern States are unfamiliar with regional security co-operation and confidence and security-building measures and often find the EU's comprehensive security agenda less immediately relevant to them than national security.[65] Also, individual States and sub-regions alike fear becoming 'lost' in macro-Mediterraneanism or being held back in their relations with the EU by the slow pace of reform in the wider Mediterranean. For example, North African governments seek distinctive relations with the EU in part lest they become marginalised even further in an all-Mediterranean co-operation scheme, which would inevitably be influenced significantly by the MEPP.[66]

In 2004 Maltese Commissioner Joe Borg conceded that 'The Euro-Mediterranean Partnership has struggled to maintain momentum as different sub-regional dynamics in the different parts of the Mediterranean have made it very hard to formulate and deliver a common programme of action among its Members.'[67] This concession leads into the second, related problem for the EU. Does the Union have the necessary framework(s) and leverage to encourage, guide and sustain political, economic and security reform in the Southern Mediterranean? An immediate issue is the policy mix of bi- and multilateralism and the multiplicity of overlapping EU policy frameworks. The bilateralism of ENP has been seen as being at odds with Mediterranean regionalism.[68] A case in point is Israel which, owing to its status as a Western democracy and a developed country tends to favour working with the EU through ENP over EMP because it has less to fear from positive conditionality than do Arab partners.[69] Also, the EU's progressive enlargement of EMP/Union for the Mediterranean has contributed to its Members operating within different expectational environments and under different frameworks. The former ranges from prospective full EU membership through to ENP membership at best. As for the latter, the Commission recently stressed in the context of the Union for the Mediterranean that it would have to be 'complementary to EU bilateral relations with these countries which will continue under existing policy frameworks such as the European Neighbourhood Policy, and, in the case of Mauritania, the African, Caribbean, Pacific framework. It will also be complementary to the regional dimension of EU enlargement policy, which includes the accession negotiations and the pre-accession process. It will also be coherent and complementary with EU–Africa strategy.'[70]

Time will tell whether the Commission can develop what was essentially a national initiative in ways compatible with existing EU policies or whether the Union for the Mediterranean will simply add another layer of complexity and potential tension to EU-Mediterranean relations. However, neither the reform incentives offered through ENP nor the political identity building through EMP currently seem sufficient to convince authoritarian Southern regimes to embark upon meaningful reform processes that potentially undermine their own foundation. Southern Mediterranean States continue to view with suspicion EU regional security initiatives. Thus the EU's security and defence policy was perceived by some as the effective construction of a new border and the creation in the 1990s of EURO-MARFOR and EUROFOR as being potentially directed against Southern Mediterranean countries in a new era of interventionism.[71] EU measures have also been seen widely as preserving the hierarchy between Europe and the Southern Mediterranean States.[72] The Barcelona process did effectively create a hub-and-spoke system that advantaged the EU[73] and ENP, though rhetorically making much of partnership and joint ownership, is highly asymmetric. The policy is of EU design, the Commission judges on progress or otherwise and positive conditionality effectively rewards progress towards EU objectives. At the same time, Southern Mediterranean States have in recent years been somewhat better able to resist external reform pressure. The US-led intervention in Iraq provoked widespread rejection of forcible democratisation. More importantly in the under-powering of ENP and EU Mediterraneanism, EU Member States' increased focus on the political-security dimension of the Euro-Mediterranean partnership and fear of further radical Islam success through the ballot box have simultaneously tempered their reformist zeal and increased impatience for solutions to pressing security problems.

This situation has thrown up some interesting problems. The first is that European Member States' focus is on the political and security aspects of the Barcelona Process/

Union for the Mediterranean and EU-Mediterranean relations have been increasingly securitised in recent years.[74] However, the political-security dimension is precisely the area in which the European Commission concedes least progress has been made.[75] Second, the grindingly slow pace of sectoral horizontal integration and its vulnerability to developments in the wider Middle East has highlighted 'the tension between a policy aiming at functional co-operation and the need to address pressing foreign policy challenges.'[76] Third, the EU is in a position of having rejected US-style imposition of reform but of concomitantly possessing insufficient leverage through EMP and ENP to encourage reform from within. Fourth, securitisation has encouraged an eliding of EU and Southern Mediterranean States' policies. Krause and Latham argued that governments' preference for comprehensive and co-operative security had already been blunted by the development during the 1990s of a 'new discourse of threat and danger' centred on rogue States and WMD proliferation.[77] 9/11 strengthened the perceived nexus between rogue States, WMD proliferation and international terrorism and encouraged a securitisation of policies that pay less attention to human rights and good governance. For example, though the Commission denies that security issues have been emphasised over political rights and freedoms,[78] it does acknowledge that promotion of democracy and human rights 'is complicated by the fact that religious extremism has emerged as a powerful political alternative. ... Freedoms of expression and association are frequently curtailed, mainly by resorting to emergency legislation.'[79] Critics argue that the EU has done little to prevent this process and has shied away from the sustained encouragement of civil society thought by many to be necessary for successful reform in Southern Mediterranean States.[80] As Youngs has observed, 'Partly reflecting political resistance, a lower share of EU aid goes through civil society actors in the Mediterranean than in any other developing region'.[81]

Turning to the third key problem, EU policies towards many Southern Mediterranean States are particularly vulnerable to spill-over from wider Middle East issues, no more so than the Arab–Israeli conflict and tensions over Iran's alleged nuclear weapons programme and its support for radical groups. In respect of the Arab–Israeli conflict, the 2003 ESS stressed that its resolution was a core strategic priority and the European Council acknowledged the following year that without a just and lasting settlement a common zone of peace, prosperity and progress would be unattainable.[82] As for Iran, analysts began warning in 2005 that it was seeking for the first time in 2000 years to play a military role in the Eastern Mediterranean.[83] In 2006 the Bush administration pinpointed Iran as arguably the greatest single threat that America faced.[84] And in 2008 the Solana review of the ESS acknowledged Iran's importance to peace in the Middle East and Afghanistan, warned that Iran's nuclear programme represented a danger for regional stability and the wider non-proliferation system, and stated bluntly that an Iranian nuclear military capability 'would be a threat to EU security that cannot be accepted'.[85] In addition, of course, Iran is a key player in hydrocarbons. This enables Teheran to insulate itself to an extent from external pressure by buying strategic security from Moscow and Beijing especially and intensifying its relations with other regional partners.[86]

The EU has in recent years adopted a more prominent role in both the MEPP and the international handling of Iran. It is part of the Quartet, has a Special Representative for the MEPP, and helped appoint former British Prime Minister Tony Blair as the Middle East Envoy. It supports the peace process through numerous civil society and confidence-building mechanisms, including the solar energy for peace project between the EC, Israel and the Palestinian Authority and the Partnership for Peace, successor to the people-to-people programme.[87] The EU provides substantial humanitarian and reconstruction assistance. For instance, the Palestinians received approximately 2.4 billion euros from a range of programmes between 2000 and 2007,[88] and in the wake of Israel's three week offensive in Gaza in December 2008 to January 2009 the EU reportedly promised the Palestinians a further $556 million.[89] Furthermore, EU troops provided the bulk of UNFIL in Lebanon in 2006 and at the end of 2008 the Union had three live ESDP missions in the Middle East, namely EUPOL COPPS (Palestine), EUJUSTLEX (Iraq) and EUBAM (Rafah).

As for Iran, the EU initiated a critical dialogue in 1995 and upgraded this two years later to a comprehensive dialogue that provided for regular discussions on global and regional issues (including terrorism, human rights, proliferation and the MEPP) and on areas of potential co-operation, such as drugs, energy, trade and investment. From October 2003 through to Iran's referral to the UN Security Council in February 2006, the EU3 took the initiative in seeking a diplomatic solution with Teheran of its nuclear programme. This may have influenced the Bush administration against precipitate military strikes on Iranian nuclear and defence facilities. It also bought temporary respite insofar as Iran agreed to suspend uranium enrichment, sign the additional protocol to the NPT and, in the Paris Agreement of 15 November 2004, confirmed its intention not to seek nuclear weapons.[90] In August 2005 the EU offered Iran its 'readiness to support the development of a safe, economically viable and proliferation-proof civilian nuclear programme in Iran in the context of objective guarantees provided by Iran'.[91] It has subsequently continued its 'dual track' approach, albeit the emphasis has generally been on tighter sanctions given Iran's resumption of uranium conversion and enrichment in 2005/06 and the IAEA's report in February 2009 that Teheran possessed a metric ton of low enriched uranium – technically sufficient to produce a nuclear weapon.[92]

Ultimately, though, little progress has been made in either the MEPP or in resolving the challenges posed by Iran. Moreover, this has helped reveal two negative things for the EU. First, the EU has had very limited success in managing spill-over from Middle East problems into its relations with the Southern Mediterranean States. The Union has tried to separate the Barcelona Process from the Palestinian–Israeli issue especially in order to avoid progress on its wider agenda with Southern Mediterranean States being held hostage to the vagaries of the MEPP. This is sensible given the seemingly intractable nature of the Palestinian–Israeli conflict but while better able than the Euro–Arab Dialogue in preventing politics from de-railing economic co-operation,[93] progress has still been slowed by political and security problems.[94] Moreover, the separation of the Barcelona Process and the Middle East conflict has always been tenuous[95]and it became harder still after the 2004 enlargement and

Turkey's securing of candidate status given that EMP partners thereafter constituted only the Mediterranean Arab States and Israel.[96] Though the expanded membership of the Union for the Mediterranean now weakens the Arab–Israeli dichotomy in EU-Mediterranean regionalism, the fact remains that it is not possible to decouple it from the MEPP. In 2008 even the Commission conceded that 'the persistence of the conflict in the Middle East has challenged and stretched the Partnership to the limits of its abilities to preserve the channels of dialogue among all partners.'[97]

Second, the EU remains very much a junior partner to the US in the Middle East. This, and the permeability of Mediterranean–Middle East agendas, renders the EU's policies in the Mediterranean vulnerable to the vagaries of US foreign policy and to the temper of transatlantic relations. The EU debacle caused by US-led intervention in Iraq in March 2003 is the most obvious and severe example of this. However, there are numerous other instances too, including Operation Desert Fox in December 1998 and Britain's conforming in 2006 with the US in delaying the call for a ceasefire in the Lebanon, which belied the EU's apparent success in generating 7,000 peace-keeping troops from five nations for UNFIL. There are also broad US–EU differences in the Middle East. The EU is more influenced by geographic proximity and while traditionally the US tends to favour Israel, the Europeans have been more sympathetic to the Palestinians.[98] Furthermore, though the EU and US each (officially) rejects the status quo in the Middle East and Mediterranean[99] and broadly subscribe to similar objectives, their co-operation is hindered by their operating within different strategic frameworks and having different policy emphases.

In the aftermath of the Cold War, European perceptions of the Mediterranean shifted from its being Europe's Southern flank and a marginal theatre to being an extension of the European security environment. This fed an inclination to treat it as a distinct region, not least because proximity rendered its diffuse security threats particularly salient to the Union. However, the US has come to view the Mediterranean as an extension of the European and the Middle Eastern security environments.[100] This is reflected in its foreign and security policy bureaucratic arrangements. As Lesser noted in 2004, 'At a time when many of America's partners in Europe and the Middle East have established bureaus focused on Mediterranean issues, the American state and defense departments, as well as the analytic branches of the intelligence community, remain firmly divided between Europe on the one hand, and the Middle East (actually "Near East and South Asia"), on the other.'[101] Subsequently it seems that American strategic conceptions of the Mediterranean region are becoming even less distinct as it is gathered together in a larger regional threat 'entity', something the Bush administration sought to capture in its conception of a 'Greater Middle East' and that is essentially an arc of crisis spanning from West Africa through the Mediterranean to the Gulf and on to South and Central Asia. Indeed, the knitting together of previously distinct regional theatres into functional (threat) entities is further suggested in the early Obama era with National Security Advisor General James L. Jones resurrecting the Near East and South Asia office at the National Security Council and staffing it with three senior directors instead of the one in place at the beginning of the Bush administration.[102]

Washington views the Mediterranean principally through the global war on terrorism, and addresses it as a part of the more expansive arc of crisis. The EU views the Mediterranean primarily through a regional neighbourhood prism and geographic proximity determines that its principal concerns include, but are much wider than, counter-terrorism. In terms of policy emphases, the US demonstrates much weaker commitment than the EU to collective frameworks of governance, despite its launch in December 2002 of the US–Middle East Partnership Initiative,[103] Bush's proposal in May 2003 for a US–Middle East Free Trade Area by 2013, and American sponsorship in June 2004 of the G-8 'Partnership for Progress and a Common Future with the Broader Middle East and North Africa'.[104] Also, and reflecting their different strategic frameworks, the EU tends to use its trade agreements to promote regional and intraregional trade while the US tends to use them to promote global economic integration and to reward and consolidate geo-strategic allies.[105]

Conclusion

In December 2008 Javier Solana described the EU as 'an anchor of stability'.[106] His analogy was evidently to how the EU provides security for its citizens and neighbours. However, an anchor is also tied to something and from a security perspective there are few things more problematic for the Union to be tied to than the Southern Mediterranean States and, by extension, the Middle East.

Successive and prospective enlargements, together with the revised post-Cold War security agenda, have drawn the EU progressively deeper into Mediterranean security to the point that it is now the region's leading security actor. The Union's size and proximity give it unrivalled gravitational pull upon the Southern littoral States and its combination of multilateral regionalism and structured bilateralism is probably the optimum approach. In addition, other European security institutions have secured limited purchase in the Mediterranean and the US has in relative terms traditionally been little interested in the region *per se*, viewing it as the space between the two more important theatres of Europe and the Middle East.

That said, can the Union for the Mediterranean deliver the promised improved visibility, co-ownership and results-orientated programmes? Possibly, but the omens are not good.[107] At the time of writing much remained to be done to operationalise the Union, for the Mediterranean and Arab States were refusing to sit alongside Israel on account of the 2008–9 military campaign in Gaza. Also, the initiative remains based on a formula of trade plus investment plus co-operation that has changed little and delivered relatively little in twenty years of promoting comprehensive security with and between the Southern Mediterranean States. Even leaving aside the EU's co-ordination and delivery problems and the internal strategic tensions between its Member States, it is doubtful whether ENP has sufficient positive attraction to lever reluctant Arab authoritarian regimes voluntarily into Western-style political and economic liberalisation. The EU also faces a very long haul in building a common security dialogue and a virtually new Mediterranean regionalism given the region's vast political, security and socio-economic differences, the strength of sub-regional dynamics and the low level of Mediterranean political identity next to Arab and Islamic identities in particular. Even reforms already made by EU partners in the Union for the Mediterranean remain vulnerable both to events in the Middle East and to domestic tensions, something demonstrated by the successful military coup in Mauritania in August 2008. Moreover, the hierarchy of privilege in the EU's relations with Southern Mediterranean States could have the effect of fracturing the region further.

The Union also faces some difficult dilemmas. Short-term security needs of EU Member States clash increasingly with the comprehensive security agenda. Reform processes within unstable authoritarian regimes could spin out of control, resulting in regional destabilisation and/or the emergence of more democratically legitimate but hostile radical Islamic governments. Also, functional integration is ill-suited to 'resolving' urgent foreign and security policy issues, especially given its apparent inability to encourage more than glacially paced reform when working across normative divides. Securitisation of EU–Mediterranean relations thus threatens to transform inclusive EU–Mediterranean regionalism into exclusive border management and to encourage downplaying of the normative agenda in favour of selective security co-operation based on coincidences of interest with the Southern Mediterranean States. Furthermore, while the EU focuses on a distinctive Mediterranean political identity, its most important security partner, the US, is moving further away from this concept as it looks towards the arc of crisis spanning from West Africa through the Mediterranean to the Gulf and on to South and Central Asia. Therefore, while the predominance of the US in Middle Eastern security and the permeability of the Mediterranean and Middle East mean that the success of the EU's Mediterranean security agenda rests in part upon co-operation with the US, the likelihood of securing close co-ordination with Washington is uncertain. Transatlantic relations have helped seriously and repeatedly divide the EU over Middle East questions in recent years and even a more multilaterally inclined Obama administration is unlikely to significantly weaken support of Israel as it builds strongholds for a new security perimeter fence.

The EU remains committed to the ideal of comprehensive security in the Mediterranean and convinced of the basic formula of past policies there. It also (rightfully) emphasises that full engagement by the Southern partners is necessary to deliver the objectives set out in the Barcelona process. Nevertheless, the Union has slipped increasingly into a position whereby it is seemingly unwilling to impose reform, unable to leverage it decisively from within and even uncertain about reform generally because of its Member States' short-term security priorities and the risk of unleashing uncontrollable radical change. With the Washington consensus questioned increasingly and the ENP and Mediterranean regionalism both underpowered in the context of the very limited progress to date and the fragile extant security situation, it seems likely that the Mediterranean – and by extension the Middle East – will remain the wildest frontier within the EU's neighbourhood for the foreseeable future.

9

CONCLUSION

The period covered in this book has been one of profound change in international relations generally and international security specifically. The end of the Cold War delivered huge geo-strategic shifts and 9/11 proceeded to reconfigure the global relations of the US. The costs of post-9/11 American foreign policy and accelerating globalisation induced further changes in the balance of power around the world. Within 20 years of the end of the Cold War the world went from the 'unipolar moment' to an era of multipolarity or, even, non-polarity. The rise of countries like Brazil, Russia, India and China (BRICs) is moving the fulcrum of power from West to East and the post-World War Two Western-styled architecture of international organisations is becoming increasingly strained and anachronistic in the face of shifting patterns of wealth, military power and influence.

Security has become much harder for actors to provide. An era for the West in which it has been freed from the threat of Armageddon has had diverse consequences for its constituent elements. Widespread and inconclusive debate has raged about the principal referents of Western security: the state, society or the individual. Threat perceptions and strategic priorities have unravelled within the Western Alliance. The absence of mortal danger has been offset by experiences of costly interventions, insurgencies and protracted state reconstruction efforts. These have served to sap the will of many Western countries to maintain critical investment in ever more expensive defence platforms and force structures, as well as the political will to undertake expeditionary operations. The removal of Cold War overlay has unleashed underlying conflicts and revealed critical fault lines, including wealth, religion and civilization. Western norms are increasingly re-interpreted or rejected by emerging centres of global power.

Within these upheavals Europe's place in the world and the security challenges it faces have changed dramatically. Europe is less central in the global distribution of power and this trend is likely to accelerate in the future. Amidst US security priorities, focus has switched from the defence of Europe to regions further afield such as the Caucasus, the Middle East and Asia. As European States examine their own security challenges, they have found it harder to prioritise between a resurgent Russia and issues rising up from their North African and Mediterranean neighbourhoods. The security agenda is both internal and external in nature and challenges emanate from sub- and non-state actors as well as from States. Traditional threats still exist, such as inter-ethnic conflict, the potential proliferation of weapons of mass destruction in the Middle East and the vulnerability of energy supplies from adjacent territories. But they have been supplemented by concerns such as the increase in illegal immigration from poor countries and the radicalisation of ethnic groupings and diaspora communities.

Placed in this context we have argued throughout this book that in a number of areas the EU has done remarkably well in transforming itself into a meaningful regional security actor and in exerting a considerable stabilising force across large swathes of Central, Southern and Eastern Europe. This owes much to recognition by EU Member States of the added security value they see the Union providing in the realisation of their objectives. This is attested to by the growing number of security tasks that the Union has been fulfilling. On European soil, the EU has taken over from NATO missions in Bosnia and in Kosovo. Outside Europe, EU personnel have undertaken operations on two occasions in the Democratic Republic of Congo, in Chad, in Aceh and in the Palestinian Occupied Territories. The increase in the number of EU agencies – such as Europol, Eurojust and Frontex – further supports this contention. Not only have these bodies been active in developing linkages between Union Members, but they have also been employed to reach out to third countries in order to draw them into patterns of virtuous co-operation.

The growing role of the EU reflects its evolution into a multi-dimensional security actor. Its influence stems partly from the fact that it is a value community, championing democracy, market economics, the rule of law and human rights. This is an important role in its own right as it upholds a particular set of priorities within the international system. It encourages other States to resolve their disputes peacefully, to engage in economic intercourse that fosters interdependence between countries and to protect the rights of their own citizens. The EU has been able to model this type of behaviour because it has embodied these values amongst its own Member States. The principles upon which the Union has been built and its demonstrable success in overcoming past antipathies among its Members have become a source of attraction to the wider international community.

The EU has drawn upon its full range of instruments to realise its security objectives. Because its principal source of power resides in its economic and trading influence, it has used this to exert compliance over neighbouring countries. For instance, all trade agreements have contained readmission policies for the return of failed asylum seekers or counter-terrorism clauses to ensure co-operation with both the EU and the United Nations. The Union has accorded Europol an external function in developing information and technology sharing with countries that are host to organised crime groups. It has provided specialist advice and the secondment of officials to work on legislation in target countries to counteract criminal activity and corrupt practices. The EU has also been willing to provide technical assistance and hardware to help countries with border management, whether in relation to illegal immigration, counter-narcotics trafficking or counter-terrorism.

A military component has been added to the EU's civilian power instruments. This has excited considerable controversy amongst analysts and encouraged a debate about the Union as a new sort of 'imperial power'. Though the scale of its military power remains modest, the EU has been able to mobilise other assets such as its contribution of expertise and resources to civilian crisis management and post-conflict stabilisation and reconstruction. Its pioneering work in these fields was derided in the past by the US, which regarded it as a poor substitute for a larger contribution to expeditionary operations. Recent experience, however, in Afghanistan and Iraq, has taught Western governments of the need to develop a wider range of capabilities beyond that of the spearhead military formations. Since the creation of ESDP (and its successor CSDP), the Union has developed a hybrid range of capabilities that are relevant to complex emergencies. Law enforcement officers, administrators and judges are just some of the many professionals available for rapid mobilisation. The EU has gone on to perform a range of missions drawing upon these skills, including security sector reform and rule of law missions – sometimes in zones where traditional state intervention would have been seen as inflammatory. For example, the post-conflict monitoring mission in Georgia demonstrated the capability of the EU to conduct an operation in a theatre where US or NATO participation would have been too sensitive.

It is no exaggeration to claim that the EU has come to contribute effectively to different types of security, in different ways, in Central and Eastern Europe, the Western Balkans, the Mediterranean and in North Africa. Its contribution has been unique and its influence has extended outwards in concentric circles. These circles mirror the degree of intimacy that the Union has been prepared to countenance with the States concerned and generally diminish with distance. This reflects the EU's two principal sources of influence, namely its process of enlargement and its economic muscle. In relation to enlargement, its influence has derived from the conditionality of membership, by insisting that countries reshape their domestic systems in order to comply with the *acquis communitaire*. Its economic strength has given the Union a range of inducements to tempt countries without an accession perspective to comply with its requests.

The EU has sought to export its own experience and values to States within its region and their absorption of these values promises the greatest amount of security for the Union's Members. Aside from the 1995 enlargement, the countries of which were already closely associated with the EU through the European Free Trade Association, the Central and East European countries were the earliest candidates for accession to the EU. The EU's influence with the latter countries was strong and it has successfully projected its values onto them. By creating stringent enlargement criteria and monitoring progress through an intrusive oversight regime, the CEECs were successfully modelled to conform to the EU. Where the policy of enlargement has not been immediately, or even ever, available, the EU has been required to develop alternative policies, notably the European Neighbourhood Policy. It has offered such countries the prospect of deeper integration with the Union, short of membership.

Hard times ahead?

In spite of the difficulties that the Union faced during the 1990s, it may be that it is nearing the end of its easiest phase as a security actor. This sobering conclusion is drawn from a number of contributory considerations. First, the Union has all but exhausted its willingness to enlarge. The EU is pushing up against perceived limits of European identity, albeit there remains some (debilitating) ambiguity in respect of certain Eastern partnership countries. Turkey is the biggest immediate enlargement issue and there is deep-seated opposition to its becoming a full EU Member, irre-spective of its candidate status and the strategic advantages it could offer. The Union is also exhibiting disturbing signs of enlargement fatigue in the face of the costs of past enlargements, concerns about institutional effectiveness and the potentially difficult and contentious future enlargements in train. Even among some of the foremost EU powers, such as France and Germany, there is a growing reluctance to embrace a new wave of enlargement. The perceived failure of the Union to honour pledges to assist the accession of Balkan countries risks setting back the region's post-conflict reconciliation and reconstruction. While renewed widespread conflict is currently unlikely, Kosovo could remain indefinitely an expensive EU protectorate and the wider region could slip into decline.

The second key problem is that past and prospective enlargements have moved and will move the EU further into more difficult territory. Its new neighbourhood is less secure, less receptive to EU norms and more dangerous than the CEECs ever were. Russia is the obvious challenge as it champions its own political and development model in contrast to the Union's and pursues hard power priorities and sphere-of-influence objectives that are rejected by Brussels. However, States such as Azerbaijan, Belarus and even Ukraine have been ambivalent at best about engaging in the reform agenda advocated by the Union. The ability of the EU, in the absence of enlargement, to change behaviour in countries such as these appears very limited. The Union would face even more profound challenges upon its borders were Turkey to finally achieve its objective of full membership.

Third, there is the question of political will, and here the Union encounters numerous problems. These include the challenges of implementing the Lisbon Treaty and the euro crisis brought on by the near collapse of the Greek economy. In addition, the rapid enlargement of the Union in an era of little conceivable mortal threat has encouraged strategic dissonance. The Union for the Mediterranean and Eastern Partnership initiatives reflect the trade-offs at the heart of the EU necessary to garner support for specific regional interests. The more disparate these regional interests become, and the further away they are from the central interests of the EU's leading powers, the harder it is to sustain political will. The reluctance to let the EU speak on behalf of its Members in foreign and security matters is reflected in the complexity of the organisation's structure and its experience of paralysis during times of tension. The appointments of Baroness Catherine Ashton and Herman van Rompuy to the positions of High Representative and EU President, respectively, underline the unwillingness of Member States to appoint high profile individuals who might eclipse the role of national foreign ministers.

Finally, and closely related to political will, the EU faces critical challenges in developing the assets, especially military, to meet its legal and rhetorical commitments. Major weaknesses include a shortage of heavy-lift aircraft, limited intelligence capability, a lack of command, control and communications assets and a paucity of precision-guided munitions. Many European countries face brutal spending cuts to rebalance national finances in the wake of the global economic crisis. Even the Union's most able and committed military powers, such as the UK and France, are reducing defence spending. Their defence agreements in November 2010 marked recognition of inability to hold the status quo let alone develop military capabilities to fulfill the EU's Petersberg tasks. Member States will also likely be deterred from embarking upon expensive expeditionary missions and there is no evidence that the EU foresees such a capability being available to it in the future. Capability development coordination with NATO is at best limited and the Berlin Plus arrangements need further examination. Though the EU has conducted operations at long distances from its Member States, it has done so with only small numbers, in a relatively benign environment and with strictly limited objectives. These limitations are likely to continue and meeting upper end demands of the Petersberg tasks will most probably remain beyond the Union.

It is also the case that the Union is finding the European security landscape more challenging. It is increasingly affected by blowback from events in the Middle East, Iraq and the Israeli–Palestine issues especially but also from, for instance, reaction to Iran's nuclear programme. In 2008 at least thirteen countries throughout the greater Middle East announced new or revived plans to explore civilian nuclear energy. Russia's resurgence and the failure of the strategic partnership to gain significant purchase in EU–Russia relations is creating a sharp zone of normative, economic and strategic competition between Europe's two leading indigenous powers. Russia's military campaign against Georgia signalled strongly Moscow's intent to re-establish by whatever means necessary its European sphere of influence and to resist the further spread of EU/transatlantic influence into its backyard. Military conflict between Russia and the EU is almost inconceivable but there remain many areas of tension and obstacles to closer cooperation.

The EU is also being impacted in numerous ways by the accelerating American shift of focus away from the EU's Eurocentric priorities. America intervened militarily in Bosnia and Kosovo but its reluctance to play a leading role in re-constructing these countries was an illustration of its desire to avoid long-term commitments to the region. This was evident in the hand-over period between the presidencies of Bill Clinton and George W. Bush when the incoming administration began to signal that it wanted to withdraw all US combat forces from the Balkans. Again, in the run up to the 2003 War against Iraq some American forces were removed from Germany and never returned. Washington has wanted its European allies to take the lead role in their own affairs and to contribute effectively to pressing global security issues such as the proliferation of weapons of mass destruction and the collapse of countries into 'failed States'. However, this has revealed sharp differences between the two sides. European countries have preferred to engage in a critical dialogue with States such as Iran, Libya and Syria, rather than isolate and attempt to de-stabilise them. In the latter part of the 1990s, the transatlantic allies diverged very publicly over the American policy of applying extra-territorial sanctions; the Union even threatened legal action before the World Trade Organisation. Iran's alleged nuclear weapons programme has the potential to again divide the EU and US over the optimum course of action.

The post-9/11 response to international terrorism further illustrated contending EU–US approaches and mutual suspicions. The US declared a 'War on Terror' and was determined to take the fight militarily to its adversaries. It argued the need for 'pre-emptive' operations, on the grounds that the threat was too great to wait until it was visited upon the American homeland. The majority of EU States were wary of using the terminology of war to counter terrorism, preferring instead to emphasise intelligence, law enforcement and criminal prosecution. They were fearful, justifiably in the event, that the US would undermine the legitimacy of its own case by heavy-handed action. This was to prove the case as the Abu Ghraib and Guantanamo Bay detention centres, extraordinary rendition and the use of torture became a stain upon America's reputation. In the meantime, the US regarded the EU's emphasis upon acting under a United Nations mandate as a deliberate attempt to constrain America's freedom of action. This was also seen to stem from European weakness, an inability to use military force that made governments within the EU cling to multilateralism to hide their own inadequacies. Conversely, many in Europe saw the George W. Bush administrations as being determined to (re)assert American hegemony. France went as far as to argue that the war against Iraq proved the need for a multipolar world order in which one power was not dominant.

The challenge for the future will be to rebuild trust within the EU–US relationship and develop a partnership around shared strategic goals. The Obama administration has taken steps to reinvigorate the transatlantic partnership and has talked up America's relations with the EU. The EU recognises that the US remains its key international partner. But for as long as the two sides remain focused on different priorities, the common ground between them will be limited. In this sense, the unimpressive EU role in training the Afghan police suggests that the Union is a long way from focusing on America's global security agenda. It also remains the case that US policies towards Europe will likely continue to have some cross-socialisation effects with those of the EU, influence Russia's relationship with the Union in unpredictable ways and affect the relative smoothness or otherwise of relations between the EU's Atlanticist- and Europeanist-inclined Members.

To truly harness the potential of its international presence the EU needs to develop greater unity; additional and more integrated capabilities; a clearer sense of strategic priorities; improved relations with the US and a more effective policy mix towards its ENP partners. The evolving nature of security challenges also requires EU States to find new and innovative ways of working together to address insecurities that will, to varying extents, impact upon all of them. This means choosing the appropriate institutional framework to facilitate common action as well as looking for imaginative solutions to problems.

It would be a bold pundit that would forecast that the Union will meet these demands. The EU is still in the process of carving space for itself within the European security architecture, an architecture that is still contested by Moscow and viewed with varying degrees of suspicion by Washington. The EU will also likely be preoccupied for a while in implementing the Lisbon Treaty and will find rapid internal reform and capability development even more difficult than in the past. At the same time, EU Member States are likely to cling to national sovereignty and in the majority remain Eurocentric in their preoccupations. The absence of anything more than a putative EU strategic culture points to continuing intra-EU divisions on key issues and at moments of international crisis. This likelihood is underscored by EU States' inability to better cohere consistently in the face of Russia's resurgence.

The EU will remain an important security actor and continue to adapt and evolve. However, though it often articulates its policies in universal terms, the Union will likely be confined to acting predominantly locally. It is also likely that compared to its experience with the CEECs, the results of EU efforts to project security into its new neighbourhood will in the future be more limited and positive results slower in coming. Engagement, socialisation and positive conditionality are inherently long-term approaches but these have worked best where coupled with the lure of membership. Countries that have no prospect of EU membership have been the most resistant to the Union's security demands – and EU Members are aware that the most proximate and potent security threats currently emanate from these very regions where their influence is weakest. These threats are complex in nature, ranging from migration to drug trafficking, a proliferation of organised crime and transnational terrorism. The experience to date of ENP suggests that in the face of this the EU will struggle in trying to draw the security policies of its more geographically distant and normatively different neighbours into harmony with its own priorities.

NOTES

Chapter 1 Introduction: The nature of security

1 B. Buzan *People, States and Fear: The National Security Problem in International Relations*, Brighton: Harvester Wheatsheaf, 1983.
2 B. Buzan, O. Waever and J. de Wilde *Security: A New Framework for Analysis*, Boulder and Colorado: Lynne Reinner Publishers, 1998.
3 R. Jervis *Perception and Misperception in International Politics*, Princeton NJ: Princeton University Press, 1976.
4 B. Buzan, *op. cit.*, 1983, pp. 24–26.
5 See E. Brimmer 'From territorial security to societal security: Implications for the transatlantic strategic outlook', in E. Brimmer, (ed.) *Transforming Homeland Security: US and European Approaches*, Center for Transatlantic Relations, Washington DC: John Hopkins University, 2006, pp. 23–42.
6 United Nations Development Programme, 'Human Development Report 1994', Oxford and New York: Oxford University Press.
7 P. Kerr 'Human security' in A. Collins, (ed.) *Contemporary Security Studies*, Oxford: Oxford University Press, 2007.
8 B. Giegerich 'European Military Crisis Management: Connecting Ambition and Reality', *Adelphi Paper 397*, Abingdon: Routledge, 2008, p. 37
9 K. Deutsch *Political Community and the North Atlantic Area: International Organization in the Light of Historical Experience*, Princeton NJ: Princeton University Press, 1957. Security communities have been defined as 'transnational regions comprised of sovereign States whose people maintain dependable expectations of peaceful change'. E. Adler and M. Barnett, eds *Security Communities,* Cambridge: Cambridge University Press, 1998, p. 30.
10 P. Cornish and G. Edwards 'The strategic culture of the European Union: A progress report', *International Affairs*, 81, 4, 2005.
11 A. Toje *America, the EU and Strategic Culture: Renegotiating the Transatlantic Bargain*, London: Routledge, 2008, p. 21: C. Meyer *The Quest for a European Strategic Culture: Changing Norms on Security and Defence in the European Union*, Basingstoke: Palgrave Macmillan, 2006.
12 European Council 'The European Security Strategy: A Secure Europe in a Better World', Brussels, 12 December, 2003.

13 R. Smith *The Utility of Force: The Art of War in the Modern World*, New York: Alfred A. Knopf, 2007 .

14 R. Hunter 'NATO and the European Union: Inevitable partners', in Serfaty, S. (ed.) *Visions of the Atlantic Alliance. The United States, the European Union and NATO,* Significant Issues Series, Volume 27, No. 8, Washington DC: Center for Strategic and International Studies, 2005, p. 60.

15 J. Howorth *Security and Defence Policy in the European Union*, Basingstoke and New York: Palgrave Macmillan, 2007, p. 129.

16 V. Nuland US Ambassador to NATO Victoria Nuland, Speech to the Press Club and American Chamber of Commerce, Paris, 22 February, 2008.

17 United Nations Report of the High Level Panel on Threats, Challenges and Change, report to the UN General Assembly, New York, December, 2004.

18 I. Daalder and J. Lindsay *America Unbound: The Bush Revolution in Foreign Policy*, Washington DC: Brookings Institution Press, 2003.

19 European Council 'EU Strategy against Proliferation of Weapons of Mass Destruction', Thessaloniki, Greece, December, 2003, http://www.consilium.europa.eu/uedocs/cms Upload/st15708.en03.pdf.

20 S. Kutchesfahani 'Iran's nuclear challenge and European diplomacy', *European Policy Centre Paper 46*, Brussels, March, 2006.

21 *The Economist* 'Sanctions begin to bite', 9 October, 2010, p. 27.

22 *United States National Security Strategy* Washington DC: The White House, 2002.

23 European Council, European Security Strategy *op. cit.* 2003.

24 M. Singer and A. Wildavsky *The Real World Order: Zones of Peace, Zones of Turmoil*, New Jersey: Chatham House Publishers, 1993.

25 The Petersberg Declaration Western European Union Council of Ministers, Bonn, 19 June, 1992.

26 D. Keohane 'The absent friend: EU foreign policy and counter-terrorism', *Journal of Common Market Studies*, 46, 1, 2008, pp. 125–46.

27 V. Mitsilegas, J. Monar and W. Rees, *The European Union and Internal Security: Guardian of the People?* Palgrave: Basingstoke, 2003.

28 A. Geddes *Immigration and European Integration. Towards Fortress Europe?* Manchester: Manchester University Press, 2000.

29 S. Simon and D. Benjamin 'America and the New Terrorism', *Survival*, 42, 1, 2000, Spring, pp. 59–75.

30 M. Dittrich 'Muslims in Europe: Addressing the Challenges of Radicalisation', Brussels: European Policy Centre, 2006. http://www.epc.eu; J. Shapiro and D. Byman 'Bridging the Transatlantic Counterterrorism Gap', *The Washington Quarterly*, 29, 4, Autumn, 2006, p. 34.

31 O. Roy 'Euro-Islam: The Jihad within', *The National Interest*, Spring, 2003, p. 64.

32 *United States National Strategy for Homeland Security* Washington DC: The Whitehouse, 2002.

33 A. Cottey *Security in the New Europe*, Basingstoke: Palgrave Macmillan, 2007, p. 192.

34 J. Nye *The Paradox of American Power*, New York: Oxford University Press, 2002.

35 E. Kirchner and J. Sperling *EU Security Governance*, Manchester: Manchester University Press, 2007.

36 European Council, European Security Strategy, *op. cit.*, 2003.

37 Barcelona Report of the Study Group on Europe's Security Capabilities 'A Human Security Doctrine for Europe', 15 September, 2004, quoted in J. Matlary, 'Much ado about little: the EU and human security', *International Affairs*, 84: 1, p. 139.

38 J. Kotsopoulos 'A human security agenda for Europe?' *European Policy Centre Issue Paper 48*, June, 2006, p. 12.

39 M. Kaldor, M. Martin and S. Selchow 'Human security: a new strategic narrative for Europe', *International Affairs*, 83: 2, 2006, pp. 273–88, at p. 273.

40 See H. Mayer 'Is it still called "Chinese whispers? The EU's rhetoric and action as a responsible global institution', *International Affairs*, 84: 1, 2008, pp. 61–79, at p. 61.

41 See, for example, S. Werthes and D. Bosold 'Caught between pretension and substantiveness: ambiguities of Human Security as a political leitmotif', in T. Debiel and S. Werthes, (eds) *Human Security on foreign policy agendas, changes, concepts and cases,* INEF Report 80/2006, pp. 21–38, http://209.85.229.132/search?q=cache:_ fcTilfaXPEJ:inef. uni-due.de/page/documents/Report80.pdf+Tobias+Debiel+and+Sascha+Werthes+ eds,+Human+Security+on+foreign+policy+agendas,+changes,+concepts+and+cases& cd=1&hl=en&ct=clnk&gl=uk.
42 The Brandt Report 'North–South: A Programme for Survival', Report of the Independent Commission on International Development Issues, Cambridge: MIT Press, 1980.
43 C. McInnes 'Health', in P. Williams, (ed.) *Security Studies: An Introduction*, London: Routledge, 2008, p. 275.
44 B. Kellman *Bioviolence: Preventing Biological Terror and Crime*, Cambridge: Cambridge University Press, 2007.
45 O. Babarinde 'The European Union's Relations with the South: a commitment to development?' in C. Rhodes (ed.) *The EU in the World Community*. Boulder, CO: Lynne Rienner, 1998, p. 130.
46 A. Cottey (2007) *op. cit.* p. 197.
47 T. Terriff, S. Croft, L. James and P. Morgan *Security Studies Today*, Cambridge: Polity Press, 1999, p. 120.
48 M. Paterson 'Post-hegemonic climate politics?' *The British Journal of Politics and International Relations*, 11, 1, February, 2009, p. 141.
49 *The Economist* (2009) 'Pipe down: Russia, Ukraine and gas', 10 January.
50 T. Terriff, S. Croft, L. James and P. Morgan, *op. cit.*, 1999, p. 132.

Chapter 2 The EU and Internal Security

1 V. Mitsilegas, J. Monar and W. Rees, *The European Union and Internal Security: Guardian of the People?* Basingstoke: Palgrave, 2003, pp. 10–15.
2 *Ibid.*, pp. 23 and 25.
3 F. Ateaga, 'The EU's Internal Security Strategy', ARI 75/2010, Real Instituto Elcano, 8 July 2010, http://www.realinstitutoelcano.org/wps/portal/rielcano_eng.
4 P. Chalk, *Non-Military Security and Global Order: The Impact of Extremism, Violence and Chaos on National and International Security*, Basingstoke: Macmillan, 2000, p. 178.
5 D. Spence, 'Introduction', in Spence, D. (ed.) *The European Union and Terrorism*, London: John Harper Publishing, 2007, p. 19.
6 S. Stetter, *EU Foreign and Interior Policies. Cross-pillar Politics and the Social Construction of Sovereignty*, London and New York: Routledge, 2007.
7 Title VI, Article 29, Treaty of European Union.
8 European Council Presidency Conclusions, Tampere, Finland, 15–16 October, 1999.
9 *Ibid.*
10 European Council Presidency Conclusions, Gothenburg, Sweden, June, 2001.
11 E. Collet, (2006) 'Foreword', in S. Bertozzi, and E. Pastore, *Towards a Common European Asylum Policy*, Multicultural Europe, European Policy Centre Paper No. 49, October, Brussels, p. 5.
12 European Council 15–16 October, 1999, *op. cit.* Paragraph 5.
13 European Council 'The Hague Programme: Strengthening Freedom, Security and Justice in the European Union', Official Journal, C 53, March 2005, pp. 1–14. The Hague Programme was superseded in 2010 by the Stockholm Programme.
14 M. den Boer, 'New dimensions in EU police-cooperation: The Hague milestones for what they are worth', in J. Zwaan, de and R. Goudappel (eds) *Freedom, Security and Justice in the European Union: Implementation of the Hague Programme*, The Hague: TMC Asser Press, 2006, p. 223.

15 D. Hamilton, 'The Lisbon Treaty: Implications for future relations between the European Union and the United States', Testimony to the House Committee on Foreign Affairs, Subcommittee on Europe, 15 December, 2009.

16 F. Ateaga, *op. cit.*, 2010.

17 B. Buzan, O. Waever and de J. Wilde, *Security: A New Framework for Analysis*, Boulder and London: Lynne Reinner, 1998; J. Huysmans, 'The European Union and the securitization of migration', *Journal of Common Market Studies*, 38, 5, 2000, 751–77 and J. Huysmans, *The Politics of Insecurity: Fear, Migration and Asylum in the EU*, London: Routledge, 2006.

18 E. Kirchner and J. Sperling, *EU Security Governance*, Manchester: Manchester University Press, 2007, p. 125.

19 E. Ucarer, 'Justice and Home Affairs', in M. Cini and N. P-S. Borragan (eds) *European Union Politics*, (Third Edition) Oxford: Oxford University Press, 2010, p. 317.

20 R. Boyes, 'Villa called Freedom where migrants wait in search for haven', *The Times*, 13 February, 2010, 52–53.

21 C. Boswell, 'The "external dimension" of EU immigration and asylum policy', *International Affairs*, 79, 3, 2003, p. 626.

22 *Economist, The* 'When East meets West', 22 November, 2003, p. 14.

23 F. Schimmelfennig and U. Sedelmeier, 'Governance by conditionality: EU rule transfer to the candidate countries of Central and Eastern Europe', *Journal of European Public Policy*, 11, 4, August, 2004, p. 671.

24 J. Apap and A. Tchorbadjijska, 'What about the Neighbours? The Impact of Schengen along the EU's External Borders', Centre for European Policy Studies, *Working Document No. 210*, October, 2004, http://www.ceps.be, p. 2.

25 European Council 'Seville Presidency Conclusions', Brussels, 24 October, 2002.

26 European Commission EU–Russia Common Space on Freedom, Security and Justice, Progress Report 2007, March, 2008, p. 31. http://ec.europa.eu/external_relations/russia/docs/commonspaces_prog_report2007.pdf. See also E. Barbe and B. Kienzle, 'Security provider or security consumer? The European Union and conflict management', *European Foreign Affairs Review*, 12, 4, 2007, pp. 517–36.

27 *Ibid.*

28 European Council 'Presidency Conclusions: Justice and Home Affairs', 21–22 June, 2007, Brussels.

29 A. Sorel, 'Asylum, Migration and Border Controls in the Hague Programme', in J. de Zwaan and F. Goudappel (eds) 2006, *op. cit*, p. 14.

30 Agence Presse 'EU/Neighbourhood', No. 9558, 6 December, 2007.

31 H. Grabbe, 'What the new Member States will bring into the European Union, in N. Nugent (ed.) *European Union Enlargement*, The European Union Series, Palgrave Macmillan, Basingstoke, 2004, p. 78.

32 European Council Laeken Presidency Conclusions, Brussels, 15 December, 2001.

33 http://www.frontex.europa.eu.

34 Europol 'EU Organised Crime Threat Assessment 2009', The Hague, 2009, www.europol.europa.eu.

35 European Commission 'Towards integrated management of the external borders of the Member States of the European Union', COM (2002) 233, final, May, 2002.

36 H. Grabbe, *The EU's Transformative Power: Europeanization through Conditionality in Central and Eastern Europe*, New York: Palgrave Macmillan, 2006.

37 Council of Ministers 'Pre-Accession Pact on Organised Crime between the Member States of the European Union and the Applicant Countries of Central and Eastern Europe and Cyprus', 98/C 220/01, 28 May, 1998, Brussels.

38 M. Beare, 'Purposeful misconceptions: organized crime and the state', in E. Viano, J. Magallanes and L. Bridel, *Transnational Organized Crime: Myth, Power, and Profit*, Carolina Academic Press: Durham, N.Ca., 2003.

39 Europol, *op. cit.*, 2009.

40 European Council 'Action Plan to Combat Organised Crime', (97/C) Brussels, 28 April, 1997.
41 European Council 15–16 October, *op. cit.*, 1999.
42 Road Map for the Common Space of Freedom, Security and Justice, Annex 2, http://www.ec.europa.eu/external_relations/russia/russia_docs/road_map_ces.pdf.
43 European Council 'Common Strategy of the European Union on Russia', Brussels, 4 June, 1999.
44 C. Malmstrom, EU Commissioner for Home Affairs, Keynote speech at the seminar 'Does Europe need "Homeland Security?"' Security and Defence Agenda, Brussels, 12 May, 2010, p. 6.
45 European Monitoring Centre for Drugs and Drug Addiction 'Annual Report 2009: The State of the Drugs Problem in Europe', Lisbon, 2009, http://www.emcdda.europa.eu/attacments.cfm/att_93236_EN.
46 *Ibid.*
47 S. Fukumi, *Cocaine Trafficking in Latin America: EU and US Policy Responses*, Aldershot: Ashgate, 2008, chapter 6.
48 A. Cordesman, 'The crisis in Afghanistan', Statement before the House Armed Services Committee, February 12, 2009, Washington DC.
49 B. Hoffman, *Inside Terrorism*, New York, Colombia University Press, 1998.
50 European Council The European Security Strategy, 'A secure Europe in a better world', 12 December, 2003, Brussels.
51 P. Bobbitt, *Terror and Consent: The Wars for the Twenty-First Century*, New York: A. Knopf, 2008.
52 E. Brimmer, 'From territorial security to societal security: Implications for the transatlantic strategic outlook', in E. Brimmer (ed.) *Transforming Homeland Security: US and European Approaches*, Center for Transatlantic Relations, Washington DC: John Hopkins University, 2006, p. 31.
53 D. Keohane, 'The absent friend: EU foreign policy and counter-terrorism', *Journal of Common Market Studies*, 46, 1, 2008, p. 129.
54 M. den Boer and J. Monar, (2002) 'Keynote article: 11 September and the challenge of global terrorism to the EU as a security actor', *Journal of Common Market Studies*, 40, pp. 11–28.
55 E. Guild, 'International terrorism and EU immigration, asylum and borders policy: The unexpected victims of 11 September 2001', *European Foreign Affairs Review*, 8, 2003, p. 332.
56 M. Dittrich, 'Muslims in Europe: Addressing the challenges of radicalisation', *European Policy Centre Working Paper 23*, Brussels, March, 2006.
57 European Council 'The European Union Counter-Terrorism Strategy', Brussels, 30 November, 2005.
58 C. Malmstrom, *op. cit.*, 2010, p. 7.
59 H. Nilsson, 'The EU Action Plan on Combating Terrorism: Assessment and Perspectives', in Mahncke, D. and Monar, J. (eds) *International Terrorism: A European Response to a Global Threat?* College of Europe Studies No. 3, Germany, PIE Peter Lang, 2006, p. 75.
60 European Commission 'Critical Infrastructure Protection in the Fight against Terrorism', Brussels, 2004.
61 J. Monar, 'Justice and home affairs', *Journal of Common Market Studies*, 43, 131–46, 2005, p. 142.
62 D. Keohane, *op. cit.*, 2008, p. 128.
63 A. Millar and E. Rosand, *Allied Against Terrorism: What's Needed to Strengthen Worldwide Commitment*, New York: A Century Foundation Report, 2006.
64 J. Shapiro and D. Byman, 'Bridging the transatlantic counterterrorism gap', *The Washington Quarterly*, 29, 4, 2006, p. 34.
65 M. O'Hanlon, 'Border protection', in M. d'Arcy, M. O'Hanlon, P. Orszag, J. Shapiro and J. Steinberg (eds) *Protecting the Homeland 2006/2007*, Washington DC: Brookings Institution Press, 2006, pp. 96–112.

66 W. Rees, *Transatlantic Counter-terrorism Cooperation: The New Imperative*, London: Routledge, 2006, p. 99.

67 House of Lords, 2007, 'The EU/US Passenger Name Record (PNR) Agreement', European Union Committee, *HL Paper 108*, London, The Stationery Office, 2007.

68 European Council, (2004), March 2005, *op. cit.*, p. 1.

Chapter 3 The EU and external security relations

1 T. Dunne, 'Good Citizen Europe', *International Affairs*, 84: 1, 2008, pp. 13–28, at p. 14, footnote 5.

2 For more on the EDC see E. Fursdon, *The European Defence Community: A History*, London: Macmillan, 1980; S. Dockrill, *Britain's Policy for West German Rearmament, 1950–55*, Cambridge: Cambridge University Press, 1991; K. Ruane, *The Rise and Fall of the European Defence Community: Anglo-American Relations and the Crisis of European Defence, 1950–55*, Basingstoke: Macmillan, 2000.

3 C. Piening, *Global Europe. The European Union in World Affairs*, London: Lynne Rienner Publishers, 1997, p. 4.

4 Judgment of the Court of 14 July 1976 (1) Cornelis Kramer and Others, 'Biological resources of the sea', Joined cases 3, 4 and 6/76, http://www.ena.lu/.

5 H. Maull, 'Germany and Japan: The new Civilian Powers', *Foreign Affairs* 69: 5, 1990, pp. 91–106; H. Maull and S. Harnisch (eds), *Germany as a Civilian Power?* Manchester: Manchester University Press, 2001.

6 For instance, scholars who emphasise economic power within civilian power effectively blur a line between that concept and Rosecrance's ideas regarding 'trading States'. R. Whitman, *From Civilian Power to Superpower? The International Identity of the European Union,* Basingstoke: Macmillan, 1998; M. Telo, *Europe: a Civilian Power?* Basingstoke: Palgrave, 2005.

7 I. Manners, 'Normative Power Europe: A contradiction in terms?', *Journal of Common Market Studies* 40: 2, 2002, pp. 235–58, at p. 238.

8 I. Manners, 'Normative Power Europe reconsidered', CIDEL Workshop, October 2004, at p. 20; K. Smith, 'Still Civilian Power Europe?', European Foreign Policy Unit Working Paper, 2005, p.11; S. Stavridis, 'Militarizing the EU: the concept of Civilian Power Europe revisited', *The International Spectator* 36: 4, 2001, pp. 43–50; S. Stavridis, 'Why the "Militarising" of the EU is strengthening the concept of a "civilian power Europe"', EUI Working Papers Series, RSC No. 2001/17, Robert Schuman Centre for Advanced Studies.

9 H. Bull, 'Civilian Power Europe: A contradiction in terms?', *Journal of Common Market Studies* 21: 2, 1982, pp. 149–64; R. Kagan, *Of Paradise and Power: America and Europe in the New World Order*, New York: Knopf, 2003.

10 M. Lerch and G. Schwellnus, 'Normative by nature? The role of coherence in justifying the EU's external human rights policy', *Journal of European Public Policy* 13: 2, 2006, pp. 304–21.

11 K. Smith, 'The end of Civilian Power Europe: A welcome demise or cause for concern?', *International Spectator* 23: 2, 2000, pp. 11–28, at p. 27; Robert Cooper, *The Breaking of Nations: Order and Chaos in the Twenty-First century*, London: Atlantic Books, 2003; F. Duchêne, 'The European Community and the uncertainties of interdependence', in M. Kohnstamm and W. Hager (eds.) *A Nation Writ Large? Foreign-Policy Problems before the European Community*, London: Macmillan, 1972, at p. 20.

12 K. Smith, 'Still Civilian Power Europe?', European Foreign Policy Unit Working Paper, 2005, p. 4.

13 Sjursen also argues that to prevent this it is necessary in presentations of civilian, ethical and normative power Europe arguments to critically unpack different types of norms and their validity and legitimacy basis. H. Sjursen, 'What kind of power?', *Journal of European Public Policy* 13: 2, 2006, pp. 169–81.

14 C. Bretherton and J. Vogler, *The European Union as a Global* Actor, 2nd edition, Abingdon: Taylor and Francis, 2005, p. 49.

15 C.M. Dent, *The European Economy: The Global Context,* London: Routledge, 1997, p. 183.

16 K. Smith, 'The use of political conditionality in the EU's relations with third countries: How effective?', *European Foreign Affairs Review* 3, 1998, pp. 253–74, at p. 253.

17 See, for example, N. Nugent, *The Government and Politics of the European Union*, 5th edition, Basingstoke: Macmillan, 2003, p. 433.

18 General Secretariat of the African, Caribbean and Pacific Group of States (2000) *Cotonou Agreement,* http://www.acpsec.org/gb/cotonou/accord1.htm.

19 Romano Prodi, cited in F. Cahrillon, 'The EU as a security regime', *European Foreign Affairs Review,* 10, 2005, pp. 517–33, at p. 529, footnote 21; ESS, p. 2.

20 Commission Staff working document, annex to the Communication from the Commission to the Council and the European Parliament, Annual Report 2005 on the European Community's Development Policy and the Implementation of External Assistance in 2004, 15 July 2005, p. 4; Annual Report 2008 on the European Community's Development and External Assistance Policies and their Implementation in 2007, p. 21.

21 See, for example, N. Woods, 'The shifting politics of foreign aid', *International Affairs* 81: 2, 2005, pp. 393–409; D. Keohane, 'The absent friend: EU foreign policy and counter-terrorism', *Journal of Common Market Studies* 46: 1, 2008, pp. 125–46.

22 European Communities (1987) *Treaties Establishing the European Communities*, Luxembourg: Office of Official Publications. For more on the development of EPC see S. Nuttall, *European Political Co-operation*, Oxford: Clarendon Press, 1992; E. Regelsberger, W. Wessels and P. de Schoutheete de Tervarent, (eds.) *Foreign Policy of the European Union: From EPC to CFSP and Beyond*, London: Lynne Rienner Publishers, 1997.

23 European Commission, 'Sanctions or restrictive measures', http://ec.europa.eu/external_relations/cfsp/sanctions/index_en.htm.

24 http://register.consilium.europa.eu/pdf/en/03/st15/st15708.en03.pdf.

25 Article 28 b (1), Lisbon Treaty.

26 European Council, 'Declaration on Strengthening Capabilities', 11 December 2008.

27 EDA, 'An Initial Long-Term Vision for European Defence Capability and Capacity Needs', 3 October 2006, p. 3.

28 *Ibid.*

29 EDA, 'Background Note – Capability Development Plan', 8 July 2008; EDA, 'European Air Transport Fleet Launched', Press Release, 10 November 2008.

30 D. Keohane, 'EU on the offensive about defence', *European Voice.com*, 22–28 July 2004.

31 'The Code of Conduct on Defence Procurement of the EU Member States Participating in the European Defence Agency', 21 November 2005; EDA, 'The Code of Best Practice in the Supply Chain', 15 May 2006; EDA, 'Key Facts on the Code of Best Practices in the Supply Chain'.

32 'The Code of Conduct on Defence Procurement', 21 November 2005.

33 Items such as nuclear weapons and propulsion systems, chemical, bacteriological and radiological goods and so forth are completely exempt from Single Market legislation. Other defence products are provided with potential exemption under Article 296 of the EC Treaty. Paragraph 1 states that:
The provisions of this Treaty shall not preclude the application of the following rules:

    (a) no Member State shall be obliged to supply information the disclosure of which it considers contrary to the essential interests of its security;

    (b) any Member State may take such measures as it considers necessary for the protection of the essential interests of its security which are connected with the production of or trade in arms, munitions and war material … ' Article 296, Consolidated Version of the Treaty Establishing the European Community.

34 M. Flournoy and J. Smith *et al.*, 'European defence integration: Bridging the gap between strategy and capabilities', Center for Strategic and International Studies, October 2005, p. 78.

35 European Commission, Communication COM(1996)10 – 'The challenges facing the European defence-related industry, a contribution for action at European level', 24 January 1996; European Commission, Communication COM(1997) p. 583; 'Implementing European Union strategy on defence-related industries', 12 January 1997; European Commission, Green Paper: Defence Procurement, COM(2004) 608 final, 23 September 2004, p. 6; European Parliament, 'MEPs launch offensive to improve EU arms procurement', 20051003IPR00969, 4 February 2005; European Commission, 'Consultation Paper on the Intra-Community circulation of products for the defence of Member States', 21 March 2006, p. 5; European Commission, 'Interpretative Communication on the application of Article 296 of the Treaty in the field of defence procurement', COM(2006) 779 final, 7 December 2006.

36 Communication from the Commission to the European Parliament, the Council, The European Economic and Social Committee and the Committee of the Regions, 'A Strategy for a stronger and more competitive European defence industry', COM (2007) 764 final, 5 December 2007; 'Proposal for a Directive of the European Parliament and of the Council on simplifying terms and conditions of transfers of defence-related products within the Community', COM (2007) 765 final, 5 December 2007; 'Proposal for a Directive of the European Parliament and of the Council on the coordination of procedures for the award of certain public works contracts, public supply contracts and public service contracts in the fields of defence and security', COM (2007) 766 final, 5 December 2007.

37 EDA, 'Defence Data of EDA participating Member States in 2007, Defence Expenditure as a Percentage of GDP', p. 6.

38 European Parliament, 'European Defence and Security Market strengthened', Press Release, http://www.europarl.europa.eu/pdfs/news/expert/infopress/20090113IPR46066/200 90113IPR46066_en.pdf; Forecast International, 'A Frugal Pax Europa', 12 November 2008; EDA, Defence Data of EDA participating Member States in 2007, 'Investment (Equipment Procurement and R&D)', p. 9.

39 In 2008, in constant (2005) US$, EU Member States' collective military expenditure totalled $254225.1 million. Figures exclude Luxembourg and are compiled by the author from SIPRI Military Expenditure Database (http://milexdata.sipri.org/) and Appendix 5A. Military expenditure data, 1999–2008, summary, 8 June 2009.

40 Nick Witney, 'The European Defence Agency – Strategic Directions and Impact on Transatlantic Relations', speech to the Press Club, Washington, 24 October 2005; J. Wither, 'Expeditionary forces for post-modern Europe: Will European military weakness provide an opportunity for the new Condottieri?', Conflict Studies Research Centre, January 2005, p. 4.

41 See, for example, Michael Ryan, US Mission to the EU, comments at 'Is a transatlantic defence industry increasingly on the cards?', Security and Defence Agenda Roundtable, 30 January 2006, p. 8.

42 EDA, Defence Data of EDA participating Member States in 2007, 'Personnel Expenditure as a Percentage of Total Defence Expenditure', p. 26.

43 B. Schmitt, 'Armaments cooperation in Europe', Institute for Security Studies, January 2005; K. Becher, 'Chairman's summing-up', IISS/CEPS European Security Forum: European and Transatlantic Industrial Strategies', 25 November 2002; B. Benoit, 'A Cooling of the once passionate Franco-German love affair', *Financial Times*, 24 June 2006; T. Guay, 'The transatlantic defence industrial base: Restructuring scenarios and their implications', Strategic Studies Institute, April 2005, p. 30.

44 For example, six EU countries are developing the Meteor air-to-air missile; Belgium, Spain and France are developing the Hélios II military observation satellite programme; and the A400M strategic airlifter, Tiger helicopter and Counter Battery Radar are overseen by OCCAR.

45 In December 2005 a British Defence White Paper noted that 'Enthusiasm from governments and industry for collaborative development programmes has undoubtedly been tempered by difficulties experienced on some high profile collaborative ventures in recent years.' UK Secretary of State for Defence, 'Defence Industrial Strategy. Defence White Paper', Command 6697, December 2005, p. 26

46 J. Mawdsley, 'The gap between rhetoric and reality: Weapons acquisition and ESDP', Paper 26, Bonn International Center for Conversion: Bonn, 2002, p. 23; Salmon and Shepherd note that contract-theory explanations of the origins and the nature of the state together with the role of external sovereignty in defining a state as a state, mean that encroachment upon the foreign, defence, and armaments policy by outside agencies threatens the very concept and existence of a state. T.C. Salmon and A. Shepherd, *Toward a European Army. A Military Power in the Making?* Boulder: Lynne Rienner, 2003, p. 181.

47 Even then Poland was reportedly close to rejecting the Code of Conduct on Defence Procurement, and Hungary and Spain initially did so – the latter reportedly from concern for its domestic contractors. G. Anderson, 'A new era for European defence procurement?', *Janes*, 4 July 2006.

48 For instance, Britain's Defence Industrial Strategy (2005) stated that 'The fragility of the wider UK industrial base is such that open international competition could put the sustainment of key industrial capacities at risk. … We must maintain the appropriate degree of sovereignty over industrial skills, capacities, capabilities and technologies to ensure *operational independence* against the range of operations that we wish to be able to conduct.' UK Secretary of State for Defence, 'Defence Industrial Strategy. Defence White Paper', Command 6697, December 2005, pp. 9 and 17.

49 M.E. Smith, 'The quest for coherence: Institutional dilemmas of external action from Maastricht to Amsterdam', in A. Stone Sweet, W. Sandholtz and N. Fligstein (eds), *The Institutionalisation of Europe*, Oxford: Oxford University Press, 2001, pp. 171–93.

50 D. Lutterbeck, 'Blurring the dividing line: The convergence of internal and external security in Western Europe', *European Security* 14:2, 2005, pp. 231–53, at p. 231.

51 There is debate about whether this de-differentiation is primarily the product of the transformation of security threat or from 'institutional games and particular practices of securitization that define the importance of security as superior to sovereignty and freedom'. See D. Bigo, 'Internal and external aspects of security', *European Security* 15: 4, 2006, pp. 405–22, quote at p. 405.

52 Australian Trade Minister Mark Vaile cited in A. Hyde-Price, 'A "tragic actor"? A realist perspective on "ethical power Europe"', *International Affairs* 84: 1, 2008, pp. 29–44, at p. 32.

53 See Pascal Gauttier, cited in S. Duke, 'Areas of Grey: Tensions in EU External Relations competencies', *EIPASCOPE* 1, 2006, pp. 21–27, at p. 24.

54 Javier Solana, Address by the EU High Representative for CFSP to the External Action Working Group of the Convention, Brussels, Belgium, 15 October 2002.

55 S. Everts and H. Grabbe, 'Why the EU needs a security strategy', CER Briefing Note, May 2003; S. Rynning, 'Less may be better in EU Security and Defence Policy', *Oxford Journal on Good Governance* 2: 1, 2005, pp. 45–50, at p. 49.

56 Javier Solana, 'Thoughts on the reception of the European Security Strategy', *Oxford Journal on Good Governance* 1: 1, 2004, pp. 17–19, at p. 19.

57 Leonard and Gowan, for instance, argued that despite some changes to the original draft ESS, 'the document remains almost Rumsfeldian in its warnings about terrorism and rogue States.' However, the ESS never mentions rogue States specifically and its assessment of the extent and imminence of threats posed by terrorism is markedly more equivocal than the 2002 US National Security Strategy. M. Leonard and R. Gowan, 'Global Europe: Implementing the European Security Strategy', The Foreign Policy Centre in association with the British Council, Brussels, 2003, p. 7.

58 A. Toje, 'The 2003 European Security Strategy: A critical appraisal', *European Foreign Affairs Review* 10:1, 2005, pp. 117–33, at p. 132; S. Rynning, 'Less may be better in EU

Security and Defence Policy', p. 46; M.E. Sangiovanni, 'Why a Common Security and Defence Policy is bad for Europe', *Survival* 45: 3, 2003, pp. 193–206.

59 Crowe argues that Iraq seemed 'to epitomise everything that is wrong with the practice and even the concept of a CFSP' and Sedivy that the lessons of Iraq and the need to respond to shifts in US strategic outlook were possibly determinants in the ESS being adopted. B. Crowe, 'A Common European Foreign Policy after Iraq?', *International Affairs* 79: 3, 2003, pp. 533–46, at p. 534; J. Sedivy, 'One year on: lessons from Iraq', ISS Chaillot Paper no. 68, Paris, 2004, p. 107.

60 C. Kelleher, 'The European Security Strategy and the United States: The past as prologue', in S. Biscop and J. J. Andersson (eds), *The EU and the European Security Strategy: Forging a Global Europe*, New York: Routledge, 2008, p. 151.

61 H. Strachan, 'The lost meaning of strategy', *Survival* 47: 3, 2005, pp. 33–54, at p. 34 and p. 48.

62 C.S. Gray, *Modern Strategy*, Oxford: Oxford University Press, 1999, p. 16.

63 ESS, p. 10.

64 For instance: 'Dealing with terrorism *may require* a mixture of intelligence, police, judicial, military and other means. In failed States, military instruments *may be needed* to restore order … Regional conflicts need political solutions but military assets and effective policing *may be needed* in the post conflict phase.' ESS, p. 7.

65 See, for instance, Van Oudenaren, 'The Solana security paper', American Institute for Contemporary German Studies, http://www.aicgs.org/analysis/c/solana.aspx.

66 A. Toje, 'The consensus–expectations gap: Explaining Europe's ineffective policy', *Security Dialogue* 39: 1, 2008, pp. 121–41, at p. 127; J. Wyllie, 'Measuring up: The strategies as strategy', in R. Dannreuther and J. Peterson eds, *Security Strategy and Transatlantic Relations,* London: Routledge, 2006, pp. 165–77, at p. 174; T. Salmon, The European Security and Defence Policy: Built on rocks or sand?', *European Foreign Affairs Review* 10, 2005, pp. 359–79, at p. 378; H. Maull, 'Europe and the new balance of global order', *International Affairs* 81: 4, 2005, pp. 775–99, at pp.792–94.

67 S. Biscop and J.J. Andersson (eds), 2008, *op. cit.* pp. 3 and 12.

68 ESS, p. 13.

69 A. Bailes, 'The European Security Strategy: An evolutionary history', SIPRI Policy Paper 10, February 2005, at p. 14.

70 Council of the European Union, European Council Presidency conclusions, 17–18 June 2004, 10679/2/04, REV 2, CONCL 2, p. 11.

71 ESS, p. 1.

72 A. Bailes, 'EU and US strategic concepts', *The International Spectator* 39:1, 2004, pp. 19–33, at p. 32.

73 ESS, p. 11. See, for instance, S. Biscop, 'The European Security Strategy in context', in S. Biscop and J. Andersson (eds), 2008, *op. cit.* p. 8; T. Valasek, 'Europe's defence and its new security strategy', CER Bulletin, 57, December 2007–January 2008.

74 ESS, p. 13 and p. 8.

75 ESS, p. 2, p. 3, p. 7 and p. 13.

76 James Wyllie, 'Measuring up: The strategies as strategy', p. 174, *op. cit.*

77 R. Gowan, 'The Battlegroups: A concept in search of a strategy?', in Sven Biscop ed., *E Pluribus Unum? Military integration in the European Union*, Egmont Papers, No.7, Brussels: Royal Institute for International Relations, 2005, pp. 13–20; M. Kaldor and A. Salmon, 'Military force and European strategy', *Survival* 48: 1, 2006, pp. 19–34.

78 M. Sangiovanni, p. 194, *op. cit.*

79 R. Whitman, 'Road map for a route march? (De-)civilianizing through the EU's security strategy', *European Foreign Affairs Review* 11, 2006, pp. 1–15, at pp. 11–14.

80 J. Matlary, 'When soft power turns hard: Is an EU strategic culture possible?', *Security Dialogue* 37: 1, 2006, pp. 105–21, at p. 109.

81 Kotsopoulos cited in J. Matlary, 'Much ado about little: the EU and human security', *International Affairs* 84: 1, 2008, pp. 131–43, at p. 140.

82 See, for instance, W. Wallace, 'Foreign policy and national identity in the United Kingdom', *International Affairs* 67: 1, 1991, pp. 65–80, at p. 78. Aggestam argues that the EU-3 had by the end of the 1990s resolved that the Union ought to be a broadly ethical actor in international politics. L. Aggestam, *A European foreign policy? Role Conceptions, and the Politics of Identity in Britain, France and Germany*, Stockholm: Stockholm University Press, 2004, pp. 241–45.

83 ESS, p. 13.

84 For soft balancing see, for example, J. Kelley, 'Strategic non-cooperation as soft balancing: Why Iraq was not just about Iraq', *International Politics* 42, 2005, pp. 153–73; S. Brooks and W. Wohlforth, 'Hard times for soft balancing', *International Security* 30: 1, 2005, pp. 72–108; T.V. Paul, 'Soft balancing in an age of US primacy', *International Security* 30: 1, 2005, pp. 46–71; R. Pape, 'Soft balancing against the United States', *International Security* 30: 1, 2005, pp. 7–45.

85 P. Schmidt and G. Geipel, *Oxford Journal on Good Governance*, 2004, 1: 1, pp. 29–32, at p. 30; J. Rickli, 'US and EU security strategies: Same planet, different hemispheres', *Oxford Journal on Good Governance* 1: 1, 2004, pp. 55–60, at p. 57.

86 C. Meyer, *The Quest for a European Strategic Culture. Changing Norms on Security and Defence in the European Union*, Basingstoke: Palgrave, 2006, p. 181.

87 P.M. Martinsen, 'Forging a strategic culture: Putting policy into the ESDP', *Oxford Journal on Good Governance* 1: 1, 2004, pp. 61–66, at p. 64.

88 K. Vrettos (Rapporteur – Greece, Socialist Group), Explanatory Memorandum, Assembly of the WEU, 'ESDP Developments and the Headline Goal 2010 – reply to the annual report of the Council', 15 June 2005, Document A/1898.

89 R. Cooper, 'The next empire', *Prospect* 67, 2001, pp. 222–26.

90 M. Webber, S. Croft, J. Howorth, T. Terriff and E. Krahmann, 'The governance of European security', *Review of International Studies* 30, 2004, 3–36, at p.17. Lantis argues that the St Malo declaration was an effort 'to prime the pump for the development of a common strategic culture'. J. Lantis, 'EU strategic culture and US ambivalence', *Oxford Journal on Good Governance* 2: 1, 2005, pp. 55–60, at p. 58.

91 A. Miskimmon, 'Continuity in the face of upheaval – British strategic culture and the impact of the Blair government', *European Security* 13: 3, 2004, 273–99. Meyer, for example, argues that there is a gradually emerging European strategic culture but that it as yet rests on a relatively narrow basis in terms of norms and social cohesion, supporting a 'humanitarian power Europe'. Cornish and Edwards describe strategic culture even more narrowly as 'the political and institutional confidence and processes to manage and deploy military force, coupled with external recognition of the EU as a legitimate actor in the military sphere.' Cristoph Meyer, 2006, *op. cit.*, p. 11; P. Cornish and G. Edwards, 'The strategic culture of the European Union: A progress report', *International Affairs* 81: 4, 2005, pp. 801–20, at p. 802.

92 L.E. Cederman, 'Political boundaries and identity tradeoffs', in LE Cederman (ed.), *Constructing Europe's Identity: the External Dimension*, Boulder CO: Lynne Rienner, 2001, pp. 1–34, at p. 3.

93 A. Hyde-Price, 'European security, strategic culture, and the use of force', *European Security* 13: 4, 2004, pp. 323–43, at p. 326.

94 For more on interaction capacity in the context of structuring international relations, see B. Buzan, C. Jones, and R. Little, *The Logic of Anarchy: Neorealism to Structural Realism*, New York: Columbia University Press, 1993, pp. 66–80.

95 For example: C.A. Kupchan and C.A. Kupchan, 'Concerts, collective security, and the future of Europe', *International Security* 16: 1, 1991, pp. 114–61; G. Flynn and D. Scheffer, 'Limited collective security', *Foreign Policy* 80, 1990, pp. 77–101; R. Ullman, 'Enlarging the zone of peace', *Foreign Policy* 80, 1990, pp. 102–20. Even at this time, though, not everyone was convinced by liberal institutionalists' claims about the ability of institutions to modify state behaviour sufficiently. See, for example, R.O. Keohane and L.L. Martin, 'The promise of institutionalist theory', *International Security*

20: 1, pp. 39–51; J. Snyder, 'Averting anarchy in the new Europe', *International Security* 14: 4, 1990, pp. 5–41; C.A. Kupchan and C.A. Kupchan, 'The promise of collective security', *International Security* 20: 1, 1995, pp. 52–61; R. Russell, 'The chimera of collective security in Europe', *European Security* 4: 2, 1995, pp. 241–55; P. Zelikow, 'The new concert of Europe', *Survival* 34: 2, 1992, pp. 12–30; J. Joffe, 'Collective security and the future of Europe: Failed dreams and dead ends', *Survival* 34: 1, 1992, pp. 36–50; J. Mearsheimer, 'The false promise of international institutions', *International Security* 19: 3, 1994/95, pp. 5–49.

 96 As cited in Bretherton, C. and Vogler, J. (1999) *The European Union as a Global Actor*, p. 145.

 97 J. Sperling and E. Kirchner, *Recasting the European Order: Security Architectures and Economic Cooperation*, Manchester: Manchester University Press, 1997, p. 16.

 98 A.J.K. Bailes, speech to St Antony's College, Oxford, 'Under a European flag? From WEU to EU', 29 November 1999.

 99 Secretary-General William Van Eekelen publicly located the WEU between NATO and the European institutions and at 'the heart of a dynamic two-fold process' of their reform. The WEU became actively involved in developing arms control and understandings, in measures to implement the Conventional Forces in Europe Treaty verification regime and in outreach programmes such as the 1992 Forum for Consultation and Associate Memberships. W. Van Eekelen, 'WEU's post-Maastricht agenda', *NATO Review* 40: 2, 1992, pp. 13–17, at p. 15. For more details see S. Croft, J. Redmond, G.W. Rees, and M. Webber, *The Enlargement of Europe*, Manchester: Manchester University Press, 1999, pp. 99–104.

100 By 1994 the annual cost of UN Balkans intervention was greater than the total spent on 30 UN peace operations world-wide since 1948. A. Blair, 'What happened in Yugoslavia? Lessons for future peacekeepers', *European Security* 3: 2, 1994, pp. 340–49, at p. 349. For just two of the many predictions of NATO's demise see J. Mearsheimer, 'Back to the future: Instability in Europe after the Cold War', *International Security* 15: 3, 1990, pp. 5–57, at p. 52; S. Lodgaard, 'Competing schemes for Europe: The CSCE, NATO and the European Union', *Security Dialogue* 23: 3, 1992, pp. 57–68, at p. 58.

101 NATO, 'The Alliance's Strategic Concept, 8 November 1991', in *NATO Handbook Documentation*, Brussels: NATO Office of Information and Press, 1999, pp. 281–300.

102 M. Wörner, 'A vigorous alliance – A motor for peaceful change in Europe', *NATO Review* 40: 6, 1992, pp. 1–8, at p. 7.

103 NATO's first out-of-area military action was to shoot down four Bosnian-Serb aircraft that violated the UN no-fly zone over Bosnia and Herzegovina in February 1994. For analysis and opinions about PFP see Richard Lugar, 'NATO Enlargement and US Public Opinion', speech at Center for Strategic and International Studies Conference on 'NATO's Role in European Security', Washington DC, 3 March 1995; R.E. Hunter, 'NATO at fifty. Maximising NATO: A relevant Alliance knows how to reach', *Foreign Affairs* 78: 3, 1999, pp. 190–203, at p. 194; R.C. Holbrooke, 'America as a European power', *Foreign Affairs* 74: 2, 1995, pp. 38–51, at p. 44; M. Rühle and N. Williams, 'Partnership for Peace after NATO enlargement' *European Security* 5: 4, 1996, pp. 521–28; H. De Santis, 'Romancing NATO: Partnership for Peace and East European stability', *Journal of Strategic Studies* 17: 4, 1994, pp. 61–81; J. Borawski, 'Partnership for Peace and beyond', *International Affairs* 71: 2, 2005, pp. 233–46; N. Williams, 'Partnership for Peace: Permanent fixture or declining asset?', *Survival* 38: 1, 1996, pp. 98–110.

104 S. Croft, 'The EU, NATO and the return of the architectural debate', *European Security* 9:3, 2000, pp. 1–20, at p. 13.

105 J. Borawski, 'Revisiting the common European home: A rejoinder', *Security Dialogue*, 31: 1, 2000, pp. 85–90.

106 E. Mlyn, 'The OSCE, the United States and European security' *European Security* 5: 3, 1996, pp. 426–47, at pp. 439–40.

107 The Quint comprises Britain, Germany, France, Italy and the US. For details see: C. Gegout, 'The Quint: Acknowledging the existence of a Big Four-US *directoire* at the heart of the European Union's foreign policy decision-making process', *Journal of Common Market Studies* 40:2, 2002, pp. 331–44. For an analysis of the EU-3 within the European Council see J. Tallberg, *Bargaining power in the European Council*, Stockholm: Swedish Institute for European Policy Studies, 2007. For a discussion of *directoires* in the EU's CFSP see S. Keukeleire, 'Directoires within the CFSP/CESDP of the European Union: a plea for "restricted crisis management groups"', *European Foreign Affairs Review* 6:1, 2001, pp. 75–101.

108 J. Wright, 'European security – post-Bosnia', *European Security* 6: 2, 1997, pp. 1–17, at p. 5.

109 P. Baev, 'External interventions in secessionist conflicts in Europe in the 1990s', *European Security* 8: 2, 1999, pp. 22–51, at p. 30; J. Lindley-French, 'In the shade of Locarno? Why European defence is failing', *International Affairs* 78: 4, 2002, pp. 789–811, at p. 799.

110 G. Aybet, *A European Security Architecture after the Cold War*, Basingstoke: Macmillan, 2000, p. 196; F. Bozo, 'The effects of Kosovo and the danger of decoupling', in J. Howorth and J.T.S. Keeler (eds), *Defending Europe: The EU, NATO and the Quest for European Autonomy*, Basingstoke: Palgrave, 2003, p. 62.

111 J. Sperling and E. Kirchner, *Recasting the European Order*, note 43, p. 27.

112 S. Duke, 'CESDP: Nice's overtrumped success?', *European Foreign Affairs Review* 6: 2, 2001, pp. 155–75, at p. 157; J. Howorth, 'Britain, France and the European defence initiative', *Survival* 42: 2, 2001, pp. 33–55, at p. 41.

113 For instance, the OSCE adopted in November 1999 at its Istanbul Summit a Charter for European Security that outlined a security architecture based on inter-organisational co-operation in which the OSCE enjoyed a co-ordinating role. Charter for European Security, www.osce.org/docs/english/1990–99/summits/istachart99e.htm. Text reproduced in: V.Y. Ghebali and D. Warner (eds.), *The Operational Role of the OSCE in South-Eastern Europe*, Aldershot: Ashgate, 2001, pp. 113–31.

114 Kurt Volker, Principal Deputy Assistant Secretary for European and Eurasian Affairs, Remarks at Media Roundtable, Brussels, Belgium, 6 February 2006; John Shimkus, Rapporteur, 170 DSTC 05 E – Progress on the Prague Capability Commitments, NATO Parliamentary Assembly, 2005 annual session; House of Commons, Select Committee on European Scrutiny, 23rd Report, 4 June 2003, item 22.

115 NATO Press Release, Defence Capabilities Initiative, NAC-S(99)69, 25 April 1999; NATO, 'The Alliance's Strategic Concept', NAC-S(99)65, 24 April 1999.

116 These were organised within eight essential fields for improvement – chemical, biological, radiological and nuclear defence; intelligence, surveillance and target acquisition; air-to-ground surveillance; deployable and secure command, control and communications; combat effectiveness, including precision-guided munitions and suppression of enemy air defences; strategic air- and sea-lift; air-to-air refuelling; and deployable combat support and combat service support units.

117 C. Taylor, 'NATO: the Istanbul Summit', House of Commons research paper 04/60, 26 July 2004, pp. 1–46, at p. 27.

118 EU-NATO Declaration on ESDP, The European Union and the North Atlantic Treaty Organisation, Press Release (2002) p. 142, 16 December 2002. For further details of the Berlin Plus package see NATO fact sheet, http://www.nato.int/shape/news/2003/shape_eu/se030822a.htm.

119 Belgium, France, Germany and Luxembourg announced agreement to enhance their defence collaboration and their desire for an EU operational planning cell (as an alternative to NATO) in Tervuren. Given these four governments led the anti-war camp and had blocked NATO aid for Turkey before the intervention in Iraq, the proposal inevitably appeared directed against NATO. J. Keeler, 'Transatlantic relations and European security and defence', *EUSA Review* 17: 2, 2004, pp. 3–4, at p. 3.

120 Sir Peter Ricketts (comments of), Permanent Representative of the UK to NATO, 'Conference Report: 'European Defence Integration: Bridging the Gap between

Strategy and Capabilities', Center for Strategic and International Studies, 12 October 2005, p. 21.

121 K. Kamp, 'NATO-summit 2006: The Alliance in search of topics', No.156/2006, Konrad Adenauer Stiftung: Berlin, February 2006. p. 7; D. Keohane, 'Unblocking EU-NATO cooperation', *CER Bulletin*, 48, June/July 2006.

122 Luca Bonsignore, 'Is cooperation the key to a European Security Architecture: Resumé of the Handlesblatt conference', pp. 33–36, at p. 35.

123 Michael Ryan, US Mission to the EU, comments at 'Is a transatlantic defence industry increasingly on the cards?', Security and Defence Agenda Roundtable', 30 January 2006, p. 8. For a convenient contrast of conclusions see: A. Menon, 'Why ESDP is dangerous and misguided for the Alliance', in J. Howorth and J.T.S. Keeler (eds), *Defending Europe: The EU, NATO and the Quest for European Autonomy*, Basingstoke: Palgrave Macmillan, 2003, pp. 203–18; J. Howorth, 'Why ESDP is necessary and beneficial for the Alliance' in *Ibid.*, pp. 219–38. See also R. Hunter, *The European Security and Defence Policy: NATO's Companion – Or Competitor*, Washington DC: RAND, 2002.

124 S. Duke, 'The future of EU–NATO relations: a case of mutual irrelevance through competition?', *Journal of European Integration* 30: 1, 2008, pp. 27–43.

125 Jaap de Hoop Scheffer, 'Speech at the high-level seminar on relations between the European Union and NATO', 7 July 2008.

126 A. Menon, 'Empowering paradise? The ESDP at ten', *International Affairs* 85: 2, 2009, pp. 227–46, at p. 237.

127 SIPRI, Military expenditure, Summary, http://www.sipri.org/yearbook/2009/05.

Chapter 4 The US, European security and EU–US relations

1 Secretary of State Albright, cited by C.W. Maynes, 'US Unilateralism and its Dangers', *Review of International Studies*, 25: 3, 1999, pp. 515–18, at p. 517.

2 Kurt Volker, Principal Deputy Assistant Secretary of State for European and Eurasian Affairs, 'From London to Moscow: New Faces, Old Alliances', 2 May 2008.

3 James Baker, 'A New Europe, A New Atlanticism. Architecture for a New Era', Berlin Press Club, 12 December, 1989, U.S. Department of State, Current Polity, no. 1233.

4 A.L. Gardner, *A New Era in US-EU Relations. The Clinton Administration and the New Transatlantic Agenda*, Aldershot: Ashgate, 1999, p. 10.

5 Declaration on US–EC Relations, htttp://www.useu.be/TransAtlantic/transdec.html.

6 Chris Patten, cited in 'The New Transatlantic Agenda', http://europa.eu.int/comm/external-relations/us/new-transatlantic, May 2001.

7 'Transatlantic Relations – The EU-US Partnership', http://www.useu.be/TransAtlantic/Index.html; For the JAP see 'Joint EU-US Action Plan', http://europa.eu.int/comm/external-relations/us/action-plan.

8 For a discussion of the CNN effect and a guide to further reading, see P. Robinson, 'The CNN effect: Can the news media drive foreign policy? *Review of International Studies* 25: 2, 1999, pp. 301–9.

9 This educational aspect of the NTA was strengthened in 1998 by the Transatlantic Donors Dialogue and Transatlantic Information Exchange Service to facilitate people-to-people projects and by the European Commission's programme of EU Centres in the US, designed to promote American interest in, and provide information about, European integration.

10 Ambassador Eizenstat, cited in T. Frellesen, 'Processes and procedures in EU-US foreign policy cooperation: From the Transatlantic Declaration to the New Transatlantic Agenda', in E. Philippart and P. Winand (eds), *Ever Closer Partnership. Policy-making in EU-US Relations*, Berlin: Peter Lang, 2001, p. 333.

11 C. Patten, 'Devotion or divorce? The future of transatlantic relations', *European Foreign Affairs Review* 6: 3, 2001, 287–90, p. 288.

12 European Presidency, 'A Strategy for the External Dimension of JHA: Global Freedom, Security and Justice', 5 December 2005.

13 European Commission, Press Release 'EU–US Summit in Washington puts global challenges at centre of discussion', IP/09/1664, 3 November 2009.

14 Reuters, 'EU-U.S. summit in doubt as Obama decides not to come', 2 February 2010.

15 The most famous example is R. Kagan, *Of Paradise and Power: America and Europe in the New World Order*, New York: Knopf, 2003.

16 P. Kennedy, *The Rise and Fall of the Great Powers*, London: Unwin Hyman, 1988, p. 666. See also D.P. Calleo, *Beyond American Hegemony*, New York: Basic Books, 1987. In counterargument see J.S. Nye, 'Understating US strength', *Foreign Policy* 72, 1998, 105–29; J.S. Nye, *Bound to Lead: the Changing Nature of American Power*, New York: Basic Books, 1990.

17 S. Brooks and W. Wohlforth, 'American primacy in perspective', *Foreign Affairs* 81: 4, 2002, pp. 20–33; E. Todd, *After the Empire: The Breakdown of American Order*, New York: Columbia University Press, 2003; S. Huntington, 'The lonely superpower', *Foreign Affairs* 78: 2, 1999, pp. 35–50, at p. 35.

18 For contrasting views see C. Krauthammer, 'America and the world', *Foreign Affairs* 70:1, 1990/91, pp. 23–33; C. Krauthammer, 'The unipolar moment revisited', *National Interest* 70, 2002–3, pp. 5–17; J. Mearsheimer, 'Back to the future: Instability in Europe after the Cold War', *International Security* 15:3, 1990, pp. 5–57; J.J. Mearsheimer, *The Tragedy of Great Power Politics*, New York: W. W. Norton, 2001; C. Kupchan, *The End of the American Era: U.S. Foreign Policy After the Cold War*, New York: Alfred Knopf, 2002.

19 M. Boot, 'What the Heck Is a Neocon?', *Wall Street Journal*, 30 December 2002; C. Krauthammer, *Democratic Realism. An American Foreign Policy for a Unipolar World*, Washington: American Enterprise Institute, 2004; R. Kagan, 2003; *op. cit.*, J.S. Nye, *The Paradox of American Power: Why the World's Only Superpower Can't Go It Alone*, New York: Oxford University Press, 2002.

20 P. Buchanan, *A Republic not an Empire: Reclaiming America's Destiny*, Washington: Regnery Publishing, Inc., 1999; P. Buchanan, *Where the Right Went Wrong: How Neoconservatives Subverted the Reagan Revolution and Hijacked the Bush Presidency*, New York: Thomas Dunne Books, 2004; P. Moreau-Defarges, 'Multilateralism and the end of history', *Politique étrangère*, 2004, n.p., http://www.diplomatie.gouv.fr/en/IMG/pdf/0104Moreau_Defarges_gb.pdf; M. Lind, 'Protect the Great Powers', *The Financial Times*, 3 July 2002; M. Lind, 'Beware Visionaries Wielding Power', *The Australian*, 14 March 2003.

21 Condoleeza Rice, speech to the Republican National Convention, 1 August 2000. All post-Cold War US Presidents have asserted that the US must not be the world's policeman: President George H. Bush, Address at West Point, 5 January 1993; Transcript of President Clinton's speech on Bosnia, 27 November 1995; George W. Bush, Presidential debate, Boston MA, 3 October 2000.

22 The idea of Bush administration strategy being rooted as much, if not more, in continuity than change is subject of debate. For similar views and an attempt to put Bush policy in the context of American history, see M. Leffler, '9/11 and American foreign policy', *Diplomatic History* 29: 3, 2005, pp. 395–413; J.L. Gaddis, *Surprise, Security, and the American Experience*, Washington, D.C.: Council on Foreign Relations, 2004. For different emphases see I.H. Daalder and J. Lindsay, *America Unbound. The Bush Revolution in Foreign Policy*, Washington DC: Brookings Institute Press, 2003; J. Newhouse, *Imperial America. The Bush Assault on the World Order*, New York: Knopf, 2003; C. Johnson, *The Sorrows of Empire: Militarism, Secrecy and the End of the Republic*, New York: Metropolitan Books, 2004.

23 For example, Director of the Policy Planning Staff Paul Nitze claimed in 1950 that 'Preponderant power must be the objective of U.S. policy', the military planning document *Joint 2020 Vision* determined that the US should have full spectrum dominance, and the leaked – and subsequently buried – Pentagon draft of the Defense

Planning Guidance in 1992 indicated American commitment to primacy. Nitze cited in M. Leffler, 2005, *op. cit.*, at p. 402; United States Department of Defense, *Joint Vision 2020*, p. 8; PBS, Frontline, 'The War Behind Closed Doors', excerpts from 1992 Wolfowitz draft; P. Tyler, 'US Strategy Plan Calls for Insuring no Rivals Develop. A One-Superpower World', *New York Times*, 8 March 1992; B. Gellman, 'Keeping the US First', *The Washington Post*, 11 March 1992.

24 Gaddis argues that it was not until the 1930s that the US even began to pursue a more multilateralist orientation in foreign policy. J.L. Gaddis, 2005, *op. cit.*, p. 50. See also A. Schlesinger Jr., 'Back to the womb? Isolationism's renewed threat', *Foreign Affairs* 74: 4, 1995, pp. 2–8.

25 For instance, the Clinton administration considered preventative strikes against North Korean nuclear sites in 1994, George H. Bush's invasion of Panama in 1989 had little pretext in a clear and present danger to American national security – unless the definition is stretched to include treaty rights to the Panama Canal – and in many ways President Theodore Roosevelt's Corollary to the Monroe Doctrine in 1904 is an embodiment of preventative military action, asserting as it did the US right to intervene in civil unrest in Western Hemisphere countries to restore order and protect American economic interests.

26 President George H. Bush, State of the Union Address, 28 January 1992. For an introduction to the impact of Congress see D.P. Calleo, 'Imperial America and its Republican constitution', in H. Gardner and R. Stefanova (eds), *The New Transatlantic Agenda: Facing the Challenges of Global Governance*, Aldershot, Ashgate, 2001, pp. 7–16; W. Pfaff, 'US Ambitions Outstrip Its Domestic Appetite, *International Herald Tribune*, 10 July 1997; S. Everts, 'Unilateral America, Lightweight Europe?', working paper, Centre for European Reform, February 2001, p. 7; D.P. Auerswald, 'The President, Congress and American missile defence policy', *Defence Studies* 1: 2, 2002, pp. 57–82.

27 Department of Defense, Quadrennial Defense Review Report, 6 February 2006, p. 3.

28 National Security Strategy of the United States of America, March 2006, p. 36.

29 National Security Strategy of the United States of America, August 1991.

30 There is considerable debate about the consequences of this. For a cross section of opinion see J. Mann, *Rise of the Vulcans: The History of Bush's War Cabinet,* New York: Viking, 2004; B. Woodward, *Bush at War*, New York: Simon and Schuster, 2002; D. Frum and R. Perle, *An End to Evil: How to Win the War on Terror*, New York: Random House, 2003; R.A. Clarke, *Against All Enemies: Inside America's War on Terror*, London: Free Press, 2004; S. Halper and J. Clarke, *America Alone: The Neo-Conservatives and the Global Order*, Cambridge: Cambridge University Press, 2004; A. Moens, *The Foreign Policy of George W Bush: Values, Strategy and Loyalty*, Aldershot: Ashgate, 2004.

31 See, for instance, President Bush, Remarks to the People of Poland, Wawel Royal Castle Krakow, Poland, 31 May 2003; Condoleezza Rice, 'A Balance of Power that Favors Freedom', article adapted from the 2002 Wriston lecture.

32 Interview of the President by Trevor Kavanagh of *The Sun*, 14 November 2003.

33 'A National Security Strategy of Engagement and Enlargement', February 1996, preface; Condoleezza Rice, 'Transformational Diplomacy', Georgetown University, 18 January 2006.

34 *US National Security Strategy, March 2006*, p.37; Jim Lehrer interview with George W. Bush, *Newshour*, 16 February 2000.

35 R. Perle, 'Next Stop Iraq', Foreign Policy Research Institute's annual dinner, 14 November 2001.

36 Condoleezza Rice, 'Transformational Diplomacy', Georgetown University, 18 January 2006.

37 *US National Security Strategy, March 2006*, p. 36.

38 President Clinton, Second Inaugural 20 January 1997; Remarks of Senator Barack Obama to the Chicago Council on Global Affairs, 23 April 2007.

39 President Obama Live From the G-20 Summit, CNN Transcript, 2 April 2009.

40 Some analysts hold that America owes its longevity as the world's leading state to its ability and willingness to exercise power within alliance and multinational frameworks.

See, for instance, J.G. Ikenberry, 'On the sustainability of US power', *The Globalist*, 12 September 2002, http://theglobalist.com/DBWeb/Storyld.aspx?StoryID=2714; J.G. Ikenberry, 'The end of the Neoconservative moment', *Survival* 46: 1, 2004, pp. 7–22.

41 President George Bush, Remarks to the Citizens in Mainz. Rheingoldhalle. Mainz, Federal Republic of Germany, 31 May 1989.

42 President Bill Clinton, speech at North Atlantic Council Summit, NATO Headquarters 10 January 1994.

43 Condoleezza Rice, 'Transformational Diplomacy', 2006, *op. cit.*

44 Elizabeth Jones (Assistant Secretary for European and Eurasian Affairs), testimony before the House International Relations Committee Subcommittee on Europe, 3 March 2004.

45 US Department of State and US Agency for International Development, 'Strategic Plan: Fiscal Years 2007–12', p. 48.

46 Elizabeth Jones, 2004, *op. cit.* PFP is a bilateral cooperation programme between NATO and partner countries that allows the latter to select priorities for cooperation and helps build a relationship between them.

47 Testimony of Daniel Fried, Assistant Secretary of State for European Affairs, before the House Committee on International Relations: Subcommittee hearing on Europe and Emerging Threats, 8 March 2006.

48 National Security Strategy of the United States of America, March 2006, p. 38; Kurt Volker, Principal Deputy Assistant Secretary for European and Eurasian Affairs, Remarks at Media Roundtable, Brussels, Belgium, 6 February 2006. There have been similar calls on Capitol Hill, e.g. Congressman Robert Wexler, Statement, House Committee on International Relations: Subcommittee hearing on Europe and Emerging Threats, 8 March 2006.

49 D.B. Cohen, 'From START to START II: Dynamism and pragmatism in the Bush administration's nuclear weapon policies', *Presidential Studies Quarterly* 27: 3, 1997, pp. 412–29.

50 Initiatives include the Nuclear Cities Initiative, Bio Redirection assistance and a twenty-year deal struck in 1994 worth $12 billion for Russia to dilute approximately 20,000 warheads of uranium for sale to utilities in the US. M. Alexseev, 'From the cold war to the cold peace: US–Russian interactions from Gorbachev to the present', in S. Ramet and C. Ingebritsen (eds), *Coming in From the Cold War. Changes in US-European Interactions Since 1980*, New York: Rowman and Littlefield, 2002, pp. 160–61.

51 This committed both sides to reducing their strategic nuclear warheads to 1,700–2,200, 200 by 31 December 2012.

52 R. Levgold, 'All the way: Crafting a U.S.–Russian alliance', *The National Interest*, 70, 2002, pp. 21–32, at p. 24; 'Bush Approves Resumed Funding for Destruction of Soviet Arms', 14 January 2003, US Office of International Information Programs. The Bush administration's FY2003 budget request for $1.04 billion for Cooperative Threat Reduction programmes marked a 37% increase on the previous year.

53 V. Socor, 'Medvedev proposes all-European security pact during Berlin visit', *Eurasia Daily Monitor*, 9 June 2008.

54 Lecture by Julian Lindley-French, 'Are reinforcing the ESDP and Improving Transatlantic Relations Compatible Objectives', at the Internal Seminar for Experts 'The Common Foreign and Security Policy – What can be Learned from the Iraq Crisis?', 10 June 2003; K. Archick, 'The United States and Europe: Possible Options for US Policy', CRS Report for Congress, RL32577, 8 March 2005, p.10.

55 J. Van Oudenaren, 'US reactions to the EU security strategy', *Oxford Journal of Good Governance* 1: 1, 2004, pp. 43–47, at p. 44. For examples of such unilateralist charges see Chancellor Schröder cited in C.R. Whitney, 'NATO AT 50: With Nations at Odds, Is it a Misalliance?', *The New York Times*, p. 7; French Foreign Minister Hubert Védrine, cited in A.J. Blinken, 'The false crisis over the Atlantic', *Foreign Affairs* 80: 3, 2001, pp. 35–48, at p. 41; C. Patten, 'Jaw-jaw, not war-war', 14 February 2002; J. Freedland, interview

with Chris Patten, *The Guardian*, 9 February 2002, p. 8; Address by Javier Solana, 'Europe's Place in the World', 23 May 2002, SO101/02; Solana, cited in unattributed, 'EU's Solana Chides Washington over Unilateralism', *Deutsche Welle*, 28 July 2004.

56 J. Van Oudenaren, 'US Reactions to the EU Security Strategy', 2004, *op. cit*, p. 44.

57 H.A. Kissinger, 'NATO's Uncertain Future in a Troubled Alliance', 1 December 2002, http://www.expandnato.org/uncertain.html; Charles Ries, Principal Deputy Assistant Secretary for European and Eurasian Affairs, 'Mars and Venus: Prospects for Transatlantic Cooperation', Remarks at the XXI German American Conference, Atlantik-Bruecke and The American Council on Germany, Berlin, Germany, 13 June 2003.

58 Rademaker's statement to the Conference on Disarmament in Geneva, 'The Commitment of the United States to Effective Multilateralism', 2003.

59 V. Pop, 'US backs Eastern Partnership eyeing energy independence', 6 April 2009.

60 See, for example, 'Interview of the President by Christian Malar', France 3 TV, 6 June 2008; President George W. Bush, comments at joint President Bush and Prime Minister Tony Blair press conference, 25 May 2006.

61 Colleen Graffy, Deputy Assistant Secretary of State for Public Diplomacy for Europe, 'What is the US doing to improve its image abroad?', Remarks at Chatham House, 1 November 2007.

62 President George W. Bush, inauguration speech, 20 January 2005; President Bush, 'Remarks at OECD Meetings in Paris', 13 June 2008; The White House, Office of the Press Secretary, 'President Bush Participates in Joint Press Availability with Slovenian Prime Minister Janša and European Commission President Barroso', 10 June 2008.

63 US National Security Strategy, March 2006, preface.

64 US Ambassador to NATO, Victoria Nuland, speech at the London School of Economics, 25 February 2008. See also The United States Mission to the EU, 'Under Secretary Burns elaborates on challenges and opportunities facing the transatlantic community', 26 March 2007.

65 Remarks as delivered by Secretary of Defense William S. Cohen, National Press Club, Washington, DC, Wednesday, 10 January 2001.

66 NATO, Understanding NATO Military Transformation, Norfolk, Allied Command Transformation, 2005, p. 6. Definitions of Effects-Based Operations vary. Davis, for example, defines EBO as 'operations conceived and planned in a systems framework that considers the full range of direct, indirect, and cascading effects – effects that may, with different degrees of probability, be achieved by the application of military, diplomatic, psychological, and economic instruments.' P. Davis, *Effects-Based Operations (EBO): A Grand Challenge for the Analytical Community*, Santa Monica: RAND, 2001, p. xiii.

67 Christopher Murray, Deputy Chief of Mission at the US Mission to the EU, 'U.S. Mission's Murray discusses the US–European security relationship', 20 September 2007, The United States Mission to the European Union; US Ambassador to NATO, Victoria Nuland, speech to Presse Club and AmCham, Paris, 22 February 2008; US Ambassador to NATO, Victoria Nuland, *op. cit*. 2008.

68 Kurt Volker, Principal Deputy Assistant Secretary of State for European and Eurasian Affairs, 'From London to Moscow: New Faces, Old Alliances', 2 May 2008; The United States Mission to the EU, 'Under Secretary Burns elaborates on challenges and opportunities facing the transatlantic community', 26 March 2007.

69 Daniel Fried, US Assistant Secretary of State for European and Eurasian Affairs, 'Transatlantic priorities: the short list', remarks before the Center for National Policy, 18 April 2007.

70 Testimony of Daniel Fried, US Assistant Secretary of State for European Affairs, before the House Committee on International Relations: Subcommittee hearing on Europe and Emerging Threats, 8 March 2006.

71 Kurt Volker, Acting Assistant Secretary for European and Eurasian Affairs, 'Bucharest: NATO and the Future of the Transatlantic Alliance', Remarks at the Heritage Foundation, 7 April 2008.

72 Remarks of President Barack Obama – As Prepared for Delivery, Address to Turkish Parliament, 6 April 2009.

73 EULEX is the EU's rule of law mission in Kosovo and the largest civilian mission it has yet deployed.

74 Daniel Fried, Assistant Secretary for European and Eurasian Affairs, Testimony Before the Senate Foreign Relations Committee Washington, DC, Kosovo: The Balkans' Moment of Truth? 4 March 2008.

75 Possible Russian actions in this respect include encouraging secession of the Crimea and Eastern regions of Ukraine. V. Socor, 'Moscow makes furious but empty threats to Georgia and Ukraine', *Eurasia Daily Monitor*, 5: 70, 14 April 2008.

76 A. Åslund and A. Kuchins, 'Pressing the "reset button" on US–Russia relations', CSIS Policy Brief, March 2009, p. 1.

77 European Security Strategy, 'A Secure Europe in a Better World', 12 December 2003, p. 6.

78 Comments of Sir Peter Ricketts, Permanent Representative of the UK to NATO, 'Conference Report: 'European Defence Integration: Bridging the Gap between Strategy and Capabilities', Center for Strategic and International Studies, 12 October 2005, p. 21; Keynote speech by NATO Secretary General, Jaap de Hoop Scheffer, 'NATO and the EU: Time for a New Chapter', 29 January 2007.

79 C4ISR: command, control, communications, computer, intelligence, surveillance and reconnaissance. Network-centric operations refer to military operations enabled by networking the military force, which 'means computer network-based provision of an integrated picture of the battlefield, available in detail to all levels of command and control down to the individual soldier.' N. Wesenten, G. Belenky and T. Balkin, 'Cognitive readiness in network-centric operations', *Parameters* 35, 2005, pp. 94–105, at p. 94

80 S. Neuman, 'Defense industries and global dependency', *Orbis* 50: 3, 2006, pp. 429–51, at p. 438.

81 G. Adams, 'Fortress America in a changing transatlantic defence market', in B. Schmitt (ed.), *Between Cooperation and Competition: The Transatlantic Defence Market*, ISS: Chaillot Paper 44, January 2001; P. Dombrowski, E. Gholz and A. Ross, 'Selling military transformation: The defense industry and innovation', *Orbis* 46: 3, 2002, pp. 523–36.

82 For instance, in March 2006 a joint report by the US Defense Science Board and the UK Defence Scientific Advisory Council concluded that Anglo-American collaboration on selected critical technologies was essential to defend against COTS. US Defense Science Board and the UK Defence Scientific Advisory Council, 'Defense Critical Technologies', March 2006.

83 This fear was reflected in the Clinton administration's decision to block the proposed merger in 1998 of Lockheed Martin and Northrop Grumman.

84 T. Guay, 'The transatlantic defence industrial base: Restructuring scenarios and their implications', Strategic Studies Institute, April 2005, p. 1; US Chamber of Commerce to the EU, 'Position paper response to the European Commission's Green Paper on Defence Procurement, 22 February 2005; F. Heisbourg, 'From European defense industrial restructuring to transatlantic deal?', CSIS working paper no.4, February 2001, p. iv; B. Tigner, 'EU Threatens To Build Own Defense Market Vents Frustration With U.S. Trade Restrictions', *Defense News*, 24 January 2005.

85 R. North, 'The wrong side of the Hill: The secret realignment of UK defence policy with the EU', Centre for Policy Studies, October 2005, p. 4.

86 Philip T. Reeker (Acting Spokesman), U.S. Department of State Office of the Spokesman, Press Statement: 'Defense Trade Security Initiative' Press Statement, 24 May 2000; US Mission to the EU, 'New Export Exemption for Closest Allies to Promote Defense Efficiency', 23 May 2000. For details see US State Department – Policy – Directorate of Defense Trade Controls, 'Defense Trade Security Initiative (DTSI) – Summary Sheet'.

87 T. Guay, 2005, *op. cit.*, p. 30.

88 Alain Picq, comments at 'Is a transatlantic defence industry increasingly on the cards?', Security and Defence Agenda Roundtable', 30 January 2006, p.13.

89 Burkard Schmitt, 'Armaments cooperation in Europe', Institute for Security Studies, updated January 2005; Secretary of State for Defence, Defence Industrial Strategy. Defence White Paper, Command 6697, December 2005, p. 26. When Poland decided to buy American made F-16 fighters rather than European models the European Commission President bluntly warned Warsaw in April 2003 '"You can't entrust your purse to Europe and your security to America."' Prodi cited in F.S. Larrabee, 'Danger and opportunity in Eastern Europe', *Foreign Affairs* 85: 6, 2006, pp. 117–31.

90 House of Commons, Select Committee on European Scrutiny - Twenty-Third Report, 4 June 2003, item 22.

91 UK Ministry of Defence, 'UK Operations in Iraq: Lessons for the Future', December 2003, pp. 34 and 36.

92 The MOD, for example, argues that this should be pursued only when it 'is compatible with, and does not threaten our links to, the US and NATO.' UK Ministry of Defence, Paper No.2 – Multi-national Defence Co-operation, p. 8.

93 Secretary of State for Defence, Defence Industrial Strategy. Defence White Paper, Command 6697, December 2005, p.27; A. Dorman, 'Reconciling Britain to Europe in the Next Millennium: The Evolution to British Defence Policy in the post-Cold War Era', Paper to the International Studies Association, March 2000, p. 41.

94 Klaus Becher, 'Chairman's summing-up', IISS/CEPS European Security Forum: European and Transatlantic Industrial Strategies', 25 November 2002; A. Ashbourne, 'Opening the US Defence Market', Center for European Reform, October 2000, p. 7.

95 D. Reveron, 'Old allies, new friends: Intelligence-sharing in the War on Terror', *Orbis* 50:3, 2006, pp. 453–68; C. Grant, 'Intimate Relations. Can Britain play a leading role in European Defence – and keep its special links to US intelligence?', Working Paper, Centre for European Reform, 2000, np; I. Carson, 'Transformed? Transformed?', *The Economist* (US), 20 July 2002.

96 BBC News, 'BAE Systems to buy US rival UDI', 7 March 2005.

97 Pierre Sabatié-Garat, comments at 'Is a transatlantic defence industry increasingly on the cards?', Security and Defence Agenda Roundtable, 30 January 2006, p. 9.

98 A. Ashbourne, 'Opening the US Defence Market', 2000, p. 15; PriceWaterhouse-Coopers, 'The Defence Industry in the 21st Century: Thinking Global ... or Thinking American?', 2005, p. 21.

99 R. North, 'The Wrong Side of the Hill', 2005, p. 16.

100 S. Neuman, 2006, *op. cit.*, p. 447.

101 *Ibid.*, p. 451. For example, it has been suggested that European anxiety for economic and technology benefits helped the US use the Joint Strike Fighter as a modern day 'trojan horse' to encourage long-term dependence on American weaponry, combat a Fortress Europe and protect market share against European alternatives – the multinational Eurofighter, French Rafale and Swedish Gripen. See E. Kapstein, 'Capturing fortress Europe: International collaboration and the Joint Strike Fighter', *Survival* 46: 3, 2004, pp. 137–60, at p. 138.

102 Council of the European Union, EU–US Summit Washington, 3 November 2009, 15352/09 (Presse 316).

Chapter 5 Russia, European security and relations with the EU

1 European Council, Common Strategy of the European Union on Russia, 4 June 1999, Brussels: Official Journal of the European Communities, L 157/1, 24 June 1999; European Security Strategy, 'A Secure Europe in a Better World', 12 December 2003, p. 14.

2 V. Merkushev, 'Relations between Russia and the EU: The view from across the Atlantic', *Perspectives on European Politics and Society* 6: 2, 2005, pp. 353–71, at p. 365; S. Karaganov, 'A new epoch of confrontation', *Russia in Global Affairs* 4, 2007, n.p., http://eng.globalaffairs.ru/region-rfp/numbers/21/1148.html

3 D. Allen, 'EPC/CFSP, the Soviet Union, and the former Soviet Republics: Do the twelve have a coherent policy? in E. Regelsberger *et al.* (eds), *Foreign Policy of the European Union: From EPC to CFSP and Beyond*, Boulder: Lynne Rienner, 1997, pp. 219–36, at p. 233.

4 European Commission (1994) Partnership and Association Agreement with Russia, http://www.europa.eu.int/comm/external_relations/russia/intro/index.htm.

5 L. Karabeshkin and D. Spechler, 'EU and NATO enlargement: Russia's expectations, responses and options for the future', *European Security* 16: 3–4, 2007, pp. 307–28, at p. 307.

6 European Commission, Communication for the Commission, The European Union and Russia: the future relationship, 31 May 1995, COM(95) 223 final, p. 9.

7 Common Strategy of the European Union on Russia, 4 June 1999, http://ec.europa.eu/external_relations/ceeca/com_strat/russia_99.pdf.

8 M. Light, J. Lowenhardt and S. White, 'Russian perspectives on European security', *European Foreign Affairs Review* 5, 2000, pp. 489–505; Medium-term Strategy for Development of Relations between the Russian Federation and the European Union (2000–2010), 1999, unofficial translation, http://europa.eu.int/comm/external_relations/russia/russian_medium_term_strategy/ (hereafter Medium Term Strategy).

9 Putin cited by H. Timmermann, 'European–Russian partnership: What future?', *European Foreign Affairs Review* 5: 2, 2000, pp. 165–74, at p.167.

10 European Commission, Factsheet – EU–Russia Common Space of External Security, November 2006.

11 H. Moroff, 'Russia, the CIS and the EU: Secondary integration by association?', in K. Malfiet, L. Verpoest and E. Vinokuroz (eds), *The CIS, the EU and Russia: The Challenges of Integration*, London: Routledge, 2007, pp. 95–120, at p. 98.

12 European Commission, Country Strategy Paper 2007–13, Russian Federation, p. 4.

13 D. Simes, 'Losing Russia: The costs of renewed confrontation', *Foreign Affairs* 86: 6, 2007, pp. 36–52; A. Arbatov, 'Is a new Cold War imminent?', *Russia in Global Affairs* 2, 2007, Conflict Studies Research Center, Russian Series, July 2007, n.p.

14 See, for instance, President Medvedev, Address to the Federal Assembly of the Russian Federation, 5 November 2008.

15 Scholarship on Russia's relationship with the West since 2000 reveals the extent of flux within Russia – and interpretations of this flux. For example, in 2001 the respected commentator Dmitri Trenin published *The End of Eurasia: Russia on the Border between Geopolitics and Globalization*; in 2002 he delivered a paper entitled 'A Russia-within-Europe: Working toward a new security arrangement'; and in 2006 he announced in *Foreign Affairs* that 'Russia leaves the West'. D. Trenin, *The End of Eurasia: Russia on the Border Between Geopolitics and Globalization*, Moscow: Carnegie Moscow Center, 2001; 'A Russia-within-Europe: Working toward a new security arrangement', Paper prepared for the IISS/CEPS European Security Forum, Brussels, January 14, 2002; 'Russia leaves the West', *Foreign Affairs* 85: 4, 2006, pp. 87–96.

16 This summary is based predominantly on S. White, 'Elite opinion and foreign policy in post-communist Russia', *Perspectives on European Politics and Society* 8: 2, 2007, pp. 147–67, at p. 149. See also T. Ambrosio, *Challenging America's Global Pre-eminence: Russia's Quest for Multipolarity*, Aldershot: Ashgate, 2005.

17 Speech by Minister of Foreign Affairs of the Russian Federation, Sergey Lavrov, at the XV Assembly of the Council of Foreign and Defence Policy, 17 March 2007.

18 P. Flenley, 'Russia and the EU: A pragmatic and contradictory relationship', *Perspectives on European Politics and Society* 6: 3, 2005, pp. 435–61, at p. 435; A. Tsygankov, 'New challenges for Putin's foreign policy', *Orbis* 50: 1, 2006, pp. 153–65, at p. 156; R. Sakwa, *Putin: Russia's Choice*, 2nd edition, London: Routledge, 2008, Chapter 10.

19 See, for instance, A. Kozyrev, 'Russia: A chance for Survival', *Foreign Affairs* 71, 1992, pp. 1–16, p. 10.

20 R. Sakwa, '"New Cold War" or twenty years' crisis? Russia and international politics', *International Affairs* 84: 2, 2008, pp. 241–67, at p. 244.

21 March stresses in this cautionary mode 'the lack of transparency and divergence of the formal and informal that often characterizes Russian politics.' See L. March, 'Security strategy and the "Russia problem"', in R. Dannreuther and J. Peterson (eds), *Security Strategy and Transatlantic Relations*, London: Routledge, 2006, pp. 97–114, at p. 101.

22 E. Rumer, *Russian Foreign Policy Beyond Putin*, Oxford: International Institute for Strategic Studies, Routledge, 2007, p. 14.

23 The Foreign Policy Concept of the Russian Federation, approved on 28 June 2000, accessed at http:www.fas.org/nuke/guide/Russia/doctrine/econcept.htm (hereafter Foreign Policy Concept, 2000, n.p.)

24 *Ibid.*

25 *Ibid.* Ministry of Foreign Affairs of the Russian Federation, A Survey of Russian Federation Foreign Policy, Unofficial translation from Russian, accessed at http:/www.mid.ru/brp (hereafter Survey of Russian Federation Foreign Policy, n.p.); Foreign Policy Concept of the Russian Federation approved by President of the Russian Federation Dmitry Medvedev on the 12 July, 2008, http://www.norway.mid.ru/pr050808_eng.html (hereafter Foreign Policy Concept, 2008, n.p.)

26 Foreign Policy Concept, 2000, n.p., *op. cit.*

27 Foreign Policy Concept, 2008, n.p., *op. cit.*

28 'The main priority in the foreign policy of the Russian Federation in international economic relations is to promote the development of the national economy, which, in conditions of globalization, is unthinkable without broad integration of Russia in the system of world economic ties.' Foreign Policy Concept, 2000, n.p., *op. cit.*

29 *Ibid.*

30 L. Shevtsosa, *Putin's Russia*, Washington: Carnegie Endowment for International Peace, 2003, p. 199.

31 Survey of Russian Federation Foreign Policy, 2007, n.p., *op. cit.*

32 Ivanov, cited in P. Baev, *Russian Energy Policy and Military Power: Putin's Quest for Greatness*, London: Routledge, 2008, p. 155.

33 F. Weir, 'Russia's resurgent military', CS Monitor, 17 August 2007; A. Cohen, 'How to confront Russia's anti-American foreign policy', Backgrounder, Heritage Foundation, 27 June 2007, pp. 1–6, at p. 4; President Medvedev, Opening Address at a Meeting with Commanders of Military Districts, 26 September 2008.

34 The 2000 Military Doctrine stresses that nuclear weapons may be used in response to 'large-scale aggression utilizing conventional weapons in situations critical to the national security of the Russian Federation'. The 2007 Survey further advises that 'Prerequisites are being created for the justification of lowering the "threshold" for using nuclear weapons.' Russian Federation, Russian Federation Military Doctrine, 21 April 2000, n.p., English translation by US Foreign Broadcast Information Service, accessed at http://www.freerepublic.com/forum/a394aa0466bfe.htm; Survey of Russian Federation Foreign Policy, 2007, n.p., *op. cit.*

35 L. Harding, 'Russia issues new missile defence threat', *The Guardian,* 4 July 2007; President Medvedev, Address to the Federal Assembly of the Russian Federation, 5 November 2008; R. Ryan, 'Join Nato and we'll target missiles at Kiev, Putin warns Ukraine', *The Guardian,* 12 February 2008; H. de Quetteville and A. Pierce, 'Russia threatens nuclear attack on Poland over US missile shield deal', *The Telegraph,* 15 August 2008; Unattributed, 'Russia's new nuclear challenge to Europe', *The Sunday Times,* 17 August 2008; H. de Quetteville and I. Wilkinson, 'Russia threatens to target US missile shield', *The Telegraph,* 19 December 2007.

36 Survey of Russian Federation Foreign Policy, 2007, n.p., *op. cit.*

37 Foreign Policy Concept, 2000, n.p. It should be noted that The National Security Concept of the Russian Federation placed slightly greater emphasis on force, stating that 'The significance of military force in international relations remains considerable. Russian Federation, National Security Concept of the Russian Federation, Presidential decree 24, 10 January 2000, n.p.

38 Survey of Russian Federation Foreign Policy, 2007, n.p., *op. cit.*

39 Foreign Policy Concept, 2008, n.p., *op. cit.*
40 For example, in March 2007 Sergey Lavrov observed that the lack of reform of a European security architecture whose 'entities and instruments' are largely inherited from the past was 'reproducing the bloc policy in present day conditions'. Speech by Minister of Foreign Affairs of the Russian Federation, Sergey Lavrov, 2007, *op. cit.*
41 Medvedev cited in Unattributed, 'Georgia signs peace deal', *The Independent*, 15 August 2008; S. Cimbala, 'Missile defenses and Mother Russia: Scarecrow or showstopper?', *European Security* 16: 3–4, 2007, pp. 289–306, at p. 292.
42 In 2006 an article in *Foreign Affairs* arguing that a long-term US objective of achieving nuclear supremacy stirred a major academic and political exchange. See K. Lieber and D. Press, 'The rise of U.S. nuclear supremacy', *Foreign Affairs* 85: 2, 2006, pp. 42–54; and responses to this article in *Foreign Affairs*, 85: 5, 2006.
43 President Medvedev, Speech at Meeting with German Political, Parliamentary and Civic Leaders, 5 June 2008. This is consistent with the Putin era. For example, Lavrov argued in 2007 that Russian reforms 'proceed in the mainstream of a European choice, but with the preservation of centuries-old traditions of Russia.' Speech by Minister of Foreign Affairs of the Russian Federation, Sergey Lavrov, 2007, *op. cit.*
44 P. Baev, 2008, *op. cit.*, p. 40.
45 R. Sakwa, 2008, *op. cit.* at p. 249.
46 President Putin, 'Annual Address to the Federal Assembly of the Russian Federation', 25 April 2005'; President Medvedev, Address to the Federal Assembly of the Russian Federation, 5 November 2008.
47 Foreign Policy Concept, 2008, n.p., *op. cit.*
48 *Ibid.*
49 Survey of Russian Federation Foreign Policy, 2007, n.p., *op. cit.*
50 Putin called in 2007 for reconsideration of the 'architecture of global security' and of the global economic architecture. Speech by President Putin at the 43rd Munich conference on security, 02/10/2007; A. Cohen, 'How to confront Russia's anti-American foreign policy', at p. 1.
51 Survey of Russian Federation Foreign Policy, 2007, n.p., *op. cit.*
52 Putin, cited in D. Averre, 'Russia and the European Union: Convergence or divergence?', *European Security* 14:2, 2005, pp. 175–202, at p. 194.
53 Survey of Russian Federation Foreign Policy, 2007, n.p., *op. cit.*
54 Foreign Policy Concept, 2008, n.p., *op. cit.*
55 President Medvedev, remarks at meeting with Members of the Council on Foreign Relations, 16 November 2008.
56 Survey of Russian Federation Foreign Policy, 2007, n.p., *op. cit.*
57 M.H. Van Herpen, 'Medvedev's proposal for a pan-European security pact: Its six hidden objectives and how the West should respond,' Cicero Foundation, 27 October 2008, p. 6.
58 See, for example, M. Smith, *Pax Russica: Russia's Monroe Doctrine*, London: Royal United Services Institute for Defence Studies, 1993.
59 Interview given by President of Russia Dmitry Medvedev to Television Channels, Channel One, Russia, NTV, 31 August 2008.
60 M. Van Herpen, 2008, *op. cit.*, p. 9.
61 Survey of Russian Federation Foreign Policy, 2007, n.p., *op. cit.*
62 H. Moroff, K. Malfiet, L. Verpoest and E. Vinokuroz (eds), 2007, *op. cit.*, at p. 99.
63 L. March, 2006, *op. cit.*, p. 113.
64 Survey of Russian Federation Foreign Policy, 2007, n.p., *op. cit.*
65 BBC News, 'Putin deplores collapse of USSR', 23 April 2005; Putin, cited in A. Cohen, 'How to confront Russia's anti-American foreign policy', at p. 5.
66 President Medvedev, Speech at the Meeting with Russian Ambassadors and Permanent Representatives to International Organisations, 15 July 2008.
67 President Medvedev. Speech at Meeting with German Political, Parliamentary and Civic Leaders, 5 June 2008.

68 Survey of Russian Federation Foreign Policy, 2007, n.p., *op. cit.*
69 W. Guanqun, 'Solana: no big need to revamp European security structures', *China View,* 21 March 2009.
70 Council of the European Union, Summary of the address by the EU High Representative for CFSP, Javier Solana, 'Where is Russia going? A new attempt for an all-European security order', at the 44th Munich Conference on Security Policy, SO55/ 08, 10 February 2008.
71 Benita Ferrero-Waldner, 'EU/Russia: a challenging partnership, but one of the most important of our times', EP Plenary Debate on EU/Russia Strasbourg, SPEECH/08/ 545, 21 October 2008.
72 A. Cohen, date, *op. cit.,* at p. 6.
73 Survey of Russian Federation Foreign Policy, 2007, n.p., *op. cit.*
74 Y. Tymoshenko, 'The sources of Russian conduct', *Foreign Affairs,* 86:3, 2007, pp. 69–82.
75 P. Finn, 'Russia, Indonesia set $1 billion arms deal', *Washington Post.com.,* 7 September 2007.
76 As Krastev has observed, 'the concept of sovereign democracy does not mark Russia's break with the European tradition. It embodies Russia's ideological ambition to be the ' other Europe – an alternative to the European Union.' Ivan Krastev, 'Russia as the "other Europe"', *Russia in Global Affairs,* 4, 2007, n.p. Opinions vary about the attractiveness and/or practicability of Russia's sovereign democracy and development model as an alternative to the EU's/West: A. Gat., 'The return of authoritarian Great Powers', *Foreign Affairs* 86:4, 2007, pp. 59–69; M. McFaul and K. Stoner-Weiss, 'The myth of the authoritarian model; How Putin's crackdown holds Russia back', *Foreign Affairs* 87:1, 2008, pp. 68–84; M. McFaul, 'Russia: more stick, less carrot', *Hoover Digest,* 1, 2008.
77 Moscow has criticised increasingly what it considers to be an anti-Russian caucus amongst the 2004 entrants that is 'turning the Russia-EU relationship into a "hostage" of their own national interests.' Sergei Yastrzhembskii, Russia's special representative for the EU–Russia common space of internal security, cited in Derek Averre, date, *op. cit.* at p.184; Chizhov cited in I. Traynor, 'Russia accused of unleashing cyberwar to disable Estonia', *The Guardian,* 17 May 2007.
78 Medium Term Strategy, n.p., *op. cit.*
79 Some have cited this as an example of the Kremlin's paranoia. See Yuliya Tymoshenko, 'The sources of Russian conduct'.
80 European Commission, Country Strategy Paper 2007–13, Russian Federation, pp. 18–19.
81 The 2008 Foreign Policy Concept makes clear Russia's determination to dominate the CIS: 'Russia's attitude towards subregional entities and other bodies to which Russia is not party in the CIS area is determined by their assessed real contribution into ensuring good neighborly relations and stability, their eagerness to take into account Russia's legitimate interests in practice and to duly respect existing cooperation mechanisms, such as the CIS, CSTO, EurAsEC, and Shanghai Cooperation Organization (SCO).' Foreign Policy Concept, 2008, n.p., *op. cit.*
82 President Medvedev, Address to the Federal Assembly of the Russian Federation, 5 November 2008.
83 The European Commission noted especially in the soft power context energy supply, trade and investment, jobs for migrant workers, cultural and linguistic influence. The Kremlin is also apparently 'getting into the game of "creating" NGOs to counter the influence of Western-funded organizations operating in its sphere of influence.' European Commission, Country Strategy Paper 2007–13, Russian Federation, p.8. See also A. Tsygankov, 'Projecting confidence, not fear: Russia's post-imperial assertiveness', *Orbis* 50: 4, 2006, pp. 677–90.
84 Announced by Medvedev in May 2008, this Agency is modelled on USAID and aimed especially at soft security in Russia's relations with its neighbours. Lindner argues that as it will above all assist Russia and Russian citizens living in the post-Soviet world – a population group that regularly serves as political justification for intervention,

including in the frozen conflicts, 'hard and soft security are very close together here.' R. Lindner, 'New realism: The making of Russia's foreign policy in the post-Soviet world', *The EU–Russia Centre Review: Russian Foreign Policy*, Issue 8, October 2008, pp. 28–37, at p. 30.

85 MNEPR Membership: EC, EURATOM, Russia, Norway, Finland, Sweden, Denmark, UK, Netherlands, Germany and Belgium. (2003) 'Signature of MNEPR, 21 May 2003, IP/03/724.

86 European Commission, 'Guidelines for the Development of a Political Declaration and Policy Framework Document for the Northern Dimension from 2007', Annex 1, p. 3.

87 Council Joint Action establishing a European Union Cooperation Programme for non-proliferation and disarmament in the Russian Federation, 1999/878/CFSP, 17 December 1999.

88 S. De Spiegeleire, 'Recoupling Russia: Staying the course. Europe's security relationship with Russia', Paper prepared for the IISS/CEPS European Security Forum, Brussels, January 2002; M. Webber, 'Third-party inclusion in European Security and Defence Policy: A case study of Russia', *European Foreign Affairs Review* 6:4, 2001, pp. 407–26, at p. 417.

89 Comments of Jonathan Stern, director of gas research at the Oxford Institute for Energy Studies, cited in *Energy Bulletin*, 22 January 2009.

90 Unattributed, '"Ice Period" ensues in Poland-Russia relations', *RIA Novosti*, 22 April 2007.

91 The celebrations of the 750th Anniversary of Kaliningrad have been seen as an 'important focal point of such a policy, enabling Russia to emphasise its natural, long-standing presence in the region.' L. Karabeshkin and D. Spechler, 'EU and NATO enlargement: Russia's expectations', 2007, at p. 314.

92 The 2007 Survey States the restoration and development of Russia's 'informational and cultural presence' abroad as a top priority and identifies as 'A major resource for the protection of compatriots' interests' the preservation of the Russian-language space in foreign countries, primarily the enhancement of the status of the Russian language. Survey of Russian Federation Foreign Policy, 2007, n.p., *op. cit.*

93 Ian Traynor, 'Russia accused of unleashing cyberwar to disable Estonia'; Tony Halpin, 'Estonia fails to appease Russia over statue', *Timesonline*, 8 May 2007.

94 European Commission, EU–Russia Common Space on Freedom, Security and Justice, Progress Report 2007, March 2008, p. 2.

95 Communication from the Commission to the Council, 'Review of EU–Russia relations', COM(2008) 740 final, 5 November 2008, p. 2; Benita Ferrero-Waldner, 'External Relations: latest developments', AFET, European Parliament Brussels, 5 November 2008, SPEECH/08/586, 6 November 2008.

96 Unattributed, 'Putin threatens to review relations with EU', *Russia Today,* 23 March 2009.

97 House of Lords, European Union Committee -Third Report 'After Georgia. The EU and Russia: Follow-Up Report', 3 February 2009.

98 L. Karabeshkin and D. Spechler, *op. cit.* 2007, at p. 312.

99 Text of the Russian Minister of Foreign Affairs Sergey Lavrov's Interview published in the newspaper "Rossiiskiye Vesti", 1 April 2009.

100 Moscow originally viewed ESDP as a potential means to weaken the transatlantic relationship. Russia's Medium Term Strategy suggested that the EU–Russia partnership over the coming decade might 'ensure pan-European security by the Europeans themselves without both the isolation of the United States and NATO and their dominance on the continent'. Medium Term Strategy, n.p., *op. cit.* See also Zhurkin cited in A. Deighton, 'The European Security and Defence Policy', *Journal of Common Market Studies* 40: 4, 2002, pp. 719–41, at p. 733.

101 D. Gowan, *How the EU can help Russia*, London: Center for European Reform, 2000, p. 24.

102 Council of the European Union, Extraordinary European Council, Presidency Conclusions, 12594/2/08, REV 2, 6 October 2008, p. 3.

103 Press release, 'Eastern Partnership', MEMO/08/762, 3 December 2008.
104 Y. Tymoshenko, date, *op. cit.* D. Trenin, 'Russia leaves the West'.
105 Russia rejected participation in the ENP.
106 V. Ivanenko, 'Russian global position after 2008', *Russia in Global Affairs* 4, 2007, n.p.
107 Views differ about the potential of the CIS and for Russian leadership of it. B. Nygren, *The Rebuilding of Greater Russia: Putin's foreign policy towards the CIS countries*, London: Routledge, 2008, p. 25; J. Willerton and M. Beznosov, 'Russia's pursuit of its Eurasian security interests: Weighing the CIS and alternative bilateral-multilateral arrangements', in K. Malfiet, L. Verpoes and E. Vinokurov (eds), 2007, *op. cit.* pp. 47–70, at p. 68; P. Baev, 'The CIS: refusing to fade away', *Russia and Eurasia Review*, 1: 10, 2002, n.p.
108 S. Cimbala, 'Missile defenses and Mother Russia',at p. 295; Survey of Russian Federation Foreign Policy, 2007, n.p., *op. cit.*
109 Common Strategy of the European Union on Russia, 4 June 1999.
110 European Commission, EU–Russia summit, 10 May 2005.
111 European Commission, Country Strategy Paper 2002–6, National Indicative Programme, 2002–3, Russian Federation, 27 December 2001, p. 15.
112 *Ibid.*, p. 9.
113 European Commission, Country Strategy Paper 2007–13, Russian Federation, p. 7.
114 European Commission, Communication for the Commission, The European Union and Russia: the future relationship, 31 May 1995, COM(95) 223 final, pp. 1–2.
115 Mark Leonard and Nicu Popescu, 'A five-point strategy for EU–Russia relations', http://www.europesworld.org.
116 President Medvedev, Speech at the Meeting with Russian Ambassadors and Permanent Representatives to International Organisations, 15 July 2008.
117 T. Bordachev, 'An odd insider's perspective: A Russian perspective', in C. Grant, J. Gedmin and T. Bordachev, *Strategic Implications of the EU crisis*, Brussels: Center for European Studies, 2006, pp. 14–21, at p.18; I. Kempe, 'Beyond bilateralism: adjusting EU–Russia relations', Bertelsmann Group for Policy Research, no.12, September 2007.
118 M. Leonard and N. Popescu, 'A power audit of EU–Russia relations', European Council of Foreign Affairs, November 2007, p. 2. The Baltic States are seen variously to have been emboldened by their EU and NATO Memberships, as carving a role for themselves as mentors by example to governments of other former Soviet republics, especially the Western CIS and the Caucasus, and to have seemingly 'chosen to play the role of permanent opponent of Russian in European politics, rather than that of bridge between the EU and Russia.' Makarychev suggests that Russia treats most of its neighbours as security challengers. L. Karabeshkin and D. Spechler, date, *op. cit.*, at p. 311; A. Makarychev, 'Russia's energy policy: between security and transparency', PONARS Memo no.425, December 2006.
119 A. Wilson, N. Popescu and P. Noël, *The Future of EU–Russia Relations: A Way Forward in Solidarity and the Rule of Law*, Brussels: European Parliament, 2009, p. 4.
120 H.M. Kloth, 'Polish Minister Attacks Schröder and Merkel', 1 May 2006, http://www.spiegel.de/international/0,1518,413969,00.html.
121 European Commission, Communication to the Council and the European Parliament on relations with Russia', COM (2004) 106, 9 February 2004; Unattributed, 'Polish Prime Minister: Europe must speak with one voice to Russia', *FT.com*, 17 February 2008; Communication from the Commission to the Council, 'Review of EU–Russia relations', COM(2008) 740 final, 5 November 2008, p. 5.
122 A report in 2009 argued that market integration and the emergence of pan-European competitive trading would turn Europe into a single export market for Gazprom. This would result in large importers of Russian gas in Western Europe feeling less incentive to accommodate Moscow politically and highly dependent Eastern European countries feeling less insecure. Europe would in turn, therefore, be better prepared to address Moscow with one voice. A. Wilson, N. Popescu and P. Noël, date, *op. cit.*, p. 23.
123 Benita Ferrero-Waldner, 'After the Russia / Ukraine gas crisis: what next?', Chatham House, London, 9 March 2009.

124 V. Ivanenko, 'Russian global position after 2008', n.p.
125 Zagorski, for instance, has argued in the case of the Ukraine that conditionality will work effectively with Kiev only if it is granted a prospective Membership option A. Zagorski, 'Policies towards Russia, Ukraine, Moldova and Belarus', in R. Dannreuther (ed.), *European Foreign and Security Policy: Towards a Neighbourhood Strategy*, London: Routledge, 2004, pp. 79–97, at p. 94.
126 US Department of State and US Agency for International Development, 'Strategic Plan: Fiscal Years 2007–12', p. 48.
127 M. Leonard and N. Popescu, 'A power audit of EU–Russia relations', European Council of Foreign Affairs, November 2007, p. 16.
128 Text of the Russian Minister of Foreign Affairs Sergey Lavrov's Interview published in the newspaper "Rossiiskiye Vesti", 1 April 2009.
129 K. Bennhold, 'Neighbors trying diplomatic approach', *International Herald Tribune*, 12 August 2008; T. Vasalek, 'What does the War in Georgia mean for EU foreign policy?', Briefing Note, Center for European Reform, 15 August 2008, p. 2; I. Traynor, 'Georgia: Divided EU prepares to review stand on Russia at emergency summit', *The Guardian*, 1 September 2008.
130 Council of the European Union, Extraordinary European Council, Presidency Conclusions, 12594/2/08, REV 2, 6 October 2008, p. 4.
131 Sergei Markedonov, 'Regional conflicts reloaded', *Russia in Global Affairs*, no.4, October – December 2008.
132 S. Prozorov, *Understanding conflict between Russia and the EU: the limits of integration*, Basingstoke: Palgrave, 2006.
133 Peter Mandelson, EU Trade Commissioner, 'Russia and the EU: building trust on a shared continent', Conference, 'Russia in the 21st century', Moscow, SPEECH/08/343, 19 June 2008; Peter Mandelson, 'The EU and Russia: our joint political challenge', speech in Bologna, 20 April, 2007. April 2007; Foreign Policy Concept, 2008, *op. cit.*, n.p.; Speech by Minister of Foreign Affairs of the Russian Federation, Sergey Lavrov, 2007, *op. cit.*
134 For instance, the naval base at Tartus is being upgraded for the Russian Navy. Subhash Kapila, 'Russia's Monroe Doctrine: Strategic Implications', Paper 2879, South Asia Analysis Group, 13 October 2008, p. 6.
135 Communication from the Commission to the Council, 'Review of EU–Russia relations', COM(2008) 740 final, 5 November 2008, p. 3.
136 Council of the European Union, Summary of the address by the EU High Representative for CFSP, Javier Solana, 'Where is Russia going? A new attempt for an all-European security order', at the 44th Munich Conference on Security Policy, SO55/08, 10 February 2008.
137 George Bovt, 'Russian foreign policy under Dmitry Medvedev', in The EU–Russia Centre Review, 'Russian Foreign Policy', Issue 8, October 2008, pp. 20–27, at p. 20; 'Medvedev Unveils Little New In Russia's Foreign-Policy Course', 16 July 2008; President Medvedev, Address to the Federal Assembly of the Russian Federation, 5 November 2008.

Chapter 6 EU Enlargement to Central and Eastern Europe

1 H. Sjursen, 'Why expand? The question of legitimacy and justification in the EU's enlargement policy', *Journal of Common Market Studies*, 40, 3, 2002, pp. 491–513, p. 508.
2 P. Gordon *France, Germany and the Western Alliance*, Boulder: Westview Press, 1995.
3 J. Janning 'A German Europe – a European Germany? On the debate over Germany's foreign policy', *International Affairs*, 72, 1, January, 1996, p. 39.
4 D. Haglund *Alliance within the Alliance? Franco-German Military Cooperation and the European Pillar of Defence*, Boulder: Westview Press, 1991.
5 European Council, 'Conclusions on Relations with the Countries of Central and Eastern Europe', Copenhagen, 21–22 June, 1993.

6 S. Croft, J. Redmond, W. Rees and M. Webber, *The Enlargement of Europe*, Manchester: Manchester University Press, 1999, p. 67.

7 Quoted in *The Economist* 'A Survey of European Enlargement', 19 May, 2001, p. 5.

8 *The Economist* 'When East meets West', 22 November, 2003, p. 5.

9 S. Arnswald *EU Enlargement and the Baltic States: The Incremental Making of New Members*, Programme on the Northern Dimension of the CFSP, Volume 7, Finland: The Finnish Institute of International Affairs, 2009.

10 European Council, 'Common Strategy of the European Union on Russia', Brussels, 4 June, 1999.

11 D. Yost *NATO Transformed: The Alliance's New Roles in International Security*, Washington DC: US Institute of Peace, 1998.

12 E. Bort 'Illegal Migration and Cross-Border Crime: Challenges at the Eastern Frontier of the European Union', Florence: European University Institute Working Paper 2000/9, 2000.

13 M. Ruhle and N. Williams 'NATO Enlargement and the European Union', *The World Today*, May, 1995.

14 D. Yost (1998) *op. cit.*

15 See A. Deighton (ed.) *Western European Union 1954–1997: Defence, Security, Integration*, European Interdependence Research Unit, Oxford: St Antony's College, 1997.

16 W. Rees *The Western European Union at the Crossroads: Between Trans-atlantic Solidarity and European Integration*, Boulder, CO: Westview Press, 1998, Chapter 6.

17 D. Mahncke 'The changing role of NATO', in D. Mahncke, W. Rees and W. Thompson, *Re-defining Transatlantic Security Relations: The Challenge of Change*, Manchester: Manchester University Press, 2004, pp. 54–55.

18 J. Sperling 'Two tiers or two speeds? Constructing a stable European security order', in J. Sperling (ed.) *Two Tiers or Two Speeds? The European Security Order and the Enlargement of the European Union and NATO*, Europe in Change Series, Manchester: Manchester University Press, 1999, p. 184.

19 G. Solomon *The NATO Enlargement Debate, 1990–1997: The Blessings of Liberty*, The Washington Papers 174, Westport: Praeger in conjunction with the Center for Strategic and International Studies, 1998, p. 37.

20 J. Goldgeier *Not Whether but When: The US Decision to Enlarge NATO*, Washington DC: Brookings Institution Press, 1999.

21 A. Menon 'Empowering paradise? ESDP at ten', *International Affairs*, 85, 2, March, 2009, pp. 211–26.

22 Madeleine Albright, US Secretary of State, 'The right balance will secure NATO's future', *The Financial Times*, 7 December, 1998.

23 *The Financial Times* 7 December, 2003.

24 Donald Rumsfeld Statement by the Secretary of Defense, Donald Rumsfeld, at the Pentagon, Washington DC, 2003.

25 John Redmond 'The Enlargement of Union', in S. Craft et al., 1999, *op. cit.* p. 58.

26 See B. Giegerich *European Security and Strategic Culture: National Responses to the EU's Security and Defence Policy*, Baden Baden: Nomos, 2006.

27 C. Kupchan 'The US-European Relationship: Opportunities and Challenges', Evidence before the Senate Foreign Relations Subcommittee, Washington DC, 25 April, 2001.

28 *The Economist* (2001) *op. cit.* p. 13.

29 J. Zielonka 'Policies without Strategy: The EU's Record in Eastern Europe', in J. Zielonka (ed) *Paradoxes of European Foreign Policy*, The Hague: Kluwer, 1998.

30 P. O'Neil 'Politics, finance and European enlargement Eastward', in J. Sperling, 1999 *op. cit.* p. 86.

31 A. Hyde-Price *Germany and European Order: Enlarging NATO and the EU*, Manchester: Manchester University Press, 2000, p. 182.

32 S. Meunier and K. Nicolaidis 'The European Union as a Trade Power', in C. Hill and M. Smith (eds) *International Relations of the European Union*, Oxford: Oxford University Press, 2005, p. 259.

33 L. Tsoukalis 'Managing Interdependence: The EU in the World Economy', in C. Hill and M. Smith (eds) 2005, *ibid*, p. 233.
34 Patrick O'Neil (1999) *op. cit*, p. 87.
35 *The Economist* 'Special report: European Union enlargement', 30 April, 2005, p. 23.
36 *The Economist* (2003) *op. cit.* p. 10.
37 Quoted in J. van Oudenaren 'The European Union: From Community to Constitution', in R. Tiersky and E. Jones (eds), *Europe Today. A Twenty-First Century Introduction*, Third edition, Lanham: Rowman and Littlefield, 2007, p. 348.
38 European Commission 'Europe and the Challenge of Enlargement', *EC Bulletin Supplement*, 3/92, Brussels, 1992.
39 European Council 'Conclusions on Relations with the Central and East European Countries', 9–10 December, 1994, Essen.
40 U. Sedelmeier 'Eastern enlargement: Risk, rationality, and role-compliance', in M. Cowles and M. Smith (eds) *The State of the European Union: Risks, Reform, Resistance and Revival*, Oxford: Oxford University Press, 2000, p. 165.
41 J. Peterson and E. Jones 'Decision making in an enlarging European Union', in J. Sperling (ed.), *op. cit.*, 1999, p. 30.
42 K. Smith *European Union Foreign Policy in a Changing World*, Cambridge: Polity, 2003, p. 33.
43 Stuart Croft (*et al.*) *op. cit.*, 1999, p. 69.
44 V. Mitsilegas, J. Monar and W. Rees *The European Union and Internal Security. Guardian of the People? One Europe or Several?* Basingstoke: Palgrave Macmillan, 2003, p. 143.
45 H. Grabbe *The EU's Transformative Power*, London and Basingstoke: Palgrave Macmillan, 2006.
46 European Commission, Standard Eurobarometer Survey Results 1999, http://ec.europa.eu/public_opinion/archives/eb/eb72/eb72_en.htm.
47 D. Leonard 'Schengen Poses Tough Hurdle For Candidates', *European Voice*, 20 September, 2006, http//:www.knoweurope.net/cgi/quick/full_rec?action.
48 *The Economist, op. cit.*, 2003, p. 10.
49 J. Apap 'Enlargement and an Area of Freedom, Security and Justice: Striking a Better Balance', Challenge of Europe, Brussels: The European Policy Centre, 18 October, 2001. http://www.theepc.net/challenge/challenge.detail.asp.
50 P. Kovács 'The Schengen Challenge and its Balkan Dimension', Centre for European Policy Studies Brief, no. 17, March, 2002, p. 7, http//:www.ceps.be.
51 European Commission 'Agenda 2000: For a Stronger and Wider Union', COM (1997) (Final) *Bulletin of the European Union*, Luxembourg. See also G. Avery and F. Cameron *The Enlargement of the European Union*, Contemporary European Studies 1, Sheffield: Sheffield Academic Press, 1998, Chapter 6.
52 M. Smith and G. Timmins *Building a Bigger Europe: EU and NATO Enlargement in Comparative Perspective*, Aldershot: Ashgate, 2000, p. 53.
53 *Agence Presse* 'EU/Enlargement', No. 7113, 4 December, 1997, p. 2.
54 James Sperling 'Enlarging the EU and NATO', in J. Sperling (ed), 1999, *op. cit.*, p. 10.
55 K. Smith 'Enlargement and European order', in C. Hill and M. Smith (eds), 2005, *op. cit.*, p. 281.
56 N. Nugent 'The unfolding of the 10 + 2 enlargement round: Opportunities and challenges', in N. Nugent (ed.) *European Union Enlargement*, The European Union Series, Basingstoke: Palgrave Macmillan, 2004, p. 37.
57 *The Economist* 'In the nick of time: A special report on EU enlargement', 31 May, 2008, p. 14.
58 *The Economist* 'Special report: European Union enlargement', 30 April, 2005, p. 25.
59 Unauthored, 'Sarkozy calls for freeze on EU enlargement', EurActiv.com, 13 January 2006, http://www.euractiv.com/en/future-eu/sarkozy-calls-freeze-eu-enlargement/article-151511;Unauthored, 'Sarkozy opposes Turkish entry into EU, vows referendum', 24 April 2008, http://www.eubusiness.com/news-eu/1209067322.58/; C. Moore, 'Sarkozy: No Lisbon Treaty, no Enlargement', 20 June 2008, Reuters, http://www.france24.com/en/20080620-lisbon-treaty-eu-france-nicolas-sarkozy&navi=MONDE.

60 European Commission, Eurobarometer 70: First Results, December 2008, p. 63, http://ec.europa.eu/public_opinion/archives/eb/eb70/eb70_first_en.pdf
61 T. Halpin and D. Charter 'Russia agrees new EU deal on troop pullout', *The Times*, 9 September, 2009, p. 37.
62 B. Buzan and T. Diez 'The European Union and Turkey', *Survival*, 41, 4, 1999, p. 41.
63 *Agence Presse* 'Turkey is not pleased with arrangement decided in Feira for European but non-EU NATO allies', No.7744, 24 June, 2000, p. 3.
64 F. Burwell, D. Gompert, L. Lebl, J. Lodal and W. Slocombe 'Transatlantic Transformation: Building a NATO-EU Security Architecture', *Policy Paper*, Washington DC: The Atlantic Council, March, 2006, p. 25.
65 *The Economist* 'Turkey's circular worries', 5 September, 2009, p. 48.
66 European Commission 'Wider Europe – Neighbourhood: A New framework for Relations with our Eastern and Southern Neighbours. Communication from the Commission to the Council and the European Parliament', COM (2003) 104 Final, 11 March 2003, Brussels.
67 European Commission 'European Neighbourhood Policy: Strategy Paper', COM (2004) 373 Final, 12 May, 2004. Brussels.

Chapter 7 The EU and the Eastern arc of instability

1 R.H. Ginsberg, *The European Union in International Politics: Baptism by Fire*, Lanham Md: Rowman and Littlefield Publishers, 2001.
2 J. Peterson and H. Sjursen (eds), *A Common Foreign and Security Policy for Europe?* London: Routledge, 1998, p. 171; T. Salmon, 'Testing times for European Political Cooperation: the Gulf and Yugoslavia', *International Affairs* 68: 2, 1992, pp. 233–53, p. 248; B. Soetendorp, *Foreign Policy in the European Union*, London: Longman, 1999, p. 128.
3 Cited in T. Salmon, 1992, *op. cit.* p. 248.
4 The ECMM primarily monitored cease-fires but was also a useful vehicle of moral pressure and a source of field intelligence. J. Gow, 'Security and Democracy: the EU and Central and Eastern Europe', in K. Henderson (ed.), *Back to Europe: Central and Eastern Europe and the European Union*, London: UCL Press, 1999, p. 26.
5 For the possible contribution of EC policy to exacerbating the Balkan situation see R. Dover, 'The EU and the Bosnian civil war 1992–95: The capability-expectations gap at the heart of EU foreign policy', *European Security* 14: 5, 2005, pp. 297–318, at p. 298; J. Gow, 'Deconstructing Yugoslavia', *Survival* 33:4, 1991, pp. 291–311, at pp. 305–6; J. Peterson and E. Bomberg, *Decision-making in the European Union*, Basingstoke: Macmillan, 1999, p. 243; A. Kintis, 'The EU's foreign policy and the war in the former Yugoslavia', in M. Holland (ed.), *Common Foreign and Security Policy*, London: Pinter Publishers, 1997, pp. 148–73, at pp. 148–49.
6 Cited in S. Anderson, 'EU, NATO and CSCE responses to the Yugoslav crisis: Testing Europe's new security architecture', *European Security* 4: 2, 1995, pp. 328–53, at p. 346.
7 C. Hill, 'The Capability-Expectation Gap, or Conceptualising Europe', *Journal of Common Market Studies* 31: 3, 1993, pp. 305–28.
8 There is a large and still growing literature on the Yugoslav crises. Useful starting points including J. Gow, *Triumph of the Lack of Will: International Diplomacy and the Yugoslav War*, London: Hurst and Company, 1997; S. Lucarelli, *Europe and the Breakup of Yugoslavia*, Boston: Kluwer Law International, 2000; S. Woodward, *Balkan Tragedy: Chaos and Dissolution after the Cold War*, Washington DC: Brookings Institution, 1995; R.H. Ullman (ed.), *The World and Yugoslavia's Wars*, New York: Council of Foreign Relations, 1996; A. Danchev and T. Halverson (eds), *International Perspectives on the Yugoslav Conflict*, Basingstoke: Macmillan, 1996; L.S.Talani (ed.), *EU and the Balkans: Policies of Integration and Disintegration*, Newcastle Upon Tyne: Cambridge Scholars Publishing, 2008; J. O'Brennan, *The EU and the Western Balkans: Stabilization and Europeanization through Enlargement*, Routledge: London, 2009.

9 Contrast, for example, J. Peterson and E. Bomberg, 1999, *op. cit.*, p. 243; B. Soetendorp, 1999, *op. cit.* p. 142; R.G. Whitman, 'CFSP after Enlargement', in V.C. Price, A. Landau and R.G. Whitman, *The Enlargement of the European Union: Issues and Strategies*, London: Routledge, 1999, p. 157.

10 The following overview of the EU's role in the Balkans during the 1990s draws in part on S. Marsh and H. Mackenstein, *The International Relations of the European Union*, Pearson: Harlow, 2005, especially pp. 143–51.

11 G. Edwards, 'The potential and limits of the CFSP: The Yugoslav example', in E. Regelsberger *et al.*, *Foreign Policy of the European Union: From EPC to CFSP and Beyond*, London: Lynne Reinner, 1997, pp. 191–92; A. Spence and D. Spence, 'The Common Foreign and Security Policy from Maastricht to Amsterdam', in K.A. Eliassen (ed.), *Foreign and Security Policy in the European Union*, London: Sage, 1998, p. 56.

12 A. Blair, 'What happened in Yugoslavia? Lessons for future peacekeepers', *European Security* 3:2, 1994, pp. 340–49, at p. 344–45; J. Monar, 'The financial dimension of the CFSP', in M. Holland (ed*.), Common Foreign and Security Policy*, London: Pinter Publishers, pp. 34–51, 1997, at pp. 38–39.

13 P.C. Wood, 'France and the post-Cold War order: The case of Yugoslavia', *European Security* 3: 1, 1994, pp. 129–52, at p. 139.

14 C.G. Jacobsen, 'Yugoslavia's successor wars reconsidered', *European Security* 4: 4, 1995, pp. 655–75, at p. 668.

15 The blockade cost FYROM approximately $58 million per month. Greece finally lifted it in 1995 and the two countries agreed to normalise relations, despite continued disagreement over the FYROM's use of "Macedonia." M. Glenny, 'The Macedonian question', in A. Danchev and T. Halverson (eds), *International Perspectives on the Yugoslav Conflict*, Basingstoke: Macmillan, 1996, p.143; H. Smith, *European Union Foreign Policy: What It Is and What It Does*, London: Pluto Press, 2002, p. 121.

16 O. Lepick, 'French perspectives', in A. Danchev and T. Halverson (eds), 1996, *op. cit.*, p. 78.

17 J. Sharp, *Anglo-American Relations and Crisis in Yugoslavia (FRY)*, IFRI Paris, 1999, p. 12; C. Hodge, *Britain and the Balkans: 1991 until present*, London: Routledge, 2006, p. 4.

18 S. Anderson, 1995, *op. cit.* p. 333.

19 Caplan suggests that Germany's unilateral recognition was motivated by suspicion that Croatia would not meet the necessary conditions and its consequent desire to circumvent the Badinter Committee's opinions. Sadakata argues that early recognition of Slovenia and Croatia owed in part to a Western differentiation that placed these countries in Central Europe and the rest of the Republics in the Balkans. R. Caplan, 'The EU's Recognition Policy Towards Republics of Former Yugoslavia', seminar paper November 1995, cited by K. Von Hippel, *Democracy by Force*, Cambridge: Cambridge University Press, 2000, p. 132; M. Sadakata, 'Regional governance: Lessons from European involvement in Yugoslav conflicts', *Japanese Journal of Political Science* 4: 2, 2003, pp. 315–26, at p. 317.

20 For example, the Badinter Committee's stipulated full referendum on independence was compromised by a large-scale Bosnian Serb boycott. This boycott did not deter Bosnia and Herzegovina, having already proclaimed sovereignty in October 1991, from declaring independence from the former Yugoslavia on 3 March 1992.

21 For a fuller exposition of Greece's underlying objections see J. Gow, *Triumph of the Lack of Will*, 1997, footnote 32, pp. 78–79.

22 C.G. Jacobsen, 'Yugoslavia's successor wars reconsidered', *European Security* 4:4, 1995, 655–75, at p. 658.

23 David Owen called in 1992 for NATO airstrikes to defend Bosnia against the Serbs and castigated the European approach of spring 1992 as another 'Munich'. John Major, however, recalls that the British military were concerned about an exit strategy and estimated that a 400,000 strong force – nearly three times the entire British army – would be needed to keep the three warring factions in Bosnia apart. Zimmermann argues similarly that 'It is difficult to conclude that even a massive show of force ...

could have slowed the momentum of Serbian, Croatian and Slovenian nationalisms, which were acting irrationally and without much regard for the eventual costs and consequences of their actions.' Owen, cited by D. Rieff, *Slaughterhouse: Bosnia and the Failure of the West*, London: Vintage Press, 1995, p. 29; David Owen open letter to British Prime Minister John Major, 30 July 1992, published in the *Evening Standard* and reprinted in D. Owen, *Balkan Odyssey*, New York: Harcourt Brace, 1995, pp. 14–16; J. Major, *John Major: The Autobiography*, London: HarperCollins, 1999, p. 535; W. Zimmermann, 'Yugoslavia: 1986–96', Chapter 11, n.p., http://www.rand.org/pubs/conf_proceedings/CF129/CF-129.chapter11.html.

24 http:www.europa.eu.int/abc/obj/treaties/en/entr2f.htm#Article_J.4.

25 For deadlock over whether the WEU should intervene in 1992 see J. Gow, 'The use of coercive action in the Yugoslav crisis', *World Today* 48, 1992, 198–202; S. Duke, 'The second death (or the second coming?) of the WEU', *Journal of Common Market Studies* 34: 2, 1996, 153–69, at p. 180.

26 NATO's eventual bombing campaign has been seen by some as perhaps more symbolic than decisive and that the ending of the conflict owed more to concessions made at Dayton to Serb war aims, especially acceptance of an ethnically cleansed *Republika Srpska*. F. Bozo, 'The effects of Kosovo and the danger of decoupling', in J. Howorth and J.T. S. Keeler (eds), *Defending Europe: The EU, NATO and the Quest for European Autonomy*, Basingstoke: Palgrave, 2003, p. 62; C. Bildt, 'Force and diplomacy, *Survival* 42: 1, 2000, 141–48, at p. 144; D.H. Allin, *NATO's Balkan Interventions*, Adelphi Paper 347, London: Oxford University Press for The International Institute for Strategic Studies, 2002, p. 40.

27 W. Bass, 'The Triage of Dayton', *Foreign Affairs* 77: 5, 1998, p. 99, cited in A. Dobson and S. Marsh, *US Foreign Policy Since 1945*, second edition, London: Routledge, 2006, p. 141. See also I.H. Daalder, *Getting to Dayton: The Making of America's Bosnia Policy*, Washington DC: Brookings Institute Press, 2000, *passim*; R. Holbrooke, *To End a War*, New York: Random House, 1998, 64–70.

28 NATO air strikes on Serb targets proved divisive within the Alliance, controversial in the context of civilian casualties and a contributory rather than necessarily decisive factor in bringing the Kosovo conflict to a close. For the latter see, for example, testimony of US Secretary of Defence Cohen to the Senate Armed Service Committee, cited in D. Leurdijk and D. Zandee, *Kosovo: From Crisis to Crisis,* Ashgate: Aldershot, 2001, p. 96. For more on the EU and Kosovo see D. Mahncke and A. Bayerl (eds), *Old Frontiers – New Frontiers. The Challenge of Kosovo and its Implications for the European Union*, Bern: Peter Lang, 2001; A. Deighton, 'The European Union and NATO's war over Kosovo: Towards the glass ceiling?', in P. Martin and M.R. Brawley (eds.), *Alliance Politics, Kosovo and NATO's War: Allied Force or Forced Allies?* New York: Palgrave, 2000, 57–74.

29 The Quint comprises Britain, Germany, France, Italy and the US. For details see: C. Gegout, 'The Quint: Acknowledging the existence of a Big Four-US *directoire* at the heart of the European Union's foreign policy decision-making process', *Journal of Common Market Studies* 40: 2, 2002, 331–44. For a discussion of *directoires* in the EU's CFSP see S. Keukeleire, 'Directoires within the CFSP/CESDP of the European Union: a plea for "restricted crisis management groups"', *European Foreign Affairs Review* 6: 1, 2001, 75–101.

30 For an analysis of European contributions to the Kosovo air campaign see J. Peters *et al.*, *European Contributions to Operation Allied Force: Implications for Transatlantic Cooperation*, Santa Monica: RAND, 2001.

31 Cited in C. Grant, 'Conclusion: The Significance of European Defence', in *A European Way of War*, London: Center for European Reform, 2004, p. 67.

32 Lord Ashdown, quoted in A. Brown and M. Attenborough, 'EU enlargement: the Western Balkans', House of Commons Research Paper 07/27, 14 March 2007, p. 9.

33 C. Bretherton and J. Vogler, *The European Union as a Global Actor*, London: Routledge, 1999, p. 142.

34 Sarkozy, speech to Friends of Europe, Brussels, 8 September 2006, cited in C. Grant, *Europe's Blurred Boundaries: Rethinking Enlargement and Neighbourhood Policy*, London: Centre for European Reform, 2006, p. 13.

35 European Commission, Communication for the Commission to the Council and the European Parliament, 'Wider Europe – Neighbourhood: A Framework for Relations with our Eastern and Southern Neighbours', COM(2003) 104, final, 2003, p. 4.

36 See, for instance, O. Kovač, 'Regional approach of the European Union to cooperation among countries of the former Yugoslavia', *Review of International Affairs* 47, 1996, 1–5.

37 A. Kotios, 'European policies for the reconstruction and development of the Balkans', in G. Petrakos and S. Totev (eds), *The Development of the Balkan Region*, Aldershot: Ashgate, 2001, pp. 242–43.

38 For more details and an assessment of progress in security-related measures see http://www.stabilitypact.org; M. Buchsbaum, 'The OSCE and the Stability Pact for South Eastern Europe', *Helsinki Monitor* 11: 4, 2000, 62–79; N. Pandurevic, 'Security aspects of the Stability Pact for South Eastern Europe', *Security Dialogue* 32: 3, 2001, 311–24.

39 Communication from the Commission to the Council and the European Parliament: Stabilisation and Association Process for the countries of South Eastern Europe, COM (99) 235 final, 26 May 1999; 'The Thessaloniki agenda for the Western Balkans: Moving towards European Integration'.

40 M. Delevic, 'Regional cooperation in the Western Balkans', Institute for Security Studies, Chaillot Paper 104, July 2007, p. 31.

41 European Commission, Communication for the Commission to the European Parliament and the Council, 'Western Balkans: Enhancing the European Perspective', COM (2008) 127 final, 5 March 2008, p. 19

42 European Commission, 'European Commission completes multi-annual planning of financial assistance to the candidate and potential candidate countries', press release, IP/07/856, 20 June 2007.

43 European Commission, Communication for the Commission to the European Parliament and the Council, 'Enlargement Strategy and Main Challenges 2007–8', COM(2007) 663, final, 6 November 2007, p. 10.

44 *Ibid.*, p. 9.

45 *Ibid.*, pp. 15–16.

46 European Commission, Communication for the Commission to the European Parliament and the Council, 'Western Balkans: Enhancing the European Perspective', 2008, pp. 11–12.

47 Barrot, quoted in Unattributed, 'EU reaffirms Western Balkan Membership perspective', *EurActiv.com,* 6 March 2008.

48 E. Roberts, 'Montenegro: Trouble ahead', *World Today* 55:12, 1999, 11–14.

49 Pippan, for example, argues that the FYROM government's restraint in responding to violent attacks by ethnic Albanian extremists would have been 'unthinkable' without the lure of EU Membership. C. Pippan, 'The rocky road to Europe: The EU's Stabilisation and Association Process for the Western Balkans and the principle of conditionality', *European Foreign Affairs Review* 9, 2004, pp. 219–45, at p. 240.

50 The operation was small-scale, comprising a budget of 6.2 million euros and 350 military personnel drawn from 13 EU Member States and fourteen non-EU countries. It drew on NATO assets and capabilities, was based on UN Security Council Resolution 1371 and was originally scheduled to last for 6 months. For an analysis of EU policy towards the crisis in FYROM see C. Piana, 'The EU's decision-making process in the Common Foreign and Security Policy: The case of the Former Yugoslav Republic of Macedonia', *European Foreign Affairs Review* 7, 2002, pp. 209–26.

51 Unattributed, 'EU reaffirms Western Balkan Membership perspective', *EurActiv.com,* 6 March 2008.

52 European Commission, Communication for the Commission to the European Parliament and the Council, 'Western Balkans: Enhancing the European Perspective', COM (2008) 127 final, 5 March 2008, p. 7.

53 *Ibid.*, p. 14.
54 *Ibid.*, p. 12.
55 *Ibid.*, p. 12.
56 László Salgó, Europol Assistant Director, 'Priorities of Europol in Western Balkans', Speaking points to European Parliament, Brussels, 1 April 2009, http://www.europol.europa.eu/Docs/PrioritiesofEuropolinWesternBalkans01April2009.pdf.
57 A. Mugui-Pippidi, 'Facing the "Desert of Tartars": The Eastern Border of Europe', in J. Zielonka (ed.), *Europe Unbound: Enlarging and Reshaping the Boundaries of the European Union*, London: Routledge, 2002, pp. 51–77.
58 Milica Delevic, 'Regional Cooperation in the Western Balkans', 2007, p. 24.
59 This included only countries from the region – Albania, Bosnia and Herzegovina, Bulgaria, Croatia, Greece, Macedonia, Moldova, Montenegro, Romania, Serbia and Turkey.
60 European Commission, Communication for the Commission to the European Parliament and the Council, 'Western Balkans: Enhancing the European Perspective', 5 March 2008, p. 34.
61 S. Recchia, *Beyond International Trusteeship: EU Peacebuilding in Bosnia and Herzegovina*, Institute for Security Studies: Paris, 2007, Summary. The Bosnian experience that sought to secure peace through ethnic self-rule within a single state has called into question the efficacy of power-sharing solutions in deeply divided societies. See, for example, S. Woehrel, 'Future of the Balkans and US Policy Concerns', CRS Report for Congress, RL32136, 10 January 2008, p.3; D. Rothchild and P. Roeder, 'Power sharing as an impediment to peace and democracy', in P. Roeder and D. Rothchild (eds), *Sustainable Peace: Power and Democracy after Civil Wars*, Ithaca NJ: Cornell University Press, 2005.
62 European Commission, Communication for the Commission to the European Parliament and the Council, 'Enlargement Strategy and Main Challenges 2007–8', COM (2007) 663 final, 6 November 2007, pp. 5–6.
63 *Ibid.*, pp. 5–7.
64 European Commission, Communication for the Commission to the European Parliament and the Council, 'Western Balkans: Enhancing the European Perspective', 5 March 2008, p. 2.
65 Olli Rehn, EU Commissioner for Enlargement, speech to Western Balkans Workshop, speech/08/140, 11 March 2008.
66 M. Abramowitz and H. Hurlburt, 'Can the EU hack the Balkans? A proving ground for Brussels', *Foreign Affairs* 81: 5, 2002, pp. 2–7; S. Woehrel, 'Future of the Balkans and US Policy Concerns', 2008, p. 1.
67 European Commission, 'Enlargement Strategy and Main Challenges 2006–7, Including Annexed Special Report on the EU's Capacity to Integrate New Members', COM (2006) 649, 8 November 2006, p. 22.
68 European Commission, Communication for the Commission to the European Parliament and the Council, 'Enlargement Strategy and Main Challenges 2007–8', COM (2007) 663 final, 6 November 2007, p. 4.
69 Alexandros P. Mallias, Ambassador of Greece to the US, '"Thessaloniki 2": European incentives for the Western Balkans', Atlantic Community: Open Think Tank article, Atlantic Community, 5 December 2007.
70 W. Petritsch, 'The EU must speed-up its Western Balkans enlargement', *Europe's World*, Spring 2008.
71 Timothy Garton Ash, 'This dependent independence is the least worst solution for Kosovo', *The Guardian*, 21 February 2008.
72 Council of the European Union, Council conclusions on Kosovo, 2851st External Relations Council Meeting, 18 February 2008.
73 European Commission, Communication for the Commission to the European Parliament and the Council, 'Enlargement Strategy and Main Challenges 2007–8', COM (2007) 663 final, 6 November 2007, p. 17.
74 Steven Woehrel, 'Future of the Balkans and US Policy Concerns', p. 9.
75 Unattributed, 'Third time lucky? Charlemagne', *The Economist (US)*, 14 January 2006

76 See R. Vlahutin, 'The Croatian exception' in J. Batt (ed.) 'The Western Balkans: Moving On', Institute for Security Studies Chaillot Paper, no.70, October 2004, 21–34.

77 European Commission, 'The Commission's Work Programme for 2002', COM(2001) 620 final, 5 December 2001, p. 8.

78 European Commission, Communication for the Commission to the Council and the European Parliament, 'Wider Europe – Neighbourhood: A Framework for Relations with our Eastern and Southern Neighbours', COM (2003) 104 final, 2003, p. 4.

79 European Commission, Communication from the Commission to the Parliament and the Council, 'On Strengthening the European Neighbourhood Policy', COM(2006) 726 final, 4 December 2006, p. 2.

80 European Commission, Communication from the Commission, 'A Strong European Neighbourhood Policy', COM(2007) 774 final, 5 December 2007, p. 6.

81 M. Smith and M. Webber, 'Political dialogue and security in the European Neighbourhood: The virtues and limits of "New Partnership Perspectives"', *European Foreign Affairs Review* 13, 2008, pp. 73–95, at p. 90.

82 European Commission, 'European Neighbourhood Policy – Azerbaijan, Memo/08/205, 3 April 2008.

83 European Commission, 'European Neighbourhood Policy – Georgia, Memo/08/207, 3 April 2008.

84 Kimana Zulueta-Fülscher, 'Elections and the European Neighbourhood Policy in Armenia', Comment, FRIEDE, May 2008, p. 8.

85 V. Socor, 'From CIS to CSTO: Can a "core" be preserved?', *Eurasia Daily Monitor*, 28 June 2005.

86 European Commission, Green Paper, 'Towards a European strategy for the security of energy supply', COM(2000) 769 final, 29 November 2000; European Commission, Green Paper, 'A European strategy for sustainable, competitive and secure energy', COM 2006 105 final, 8 March 2006. EU Member States possess only approximately 0.6 per cent of the world's proven oil reserves and 2 per cent of proven natural gas reserves. By 2020 it is predicted that Russia will supply 50 per cent of EU oil imports and 70 per cent of its natural gas imports. Figures from G. Bahgat, 'Europe's energy security: challenges and opportunities', *International Affairs* 82: 5, 2006, pp. 961–75, at p. 963; F. Proedrou, 'The EU-Russia energy approach under the prism of interdependence', *European Security* 16: 3–4, 2007, pp. 329–55, at p. 334.

87 See, for instance, Benita Ferrero-Waldner, European Commissioner for External Relations and European Neighbourhood Policy, speech to the Perspectives of the European Neighbourhood Policy Parliamentary conference on the 'European Neighbourhood Policy East', Brussels, speech/08/306, 5 June 2008.

88 European Commission, Communication from the Commission, 'A Strong European Neighbourhood Policy', COM(2007) 774 final, 5 December 2007, p. 6. EU External Affairs Commissioner Ferrero-Waldner has stressed similarly that 'through promoting democracy and regional cooperation, boosting national reform programmes and improving the socio-economic prospects of the region, it can contribute to a more positive climate for conflict settlement.' Ferrero-Waldner cited in T. German, 'Visibly invisible: EU engagement in conflict resolution in the Southern Caucasus', *European Security* 16: 3–4, 2007, pp. 357–74, at p. 360.

89 General Affairs and External Relations Council, 2590th Council Meeting, Luxembourg, 10189/4 (Presse 195), 14 June 2004; European Commission, 'European Neighbourhood Policy', General Context, http://ec.europa.eu/justice_home/fsj/external/neighbourhood/fsj_external_neighbourhood_en.htm.

90 European Commission, Communication for the Commission to the Council and the European Parliament, 'Wider Europe – Neighbourhood: A Framework for Relations with our Eastern and Southern Neighbours', COM(2003) 104 final, p. 4.

91 *Ibid.*, p. 15.

92 K. Zulueta-Fülscher, 2008, *op. cit.*, p. 7.

93 S.N. MacFarlane, 'The Caucasus and Central Asia: towards a non-strategy', in R. Dannreuther (ed.), *European Foreign and Security Policy: Towards a Neighbourhood Strategy*, London: Routledge, 2004, pp. 118–34, at p. 131. See also T. German, 'Visibly invisible', p. 360.

94 European Commission, Communication from the Commission to the Parliament and the Council, 'On Strengthening the European Neighbourhood Policy', COM(2006) 726 final, 4 December 2006, p. 4. Two years later, the Commission again conceded that there was still 'very limited' progress towards resolving frozen conflicts in Abkhazia and South Ossetia. Progress regarding the Nagorno-Karabakh conflict was apparently slightly better, being described only as 'limited'. European Commission, Communication from the Commission to the Parliament and the Council, 'Implementation of the European Neighbourhood Policy in 2007, COM(2008) 164, 3 April 2008, p. 5.

95 European Council, Common Strategy on Ukraine, 11 December 1999, 1999/877/CFSP, p. 1.

96 A. Riley, 'EU-Ukraine Gas Deal Is No Pipe Dream', *Wall Street Journal Europe*, 22 April 2009.

97 European Commission, 'The Revised EU-Ukraine Action Plan of Freedom, Security and Justice: Challenges and Strategic Aims', p. 3.

98 I. Gatev, 'Border security in the Eastern Neighbourhood: Where bio-politics and Geo-politics meet', *European Foreign Affairs Review* 13, 2008, pp. 97–116, at pp. 98 and 115.

99 European Commission, 'European Neighbourhood Policy – Ukraine, Memo/08/215, 3 April 2008.

100 European Commission, Communication from the Commission, 'A Strong European Neighbourhood Policy', COM(2007) 774 final, 5 December 2007, p. 2.

101 *Ibid.*

102 K. Smith, 'The outsiders: The European Neighbourhood Policy', *International Affairs* 81: 4, 2005, pp. 757–73, at p. 773.

103 Unattributed, 'Poland, Sweden propose new EU outreach for Eastern Europe', *International Herald Tribune*, 26 May 2008.

104 Antonio Missiroli, Introduction, in R. Balfour and A. Missiroli, 'Reassessing the European Neighbourhood Policy', Eurpean Policy Centre Issue Paper no. 54, 2007, p. 6.

105 European Commission, 'European Neighbourhood Policy – Moldova, Memo/08/212, 3 April 2008; European Commission, Communication for the Commission to the European Parliament and the Council, 'Western Balkans: Enhancing the European Perspective', COM(2008) 127 final, 5 March 2008, p. 19

106 European Commission, Communication from the Commission to the Parliament and the Council, 'Implementation of the European Neighbourhood Policy in 207, COM (2008) 164, 3 April 2008, p. 9.

107 Freedom House, 'Freedom in the world 2009', http://www.freedomhouse.org/uploads/fiw09/FIW09_Tables&GraphsForWeb.pdf.

108 N. Tangiashvili and M. Kobaladze, 'EU-Georgia neighbourhood relations', Central European University, 2006, p. 13; http://web.ceu.hu/cens/assets/files/georgia.

109 UK European Presidency, 'A Strategy for the External Dimension of JHA: Global Freedom, Security and Justice', 5 December 2005.

110 Rosa Balfour, 'Promoting Human Rights and Democracy in the EU's Neighbourhood: Tolls, Strategies and Dilemmas', in Rosa Balfour and Antonio Missiroli, 2007, *op. cit.*, p. 19.

111 K. Zulueta-Fülscher, 2008, *op. cit.*, p. 1.

112 Cited in *Ibid.*, p. 3.

113 See, for example, M. Vachudova, *Europe Undivided: Democracy, Leverage and Integration After Communism*, New York: Oxford University Press, 2005, pp. 72–73.

114 European Commission, Communication from the Commission to the Parliament and the Council, 'On Strengthening the European Neighbourhood Policy', COM(2006) 726 final, 4 December 2006, p. 3.

115 R. Youngs, 'Is European democracy promotion on the wane?', Center for Europen Policy Studies Working Document, no. 292, May 2008, p. 2.
116 *Ibid.*, Abstract.
117 European Commission, Communication from the Commission, 'A Strong European Neighbourhood Policy', COM(2007) 774 final, 5 December 2007, p. 7.
118 M. Smith and M. Webber, 2008, *op. cit.*, pp. 73–95, at p. 81.
119 See, for example, S. Lavenex, '"Passing the buck": European refugee policies towards Central and Eastern Europe', *Journal of Refugee Studies* 11: 2, 1998, pp. 126–45; G. Eisl, 'EU enlargement and co-operation in Justice and Home Affairs', in K. Henderson (ed.), *Back to Europe: Central and Eastern Europe and the European Union*, London: UCL Press, 1999, p. 173.
120 European Commission, Communication from the Commission, 'A Strong European Neighbourhood Policy', COM(2007) 774 final, 5 December 2007, p. 4.
121 J. Kelley, 'New wine into old wineskins: Promoting political reforms through the New Neighbourhood Policy', *Journal of Common Market Studies* 44: 1, 2006, pp. 29–55, at p. 48.
122 E. Barbé and E. Johansson-Nogués, 'The EU as a modest "force for good": the European Neighbourhood Policy', *International Affairs* 84: 1, 2008, pp. 81–96, at p. 90.
123 Poland and Sweden officially proposed a new Eastern Partnership in May 2008 as a counterpart to the Union for the Mediterranean initiative. Council of the European Union, General Affairs and External Relations, 2870th meeting, press release 9868/08 (Presse 141), 26–27 May 2008, p. 24.
124 European Commission, Communication from the Commission to the European Parliament and the Council, 'Eastern Partnership', COM(2008) 823 final, 3 December 2008, p. 15; Press release, 'Eastern Partnership', MEMO/08/762, 3 December 2008.
125 European Commission, Communication from the Commission to the European Parliament and the Council, 'Eastern Partnership', COM(2008) 823 final, 3 December 2008, p. 14.
126 *Ibid.*, p. 13.
127 Ukraine Foreign Ministry statement, cited in unattributed, 'Poland, Sweden propose new EU outreach for Eastern Europe', *International Herald Tribune*, 26 May 2008.

Chapter 8 The EU and its Southern Mediterranean neighbours

1 European Council, 'The European Security Strategy: A Secure Europe in a Batter World', Brussels, 12 December 2003, p. 8.
2 Calleya, for instance, described the CEECs as the 'Mediterranean archrivals'. S.C. Calleya, 'Post-Cold War regional dynamics in the Mediterranean,' *Mediterranean Quarterly* 7: 3, 1996, pp. 42–54, at p. 48.
3 http://www.turkish-embassy.si/About_Turkey.htm.
4 For a discussion of non-Mediterranean state attitudes see, for instance, R. Gillespie, 'Northern European perceptions of the Barcelona Process', Revista Cidob d'Afers Internationals, 37, Estabilidad y conflictos en el Mediterráneo, pp. 65–75; G. Joffé, 'The British Presidency of the European Union and the Mediterranean in 2005', iemed, 2006, pp. 95–97.
5 F.S. Larrabee, J.D. Green, I.O. Lesser, and M. Zanini, *NATO's Mediterranean Initiative: Policy Issues and Dilemmas,* Washington DC: RAND, 1998, p. 14.
6 See, for instance, J. Haqhaqi, 'Small arms and regional security in the Western Mediterranean: Reflections on European views', *Mediterranean Quarterly* 15: 3, 2004, pp. 55–74.
7 European Council, 2003 , *op. cit.*, pp. 3–4.
8 Institute of Strategic Studies, Nuclear Programmes in the Middle East: In the shadow of Iran, 2008.
9 S. Biscop, 'The European Security Strategy and the Neighbourhood Policy: A new starting point for a Euro-Mediterranean security partnership?', paper presented at EUSA Ninth Biannual International Conference, Austin, Texas, 31 March–2 April 2005, p. 4.

10 B. Lia, 'Security dilemmas in Europe's Mediterranean periphery – perspectives and policy dilemmas' *European Security* 8: 4, 1999, pp. 27–56, at p. 44.

11 Javier Solana, 'Report on the Implementation of the European Security Strategy: Providing Security in a Changing World', S407/08, 11 December 2008, p. 4.

12 European Commission, European Neighbourhood and Partnership Instrument (ENPI): Regional Strategy Paper (2007–13) and Regional Indicative Programme (2007–10) for the Euro-Mediterranean Partnership, p. 3.

13 CIA – World Factbook, https://www.cia.gov/library/publications/the-world-factbook/geos/ee.html#Econ.

14 Europol, OCTA 2008, EU Organised Crime Threat Assessment 2008.

15 P. Norman and M. Button, 'International Crime in the Mediterranean', in B. George (ed.), *Mediterranean Security and Beyond*, London: 2004.

16 Verduyn (2000) cited in A. Aronowitz, 'Smuggling and trafficking in human beings: The phenomena, the markets that drive it and the organisations that promote it', *European Journal of Criminal Policy and Research* 9: 2, 2001, pp. 163–95.

17 EU Energy Security and Solidarity Action Plan: 2nd Strategic Energy Review, MEMO/08/703, 13/11/2008; Unattributed, 'Ministers give nod to EU energy security agenda', *euractiv.com*, 20 February 2009.

18 European Commission, European Neighbourhood and Partnership Instrument (ENPI): Regional Strategy Paper (2007–13) and Regional Indicative Programme (2007–10) for the Euro-Mediterranean Partnership, p. 30.

19 Final Report on an EU Strategic Partnership with the Mediterranean and the Middle East (approved by the European Council in June 2004), p. 2.

20 GMP agreements revolved around three main chapters – commercial cooperation, financial and economic cooperation and social cooperation (focused principally on immigrant workers). By 1977 the EU had signed such agreements with Israel, Morocco, Algeria, Tunisia, Egypt, Jordan, Lebanon and Syria. For a detailed discussion of Euro-Arab Dialogue see D. Hopwood (ed.), *Euro-Arab Dialogue: The Relations Between Two Cultures*, London: Routledge, 1985.

21 Cannes European Council, Presidency Conclusions, 26–27 June 1995.

22 Barcelona Declaration and Euro-Mediterranean partnership, http://europa.eu/scadplus/leg/en/lvb/r15001.htm.

23 S.C. Calleya, 'Cross-cultural currents in the Mediterranean: What prospects?' *Mediterranean Quarterly* 9: 3, 1998, pp. 46–60, at p. 47. The Anna Lindh Foundation is arguably the best known initiative in this area but other intercultural exchange and education programmes now include the EuroMeSCo network of foreign policy institutions, the Femise network of economic research institutes, the Euromed Youth programme and the Euro-Mediterranean Parliamentary Assembly.

24 European Commission, 'Reinvigorating the Barcelona Process', Communication from the Commission to the Council and the European Parliament to prepare the Fourth Meeting of the Euro-Mediterranean Foreign Ministers, COM(2000) 497 final, 6 September 2000.

25 Between 1995 and 2003 South–South trade increased only marginally from 4.4 per cent to 5 per cent of foreign trade. European Commission, European Neighbourhood and Partnership Instrument (ENPI): Regional Strategy Paper (2007–13) and Regional Indicative Programme (2007–10) for the Euro-Mediterranean Partnership, p. 8.

26 European Commission, 'Reinvigorating the Barcelona Process', Communication from the Commission to the Council and the European Parliament to prepare the Fourth Meeting of the Euro-Mediterranean Foreign Ministers, COM(2000) 497 final, 6 September 2000.

27 Common Strategy 2000/458/CFSP of the European Council of 19 June 2000 on the Mediterranean region.

28 The focus was to be on the right of asylum, co-operation in combating illegal immigration (particularly trafficking in human beings); migration and co-operation in the fight against organised crime. European Commission, 'Reinvigorating the Barcelona Process', Communication from the Commission to the Council and the European Parliament to

prepare the Fourth Meeting of the Euro-Mediterranean Foreign Ministers, COM (2000) 497 final, 6.9.2000.

29 European Commission, Communication for the Commission to the Council and the European Parliament, 'Reinvigorating EU actions on Human Rights and democratisation with Mediterranean partners: strategic guidelines', COM(2003) 294 final 21 May 2003, 2–4.

30 Council of the European Union, Council Conclusions: Strengthening of the European Union's bilateral relations with its Mediterranean partners, 2915th External Relations Council meeting, 8–9 December 2008.

31 R. Aliboni, A. Driss, T. Schumacher and A. Tovias, 'Putting the Mediterranean Union in perspective', Euromesco paper 68, June 2008, p. 26.

32 http://www.euromedinfo.eu/site.151.content.en.html. For further details see Council of the European Union, 10th Anniversary Euro-Mediterranean Summit, Barcelona, 27 and 28 November 2005, Five Year Work Programme, 28 November 2005, 15074/05 (Presse 327).

33 Editorial: 'Summit Drama – and Beyond', Euromesco, December 2005, http://www. euromesco.net/images/enews_2_en.pdf.

34 Communication for the Commission to the European Parliament and the Council, 'Barcelona Process: Union for the Mediterranean', COM(2008) 319 (final), 20 May 2008, p. 5.

35 *Ibid.*, p. 8.

36 Council of the European Union, Barcelona Process: Union for the Mediterranean ministerial conference, Marseille, 3–4 November 2008, Final declaration, 4 November 2008, 15187/08 (Presse 314), p. 3.

37 European Commission, 'Reinvigorating the Barcelona Process', Communication from the Commission to the Council and the European Parliament to prepare the Fourth Meeting of the Euro-Mediterranean Foreign Ministers, COM (2000) 497 final, 6 September 2000, p. 4.

38 European Commission, Fact Sheet: The Euro-Mediterranean Partnership (EMP) – the Barcelona Process, February 2005, pp. 2 and 4.

39 Communication for the Commission to the European Parliament and the Council, 'Barcelona Process: Union for the Mediterranean', COM(2008) 319 (final), 20 May 2008, p. 3.

40 A. Geiger and E. Stetter, '"Barcelona Process: Union for the Mediterranean". Readjusting the Euro-Mediterranean Partnership', Friedrich Ebert Stiftung, April 2008.

41 Communication for the Commission to the European Parliament and the Council, 'Barcelona Process: Union for the Mediterranean', COM(2008) 319 final, 20 May 2008, p. 3.

42 R. Youngs, 'Ten years of the Barcelona Process: A model for supporting Arab reform?', FRIDE working paper, January 2005, p. 10; R. Gillespie and R. Youngs (eds), *The European Union and Democracy Promotion: the Case of North Africa*, London: Frank Cass, 2002.

43 F. Galli, 'The legal and political implications of the securitization of counter-terrorism measures across the Mediterranean', Euromesco Paper, 71, September 2008, p.19. See also G. Joffé, 'Morocco's reform process: Wider implications', *Mediterranean Politics* 14: 2, 2009, pp. 151–64; C. Spencer, 'North Africa: The hidden risks to regional stability', Chatham House briefing paper, Middle East and North Africa Programme, April 2009.

44 Communication from the Commission to the Council, Re-directing the Community's Mediterranean Policy – Proposals for the period 1992–96, SEC(90) 192 final, 1 June 1990, p. 2.

45 Communication for the Commission to the European Parliament and the Council, 'Barcelona Process: Union for the Mediterranean', COM(2008) 319 final, 20 May 2008, p. 2.

46 *Ibid.*, p. 3.

47 European Commission, 'Reinvigorating the Barcelona Process',

Communication from the Commission to the Council and the European Parliament to prepare the Fourth Meeting of the Euro-Mediterranean Foreign Ministers, COM (2000) 497 final, 6 September 2000, p. 14; European Council, Final Report on an EU Strategic Partnership with the Mediterranean and the Middle East (approved by the European Council in June 2004), p. 1; Communication for the Commission to the European Parliament and the Council, 'Barcelona Process: Union for the Mediterranean', COM(2008) 319 final, 20 May 2008, p. 4.

48 European Commission, 'Reinvigorating the Barcelona Process',
    Communication from the Commission to the Council and the European Parliament to prepare the Fourth Meeting of the Euro-Mediterranean Foreign Ministers, COM (2000) 497 final, 6 September 2000, p. 4; Communication for the Commission to the European Parliament and the Council, 'Barcelona Process: Union for the Mediterranean', COM(2008) 319 final, 20 May 2008, p. 4.

49 J. Monar, 'Institutional constraints of the European Union's Mediterranean policy', *European Foreign Affairs Review* 3: 2, 1998, pp. 39–60; C. Spencer, 'The EU as a security actor in the Mediterranean: Problems and prospects', *The Quarterly Journal* 2, 2002, pp. 135–42.

50 Philippart, 2001, p. 124, cited in A. Boening, 'Vortex of a regional security complex: The EuroMed Partnership and its security relevance', Miami-Florida European Union Center of Excellence, May 2008, p. 4.

51 Cannes European Council, Presidency Conclusions 26–27 June 1995.

52 I. Traynor, 'Love tops agenda as Sarkozy launches Mediterranean Union', *The Guardian*, Monday 14 July 2008; A. Borowiec, 'EU wary of French initiative: Mediterranean Union proposal seen as threat', *The Washington Times*, 13 March 2008; T. Barber, 'Med Union blueprint avoids key questions', *Financial Times*, 12 March 2008.

53 Unattributed, 'Merkel Slams Sarkozy's 'Club Med' Plans', *Spiegel on-line*, 6 December 2007.

54 R. Aliboni *et al.*, 2008, *op. cit.*, p. 17.

55 An updated Association Agreement with Syria was initialled in December 2008.

56 R. Aliboni, *European Security Across the Mediterranean*, Institute for security studies, Chaillot Paper 2, March 1991.

57 See, for instance, G. Joffé, 'Southern attitudes towards an integrated Mediterranean region', in R. Gillespie (ed.), *The Euro-Mediterranean Partnership: Political and Economic Perspectives,* London: Frank Cass, 1997, pp. 12–32; G. Joffé and A. Vasconcelos (eds), *The Barcelona Process: Building a Euro-Mediterranean Regional Community*, London: Frank Cass, 2000.

58 B. Lia, 1999, *op. cit.*, p., 30.

59 Z. Abi and A. Bojinovi, 'Mapping a regional institutional architecture: the case of the Mediterranean', *Mediterranean Quarterly* 12: 3, 2007, pp. 317–36.

60 S.C. Calleya, 'Is the Barcelona Process working? EU Policy in the Mediterranean', Zentrum für Europäische Integrationsforschung, Center for European Integration Studies, Rheinische Friedrich Wilhelms-Universität Bonn, 2000, p. 43.

61 A. Geiger and E. Stetter, 2008, *op. cit.*, p. 3.

62 E. Bielsa, 'The pivotal role of news agencies in the context of globalization: a historic approach', *Global Networks* 8: 3, 2008, pp. 347–66, at p. 349; H. Kandil, 'The media and Arab integration', in G. Luciani and G. Salame (eds), *The Politics of Arab Integration,* London: Croom Helm, 1988, pp. 54–72.

63 Demmelhuber argues that 'one should refer to a substantial Mediterranean entity which is a historical and cultural *acquis* and in case of the EMP to a virtually (new) political, economic and cultural entity that converted the Euro-Mediterranean idea into reality.' T. Demmelhuber, 'The Euro-Mediterranean space as an imagined (Geo-)political, economic and cultural entity', Zentrum für Europäische Integrationsforschung, Center for European Integration Studies, Rheinische Friedrich-Wilhelms-Universität Bonn, 2006, p. 9.

64 Cannes European Council, Presidency Conclusions 26–27 June 1995.

65 F. Attina, 'The Euro-Mediterranean project of security partnership in comparative perspective', Jean Monnet Working Papers in Comparative and International Politics, no. 52,

2004, p. 13; S. Biscop, 'The European Security Strategy and the Neighbourhood Policy', p. 11.

66 S. Haddadi, 'The Western Mediterranean as a security complex: A *liaison* between the European Union and the Middle East?', Jean Monnet Working Paper in Comparative and International Politics, no. 24, 1999, p. 7.

67 Borg cited in G. Edwards, 'The construction of ambiguity and the limits of attraction: Europe and its Neighbourhood Policy', *Journal of European Integration* 30: 1, 2008, pp. 45–62, at p. 49.

68 R.A. Del Sarto and T. Schumacher, 'From EMP to ENP', *European Foreign Affairs Review* 10, 2005, pp. 17–38.

69 R. Aliboni *et al.*, 2008, *op. cit.*, p. 26.

70 Communication for the Commission to the European Parliament and the Council, 'Barcelona Process: Union for the Mediterranean', COM(2008) 319 (final), 20 May 2008, pp. 4–5.

71 Javier Solana, 'Old and New Challenges of the Barcelona Process', 28 November 2003.

72 S. Blank, 'The Mediterranean and its security agenda,' *Mediterranean Quarterly* 11: 1, 2000, pp. 24–48, at pp. 30–31.

73 T. Baert, 'The Euro-Mediterranean Partnership/Barcelona Process', in G. Sampson and S. Woolcock (eds), *Regionalism, Multilateralism and Economic Integration: The Recent Experience*, Japan: United Nations University 2003, pp. 100–134, at p. 110.

74 See, for instance, G. Joffé, 'The European Union, democracy and counter-terrorism in the Maghreb', *Journal of Common Market Studies* 46: 1, 2008, pp. 147–71; S. Collinson, 'Security or securitization? Migration and the pursuit of freedom, security and justice in the Euro-Mediterranean area', Euromesco e-news, 19, November 2007.

75 European Commission, European Neighbourhood and Partnership Instrument (ENPI): Regional Strategy Paper (2007–13) and Regional Indicative Programme (2007–10) for the Euro-Mediterranean Partnership, p. 23.

76 S. Lavenex and F. Schimmelfennig, 'Relations with wider Europe', *Journal of Common Market Studies* 45: Annual Review, 2007,pp. 143–62, at p. 156.

77 K. Krause and A. Latham, 'Constructing non-proliferation and arms control: the norms of Western practice', in K. Frause (ed.), *Culture and Security: Multilateralism, Arms Control and Security Building,* London: Routledge, 1999, pp. 23–54, at pp. 38–39.

78 European Commission, European Neighbourhood and Partnership Instrument (ENPI): Regional Strategy Paper (2007–13) and Regional Indicative Programme (2007–10) for the Euro-Mediterranean Partnership, p. 7.

79 European Commission, communication for the Commission to the Council and the European Parliament, 'Reinvigorating EU actions on Human Rights and democratisation with Mediterranean partners: strategic guidelines', COM(2003) 294 final, 21 May 2003, p. 4.

80 See, for example, B. Huber, 'Ten Years of Euro-Med cooperation: Views of civil society representatives for the Middle East and Maghreb on the Euro-Mediterranean Partnership', Heinrich Boell Stiftung, Middle East Occasional Papers, no. 1.

81 Richard Youngs, date, *op. cit.*, p. 10.

82 European Council, Final Report on an EU Strategic Partnership with the Mediterranean and the Middle East (approved by the European Council in June 2004).

83 F. Halliday, 'The "Barcelona Process": ten years on', *Open Democracy,* 11 November 2005.

84 United States National Security Strategy, March 2006, p. 20.

85 ESS Review, December 2008.

86 S. Marsh, 'Thirty years on: Iran's silent revolution', *Iranian Studies* 42: 2, 2009, pp. 213–29; D. Ross, "The Middle East predicament", *Foreign Affairs* 84: 1, 2005, pp. 61–74; S. Kapila, 'Iran in the strategic matrix of Russia, China and India', South Asia Analysis Group, paper no. 1284, 9 March 2005; E. Ahrari, "Iran, China and Russia: The emerging anti-US nexus?", *Security Dialogue* 32: 4, 2001, pp. 453–66; H. Pant, 'The

Moscow-Beijing-Delhi "strategic triangle": An idea whose time may never come', *Security Dialogue* 35: 3, 2004, pp. 311–28.

87 European Commission, European Neighbourhood and Partnership Instrument (ENPI): Regional Strategy Paper (2007–13) and Regional Indicative Programme (2007–10) for the Euro-Mediterranean Partnership, p. 19.

88 Programmes included MEDA and ENPI budget lines, ECHO (humanitarian aid), Food Aid and Food Security budget line, Peace Process and UNRWA (providing social services for 4.5 million refugees). Communication for the Commission to the European Parliament and the Council, 'Barcelona Process: Union for the Mediterranean', COM (2008) 319 final, 20 May 2008, Annex II, p. 13.

89 Unattributed, 'EU to pledge $556 million in Palestinian aid', *Associated Press,* 27 February 2009.

90 S. Biscop, 'The EU and Middle-Eastern security: A new departure?', Paper presented at the 10th EUSA Biennial Conference Montreal, 17–19 May 2007, p. 3.

91 Statement by the United Kingdom on behalf of the European Union at the IAEA Board of Governors, pt. 5, 9 August 2005.

92 J. Berger, 'Iran has enriched enough uranium to make bomb, IAEA says', *The Guardian*, 19 February 2009.

93 R. Miller and A. Mishrif, 'The Barcelona Process and Euro-Arab economic relations, 1995–2005', *Middle East Review of International Affairs* 9: 2, 2005, pp. 94–108, at p. 99.

94 R. Balfour, 'Re thinking the Euro-Mediterranean political and security dialogue', Institute for Security Studies, Occasional Papers, no. 52, May 2004, p. 8.

95 M. Ortega, 'A new EU policy on the Mediterranean?', in Judy Batt, Dov Lynch, J. Van Oudenaren, 'The Solana security paper', American Institute for Contemporary German Studies, pp. 86–101, at p. 92.

96 F. Tanner, 'North Africa. Partnership, exceptionalism and neglect', in R. Dannreuther (ed), *European Foreign and Security Policy. Towards a Neighbourhood Strategy*, Routledge: London, 2004, pp. 130–50, at p. 140.

97 Communication for the Commission to the European Parliament and the Council, 'Barcelona Process: Union for the Mediterranean', COM(2008) 319 final, 20 May 2008, p. 2.

98 This broad difference was the source of one example of the EC's growing willingness to assert itself collectively vis-à-vis US policies in the 1980s. In June 1980 it declared against US Middle Eastern policy and in favour of a Palestinian homeland and of Palestinian participation in Arab–Israeli peace talks. For a concise discussion of different European and US approaches to the Mediterranean pre-9/11 see G. Joffé, 'Cooperation or conflict? The Euro-Mediterranean Partnership Initiative and American interests in the Maghreb', http://www.george-joffe.com/art/100.pdf.

99 For example, in November 2003 President George W. Bush argued that 'it would be reckless to accept the status quo' because for 'as long as the Middle East remains a place where freedom does not flourish, it will remain a place of stagnation, resentment, and violence ready for export'. President Bush's speech at the Twentieth Anniversary of the National Endowment for Democracy, US Chamber of Commerce, Washington DC, 6 November 2003; President Bush's speech at the Royal Banqueting House, London, 19 November 2003.

100 I. Lesser, 'Mediterranean Security: New Perspectives and Implications for US Policy', Santa Monica: RAND, 1992.

101 I. Lesser, 'The United States and Euro-Mediterranean relations: Evolving attitudes and strategies', EuroMeSCobrief, 10, July 2004, p. 5.

102 J.B. Alterman, 'The Middle East moves East', CSIS Middle East Notes and Comment, 10 February 2009.

103 This was established to promote education reform, private sector development, civil society, rule of law and economic opportunity. It was organised around four pillars of economic, political, educational and women's empowerment and designed to include governments, academic institutions, the private sector and NGOs.

104 Initiatives therein include democracy assistance dialogue, promoting education reform, training in microfinance, promotion of entrepreneurship, developing measures to encourage investment and a 'Forum for the Future' that brings together the G-8 and regional partners.

105 Ayse Kaya, 'The USA's and the EU's bilateral and regional trade agreement: divergent paths, Divergent ends?', Paper presented at the Venice Summer Institute, 19–20 July 2006, cited in B. Momani, 'The EU, the Middle East, and regional integration', *World Economics* 8: 1, 2007, pp. 1–10, at p. 4.

106 Report on the Implementation of the European Security Strategy – Providing Security in a Changing World, S407/08, 11 December 2008, p. 1.

107 For a similarly pessimistic perspective see K. Kausch and R. Youngs, 'The end of the Euro-Mediterranean vision', *International Affairs* 85: 5, 2009, pp. 963–75.

BIBLIOGRAPHY

Official reports, documents and press releases

Brandt Report, 'North–South: A Programme for Survival', Report of the Independent Commission on International Development Issues, Cambridge: MIT Press, 1980.

European Commission, Communication from the Commission to the European Parliament and the Council, 'Eastern Partnership', COM(2008) 823 final, 3 December 2008.

European Commission, Press release, 'Eastern Partnership', MEMO/08/762, 3 December 2008.

European Commission, 'Eurobarometer 70: First Results', December 2008.

———, 'EU Energy Security and Solidarity Action Plan: 2nd Strategic Energy Review', MEMO/08/703, 13 November 2008.

European Commission, Communication from the Commission to the Council, 'Review of EU–Russia relations', COM(2008) 740 final, 5 November 2008.

European Commission, Press Release 'EU–US Summit in Washington puts global challenges at centre of discussion', IP/09/1664, 3 November 2009.

European Commission, Communication from the Commission to the European Parliament and the Council, 'Barcelona Process: Union for the Mediterranean', COM(2008) 319 final, 20 May 2008.

European Commission, Communication from the Commission to the Parliament and the Council, 'Implementation of the European Neighbourhood Policy in 2007, COM(2008) 164, 3 April 2008.

European Commission, 'European Neighbourhood Policy – Moldova', Memo/08/212, 3 April 2008.

European Commission, 'European Neighbourhood Policy – Ukraine', Memo/08/215, 3 April 2008.

European Commission, 'European Neighbourhood Policy – Azerbaijan', Memo/08/205, 3 April 2008.

European Commission, 'European Neighbourhood Policy – Georgia', Memo/08/207, 3 April 2008.

European Commission, 'EU-Russia Common Space on Freedom, Security and Justice, Progress Report 2007', March 2008.

European Commission, Communication for the Commission to the European Parliament and the Council, 'Western Balkans: Enhancing the European Perspective', COM(2008) 127 final, 5 March 2008.

European Commission, 'The Revised EU–Ukraine Action Plan of Freedom, Security and Justice: Challenges and Strategic Aims'. http://ec.europa.eu/world/enp/pdf/action_plans/ukraine_enp_ap_jls-rev_en.pdf.

——, 'Annual Report 2008 on the European Community's Development and External Assistance Policies and their Implementation in 2007'. http://ec.europa.eu/europeaid/multimedia/publications/documents/annual-reports/europeaid_annual_report_2008_en.pdf.

European Commission, Communication from the Commission, 'A Strong European Neighbourhood Policy', COM(2007) 774 final, 5 December 2007.

European Commission,.Proposal for a Directive of the European Parliament and of the Council on the coordination of procedures for the award of certain public works contracts, public supply contracts and public service contracts in the fields of defence and security', COM(2007) 766, final, 5 December 2007.

European Commission,.Proposal for a Directive of the European Parliament and of the Council on simplifying terms and conditions of transfers of defence-related products within the Community', COM(2007) 765 final, 5 December 2007.

European Commission, Communication from the Commission to the European Parliament, the Council, The European Economic and Social Committee and the Committee of the Regions, 'A Strategy for a stronger and more competitive European defence industry', COM(2007) 764 final, 5 December 2007.

European Commission, Communication from the Commission to the European Parliament and the Council, 'Enlargement Strategy and Main Challenges 2007–8', COM(2007) 663 final, 6 November 2007.

European Commission, 'European Neighbourhood and Partnership Instrument (ENPI): Regional Strategy Paper (2007–13) and Regional Indicative Programme (2007–10) for the Euro-Mediterranean Partnership'.

European Commission, 'Country Strategy Paper 2007–13, Russian Federation'.

European Commission, Press release, 'European Commission completes multi-annual planning of financial assistance to the candidate and potential candidate countries', IP/07/856, 20 June 2007.

European Commission, 'Guidelines for the Development of a Political Declaration and Policy Framework Document for the Northern Dimension from 2007'.

European Commission, 'Interpretative Communication on the application of Article 296 of the Treaty in the field of defence procurement', COM(2006) 779 final, 7 December 2006.

European Commission, Communication from the Commission to the Parliament and the Council, 'On Strengthening the European Neighbourhood Policy', COM(2006) 726 final, 4 December 2006.

European Commission, 'Factsheet – EU-Russia Common Space of External Security, November 2006'.

European Commission, 'Enlargement Strategy and Main Challenges 2006–7, Including Annexed Special Report on the EU's Capacity to Integrate New Members', COM(2006) 649, 8 November 2006.

European Commission, 'Consultation Paper on the Intra-Community circulation of products for the defence of member states', 21 March 2006.

European Commission, 'Green Paper: a European strategy for sustainable, competitive and secure energy', COM(2006) 105 final, 8 March 2006.

European Commission Staff working document, 'Annex to the Communication from the Commission to the Council and the European Parliament, Annual Report 2005 on the European Community's Development Policy and the Implementation of External Assistance in 2004', 15 July 2005.

European Commission, EU-Russia summit, 10 May 2005, http://ec.europa.eu/external_relations/russia/summit_05_05/#fsj1.

European Commission, 'Fact Sheet: The Euro-Mediterranean Partnership (EMP) – the Barcelona Process', February 2005.

European Commission, 'Green Paper: Defence Procurement', COM (2004) 608 final, 23 September 2004.

European Commission, 'Communication to the Council and the European Parliament on relations with Russia', COM (2004) 106, 9 February 2004.

European Commission, 'European Neighbourhood Policy', General Context, http://ec. europa.eu/justice_home/fsj/external/neighbourhood/fsj_external_neighbourhood_en.htm.

European Commission, 'European Neighbourhood Policy: Strategy Paper', COM (2004) 373 final, 12 May 2004.

European Commission, Communication from the Commission to the Council and the European Parliament, 'Wider Europe – Neighbourhood: A New framework for Relations with our Eastern and Southern Neighbours.', COM(2003) 104 final, 11 March 2003.

European Commission, communication from the Commission to the Council and the European Parliament, 'Reinvigorating EU actions on Human Rights and democratisation with Mediterranean partners: strategic guidelines', COM(2003) 294 final, 21 May 2003.

European Commission, 'Towards integrated management of the external borders of the Member States of the European Union', COM (2002) 233 final, May 2002.

European Commission, 'The Commission's Work Programme for 2002', COM(2001) 620 final, 5 December 2001.

European Commission, 'Country Strategy Paper 2002–6, National Indicative Programme, 2002–3, Russian Federation', 27 December 2001.

European Commission, 'Green Paper: Towards a European strategy for the security of energy supply', COM(2000) 769 final, 29 November 2000.

European Commission, Communication from the Commission to the Council and the European Parliament to prepare the Fourth Meeting of the Euro-Mediterranean Foreign Ministers, 'Reinvigorating the Barcelona Process', COM(2000) 497 final, 6 September 2000.

European Commission, 'Standard Eurobarmoter Survey Results 1999'.

European Commission, Communication from the Commission to the Council and the European Parliament, 'Stabilisation and Association Process for the countries of South Eastern Europe', COM(1999)235 final, 26 May 1999.

European Commission, 'Implementing European Union strategy on defence-related industries', COM (1997) 583, 12 January 1997.

European Commission, 'Agenda 2000: For a Stronger and Wider Union', COM(1997) final *Bulletin of the European Union*, Luxembourg, 1997.

European Commission, 'The challenges facing the European defence-related industry, a contribution for action at European level', COM(1996) 10–24 January 1996.

European Commission, 'The European Union and Russia: the future relationship', COM (1995) 223 final, 31 May 1995.

European Commission (1994) 'Partnership and Association Agreement with Russia', http:// www.europa.eu.int/comm/external_relations/russia/intro/index.htm.

European Commission, 'Europe and the Challenge of Enlargement', *EC Bulletin Supplement*, 3/92, Brussels, 1992.

European Commission, Communication from the Commission to the Council, Re-directing the Community's Mediterranean Policy – Proposals for the period 1992–96, SEC(1990) 192 final, 1 June 1990.

European Council, EU-US Summit Washington, Presse 316, 15352/09, 3 November 2009.

European Council, 'Declaration on Strengthening Capabilities', 11 December 2008.

European Council, 'Council Conclusions: Strengthening of the European Union's bilateral relations with its Mediterranean partners', 2915th External Relations Council meeting, 8–9 December 2008.

European Council, 'Barcelona Process: Union for the Mediterranean ministerial conference', Marseille, 3–4 November 2008, final declaration, 15187/08 (Presse 314), 4 November 2008.

European Council, Extraordinary European Council, 'Presidency Conclusions', 12594/2/ 08, REV 2, 6 October 2008.

European Council General Affairs and External Relations, 2870th meeting, press release 9868/08 (Presse 141), 26–27 May 2008.

European Council, 'Council conclusions on Kosovo', 2851st External relations Council Meeting, 18 February 2008.

European Council, 'Presidency Conclusions: Justice and Home Affairs', 21–22 June, 2007.

European Council, 'The European Union Counter-Terrorism Strategy', 30 November 2005.

European Council, 10th Anniversary Euro-Mediterranean Summit, Barcelona, 27 and 28 November 2005, Five Year Work Programme, 15074/05 (Presse 327), 28 November 2005.

European Council, 'The Hague Programme: Strengthening Freedom, Security and Justice in the European Union', Official Journal, C 53, March 2005, pp.1–14.

European Council, 'Presidency Conclusions', 10679/2/04, REV 2, CONCL 2, 17–18 June 2004, p.11.

European Council, General Affairs and External Relations Council, 2590th Council Meeting, Luxembourg, 10189/4 (Presse 195), 14 June 2004.

European Council, Final Report on an EU Strategic Partnership with the Mediterranean and the Middle East (approved by the European Council in June 2004).

European Council, European Security Strategy, 'A Secure Europe in a Better World', 12 December 2003.

European Council, 'EU Strategy against Proliferation of Weapons of Mass Destruction', Thessaloniki, Greece, December 2003.

European Council, General Affairs and External Relations, 2518th Council meeting, 'The Thessaloniki agenda for the Western Balkans: Moving towards European Integration', 16 June 2003.

European Council, 'Seville Presidency Conclusions', 24 October 2002.

European Council, 'Laeken Presidency Conclusions', 15 December 2001.

European Council, 'Presidency Conclusions', June 2001.

European Council, 'Common Strategy 2000/458/CFSP of the European Council on the Mediterranean region',19 June 2000.

European Council, 'Council Joint Action establishing a European Union Cooperation Programme for non-proliferation and disarmament in the Russian Federation', 1999/878/CFSP, 17 December 1999.

European Council, 'Common Strategy on Ukraine', 1999/877/CFSP, 11 December 1999.

European Council, 'Presidency Conclusions', Tampere, 15–16 October 1999.

European Council, 'Common Strategy of the European Union on Russia', 4 June 1999.

European Council, 'Pre-Accession Pact on Organised Crime between the Member States of the European Union and the Applicant Countries of Central and Eastern Europe and Cyprus', 98/C 220/01, 28 May 1998.

European Council, 'Action Plan to Combat Organised Crime', 97/C251/01, 28 April 1997.

European Council, 'Cannes Presidency Conclusions', 26–27 June 1995.

European Council, 'Conclusions on Relations with the Central and East European Countries', 9–10 December 1994.

European Council, 'Conclusions on Relations with the Countries of Central and Eastern Europe', Copenhagen, 21–22 June 1993.

European Defence Agency, DA, 'European Air Transport Fleet Launched', Press Release, 10 November 2008.

EDA, 'Background Note – Capability Development Plan', 8 July 2008.

EDA, Defence Data of EDA participating Member States in 2007, 'Personnel Expenditure as a Percentage of Total Defence Expenditure'.

EDA, Defence Data of EDA participating Member States in 2007, Defence Expenditure as a Percentage of GDP.

EDA, Defence Data of EDA participating Member States in 2007, 'Investment (Equipment Procurement and R&D)'.

EDA, 'An Initial Long-Term Vision for European Defence Capability and Capacity Needs', 3 October 2006.

EDA, 'The Code of Conduct on Defence Procurement of the EU Member States Participating in the European Defence Agency', 21 November 2005.

EDA, 'The Code of Best Practice in the Supply Chain', 15 May 2006.

European Monitoring Centre for Drugs and Drug Addiction (2009) 'Annual Report 2009: The State of the Drugs Problem in Europe'.

European Parliament, 'MEPs launch offensive to improve EU arms procurement', 20051003IPR00969, 4 February 2005.

European Parliament, 'European Defence and Security Market strengthened', Press Release.

Europol, 'EU Organised Crime Threat Assessment 2009', The Hague, 2009.

Europol, Organised Crime Threat Assessment 2008.

European Union High Representative Javier Solana, in association with the European Commission on the implementation of the European Security Strategy: Providing Security in a Changing World, S407/08, 11 December 2008.

North Atlantic Treaty Organisation, 'Understanding NATO Military Transformation, Norfolk, Allied Command Transformation', 2005.

NATO, John Shimkus, Rapporteur, 170 DSTC 05 E – 'Progress on the Prague Capability Commitments', NATO Parliamentary Assembly, 2005 annual session.

NATO, Prague Capabilities Commitment.

NATO, 'EU–NATO Declaration on ESDP, The European Union and the North Atlantic Treaty Organisation', Press Release (2002) 142, 16 December 2002.

NATO, 'Defence Capabilities Initiative', Press Release, NAC-S(99)69, 25 April 1999.

NATO, 'The Alliance's Strategic Concept', NAC-S(99)65, 24 April 1999.

NATO, 'The Alliance's Strategic Concept, 8 November 1991' in *NATO Handbook Documentation*, Brussels: NATO Office of Information and Press, 1999.

Russian Federation, 'Foreign Policy Concept of the Russian Federation approved by President of the Russian Federation Dmitry Medvedev on the 12th of July 2008', English translation at http://www.norway.mid.ru/pr050808_eng.html.

Russian Federation, Ministry of Foreign Affairs, 'A Survey of Russian Federation Foreign Policy 2007', unofficial translation at http:/www.mid.ru/brp.

Russian Federation, 'The Foreign Policy Concept of the Russian Federation, approved on 28 June 2000', translation accessed at http:www.fas.org/nuke/guide/Russia/doctrine/econcept.htm.

Russian Federation, 'Russian Federation Military Doctrine', 21 April 2000, English translation by US Foreign Broadcast Information Service.

Russian Federation, 'National Security Concept of the Russian Federation', Presidential decree 24, 10 January 2000, English translation accessed at http://www.fas.org/nuke/guide/russia/doctrine/gazeta012400.htm.

Russian Federation, 'Medium-term Strategy for Development of Relations between the Russian Federation and the European Union (2000–2010)', 1999, unofficial translation, http://europa.eu.int/comm/external_relations/russia/russian_medium_term_strategy/.

United Kingdom European Presidency, 'A Strategy for the External Dimension of JHA: Global Freedom, Security and Justice', 5 December 2005.

UK House of Commons, Select Committee on European Scrutiny -Twenty-Third Report, 4 June 2003.

UK House of Lords, European Union Committee –Third Report After Georgia. 'The EU and Russia: Follow-Up Report', 3 February 2009.

UK Ministry of Defence, 'Paper No.2 – Multi-national Defence Co-operation', http:www.mod.uk/issues/cooperation/multinational.htm.

UK Ministry of Defence, 'UK Operations in Iraq: Lessons for the Future', December 2003.

UK Secretary of State for Defence, 'Defence Industrial Strategy. Defence White Paper', Command 6697, December 2005.

United Nations Development Programme, 'Human Development Report 1994', Oxford University Press: Oxford and New York.

United Nations, 'Report of the High Level Panel on Threats, Challenges and Change', report to the UN General Assembly, New York, December 1994.

United States Chamber of Commerce to the EU, 'Position paper response to the European Commission's Green Paper on Defence Procurement', 22 February 2005.

US Defense Science Board and the UK Defence Scientific Advisory Council, 'Defense Critical Technologies', March 2006.

US Department of Defense, 'Quadrennial Defense Review Report', 6 February 2006

United States Department of Defense, *Joint Vision 2020*, May 2000.

US Mission to the EU, 'Under Secretary Burns elaborates on challenges and opportunities facing the transatlantic community', 26 March 2007.

US Mission to the EU, 'New Export Exemption for Closest Allies to Promote Defense Efficiency', 23 May 2000.

US National Security Strategy 2006, Washington DC: The Whitehouse.

US National Security Strategy 2002, Washington DC: The Whitehouse.

US National Strategy for Homeland Security 2002, Washington DC: The Whitehouse.

US National Security Strategy 1991, Washington DC: The Whitehouse.

US Office of International Information Programs, 'Bush Approves Resumed Funding for Destruction of Soviet Arms', 14 January 2003.

US State Department and US Agency for International Development, 'Strategic Plan: Fiscal Years 2007–12'.

US State Department – Policy – Directorate of Defense Trade Controls, 'Defense Trade Security Initiative (DTSI) – Summary Sheet'.

Western European Union, K. Vrettos (Rapporteur – Greece, Socialist Group), Explanatory Memorandum, Assembly of the WEU, 'ESDP Developments and the Headline Goal 2010 – reply to the annual report of the Council', Document A/1898, 15 June 2005.

Western European Union, 'The Petersberg Declaration', Western European Union Council of Ministers, 19 June 1992.

Speeches, testimonies and news conferences

J. Baker, 'A new Europe, a new Atlanticism. Architecture for a new era', Berlin Press Club, 12 December 1989, U.S. Department of State, Current Polity, no. 1233 (December 1989).

A.J.K. Bailes, speech to St Antony's College, Oxford, 'Under a European flag? From WEU to EU', 29 November 1999.

President George H. Bush, 'Remarks to the citizens in Mainz. Rheingoldhalle. Mainz, Federal Republic of Germany', 31 May 1989.

President George H. Bush, 'State of the Union Address', 28 January 1992.

President George H. Bush, Address at West Point, 5 January 1993.

President George W. Bush, 'Remarks at OECD Meetings in Paris', 13 June 2008.

President George W. Bush, 'Interview of the President by Christian Malar', France 3 TV, 6 June 2008.

President George W. Bush, 'Remarks to the People of Poland', Wawel Royal Castle Krakow, Poland, 31 May 2003.

President George W. Bush, 'Comments at joint President Bush and Prime Minister Tony Blair press conference', 25 May 2006.

President George W. Bush, inauguration speech, 20 January 2005.

President George W. Bush, 'Speech at the Twentieth Anniversary of the National Endowment for Democracy', US Chamber of Commerce, Washington DC, 6 November 2003.

President George W. Bush, 'Speech at the Royal Banqueting House', London, 19 November 2003.

George W. Bush, Presidential debate, Boston MA, 3 October 2000.

President Clinton's speech on Bosnia, Transcript, 27 November 1995.

President Bill Clinton, 'Speech at North Atlantic Council Summit', NATO Headquarters 10 January 1994.

President Bill Clinton, Second Inaugural speech, 20 January 1997.

Secretary of Defense William S. Cohen, Remarks as Delivered to National Press Club, Washington, DC, Wednesday, January 10, 2001.

Anthony Cordesman, 'The crisis in Afghanistan', Statement before the House Armed Services Committee, Washington DC, 12 February 2009.

Jaap de Hoop Scheffer, 'Speech at the High-level seminar on relations between the European Union and NATO', 7 July 2008.

Jaap de Hoop Scheffer, Keynote speech by NATO Secretary General, 'NATO and the EU: Time for a New Chapter', 29 January 2007.

Benita Ferrero-Waldner, 'After the Russia / Ukraine gas crisis: what next?' Chatham House, London, 9 March 2009.

Benita Ferrero-Waldner, 'External Relations: latest developments', AFET, European Parliament Brussels, 5 November 2008, SPEECH/08/586, 6 November 2008.

Benita Ferrero-Waldner, 'EU/Russia: a challenging partnership, but one of the most important of our times', EP Plenary Debate on EU/Russia Strasbourg, SPEECH/08/545, 21 October 2008.

Benita Ferrero-Waldner, Speech to the Perspectives of the European Neighbourhood Policy Parliamentary conference on the 'European Neighbourhood Policy East', Brussels, speech/08/306, 5 June 2008.

Daniel Fried, US Assistant Secretary of State for European and Eurasian Affairs, 'Transatlantic priorities: the short list', remarks before the Center for National Policy, 18 April 2007.

Daniel Fried, Assistant Secretary of State for European Affairs, Testimony before the House Committee on International Relations: Subcommittee hearing on Europe and Emerging Threats, 8 March 2006.

Daniel Fried, Assistant Secretary for European and Eurasian Affairs, Testimony Before the Senate Foreign Relations Committee Washington, DC, Kosovo: The Balkans' Moment of Truth? 4 March 2008.

Colleen Graffy, Deputy Assistant Secretary of State for Public Diplomacy for Europe, 'What is the US doing to improve its image abroad?', Remarks at Chatham House, 1 November 2007.

Daniel Hamilton, 'The Lisbon Treaty: Implications for future relations between the European Union and the United States', Testimony to the House Committee on Foreign Affairs, Subcommittee on Europe, 15 December 2009.

Elizabeth Jones (Assistant Secretary for European and Eurasian affairs), testimony before the House International Relations Committee Subcommittee on Europe, 3 March 2004.

Charles Kupchan, 'The US-European Relationship: Opportunities and Challenges', Evidence before the Senate Foreign Relations Subcommittee, Washington DC, 25 April 2001.

Sergey Lavrov, Russian Minister of Foreign Affairs, interview published in the newspaper "Rossiiskiye Vesti", 1 April 1 2009.

Sergey Lavrov, Minister of Foreign Affairs of the Russian Federation, speech at the XV Assembly of the Council of Foreign and Defence Policy, 17 March 2007.

Richard Lugar, 'NATO Enlargement and US Public Opinion', speech at Center for Strategic and International Studies Conference on 'NATO's Role in European Security', Washington DC, 3 March 1995.

Celia Malmstrom, EU Commissioner for Home Affairs, 'Keynote speech at the seminar 'Does Europe need "Homeland Security?"' Security and Defence Agenda', Brussels, 12 May 2010.

Peter Mandelson, EU Trade Commissioner, 'Russia and the EU: building trust on a shared continent', Conference "Russia in the 21st century", Moscow, SPEECH/08/343, 19 June 2008.

Peter Mandelson, 'The EU and Russia: our joint political challenge', speech in Bologna, 20 April 2007.

President Medvedev, remarks at meeting with Members of the Council on Foreign Relations, 16 November 2008.

President Medvedev, Address to the Federal Assembly of the Russian Federation, 5 November 2008.

President Medvedev, Opening Address at a Meeting with Commanders of Military Districts, 26 September 2008.

President Medvedev, Interview given to Television Channels Channel One, Rossia, NTV, 31 August 2008.

President Medvedev, Speech at the Meeting with Russian Ambassadors and Permanent Representatives to International Organisations, 15 July 2008.

President Medvedev, Speech at Meeting with German Political, Parliamentary and Civic Leaders, 5 June 2008.

Christopher Murray, Deputy Chief of Mission at the US Mission to the EU, 'U.S. Mission's Murray discusses the US-European security relationship', 20 September 2007.

Victoria Nuland, US Ambassador to NATO, Speech at the London School of Economics, 25 February 2008.

Victoria Nuland, US Ambassador to NATO, Speech to Presse Club and AmCham, Paris, 22 February 2008.

President Barack Obama, Remarks of President – As Prepared for Delivery, Address to Turkish Parliament, 6 April 2009.

President Obama, Live From the G-20 Summit, CNN Transcript, 2 April 2009.

Remarks of Senator Barack Obama to the Chicago Council on Global Affairs, 23 April 2007.

Richard Perle, 'Next Stop Iraq', Foreign Policy Research Institute's annual dinner, 14 November 2001.

Alain Picq, comments at 'Is a transatlantic defence industry increasingly on the cards?' Security and Defence Agenda Roundtable' 30 January 2006.

President Putin, speech at the 43rd Munich conference on security, 2 October 2007.

President Putin, 'Annual Address to the Federal Assembly of the Russian Federation', 25 April 2005'.

Rademaker, statement to the Conference on Disarmament in Geneva, 'The Commitment of the United States to Effective Multilateralism', 13 February 2003.

Philip T. Reeker (Acting Spokesman), U.S. Department of State Office of the Spokesman, Press Statement: 'Defense Trade Security Initiative' Press Statement, 24 May 2000.

Olli Rehn, EU Commissioner for Enlargement, speech to Western Balkans Workshop, speech/08/140, 11 March 2008.

Condoleeza Rice, speech to the Republican National Convention, 1 August 2000.

Condoleezza Rice, 'A Balance of Power that Favors Freedom', article adapted from the 2002 Wriston lecture.

Condoleezza Rice, 'Transformational Diplomacy', Georgetown University, 18 January 2006.

Sir Peter Ricketts (comments of), Permanent Representative of the UK to NATO, 'Conference Report: 'European Defence Integration: Bridging the Gap between Strategy and Capabilities', Center for Strategic and International Studies, 12 October 2005.

Charles Ries, Principal US Deputy Assistant Secretary for European and Eurasian Affairs, 'Mars and Venus: Prospects for Transatlantic Cooperation', Remarks at the XXI German American Conference, Atlantik-Bruecke and The American Council on Germany, Berlin, Germany, 13 June 2003.

Donald Rumsfeld, Statement by the Secretary of Defense, Donald Rumsfeld, at the Pentagon, Washington DC 2003.

Michael Ryan, US Mission to the EU, comments at 'Is a transatlantic defence industry increasingly on the cards?' Security and Defence Agenda Roundtable' 30 January 2006.

László Salgó, Europol Assistant Director, 'Priorities of Europol in Western Balkans', Speaking points to European Parliament, Brussels, 1 April 2009.

Javier Solana, Summary of the address by the EU High Representative for CFSP, 'Where is Russia going? A new attempt for an all-European security order', at the 44th Munich Conference on Security Policy, SO55/08, 10 February 2008.

Javier Solana, address by the EU High Representative for CFSP, 'Old and New Challenges of the Barcelona Process', 28 November 2003.

Javier Solana, address by the EU High Representative for CFSP to the External Action Working Group of the Convention, Brussels, Belgium, 15 October 2002.

Javier Solana, address by the EU High Representative for CFSP, 'Europe's Place in the World', SO101/02, 23 May 2002.

US White House, Office of the Press Secretary, 'President Bush Participates in Joint Press Availability with Slovenian Prime Minister Janša and European Commission President Barroso', 10 June 2008.

Kurt Volker, Principal Deputy Assistant Secretary of State for European and Eurasian Affairs, 'From London to Moscow: New Faces, Old Alliances', 2 May 2008.

Kurt Volker, Acting Assistant Secretary for European and Eurasian Affairs, 'Bucharest: NATO and the Future of the Transatlantic Alliance', Remarks at the Heritage Foundation, 7 April 2008.

Kurt Volker, Principal Deputy Assistant Secretary for European and Eurasian Affairs, Remarks at Media Roundtable, Brussels, Belgium, 6 February 2006.

Robert Wexler, US Congressman, Statement, House Committee on International Relations: Subcommittee hearing on Europe and Emerging Threats, 8 March 2006.

Nick Witney, 'The European Defence Agency – Strategic Directions and Impact on Transatlantic Relations', speech to the Press Club, Washington, 24 October 2005.

Books

E. Adler and M. Barnett (eds), *Security Communities*, Cambridge: Cambridge University Press, 1998.

L. Aggestam, *A European foreign policy? Role Conceptions, and the Politics of Identity in Britain, France and Germany*, Stockholm: Stockholm University Press, 2004.

D.H. Allin, *NATO's Balkan Interventions*, Adelphi Paper 347, London: Oxford University Press for The International Institute for Strategic Studies, 2002.

T. Ambrosio, *Challenging America's Global Pre-eminence: Russia's Quest for Multipolarity*, Aldershot: Ashgate, 2005.

S. Arnswald, *EU Enlargement and the Baltic States: The Incremental Making of New Members*, Finland: The Finnish Institute of International Affairs, 2000.

G. Avery and F. Cameron. *The Enlargement of the European Union*, Sheffield: Sheffield Academic Press, 1998.

G. Aybet, *A European Security Architecture after the Cold War*, Basingstoke: Macmillan, 2000.

P. Baev, *Russian Energy Policy and Military Power: Putin's Quest for Greatness*, London: Routledge, 2008.

S. Biscop and J.J. Andersson (eds), *The EU and the European Security Strategy: Forging a Global Europe*, New York: Routledge, 2008.

P. Bobbitt, *Terror and Consent: The Wars for the Twenty-First Century*, New York: A. Knopf, 2008.

C. Bretherton and J. Vogler, *The European Union as a Global Actor*, 2nd edition, Abingdon: Taylor and Francis, 2005.

P. Buchanan, *A Republic not an Empire: Reclaiming America's Destiny*, Washington: Regnery Publishing, Inc., 1999.

P. Buchanan, *Where the Right Went Wrong: How Neoconservatives Subverted the Reagan Revolution and Hijacked the Bush Presidency*, New York: Thomas Dunne Books, 2004.

B. Buzan, *People, States and Fear: The National Security Problem in International Relations*, Brighton: Harvester Wheatsheaf, 1983.

B. Buzan, C. Jones, and R. Little, *The Logic of Anarchy: Neorealism to Structural Realism*, New York: Columbia University Press, 1993.

B. Buzan, O. Waever and J. de Wilde, *Security: A New Framework for Analysis*, Boulder and Colorado: Lynne Reinner Publishers, 1998.

D.P. Calleo, *Beyond American Hegemony*, New York: Basic Books, 1987.

P. Chalk, *Non-Military Security and Global Order: The Impact of Extremism, Violence and Chaos on National and International Security*, Basingstoke: Macmillan, 2000.

R.A. Clarke, *Against All Enemies: Inside America's War on Terror*, London: Free Press, 2004.

R. Cooper, *The Breaking of Nations: Order and Chaos in the Twenty-First Century*, London: Atlantic Books, 2003.

A. Cottey, *Security in the New Europe*, Basingstoke: Palgrave Macmillan, 2007.

S. Croft, J. Redmond, G.W. Rees, and M. Webber, *The Enlargement of Europe*, Manchester: Manchester University Press, 1999.

I.H. Daalder, *Getting to Dayton: The Making of America's Bosnia Policy*, Washington DC: Brookings Institute Press, 2000.

I.H. Daalder and J. Lindsay, *America Unbound. The Bush Revolution in Foreign Policy*, Washington DC: Brookings Institute Press, 2003.

A. Danchev and T. Halverson (eds), *International Perspectives on the Yugoslav Conflict*, Basingstoke: Macmillan, 1996.

P. Davis, *Effects-Based Operations (EBO): A Grand Challenge for the Analytical Community*, Santa Monica: RAND, 2001.

A. Deighton (ed.), *Western European Union 1954–1997: Defence, Security, Integration*, European Oxford: Interdependence Research Unit, St. Antony's College, 1997.

C.M. Dent, *The European Economy: The Global Context*, London: Routledge, 1997.

K. Deutsch, *Political Community and the North Atlantic Area: International Organization in the Light of Historical Experience*, Princeton NJ: Princeton University Press, 1957.

A.P. Dobson and S. Marsh, *US Foreign Policy Since 1945*, second edition, Routledge: London, 2006.

S. Dockrill, *Britain's Policy for West German Rearmament, 1950–1955*, Cambridge: Cambridge University Press, 1991.

D. Frum and R. Perle, *An End to Evil: How to Win the War on Terror*, New York: Random House, 2003.

S. Fukumi, *Cocaine Trafficking in Latin America: EU and US Policy Responses*, Aldershot: Ashgate, 2008.

E. Fursdon, *The European Defence Community: A History*, London: Macmillan, 1980.

J.L. Gaddis, *Surprise, Security, and the American Experience*, Washington, D.C.: Council on Foreign Relations, 2004.

A.L. Gardner, *A New Era in US-EU Relations. The Clinton Administration and the New Transatlantic Agenda*, Aldershot: Ashgate, 1999.

A. Geddes, *Immigration and European Integration. Towards Fortress Europe?* Manchester: Manchester University Press, 2000.

V.Y. Ghebali and D. Warner (eds.), *The Operational Role of the OSCE in South-Eastern Europe*, Aldershot: Ashgate, 2001.

B. Giegerich, 'European Military Crisis Management: Connecting Ambition and Reality, Adelphi Paper 397, Abingdon: Routledge, 2008.

B. Giegerich, *European Security and Strategic Culture: National Responses to the EU's Security and Defence Policy*, Baden Baden: Nomos, 2006.

R. Gillespie and R. Youngs (eds), *The European Union and Democracy Promotion: the Case of North Africa*, London: Frank Cass, 2002.

R.H. Ginsberg, *The European Union in International Politics: Baptism by Fire*, Lanham Md: Rowman and Littlefield Publishers, 2001.

J. Goldgeier, *Not Whether But When: The US Decision to Enlarge NATO*, Washington DC: Brookings Institution Press, 1999.

P. Gordon, *France, Germany and the Western Alliance*, Boulder: Westview Press, 1995.

J. Gow, *Triumph of the Lack of Will: International Diplomacy and the Yugoslav War*, London: Hurst and Company, 1997.

H. Grabbe, *The EU's Transformative Power: Europeanization through Conditionality in Central and Eastern Europe*, New York: Palgrave Macmillan, 2006.

C.S. Gray, *Modern Strategy*, Oxford: Oxford University Press, 1999.

David Haglund, *Alliance Within the Alliance? Franco-German Military Cooperation and the European Pillar of Defence*, Boulder: Westview Press, 1991.

S. Halper and J. Clarke, *America Alone: The Neo-Conservatives and the Global Order*, Cambridge: Cambridge University Press, 2004.

C. Hodge, *Britain and the Balkans: 1991 until present*, London: Routledge, 2006.

B. Hoffman, *Inside Terrorism*, New York: Colombia University Press, 1998.

R. Holbrooke, *To End a War*, New York: Random House, 1998.

D. Hopwood (ed.), *Euro-Arab Dialogue: The Relations Between two Cultures*, London: Routledge, 1985.

J. Howorth, *Security and Defence Policy in the European Union*, Basingstoke and New York: Palgrave Macmillan, 2007.

R. Hunter, *The European Security and Defence Policy: NATO's Companion – Or Competitor*, Washington DC: RAND, 2002.

J. Huysmans, *The Politics of Insecurity: Fear, Migration and Asylum in the EU*, London: Routledge, 2006.

A. Hyde-Price, *Germany and European Order: Enlarging NATO and the EU*, Manchester: Manchester University Press, 2000.

R. Jervis, *Perception and Misperception in International Politics*, Princeton NJ: Princeton University Press, 1976.

G. Joffe and A. Vasconcelos (eds), *The Barcelona Process: Building a Euro-Mediterranean Regional Community*, London: Frank Cass, 2000.

C. Johnson, *The Sorrows of Empire: Militarism, Secrecy and the End of the Republic*, New York: Metropolitan Books, 2004.

R. Kagan, *Of Paradise and Power: America and Europe in the New World Order*, New York: Knopf, 2003.

B. Kellman, *Bioviolence: Preventing Biological Terror and Crime*, Cambridge: Cambridge University Press, 2007.

P. Kennedy, *The Rise and Fall of the Great Powers*, London: Unwin Hyman, 1988.

E. Kirchner and J. Sperling, *EU Security Governance*, Manchester: Manchester University Press, 2007.

C. Krauthammer, *Democratic Realism. An American Foreign Policy for a Unipolar World*, Washington: American Enterprise Institute, 2004.

C. Kupchan, *The End of the American Era: U.S. Foreign Policy After the Cold War*, New York: Alfred Knopf, 2002.

F.S. Larrabee, J.D. Green, I.O. Lesser, and M. Zanini, *NATO's Mediterranean Initiative: Policy Issues and Dilemmas*, Washington DC: RAND, 1998.

I. Lesser, 'Mediterranean Security: New Perspectives and Implications for US Policy', Santa Monica: RAND, 1992.

D. Leurdijk and D. Zandee, *Kosovo: From Crisis to Crisis*, Ashgate: Aldershot, 2001.

S. Lucarelli, *Europe and the Breakup of Yugoslavia*, Boston: Kluwer Law International, 2000.

D. Mahncke and A. Bayerl (eds.), *Old Frontiers – New Frontiers. The Challenge of Kosovo and its Implications for the European Union*, Bern: Peter Lang, 2001.

S. Marsh and H. Mackenstein, *The International Relations of the European Union*, Harlow: Pearson, 2005.

H. Maull and S. Harnisch (eds), *Germany as a Civilian Power?* Manchester: Manchester University Press, 2001.

J.J. Mearsheimer, *The Tragedy of Great Power Politics*, New York: W. W. Norton, 2001.

J. Major, *John Major: The Autobiography*, London: HarperCollins, 1999.

J. Mann, *Rise of the Vulcans: The History of Bush's War Cabinet*, New York: Viking, 2004.

C. Meyer, *The Quest for a European Strategic Culture. Changing Norms on Security and Defence in the European Union*, Basingstoke: Palgrave, 2006.

V. Mitsilegas, J. Monar and W. Rees, *The European Union and Internal Security: Guardian of the People?* Basingstoke: Palgrave, 2003.

A. Moens, *The Foreign Policy of George W Bush: Values, Strategy and Loyalty*, Aldershot: Ashgate, 2004.

J. Newhouse, *Imperial America. The Bush Assault on the World Order*, New York: Knopf, 2003.

S Nuttall, *European Political Co-operation*, Oxford: Clarendon Press, 1992.

J.S. Nye, *The Paradox of American Power: Why the World's Only Superpower Can't Go It Alone*, New York: Oxford University Press, 2002.

J.S. Nye, *Bound to Lead: the Changing Nature of American Power*, New York: Basic Books, 1990.

B. Nygren, *The Rebuilding of Greater Russia: Putin's Foreign Policy towards the CIS Countries*, London: Routledge, 2008.

D. Owen, *Balkan Odyssey*, New York: Harcourt Brace, 1995.

J. O'Brennan, *The EU and the Western Balkans: Stabilization and Europeanization Through Enlargement*, London: Routledge, 2009.

J. Peters *et al.*, *European Contributions to Operation Allied Force: Implications for Transatlantic Cooperation*, Santa Monica: RAND, 2001.

J. Peterson and E. Bomberg, *Decision-making in the European Union*, Basingstoke: Macmillan, 1999.

J. Peterson and H. Sjursen (eds), *A Common Foreign and Security Policy for Europe?* London: Routledge, 1998.

C. Piening, *Global Europe. The European Union in World Affairs*, London: Lynne Rienner Publishers, 1997.

S. Prozorov, *Understanding Conflict between Russia and the EU: The Limits of Integration*, Basingstoke: Palgrave, 2006.

S. Recchia, *Beyond International Trusteeship: EU Peacebuilding in Bosnia and Herzegovina*, Institute for Security Studies: Paris, 2007.

W. Rees, *The Western European Union at the Crossroads: Between Trans-Atlantic Solidarity and European Integration*, Boulder, CO: Westview Press, 1998.

E. Regelsberger, W. Wessels and P. de Schoutheete de Tervarent, (eds.) *Foreign Policy of the European Union: From EPC to CFSP and Beyond*, London: Lynne Rienner Publishers, 1997.

D. Rieff, *Slaughterhouse: Bosnia and the Failure of the West*, London: Vintage Press, 1995.

K. Ruane, *The Rise and Fall of the European Defence Community: Anglo-American Relations and the Crisis of European Defence, 1950–55*, Basingstoke: Macmillan, 2000.

E. Rumer, *Russian Foreign Policy beyond Putin*, Oxford: International Institute for Strategic Studies, Routledge, 2007.

R. Sakwa, *Putin: Russia's choice*, 2nd edition, London: Routledge, 2008.

T.C. Salmon and A. Shepherd, *Toward a European Army. A Military Power in the Making?* Boulder: Lynne Rienner, 2003.

J. Sharp, *Anglo-American Relations and Crisis in Yugoslavia (FRY)*, IFRI: Paris, 1999.

L. Shevtsosa, *Putin's Russia*, Washington: Carnegie Endowment for International Peace, 2003.

M. Singer and A. Wildavsky, *The Real World Order: Zones of Peace, Zones of Turmoil*, New Jersey: Chatham House Publishers, 1993.

H. Smith, *European Union Foreign Policy: What It Is and What It Does*, London: Pluto Press, 2002.

K. Smith, *European Union Foreign Policy in a Changing World*, Cambridge: Polity, 2003.

M. Smith, *Pax Russica: Russia's Monroe Doctrine*, London: Royal United Services Institute for Defence Studies, 1993.

M. Smith and G. Timmins, *Building a Bigger Europe: EU and NATO Enlargement in Comparative Perspective*, Aldershot: Ashgate, 2000.

R. Smith, *The Utility of Force: The Art of War in the Modern World*, New York: Alfred A Knopf, 2007.

B. Soetendorp, *Foreign Policy in the European Union*, London: Longman, 1999.

G. Solomon, *The NATO Enlargement Debate, 1990–1997: The Blessings of Liberty*, Westport: Praeger in conjunction with the Center for Strategic and International Studies, 1998.

L.S. Talani (ed.), *EU and the Balkans: Policies of Integration and Disintegration*, Newcastle Upon Tyne: Cambridge Scholars Publishing, 2008.

J. Sperling and E. Kirchner, *Recasting the European Order: Security Architectures and Economic Cooperation*, Manchester: Manchester University Press, 1997.

S. Stetter, *EU Foreign and Interior Policies. Cross-pillar Politics and the Social Construction of Sovereignty*, London and New York: Routledge, 2007.

J. Tallberg, *Bargaining power in the European Council*, Stockholm: Swedish Institute for European Policy Studies, 2007.

M. Telo, *Europe: a Civilian Power ?* Basingstoke: Palgrave, 2005.

T. Terriff, S. Croft, L. James and P. Morgan, *Security Studies Today*, Cambridge: Polity Press, 1999.

E. Todd, *After the Empire: The Breakdown of American Order*, New York: Columbia University Press, 2003.

A. Toje, *America, the EU and Strategic Culture: Renegotiating the Transatlantic Bargain*, London: Routledge, 2008.

D. Trenin, *The End of Eurasia: Russia on the Border Between Geopolitics and Globalization*, Moscow: Carnegie Moscow Center, 2001.

R.H. Ullman (ed.), *The World and Yugoslavia's Wars*, New York: Council of Foreign Relations, 1996.

M. Vachudova, *Europe Undivided: Democracy, Leverage and Integration After Communism*, New York: Oxford University Press, 2005.

K. Von Hippel, *Democracy by Force*, Cambridge: Cambridge University Press, 2000.

R. Whitman, *From Civilian Power to Superpower? The International Identity of the European Union*, Basingstoke: Macmillan, 1998.

B. Woodward, *Bush at War*, New York: Simon and Schuster, 2002.

S. Woodward, *Balkan Tragedy: Chaos and Dissolution After the Cold War*, Washington DC: Brookings Institution, 1995.

D. Yost, *NATO Transformed: The Alliance's New Roles in International Security*, Washington DC: US Institute of Peace, 1998.

Book chapters

M. Alexseev, 'From the cold war to the cold peace: US-Russian interactions from Gorbachev to the present', in S. Ramet and C. Ingebritsen (eds), *Coming in From the Cold War. Changes in US-European Interactions Since 1980*, New York: Rowman and Littlefield, 2002.

D. Allen, 'EPC/CFSP, the Soviet Union, and the former Soviet Republics: Do the twelve have a coherent policy? in E. Regelsberger *et al.* (eds), *Foreign Policy of the European Union: From EPC to CFSP and Beyond*, Boulder: Lynne Rienner, 1997.

O. Babarinde, 'The European Union's relations with the South: a commitment to development?' in C. Rhodes (ed.), *The EU in the World Community*, Boulder, CO: Lynne Rienner, 1998.

T. Baert, 'The Euro-Mediterranean Partnership/Barcelona Process', in G. Sampson and S. Woolcock (eds), *Regionalism, Multilateralism and Economic Integration: The Recent Experience*, Japan: United Nations University 2003.

M. Beare, 'Purposeful misconceptions: organized crime and the state', in E. Viano, J. Magallanes and L. Bridel, *Transnational Organized Crime: Myth, Power, and Profit*, Durham, N.Ca.: Carolina Academic Press, 2003.

S. Biscop, 'The European Security Strategy in context', in S. Biscop and J. Andersson (eds), *The EU and the European Security Strategy: Forging a Global Europe*, London: Routledge, 2008.

M. den Boer, 'New dimensions in EU police-cooperation: The Hague milestones for what they are worth', in J. de Zwaan and R. Goudappel (eds), *Freedom, Security and Justice in the European Union: Implementation of the Hague Programme*, The Hague: TMC Asser Press, 2006.

T. Bordachev, 'An odd insider's perspective: A Russian perspective', in C. Grant, J. Gedmin and T. Bordachev, *Strategic Implications of the EU Crisis*, Brussels: Center for European Studies, 2006.

F. Bozo, 'The effects of Kosovo and the danger of decoupling', in J. Howorth and J.T.S. Keeler (eds), *Defending Europe: The EU, NATO and the Quest for European Autonomy*, Basingstoke: Palgrave, 2003.

E. Brimmer 'From territorial security to societal security: Implications for the transatlantic strategic outlook', in E. Brimmer (ed.), *Transforming Homeland Security: US and European Approaches*, Center for Transatlantic Relations, Washington DC: John Hopkins University, 2006.

D.P. Calleo, 'Imperial America and its Republican constitution', in H. Gardner and R. Stefanova (eds), *The New Transatlantic Agenda: Facing the Challenges of Global Governance*, Aldershot, Ashgate, 2001.

L.E. Cederman, 'Political boundaries and identity tradeoffs', in L.E. Cederman (ed.), *Constructing Europe's Identity: the External Dimension*, Boulder CO: Lynne Rienner, 2001.

A. Deighton, 'The European Union and NATO's war over Kosovo: Towards the glass ceiling?' in P. Martin and M.R. Brawley (eds.), *Alliance Politics, Kosovo and NATO's War: Allied Force of Forced Allies?* New York: Palgrave, 2000.

F. Duchêne, 'The European Community and the uncertainties of interdependence', in M. Kohnstamm and W. Hager (eds.), *A Nation Writ Large? Foreign-Policy Problems before the European Community*, London: Macmillan, 1972.

G. Edwards, 'The potential and limits of the CFSP: The Yugoslav example', in E. Regelsberger *et al.*, *Foreign Policy of the European Union: From EPC to CFSP and Beyond*, London: Lynne Reinner, 1997.

G. Eisl, 'EU enlargement and co-operation in Justice and Home Affairs', in K. Henderson (ed.), *Back to Europe: Central and Eastern Europe and the European Union*, London: UCL Press, 1999.

S. Everts *et al.*, *A European Way of War*, London: Center for European Reform, 2004.

T. Frellesen, 'Processes and procedures in EU-US foreign policy cooperation: From the Transatlantic Declaration to the New Transatlantic Agenda', in E. Philippart and P. Winand (eds), *Ever Closer Partnership. Policy-making in EU-US Relations*, Berlin: Peter Lang, 2001.

M. Glenny, 'The Macedonian question', in A. Danchev and T. Halverson (eds), *International Perspectives on the Yugoslav Conflict*, Basingstoke: Macmillan, 1996.

J. Gow, 'Security and Democracy: the EU and Central and Eastern Europe', in K. Henderson (ed.), *Back to Europe: Central and Eastern Europe and the European Union*, London: UCL Press, 1999.

H. Grabbe, 'What the new Member States will bring into the European Union', in N. Nugent (ed.), *European Union Enlargement*, Basingstoke: Palgrave Macmillan, 2004.

G. Joffe, 'Southern attitudes towards an integrated Mediterranean region', in R. Gillespie (ed.), *The Euro-Mediterranean Partnership: Political and Economic Perspectives*, London: Frank Cass, 1997.

J. Howorth, 'Why ESDP is necessary and beneficial for the Alliance' in J. Howorth and J.T.S. Keeler (eds), *Defending Europe: The EU, NATO and the Quest for European Autonomy*, Basingstoke: Palgrave Macmillan, 2003.

R. Hunter, 'NATO and the European Union: Inevitable partners', in S. Serfaty (ed.), *Visions of the Atlantic Alliance. The United States, the European Union and NATO*, Significant Issues Series, Washington DC: Center for Strategic and International Studies, 2005.

H. Kandil, 'The media and Arab integration', in G. Luciani and G. Salame (eds), *The Politics of Arab Integration*, London: Croom Helm, 1988.

C. Kelleher, 'The European Security Strategy and the United States: The past as prologue', in S. Biscop and J. J. Andersson (eds), *The EU and the European Security Strategy: Forging a Global Europe*, New York: Routledge, 2008.

P. Kerr, 'Human security' in A. Collins (ed.), *Contemporary Security Studies*, Oxford: Oxford University Press, 2007.

A. Kintis, 'The EU's foreign policy and the war in the former Yugoslavia', in M. Holland (ed.), *Common Foreign and Security Policy*, London: Pinter Publishers, 1997.

A. Kotios, 'European policies for the reconstruction and development of the Balkans', in G. Petrakos and S. Totev (eds), *The Development of the Balkan Region*, Aldershot: Ashgate, 2001.

K. Krause and A. Latham, 'Constructing non-proliferation and arms control: the norms of Western practice', in K. Frause (ed.), *Culture and Security: Multilateralism, Arms Control and Security Building*, London: Routledge, 1999.

O. Lepick, 'French perspectives', in A. Danchev and T. Halverson (eds), *International Perspectives on the Yugoslav Conflict*, Basingstoke: Macmillan, 1996.

D. Mahncke, 'The changing role of NATO', in D. Mahncke, W. Rees and W. Thompson, *Re-defining Transatlantic Security Relations: The Challenge of Change*, Manchester: Manchester University Press, 2004.

L. March, 'Security strategy and the "Russia problem"', in R. Dannreuther and J. Peterson (eds), *Security Strategy and Transatlantic Relations*, London: Routledge, 2006.

S.N. MacFarlane, 'The Caucasus and Central Asia: towards a non-strategy', in R. Dannreuther (ed.), *European Foreign and Security Policy: Towards a Neighbourhood Strategy*, London: Routledge, 2004.

C. McInnes, 'Health', in P. Williams (ed.), *Security Studies: An Introduction*, London: Routledge, 2008.

A. Menon, 'Why ESDP is dangerous and misguided for the Alliance', in J. Howorth and J.T.S. Keeler (eds), *Defending Europe: The EU, NATO and the Quest for European Autonomy*, Basingstoke: Palgrave Macmillan, 2003.

S. Meunier and K. Nicolaidis, 'The European Union as a trade power', in C. Hill and M. Smith (eds), *International Relations of the European Union*, Oxford: Oxford University Press, 2005.

J. Monar, 'The financial dimension of the CFSP', in M. Holland (ed.), *Common Foreign and Security Policy*, London: Pinter Publishers.

H. Moroff, 'Russia, the CIS and the EU: Secondary integration by association?' in K. Malfiet, L. Verpoest and E. Vinokuroz (eds), *The CIS, the EU and Russia: The Challenges of Integration*, London: Routledge, 2007.

A. Mugui-Pippidi, 'Facing the "Desert of Tartars": The Eastern Border of Europe', in J. Zielonka (ed.), *Europe Unbound: Enlarging and Reshaping the Boundaries of the European Union*, London: Routledge, 2002.

H. Nilsson, 'The EU Action Plan on Combating Terrorism: Assessment and Perspectives', in D. Mahncke and J. Monar (eds), *International Terrorism: A European Response to a Global Threat?* Brussels: Peter Lang, 2006.

P. Norman and M. Button, 'International Crime in the Mediterranean', in B. George (ed.), *Mediterranean Security and Beyond*, London: 2004.

N. Nugent, 'The unfolding of the 10 + 2 enlargement round: Opportunities and challenges', in N. Nugent (ed.), *European Union Enlargement*, Basingstoke: Palgrave Macmillan, 2004.

P. O'Neil, 'Politics, finance and European enlargement eastward', in J. Sperling (ed.), *Two Tiers or Two Speeds? The European Security Order and the Enlargement of the European Union and NATO*, Manchester: Manchester University Press, 1999.

J. Van Oudenaren, 'The European Union: From Community to constitution', in R. Tiersky and E. Jones (eds), *Europe Today. A Twenty-First Century Introduction*, Lanham: Rowman and Littlefield, 2007.

D. Rothchild and P. Roeder, 'Power sharing as an impediment to peace and democracy', in P. Roeder and D. Rothchild (eds), *Sustainable Peace: Power and Democracy after Civil Wars*, Ithaca NJ: Cornell University Press, 2005.

U. Sedelmeier, 'Eastern enlargement: Risk, rationality, and role-compliance', in M. Cowles and M. Smith (eds), *The State of the European Union: Risks, Reform, Resistance and Revival*, Oxford: Oxford University Press, 2000.

K. Smith, 'Enlargement and European order', in C. Hill and M. Smith (eds) *International Relations and the European Union*, Oxford: Oxford University Press, 2005.

M.E. Smith, 'The quest for coherence: Institutional dilemmas of external action from Maastricht to Amsterdam', in A. Stone Sweet, W. Sandholtz and N. Fligstein (eds), *The Institutionalisation of Europe*, Oxford: Oxford University Press, 2001.

J. Peterson and E. Jones, 'Decision making in an enlarging European Union', in J. Sperling (ed.), *Two Tiers or Two Speeds? The European Security Order and the Enlargement of the European Union and NATO*, Manchester: Manchester University Press, 1999.

A. Sorel, 'Asylum, Migration and Border Controls in the Hague Programme', in J. de Zwaan and F. Goudappel (eds), *Freedom, Security and Justice in the European Union: Implementation of the Hague Programme*, The Hague: TMC Asser Press 2006.

D. Spence, 'Introduction' in D. Spence (ed.), *The European Union and Terrorism*, London: John Harper Publishing, 2007.

J. Sperling, 'Two tiers or two speeds? Constructing a stable European security order', in J. Sperling (ed.), *Two Tiers or Two Speeds? The European Security Order and the Enlargement of the European Union and NATO*, Manchester: Manchester University Press, 1999.

J. Sperling (1999) 'Enlarging the EU and NATO', in J. Sperling (ed.), *Two Tiers or Two Speeds? The European Security Order and the Enlargement of the European Union and NATO*, Manchester: Manchester University Press, 1999.

F. Tanner, 'North Africa. Partnership, exceptionalism and neglect', in R. Dannreuther (ed.), *European Foreign and Security Policy. Towards a Neighbourhood Strategy*, Routledge: London, 2004.

L. Tsoukalis, 'Managing interdependence: The EU in the world economy', in C. Hill and M. Smith (eds), *International Relations of the European Union*, Oxford: Oxford University Press, 2005.

J. Willerton and M. Beznosov, 'Russia's pursuit of its Eurasian security interests: Weighing the CIS and alternative bilateral-multilateral arrangements', in K. Malfiet, L. Verpoes and E. Vinokurov (eds), *The CIS, the EU and Russia: The Challenges of Integration*, London: Palgrave, 2007.

A. Spence and D. Spence, 'The Common Foreign and Security Policy from Maastricht to Amsterdam', in K.A. Eliassen (ed.), *Foreign and Security Policy in the European Union*, London: Sage, 1998.

E. Ucarer, 'Justice and Home Affairs', in M. Cini and N. Borragan (eds), *European Union Politics*, Oxford: Oxford University Press, 2010.

R.G. Whitman, 'CFSP after Enlargement', in V.C. Price, A. Landau and R.G. Whitman, *The Enlargement of the European Union: Issues and Strategies*, London: Routledge, 1999.

J. Wyllie, 'Measuring up: The strategies as strategy', in R. Dannreuther and J. Peterson eds, *Security Strategy and Transatlantic Relations,* London: Routledge, 2006.

A. Zagorski, 'Policies towards Russia, Ukraine, Moldova and Belarus', in R. Dannreuther (ed.), *European Foreign and Security Policy: Towards a Neighbourhood Strategy*, London: Routledge, 2004.

J. Zielonka. 'Policies without strategy: The EU's record in Eastern Europe', in J. Zielonka (ed.), *Paradoxes of European Foreign Policy*, The Hague: Kluwer, 1998.

Articles

M. Abramowitz and H. Hurlburt, 'Can the EU hack the Balkans? A proving ground for Brussels', *Foreign Affairs* 81: 5, 2002, 2–7.

E. Ahrari, 'Iran, China and Russia: The emerging anti-US nexus?', *Security Dialogue* 32: 4, 2001, 453–66.

S. Anderson, 'EU, NATO and CSCE responses to the Yugoslav crisis: Testing Europe's new security architecture', *European Security* 4: 2, 1995, 328–53.

A. Arbatov, 'Is a new Cold War imminent?', *Russia in Global Affairs* 2, 2007, n.p., http://eng.globalaffairs.ru/numbers/20/1130.html.

A. Aronowitz, 'Smuggling and trafficking in human beings: The phenomena, the markets that drive it and the organisations that promote it', *European Journal of Criminal Policy and Research* 9: 2, 2001, 163–95.

D.P. Auerswald, 'The President, Congress and American missile defence policy', *Defence Studies* 1: 2, 2002, 57–82.

D. Averre, 'Russia and the European Union: Convergence or divergence?', *European Security* 14: 2, 2005, 175–202.

P. Baev, 'The CIS: refusing to fade away', *Russia and Eurasia Review*, 1: 10, 2002, n.p., http://www.jamestown.org/print_friendly.php?volume_id=15&issue_id=608&article_id.

P. Baev, 'External interventions in secessionist conflicts in Europe in the 1990s', *European Security* 8: 2, 1999, 22–51.

G. Bahgat, 'Europe's energy security: challenges and opportunities', *International Affairs* 82: 5, 2006, 961–75.

A. Bailes, 'EU and US strategic concepts', *The International Spectator* 39: 1, 2004, 19–33.

E. Barbe and B. Kienzle, 'Security provider or security consumer? The European Union and conflict management', *European Foreign Affairs Review* 12: 4, 2007, 517–36.

E. Barbé and E. Johansson-Nogués, 'The EU as a modest "force for good": the European Neighbourhood Policy', *International Affairs* 84: 1, 2008, 81–96.

E. Bielsa, 'The pivotal role of news agencies in the context of globalization: a historic approach', *Global Networks* 8: 3, 2008, 347–66.

D. Bigo, 'Internal and external aspects of security', *European Security* 15: 4, 2006, 405–22.

C. Bildt, 'Force and diplomacy, *Survival* 42: 1, 2000, 141–48.

A. Blair, 'What happened in Yugoslavia? Lessons for future peacekeepers', *European Security* 3:2, 1994, 340–49.

S. Blank, 'The Mediterranean and its security agenda', *Mediterranean Quarterly* 11: 1, 2000, 24–48.

A.J. Blinken, 'The false crisis over the Atlantic', *Foreign Affairs* 80: 3, 2001, 35–48.

M. den Boer and J. Monar, 'Keynote article: 11 September and the challenge of global terrorism to the EU as a security actor', *Journal of Common Market Studies* 40, 2002, 11–28.

J. Borawski, 'Revisiting the common European home: A rejoinder', *Security Dialogue*, 31: 1, 2000, 85–90.

J. Borawski, 'Partnership for Peace and beyond', *International Affairs* 71: 2, 2005, 233–46.

C. Boswell, 'The "external dimension" of EU immigration and asylum policy', *International Affairs* 79: 3, 2003, 619–38.

S. Brooks and W. Wohlforth, 'Hard times for soft balancing', *International Security* 30: 1, 2005, 72–108.

S. Brooks and W. Wohlforth, 'American primacy in perspective', *Foreign Affairs* 81: 4, 2002, 20–33.

M. Buchsbaum, 'The OSCE and the Stability Pact for South Eastern Europe', *Helsinki Monitor* 11: 4, 2000, 62–79.

H. Bull, 'Civilian Power Europe: A contradiction in terms?', *Journal of Common Market Studies* 21: 2, 1982, 149–64.

B. Buzan and T. Diez, 'The European Union and Turkey', *Survival* 41: 1, 1999, 41–57.

F. Cahrillon, 'The EU as a security regime', *European Foreign Affairs Review* 10, 2005, 517–33.

S.C. Calleya, 'Post-Cold War regional dynamics in the Mediterranean,' *Mediterranean Quarterly* 7: 3, 1996, 42–54.

S.C. Calleya, 'Cross-cultural currents in the Mediterranean: What prospects?', *Mediterranean Quarterly* 9: 3, 1998, 46–60.

S. Cimbala, 'Missile defenses and Mother Russia: Scarecrow or showstopper?', *European Security* 16: 3–4, 2007, 289–306.

D.B. Cohen, 'From START to START II: Dynamism and pragmatism in the Bush administration's nuclear weapon policies', *Presidential Studies Quarterly* 27: 3, 1997, 412–29.

R. Cooper, 'The next empire', *Prospect* 67, 2001, 222–26.

P. Cornish and G. Edwards, 'The strategic culture of the European Union: A progress report', *International Affairs* 81: 4, 2005, 801–20.

S. Croft, 'The EU, NATO and the return of the architectural debate', *European Security* 9: 3, 2000, 1–20.

B. Crowe, 'A Common European Foreign Policy after Iraq?', *International Affairs* 79: 3, 2003, 533–46.

H. De Santis, 'Romancing NATO: Partnership for Peace and East European stability', *Journal of Strategic Studies* 17: 4, 1994, 61–81.

A. Deighton, 'The European Security and Defence Policy', *Journal of Common Market Studies* 40: 4, 2002, 719–41.

R.A. Del Sarto and T. Schumacher, 'From EMP to ENP', *European Foreign Affairs Review* 10, 2005, 17–38.

P. Dombrowski, E. Gholz and A. Ross, 'Selling military transformation: The defense industry and innovation', *Orbis* 46: 3, 2002, 523–36.

R. Dover, 'The EU and the Bosnian civil war 1992–95: The capability-expectations gap at the heart of EU foreign policy', *European Security* 14: 5, 2005, 297–318.

S. Duke, 'The future of EU–NATO relations: a case of mutual irrelevance through competition?', *Journal of European Integration* 30: 1, 2008, 27–43.

S. Duke, 'Areas of Grey: Tensions in EU External Relations competencies', *EIPASCOPE* 1, 2006, 21–27.

S. Duke, 'CESDP: Nice's overtrumped success?', *European Foreign Affairs Review* 6: 2, 2001, 155–75.

S. Duke, 'The second death (or the second coming?) of the WEU', *Journal of Common Market Studies* 34: 2, 1996, 153–69.

T. Dunne, 'Good Citizen Europe', *International Affairs* 84: 1, 2008, 13–28.

G. Edwards, 'The construction of ambiguity and the limits of attraction: Europe and its Neighbourhood Policy', *Journal of European Integration* 30: 1, 2008, 45–62.

W. Van Eekelen, 'WEU's post-Maastricht agenda', *NATO Review* 40: 2, 1992, 13–17.

P. Flenley, 'Russia and the EU: A pragmatic and contradictory relationship', *Perspectives on European Politics and Society* 6: 3, 2005, 435–61.

G. Flynn and D. Scheffer, 'Limited collective security', *Foreign Policy* 80, 1990, 77–101.

A. Gat, 'The return of authoritarian Great Powers', *Foreign Affairs* 86: 4, 2007, 59–69.

I. Gatev, 'Border security in the Eastern Neighbourhood: Where bio-politics and Geo-politics meet', *European Foreign Affairs Review* 13, 2008, 97–116.

C. Gegout, 'The Quint: Acknowledging the existence of a Big Four-US *directoire* at the heart of the European Union's foreign policy decision-making process', *Journal of Common Market Studies* 40: 2, 2002, 331–44.

T. German, 'Visibly invisible: EU engagement in conflict resolution in the South Caucasus', *European Security* 16: 3–4, 2007, 357–74.

J. Gow, 'Deconstructing Yugoslavia', *Survival* 33: 4, 1991, 291–311.

J. Gow, 'The use of coercive action in the Yugoslav crisis', *World Today* 48, 1992, 198–202.

E. Guild, 'International terrorism and EU immigration, asylum and borders policy: The unexpected victims of 11 September 2001', *European Foreign Affairs Review* 8:3, 2003, 331–46.

J. Haqhaqi, 'Small arms and regional security in the Western Mediterranean: Reflections on European views', *Mediterranean Quarterly* 15:3, 2004, 55–74.

C. Hill, 'The Capability-Expectation Gap, or Conceptualising Europe', *Journal of Common Market Studies* 31: 3, 1993, 305–28.

R.C. Holbrooke, 'America as a European power', *Foreign Affairs* 74: 2, 1995, 38–51.

J. Howorth, 'Britain, France and the European defence initiative', *Survival* 42: 2, 2001, 33–55.

R.E. Hunter, 'NATO at fifty. Maximising NATO: A relevant Alliance knows how to reach', *Foreign Affairs* 78: 3, 1999, 190–203.

S. Huntington, 'The lonely superpower', *Foreign Affairs* 78: 2, 1999, 35–50.

J. Huysmans, 'The European Union and the securitization of migration', *Journal of Common Market Studies* 38: 5, 2000, 751–77.

A. Hyde-Price, 'A "tragic actor"? A realist perspective on "ethical power Europe"', *International Affairs* 84: 1, 2008, 29–44.

A. Hyde-Price, 'European security, strategic culture, and the use of force', *European Security* 13: 4, 2004, 323–43.

J.G. Ikenberry, 'The end of the Neoconservative moment', *Survival* 46: 1, 2004, 7–22.

V. Ivanenko, 'Russian global position after 2008', *Russia in Global Affairs* 4, 2007, np, http://www.eng.globalaffairs.ru/printver/1158.html.

C.G. Jacobsen, 'Yugoslavia's successor wars reconsidered', *European Security* 4: 4, 1995, 655–75.

J. Janning, 'A German Europe – a European Germany? On the debate over Germany's foreign policy', *International Affairs* 72: 1, 1996, 33–41.

G. Joffé, 'Morocco's reform process: Wider implications', *Mediterranean Politics* 14: 2, 2009, 151–64.

G. Joffé, 'The European Union, democracy and counter-terrorism in the Maghreb', *Journal of Common Market Studies* 46: 1, 2008, 147–71.

J. Joffe, 'Collective security and the future of Europe: Failed dreams and dead ends', *Survival* 34: 1, 1992, 36–50.

M. Kaldor and A. Salmon, 'Military force and European strategy', *Survival* 48: 1, 2006, 19–34.

M. Kaldor, M. Martin and S. Selchow, 'Human security: a new strategic narrative for Europe', *International Affairs* 83: 2, 2007, 273–88.

E. Kapstein, 'Capturing fortress Europe: International collaboration and the Joint Strike Fighter', *Survival* 46: 3, 2004, 137–60.

L. Karabeshkin and D. Spechler, 'EU and NATO enlargement: Russia's expectations, responses and options for the future', *European Security* 16: 3–4, 2007, 307–28.

S. Karaganov, 'A new epoch of confrontation', *Russia in Global Affairs* 4, 2007, n.p., http://eng.globalaffairs.ru/region-rfp/numbers/21/1148.html.

K. Kausch and R. Youngs, 'The end of the Euro-Mediterranean vision', *International Affairs* 85: 5, 2009, 963–75.

J. Keeler, 'Transatlantic relations and European security and defence', *EUSA Review* 17: 2, 2004, 3–4.

J. Kelley, 'Strategic non-cooperation as soft balancing: Why Iraq was not just about Iraq', *International Politics* 42, 2005, 153–73.

J. Kelley, 'New wine into old wineskins: Promoting political reforms through the New Neighbourhood Policy', *Journal of Common Market Studies* 44: 1, 2006, 29–55.

D. Keohane, 'The absent friend: EU foreign policy and counter-terrorism', *Journal of Common Market Studies* 46: 1, 2008, 125–46.

R.O. Keohane and L.L. Martin, 'The promise of institutionalist theory', *International Security* 20: 1, 39–51.

S. Keukeleire, 'Directoires within the CFSP/CESDP of the European Union: a plea for "restricted crisis management groups"', *European Foreign Affairs Review* 6: 1, 2001, 75–101.

O. Kovač, 'Regional approach of the European Union to cooperation among countries of the former Yugoslavia', *Review of International Affairs* 47, 1996, 1–5.

A. Kozyrev, 'Russia: A chance for survival', *Foreign Affairs* 71, 1992, 1–16.

I. Krastev, 'Russia as the "other Europe"', *Russia in Global Affairs* 4, 2007, np, http://www.eng.globalaffairs.ru/printver/1151.html.

C. Krauthammer, 'America and the world', *Foreign Affairs* 70: 1, 1990–1, 23–33.

C. Krauthammer, 'The unipolar moment revisited', *National Interest* 70, 2002–3, 5–17.

C.A. Kupchan and C.A. Kupchan, 'The promise of collective security', *International Security* 20: 1, 1995, 52–61.

C.A. Kupchan and C.A. Kupchan, 'Concerts, collective security, and the future of Europe', *International Security* 16: 1, 1991, 114–61.

J. Lantis, 'EU strategic culture and US ambivalence', *Oxford Journal on Good Governance* 2: 1, 2005, 55–60.

F.S. Larrabee, 'Danger and opportunity in Eastern Europe', *Foreign Affairs* 85: 6, 2006, 117–31.

S. Lavenex and F. Schimmelfennig, 'Relations with wider Europe', *Journal of Common Market Studies* 45: Annual Review, 2007, 143–62.

S. Lavenex, '"Passing the buck": European refugee policies towards Central and Eastern Europe', *Journal of Refugee Studies* 11: 2, 1998, 126–45.

M. Leffler, '9/11 and American foreign policy', *Diplomatic History* 29: 3, 2005, 395–413.

R. Legvold, 'All the way: Crafting a U.S.–Russian alliance', *The National Interest*, 70, 2002, 21–32.

M. Lerch and G. Schwellnus, 'Normative by nature? The role of coherence in justifying the EU's external human rights policy', *Journal of European Public Policy* 13: 2, 2006, 304–21.

B. Lia, 'Security dilemmas in Europe's Mediterranean periphery – perspectives and policy dilemmas', *European Security* 8: 4, 1999, 27–56.

K. Lieber and D. Press, 'The rise of U.S. nuclear supremacy', *Foreign Affairs* 85: 2, 2006, 42–54.

M. Light, J. Lowenhardt and S. White, 'Russian perspectives on European security', *European Foreign Affairs Review* 5, 2000, 489–505.

J. Lindley-French, 'In the shade of Locarno? Why European defence is failing', *International Affairs* 78: 4, 2002, 789–811.

S. Lodgaard, 'Competing schemes for Europe: The CSCE, NATO and the European Union', *Security Dialogue* 23: 3, 1992, 57–68.

D. Lutterbeck, 'Blurring the dividing line: The convergence of internal and external security in Western Europe', *European Security* 14: 2, 2005, 231–53.

I. Manners, 'Normative Power Europe: A contradiction in terms?', *Journal of Common Market Studies* 40: 2, 2002, 235–58.

S. Markedonov, 'Regional conflicts reloaded', *Russia in Global Affairs* 4, 2008, np, http://eng.globalaffairs.ru/region-rfp/numbers/25/1247.html.

S. Marsh, 'Thirty years on: Iran's silent revolution', *Iranian Studies* 42: 2, 2009, 213–29.

P.M. Martinsen, 'Forging a strategic culture: Putting policy into the ESDP', *Oxford Journal on Good Governance* 1: 1, 2004, 61–66.

J. Matlary, 'Much ado about little: the EU and human security', *International Affairs* 84: 1, 2008, 131–43.

J. Matlary, 'When soft power turns hard: Is an EU strategic culture possible?', *Security Dialogue* 37: 1, 2006, 105–21.

H. Maull, 'Europe and the new balance of global order', *International Affairs* 81: 4, 2005, 775–99.

H. Maull, 'Germany and Japan: The new Civilian Powers', *Foreign Affairs* 69: 5, 1990, 91–106.

H. Mayer, 'Is it still called "Chinese whispers? The EU's rhetoric and action as a responsible global institution', *International Affairs* 84: 1, 2008, 61–79.

M. McFaul and K. Stoner-Weiss, 'The myth of the authoritarian model; How Putin's crackdown holds Russia back', *Foreign Affairs* 87: 1, 2008, 68–84.

C.W. Maynes, 'US unilateralism and its dangers', *Review of International Studies* 25: 3, 1999, 515–18.

J. Mearsheimer, 'The false promise of international institutions', *International Security* 19: 3, 1994/95, 5–49.

J. Mearsheimer, 'Back to the future: Instability in Europe after the Cold War', *International Security* 15: 3, 1990, 5–57.

A. Menon, 'Empowering paradise? The ESDP at ten', *International Affairs* 85: 2, 2009, 227–46.

V. Merkushev, 'Relations between Russia and the EU: The view from across the Atlantic', *Perspectives on European Politics and Society* 6: 2, 2005, 353–71.

R. Miller and A. Mishrif, 'The Barcelona Process and Euro-Arab economic relations, 1995–2005', *Middle East Review of International Affairs* 9: 2, 2005, 94–108.

A. Miskimmon, 'Continuity in the face of upheaval – British strategic culture and the impact of the Blair government', *European Security* 13: 3, 2004, 273–99.

E. Mlyn, 'The OSCE, the United States and European security', *European Security* 5: 3, 1996, 426–47.

B. Momani, 'The EU, the Middle East, and regional integration', *World Economics* 8: 1, 2007, 1–10.

J. Monar, 'Institutional constraints of the European Union's Mediterranean policy', *European Foreign Affairs Review* 3: 2, 1998, 39–60.

P. Moreau-Defarges, 'Multilateralism and the end of history', *Politique étrangère*, 2004, n.p., http://www.diplomatie.gouv.fr/en/IMG/pdf/0104Moreau_Defarges_gb.pdf.

S. Neuman, 'Defense industries and global dependency', *Orbis* 50: 3, 2006, 429–51.

J.S. Nye, 'Understating US strength', *Foreign Policy* 72, 1998, 105–29.

J. Van Oudenaren, 'US reactions to the EU security strategy', *Oxford Journal of Good Governance* 1: 1, 2004, 43–47.

N. Pandurevic, 'Security aspects of the Stability Pact for South Eastern Europe', *Security Dialogue* 32: 3, 2001, 311–24.

H. Pant, "The Moscow-Beijing-Delhi 'strategic triangle': An idea whose time may never come", *Security Dialogue* 35: 3, 2004, 311–28.

R. Pape, 'Soft balancing against the United States', *International Security* 30: 1, 2005, 7–45.

M. Paterson, 'Post-hegemonic climate politics?', *The British Journal of Politics and International Relations* 11: 1, 2009, 140–58.

C. Patten, 'Devotion or divorce? The future of transatlantic relations', *European Foreign Affairs Review* 6: 3, 2001, 287–90.

T.V. Paul, 'Soft balancing in an age of US primacy', *International Security* 30: 1, 2005, 46–71.

C. Piana, 'The EU's decision-making process in the Common Foreign and Security Policy: The case of the Former Yugoslav Republic of Macedonia', *European Foreign Affairs Review* 7, 2002, 209–26.

C. Pippan, 'The rocky road to Europe: The EU's Stabilisation and Association Process for the Western Balkans and the principle of conditionality', *European Foreign Affairs Review* 9, 2004, 219–45.

F. Proedrou, 'The EU-Russia energy approach under the prism of interdependence', *European Security* 16: 3–4, 2007, 329–55.

D. Reveron, 'Old allies, new friends: Intelligence-sharing in the War on Terror', *Orbis* 50: 3, 2006, 453–68.

J. Rickli, 'US and EU security strategies: Same planet, different hemispheres', *Oxford Journal on Good Governance* 1: 1, 2004, 55–60.

E. Roberts, 'Montenegro: Trouble ahead', *World Today* 55: 12, 1999, 11–14.

P. Robinson, 'The CNN effect: Can the news media drive foreign policy?' *Review of International Studies* 25: 2, 1999, 301–9.

D. Ross, 'The Middle East predicament', *Foreign Affairs* 84: 1, 2005, 61–74.

O. Roy, 'Euro-Islam: The Jihad within', *The National Interest* Spring, 2003, np, http://findarticles.com/p/articles/mi_m2751/is_2003_Spring/ai_99377576/?tag=content;col1.

R. Russell, 'The chimera of collective security in Europe', *European Security* 4: 2, 1995, 241–55.

M. Rühle and N. Williams, 'Partnership for Peace after NATO enlargement', *European Security* 5: 4, 1996, 521–28.

S. Rynning, 'Less may be better in EU Security and Defence Policy', *Oxford Journal on Good Governance* 2: 1, 2005, 45–50.

Z. Sabi and A. Bojinovi, 'Mapping a regional institutional architecture: the case of the Mediterranean', *Mediterranean Quarterly* 12: 3, 2007, 317–36.

M. Sadakata, 'Regional governance: Lessons from European involvement in Yugoslav conflicts', *Japanese Journal of Political Science* 4: 2, 2003, 315–26.

R. Sakwa, '"New Cold War" or twenty years' crisis? Russia and international politics', *International Affairs* 84: 2, 2008, 241–67.

T. Salmon, 'The European Security and Defence Policy: Built on rocks or sand?', *European Foreign Affairs Review* 10, 2005, 359–79.

T. Salmon, 'Testing times for European Political Cooperation: the Gulf and Yugoslavia', *International Affairs* 68: 2, 1992, 233–53.

M.E. Sangiovanni, 'Why a Common Security and Defence Policy is bad for Europe', *Survival* 45: 3, 2003, 193–206.

F. Schimmelfennig and U. Sedelmeier, 'Governance by conditionality: EU rule transfer to the candidate countries of Central and Eastern Europe', *Journal of European Public Policy* 11: 4, 2004, 669–87.

A. Schlesinger Jr., 'Back to the womb? Isolationism's renewed threat', *Foreign Affairs* 74: 4, 1995, 2–8.

J. Shapiro and D. Byman, 'Bridging the transatlantic counterterrorism gap', *The Washington Quarterly* 29: 4, 2006, 33–50.

D. Simes, 'Losing Russia: The costs of renewed confrontation', *Foreign Affairs* 86: 6, 2007, 36–52.

S. Simon and D. Benjamin, 'America and the new terrorism', *Survival* 42: 1, 2000, 59–75.

K. Smith, 'The outsiders: The European Neighbourhood Policy', *International Affairs* 81: 4, 2005, 757–73.

K. Smith, 'The end of Civilian Power Europe: A welcome demise or cause for concern?', *International Spectator* 23: 2, 2000, 11–28.

K. Smith, 'The use of political conditionality in the EU's relations with third countries: How effective?', *European Foreign Affairs Review* 3, 1998, 253–74.

M. Smith and M. Webber, 'Political dialogue and security in the European Neighbourhood: The virtues and limits of "New Partnership Perspectives', *European Foreign Affairs Review* 13, 2008, 73–95.

J. Snyder, 'Averting anarchy in the new Europe', *International Security* 14: 4, 1990, 5–41.

J. Solana, 'Thoughts on the reception of the European Security Strategy', *Oxford Journal on Good Governance* 1: 1, 2004, 17–19.

C. Spencer, 'The EU as a security actor in the Mediterranean: Problems and prospects', *The Quarterly Journal* 2, 2002, 135–42.

S. Stavridis, 'Militarizing the EU: the concept of Civilian Power Europe revisited', *The International Spectator* 36: 4, 2001, 43–50.

H. Sjursen, 'What kind of power? ' *Journal of European Public Policy* 13: 2, 2006, 169–81.

H. Sjursen, 'Why expand? The question of legitimacy and justification in the EU's enlargement policy', *Journal of Common Market Studies* 40: 3, 2002, 491–513.

H. Strachan, 'The lost meaning of strategy', *Survival* 47: 3, 2005, 33–54.

H. Timmermann, 'European-Russian partnership: What future?' *European Foreign Affairs Review* 5: 2, 2000, 165–74.

A. Toje, 'The consensus-expectations gap: Explaining Europe's ineffective policy', *Security Dialogue* 39: 1, 2008, 121–41.

A. Toje, 'The 2003 European Security Strategy: A critical appraisal', *European Foreign Affairs Review* 10: 1, 2005, 117–33.

D. Trenin, 'Russia leaves the West', *Foreign Affairs* 85: 4, 2006, 87–96.

A. Tsygankov, 'New challenges for Putin's foreign policy', *Orbis* 50: 1, 2006, 153–65.

A. Tsygankov, 'Projecting confidence, not fear: Russia's post-imperial assertiveness', *Orbis* 50: 4, 2006, 677–90.

Y. Tymoshenko, 'The sources of Russian conduct', *Foreign Affairs*, 86: 3, 2007, 69–82.

R. Ullman, 'Enlarging the zone of peace', *Foreign Policy* 80, 1990, 102–20.

W. Wallace, 'Foreign policy and national identity in the United Kingdom', *International Affairs* 67: 1, 1991, 65–80.

M. Webber, S. Croft, J. Howorth, T. Terriff and E. Krahmann, 'The governance of European security', *Review of International Studies* 30, 2004, 3–36.

M. Webber, 'Third-party inclusion in European Security and Defence Policy: A case study of Russia', *European Foreign Affairs Review* 6: 4, 2001, 407–26.

N. Wesenten, G. Belenky and T. Balkin, 'Cognitive readiness in network-centric operations', 35, 2005, 94–105.

S. White, 'Elite opinion and foreign policy in post-communist Russia', *Perspectives on European Politics and Society* 8: 2, 2007, 147–67.

R. Whitman, 'Road map for a route march? (De-)civilianizing through the EU's security strategy', *European Foreign Affairs Review* 11, 2006, 1–15.

N. Williams, 'Partnership for Peace: Permanent fixture or declining asset?', *Survival* 38: 1, 1996, 98–110.

P.C. Wood, 'France and the post-Cold War order: The case of Yugoslavia', *European Security* 3: 1, 1994, 129–52.

N. Woods, 'The shifting politics of foreign aid', *International Affairs* 81:2, 2005, 393–409.

M. Wörner, 'A vigorous alliance – A motor for peaceful change in Europe', *NATO Review* 40: 6, 1992, 1–8.

J. Wright, 'European security – post-Bosnia', *European Security* 6: 2, 1997, 1–17.

P. Zelikow, 'The new concert of Europe', *Survival* 34: 2, 1992, 12–30.

Papers and reports

G. Adams, 'Fortress America in a changing transatlantic defence market', in B. Schmitt (ed.), *Between Cooperation and Competition: The Transatlantic Defence Market*, ISS: Chaillot Paper 44, January 2001.

R. Aliboni, *European Security across the Mediterranean*, ISS: Chaillot Paper 2, March 1991.

R. Aliboni, A. Driss, T. Schumacher and A. Tovias, 'Putting the Mediterranean Union in perspective', Euromesco paper 68, June 2008.

J.B. Alterman, 'The Middle East moves East', CSIS Middle East Notes and Comment, 10 February 2009.

J. Apap, 'Enlargement and an Area of Freedom, Security and Justice: Striking a better balance', The European Policy Centre, 18 October 2001.

J. Apap and A. Tchorbadjijska, 'What about the neighbours? The impact of Schengen along the EU's external borders', Centre for European Policy Studies, *Working Document No. 210*, October 2004.

K. Archick, 'The United States and Europe: Possible options for US policy', CRS Report for Congress, RL32577, 8 March 2005.

A. Ashbourne, 'Opening the US defence market', Center for European Reform, October 2000.

A. Åslund and A. Kuchins, 'Pressing the "reset button" on US–Russia relations', CSIS Policy Brief, March 2009.

F. Ateaga, 'The EU's internal security strategy', ARI 75/2010, Real Instituto Elcano, 8 July 2010.

F. Attina, 'The Euro-Mediterranean project of security partnership in comparative perspective', Jean Monnet Working Papers in Comparative and International Politics, no.52, 2004.

R. Balfour and A. Missiroli, 'Reassessing the European Neighbourhood Policy', EPC Issue Paper no.54, 2007.

R. Balfour, 'Re thinking the Euro-Mediterranean political and security dialogue', Institute for Security Studies, Occasional Papers, no.52, May 2004.

A. Bailes, 'The European Security Strategy: An evolutionary history', SIPRI Policy Paper 10, February 2005.

K. Becher, 'Chairman's summing-up', IISS/CEPS European Security Forum: European and Transatlantic Industrial Strategies', 25 November 2002.

S. Biscop, 'The European Security Strategy and the Neighbourhood Policy: A new starting point for a Euro-Mediterranean security partnership?' paper presented at EUSA Ninth Biannual International Conference, Austin, Texas, 31 March–2 April 2005.

S. Biscop, 'The EU and Middle-Eastern security: A new departure?' Paper presented at the 10th EUSA Biennial Conference Montreal, 17–19 May 2007.

A. Boening, 'Vortex of a regional security complex: The EuroMed Partnership and its security relevance', Miami-Florida European Union Center of Excellence, May 2008.

Erhard Bort 'Illegal migration and cross-border crime: Challenges at the Eastern frontier of the European Union', Florence: European University Institute Working Paper 2000/9, 2000.

G. Bovt, 'Russian foreign policy under Dmitry Medvedev', The EU-Russia Centre Review, 'Russian Foreign Policy', Issue 8, October 2008, 20–27.

A. Brown and M. Attenborough, 'EU enlargement: the Western Balkans', House of Commons Research Paper 07/27, 14 March 2007.

F. Burwell, D. Gompert, L. Lebl, J. Lodal and W.Slocombe, 'Transatlantic transformation: Building a NATO-EU security architecture', *Policy Paper*, The Atlantic Council, March 2006.

S.C. Calleya, 'Is the Barcelona Process working? EU Policy in the Mediterranean', Zentrum für Europäische Integrationsforschung, Center for European Integration Studies, Rheinische Friedrich Wilhelms-Universität Bonn, 2000.

A. Cohen, 'How to confront Russia's anti-American foreign policy', Backgrounder, Heritage Foundation, 27 June 2007, 1–6.

E. Collet, 'Foreword', in Bertozzi, S. and Pastore, E. *Towards a Common European Asylum Policy*, Multicultural Europe, European Policy Centre Paper No. 49, October 2006.

S. Collinson, 'Security or securitization? Migration and the pursuit of freedom, security and justice in the Euro-Mediterranean area', Euromesco e-news, 19, November 2007.

S. De Spiegeleire, 'Recoupling Russia: Staying the course. Europe's security relationship with Russia', Paper prepared for the IISS/CEPS European Security Forum, Brussels, January 2002.

M. Delevic, 'Regional cooperation in the Western Balkans', Institute for Security Studies, Chaillot Paper 104, July 2007.

T. Demmelhuber, 'The Euro-Mediterranean space as an imagined (Geo-)political, economic and cultural entity', Zentrum für Europäische Integrationsforschung, Center for European Integration Studies, Rheinische Friedrich-Wilhelms-Universität Bonn, 2006.

M. Dittrich, 'Muslims in Europe: Addressing the challenges of radicalisation', European Policy Centre, Brussels, 2006.

A. Dorman, 'Reconciling Britain to Europe in the next millennium: The Evolution to British defence policy in the post-Cold War era', Paper to the International Studies Association, March 2000.

S. Everts, 'Unilateral America, lightweight Europe?', Working Paper, Centre for European Reform, February 2001.

S. Everts and H. Grabbe, 'Why the EU needs a security strategy', CER Briefing Note, May 2003.

M. Flournoy and J. Smith *et al.*, 'European defence integration: Bridging the gap between strategy and capabilities', Center for Strategic and International Studies, October 2005.

Freedom House, 'Freedom in the world 2009'.

F. Galli, 'The legal and political implications of the securitization of counter-terrorism measures across the Mediterranean', Euromesco Paper, 71, September 2008.

A. Geiger and E. Stetter, '"Barcelona Process: Union for the Mediterranean". Readjusting the Euro-Mediterranean Partnership', Friedrich Ebert Stiftug, April 2008.

R. Gillespie, 'Northern European perceptions of the Barcelona Process', Revista Cidob d'Afers Internationals 37, Estabilidad y conflictos en el Mediterráneo.

D. Gowan, *How the EU can help Russia*, London: Center for European Reform, 2000.

R. Gowan, 'The Battlegroups: A concept in search of a strategy?' in Sven Biscop (ed.), *E Pluribus Unum? Military integration in the European Union*, Egmont Papers, No.7, Brussels: Royal Institute for International Relations, 2005, 13–20.

C. Grant, 'Intimate Relations. Can Britain play a leading role in European defence – and keep its special links to US intelligence?', Working Paper, Centre for European Reform, 2000.

C. Grant, 'Europe's Blurred Boundaries: Rethinking Enlargement and Neighbourhood Policy', Centre for European Reform, 2006.

T. Guay, 'The transatlantic defence industrial base: Restructuring scenarios and their implications', Strategic Studies Institute, April 2005.

S. Haddadi, 'The western Mediterranean as a security complex: A *liaison* between the European Union and the Middle East?', Jean Monnet Working Paper in Comparative and International Politics, no.24, 1999.

F. Heisbourg, 'From European defense industrial restructuring to transatlantic deal?', CSIS working paper no.4, February 2001.

B. Huber, 'Ten Years of Euro-Med cooperation: Views of civil society representatives for the Middle East and Maghreb on the Euro-Mediterranean Partnership', Heinrich Boell Stiftung, Middle East Occasional Papers, no.1.

Institute of Strategic Studies dossier, Nuclear programmes in the Middle East: In the shadow of Iran, 2008.

G. Joffé, 'Cooperation or conflict? The Euro-Mediterranean Partnership Initiative and American interests in the Maghrib', http://www.george-joffe.com/art/100.pdf.

G. Joffé, 'The British Presidency of the European Union and the Mediterranean in 2005', iemed, 2006, pp. 95–97.

K. Kamp, 'NATO-summit 2006: The Alliance in search of topics', No.156/2006, Konrad Adenauer Stiftung: Berlin, February 2006.

S. Kapila, 'Iran in the strategic matrix of Russia, China and India', South Asia Analysis Group, paper no.1284, 9 March 2005.

S. Kapila, 'Russia's Monroe Doctrine: Strategic implications', Paper 2879, South Asia Analysis Group, 13 October 2008.

I. Kempe, 'Beyond bilateralism: adjusting EU-Russia relations', Bertelsmann Group for Policy Research, no.12, September 2007.

D. Keohane, 'Unblocking EU–NATO cooperation', *CER Bulletin*, 48, June/July 2006.

J. Kotsopoulos, 'A human security agenda for Europe?', *European Policy Centre Issue Paper 48*, June 2006.

P. Kovács, 'The Schengen challenge and its Balkan dimension', Centre for European Policy Studies Brief, no.17, March 2002.

S. Kutchesfahani, 'Iran's nuclear challenge and European diplomacy', *European Policy Centre Paper 46*, Brussels, March 2006.

M. Leonard and N. Popescu, 'A five-point strategy for EU-Russia relations', http://www.europesworld.org.

M. Leonard and N. Popescu, 'A power audit of EU-Russia relations', European Council of Foreign Affairs, November 2007.

M. Leonard and R. Gowan, 'Global Europe: Implementing the European Security Strategy', The Foreign Policy Centre in association with the British Council Brussels, 2003.

I. Lesser, 'The United States and Euro-Mediterranean relations: Evolving attitudes and strategies', EuroMeSCobrief, 10, July 2004.

R. Lindner, 'New realism: The making of Russia's foreign policy in the post-Soviet world', *The EU-Russia Centre Review: Russian Foreign Policy*, Issue 8, October 2008, pp.28–37.

M. McFaul, 'Russia: more stick, less carrot', *Hoover Digest*, 1, 2008.

A. Makarychev, 'Russia's energy policy: between security and transparency', PONARS Memo no. 425, December 2006.

A.P. Mallias, Ambassador of Greece to the US, '"Thessaloniki 2": European incentives for the Western Balkans', Atlantic Community: Open Think Tank article, Atlantic Community, 5 December 2007.

I. Manners, 'Normative Power Europe reconsidered', CIDEL Workshop, October 2004.

J. Mawdsley, 'The gap between rhetoric and reality: Weapons acquisition and ESDP', Paper 26, Bonn International Center for Conversion: Bonn, 2002.

Antonio Missiroli, Martin Ortega, Dimitrios Triantaphyllou, 'Partners and neighbours: a CFSP for a wider Europe', EU-ISS Chaillot Paper No.64, September 2003, pp.86–101.

R. North, 'The wrong side of the Hill: The secret realignment of UK defence policy with the EU', Centre for Policy Studies, October 2005.

M. Ortega, 'A new EU policy on the Mediterranean?' in Judy Batt, Dov Lynch, J. Van Oudenaren, 'The Solana security paper', American Institute for Contemporary German Studies, http://www.aicgs.org/analysis/c/solana.aspx.

PriceWaterhouseCoopers, 'The defence industry in the 21st Century: Thinking global … or thinking American?' 2005.

B. Schmitt, 'Armaments cooperation in Europe', Institute for Security Studies, January 2005.

J. Sedivy, 'One year on: lessons from Iraq', ISS Chaillot Paper no. 68, Paris, 2004.

K. Smith, 'Still Civilian Power Europe?', European Foreign Policy Unit Working Paper, 2005.

M. Smith, 'A review of Russian foreign policy', Conflict Studies Research Center, Russian Series, July 2007.

C. Spencer, 'North Africa: The hidden risks to regional stability', Chatham House briefing paper, Middle East and North Africa Programme, April 2009.

S. Stavridis, Why the 'Militarising' of the EU is strengthening the concept of a 'civilian power Europe', EUI Working Papers Series, RSC No. 2001/17, Robert Schuman Centre for Advanced Studies.

N. Tangiashvili and M. Kobaladze, 'EU-Georgia neighbourhood relations', Central European University, 2006.

C. Taylor, 'NATO: the Istanbul Summit', House of Commons research paper 04/60, 26 July 2004, pp. 1–46.

D. Trenin, 'A Russia-within-Europe: Working toward a new security arrangement', Paper prepared for the IISS/CEPS European Security Forum, Brussels, 14 January 2002.

T. Vasalek, 'What does the war in Georgia mean for EU foreign policy?' Briefing Note, Center for European Reform, 15 August 2008.

T. Valasek, 'Europe's defence and its new security strategy', CER Bulletin, 57, December 2007-January 2008.

M.H. Van Herpen, 'Medvedev's proposal for a pan-European security pact: Its six hidden objectives and how the west should respond', Cicero Foundation, 27 October 2008.

R. Vlahutin, 'The Croatian exception' in J. Batt (ed.) 'The Western Balkans: Moving On', ISS Chaillot Paper, no.70, October 2004, pp. 21–34.

S. Werthes and D. Bosold, 'Caught between pretension and substantiveness: ambiguities of human security as a political leitmotif', in Debiel, T. and Werthes, S. (eds) *Human Security on foreign policy agendas, changes, concepts and cases*, INEF Report, 2006.

A. Wilson, N. Popescu and P. Noël, 'The future of EU-Russia relations: a way forward in solidarity ad the rule of law', Brussels: European Parliament, 2009.

J. Wither, 'Expeditionary forces for post-modern Europe: Will European military weakness provide an opportunity for the new Condottieri?', Conflict Studies Research Centre, January 2005.

S. Woehrel, 'Future of the Balkans and US Policy Concerns', CRS Report for Congress, RL32136, 10 January 2008.

R. Youngs, 'Is European democracy promotion on the wane?', CEPS Working Document, no. 292, May 2008.

R. Youngs, 'Ten years of the Barcelona Process: A model for supporting Arab reform?', FRIDE working paper, January 2005.

K. Zulueta-Fülscher, 'Elections and the European Neighbourhood Policy in Armenia', Comment, FRIEDE, May 2008.

Newspaper articles

M. Albright, 'The right balance will secure NATO's future', *The Financial Times*, 7 December 1998.

G. Anderson, 'A new era for European defence procurement?', *Janes*, 4 July 2006.

T. Barber, 'Med Union blueprint avoids key questions', *Financial Times*, 12 March 2008.

BBC News, 'Putin deplores collapse of USSR', 23 April 2005.

BBC News, 'BAE Systems to buy US rival UDI', 7 March 2005.

K. Bennhold, 'Neighbors trying diplomatic approach', *International Herald Tribune*, 12 August 2008.

B. Benoit, 'A Cooling of the once passionate Franco-German love affair', *Financial Times*, 24 June 2006.

J. Berger, 'Iran has enriched enough uranium to make bomb, IAEA says', *The Guardian*, 19 February 2009.

M. Boot, 'What the Heck Is a Neocon?' *Wall Street Journal*, 30 December 2002.

A. Borowiec, 'EU wary of French initiative: Mediterranean Union proposal seen as threat', *The Washington Times*, 13 March 2008.

R. Boyes, 'Villa called freedom where migrants wait in search for haven', *The Times*, 13 February 2010.

I. Carson, 'Transformed? Transformed?' *The Economist* (US), 20 July 2002.

P. Finn, 'Russia, Indonesia set $1 billion arms deal', *Washington Post.com,*7 September 2007.

J. Freedland, 'Interview with Chris Patten', *The Guardian*, 9 February 2002.

T. Garton Ash, 'This dependent independence is the least worst solution for Kosovo', *The Guardian*, 21 February 2008.

B. Gellman, 'Keeping the US first', *The Washington Post*, 11 March 1992.

W. Guanqun, 'Solana: no big need to revamp European security structures', *China View*, 21 March 2009.

F. Halliday, 'The "Barcelona Process": ten years on', *Open Democracy*, 11 November 2005.

T. Halpin, 'Estonia fails to appease Russia over statue', *Timesonline*, 8 May 2007.

T. Halpin and D. Charter, 'Russia agrees new EU deal on troop pullout', *The Times*, 9 September, 2009.

L. Harding, 'Russia issues new missile defence threat', *The Guardian,* 4 July 2007.

T. Kavanagh, 'Interview of President George W. Bush', *The Sun,* 14 November 2003.

D. Keohane, 'EU on the offensive about defence', *European Voice.com,* 22–28 July 2004.

H.M. Kloth, 'Polish Minister attacks Schröder and Merkel', 1 May 2006, http://www.spiegel.de/international/0,1518,413969,00.html.

J. Ikenberry, 'On the sustainability of US power', *The Globalist,* 12 September 2002.

J. Lehrer, 'Interview with George W Bush', *Newshour,* 16 February 2000.

D. Leonard, 'Schengen poses tough hurdle for candidates', *European Voice,* 20 September 2001.

M. Lind, 'Beware visionaries wielding power', *The Australian,* 14 March 2003.

M. Lind, 'Protect the Great Powers', *The Financial Times,* 3 July 2002.

C. Moore, 'Sarkozy: No Lisbon Treaty, no Enlargement', *Reuters,* 20 June 2008.

PBS, Frontline, 'The war behind closed doors', excerpts from 1992 Wolfowitz draft, http://www.pbs.org/wgbh/pages/frontline/shows/iraq/etc/wolf.html.

C. Patten, 'Jaw-jaw, not war-war', *Financial Times,* 14 February 2002.

W. Petritsch, 'The EU must speed-up its Western Balkans enlargement', *Europe's World,* spring 2008.

W. Pfaff, 'US ambitions outstrip its domestic appetite', *International Herald Tribune,* 10 July 1997.

V. Pop, 'US backs Eastern Partnership eyeing energy independence', 6 April 2009, http://euobserver.com/880/27920.

H. de Quetteville and A. Pierce, 'Russia threatens nuclear attack on Poland over US missile shield deal', *The Telegraph,* 15 August 2008.

H. de Quetteville and I. Wilkinson, 'Russia threatens to target US missile shield', *The Telegraph,* 19 December 2007.

A. Riley, 'EU-Ukraine Gas Deal Is No Pipe Dream', *Wall Street Journal Europe,* 22 April 2009.

M. Ruhle and N. Williams, 'NATO enlargement and the European Union', *The World Today,* May 1995.

R. Ryan, 'Join Nato and we'll target missiles at Kiev, Putin warns Ukraine', *The Guardian,* 12 February 2008.

V. Socor, 'Medvedev proposes all-European security pact during Berlin Visit', *Eurasia Daily Monitor,* 9 June 2008.

V. Socor, 'Moscow makes furious but empty threats to Georgia and Ukraine', *Eurasia Daily Monitor,* 14 April 2008.

V. Socor, 'From CIS to CSTO: Can a "core" be preserved?', *Eurasia Daily Monitor,* 28 June 2005.

B. Tigner, 'EU threatens to build own defense market. Vents frustration with U.S. trade restrictions', *Defense News,* 24 January 2005.

I. Traynor, 'Russia accused of unleashing cyberwar to disable Estonia', *The Guardian,* 17 May 2007.

I. Traynor, 'Georgia: Divided EU prepares to review stand on Russia at emergency summit', *The Guardian,* 1 September 2008.

I. Traynor, 'Love tops agenda as Sarkozy launches Mediterranean Union', *The Guardian,* Monday 14 July 2008.

P. Tyler, 'US strategy plan calls for insuring no rivals develop. A one-superpower world', *New York Times,* 8 March 1992.

Unattributed, 'Sanctions begin to bite', *The Economist,* 9 October 2010.

Unattributed, 'EU-U.S. summit in doubt as Obama decides not to come', *Reuters,* 2 February 2010.

Unattributed, 'Turkey's circular worries', *The Economist,* 5 September 2009.

Unattributed, 'In the nick of time: A special report on EU enlargement', *The Economist,* 31 May 2008.

Unattributed, 'Putin threatens to review relations with EU', *Russia Today,* 23 March 2009.

Unattributed, 'EU to pledge $556 million in Palestinian aid', *Associated Press,* 27 February 2009.

Unattributed, 'Ministers give nod to EU energy security agenda', *euractiv.com,* 20 February 2009.

Unattributed, *Energy Bulletin,* 22 January 2009.

Unattributed, 'Pipe down: Russia, Ukraine and gas', *The Economist,* 10 January 2009.

Unattributed, 'A frugal Pax Europa', *Forecast International,* 12 November 2008.

Unattributed, 'Russia's new nuclear challenge to Europe', *The Sunday Times,* 17 August 2008.

Unattributed, 'Georgia signs peace deal', *The Independent,* 15 August 2008.

Unattributed, 'Medvedev unveils little new in Russia's foreign-policy course', rferl.org, 16 July 2008.

Unattributed, 'Poland, Sweden propose new EU outreach for eastern Europe', *International Herald Tribune,* 26 May 2008.

Unattributed, 'Poland, Sweden defend "Eastern initiative"', *EurActiv.com,* 26 May 2008.

Unattributed, 'Sarkozy opposes Turkish entry into EU, vows referendum', *eubusiness.com,* 24 April 2008.

Unattributed, 'EU reaffirms Western Balkan membership perspective', *EurActiv.com,* 6 March 2008.

Unattributed, 'Polish Prime Minister: Europe must speak with one voice to Russia', *FT.com,* 17 February 2008.

Unattributed, 'EU/Neighbourhood', *Agence Presse,* 6 December 2007.

Unattributed, 'Merkel Slams Sarkozy's 'Club Med' Plans', *Spiegel on-line,* 6 December 2007.

Unattributed, '"Ice Period" ensues in Poland-Russia relations', *RIA Novosti,* 22 April 2007.

Unattributed, 'Third time lucky? Charlemagne', *The Economist (US),* 14 January 2006.

Unattributed, 'Sarkozy calls for freeze on EU enlargement', *EurActiv.com,* 13 January 2006.

Unattributed, 'Special report: European Union enlargement', *The Economist,* 30 April 2005.

Unattributed, 'EU's Solana chides Washington over unilateralism', *Deutsche Welle,* 28 July 2004.

Unattributed, *The Financial Times,* 7 December 2003.

Unattributed, 'When east meets west', *The Economist,* 22 November 2003.

Unattributed, 'A survey of European enlargement', *The Economist,* 19 May 2001.

Unattributed, 'Turkey is not pleased with arrangement decided in Feira for European but non-EU NATO allies', *Agence Presse,* 24 June 2000.

Unattributed, 'EU/Enlargement', *Agence Presse,* 4 December 1997.

F. Weir, 'Russia's resurgent military', *CS Monitor,* 17 August 2007.

C.R. Whitney, 'NATO at 50: With nations at odds, is it a misalliance?', *The New York Times,* 15 February 1999.

INDEX

Note: A number in brackets following the locator indicates the note number on that page.

Abdul Qadeer Khan 144
Abkhazia 89, 94, 132, 139
accession to EU *see also* enlargement of EU:
  Balkans 10, 130–1; Central and East
  European Countries (CEEC) 10, 15;
  conditions 24–5, 27, 102, 112–13; drug
  trafficking 28
Aceh 161
Action Plan to Combat Organised Crime
  27–28
Afghanistan: conflict 7, 8; drugs 28, 29; EU
  actions in 17, 32, 56, 71, 73, 165; Iran 155;
  Southern Caucasus region 132; Turkey
  116; US military intervention 64, 65, 66
African, Caribbean and Pacific States (ACP)
  13, 41
African Union in Sudan 55
Agenda 2000: For a Stronger and Wider Union
  27, 114
Albania: admission to EMP 152; asylum
  seekers 25; crisis 122, 123; and EU
  127–30; NATO membership 71, 129;
  organised crime 21; support for US 106
Albright, Madeleine 106
Algeria 145, 146, 152
Al-Qaeda 11, 29
America *see* United States (of America)
Amsterdam Treaty 17, 18, 21, 43, 46, 81,
  110–11
Anglo-French Declaration on Defence and
  Security Co-operation 45
Anglo-French policy on ESDP 51, 58

Annan, Kofi 117
Arab-Israeli conflict 20, 155, 157
arc of instability 119–20
Area of Freedom, Security and Justice (AFSJ)
  18, 21–2
Armenia 125, 131–3, 137, 138, 143; relations
  with Russia 95
arms control 9, 16, 68, 91
Arms Trade Treaty 42
Ashton Catherine (Baroness) 47, 164
Asia 17, 125, 132
assurance security policy 11
asylum seekers 9, 21–6, 146
Atlanticism 51, 61, 67, 74, 77, 78, 91
Austria 5, 51, 97, 106
avant garde groups of States 111
Azerbaijan 71, 125, 131–3, 137, 139, 143, 163

Baker, James 61
Balkan conflict 5, 20–1, 53–4, 104, 198(23);
  and EU 119–23, 140–1; re-division of
  Europe 123–5
'Balkan Route' 10
Balkans: accession to EU 10, 27, 163; division
  in inner Europe 125–31; drug trafficking
  28; ethnic cleansing 8, 20–1; and EU
  15–16, 25, 49, 140–1, 162; immigration 24
Ballistic Missile Defence (BMD) 70, 73, 74,
  86, 87, 144
Baltic Fleet 86
Baltic States 5, 94, 103, 106
Barcelona Process 49, 147–56, 158, 159

Belarus: ENP 132, 135, 137, 138, 139, 141;
EU neighbours 104, 124, 125; EU values
163; organised crime 26; outer Europe
131–3; Partnership and Cooperation
Agreements (PCAs) 118; relations with
Russia 95; Russian army units 89; trade
with Poland 113
Belgium 20, 97
Berezovsky, Boris 94
Berlin Plus 50, 55–7, 74, 164
'bio-violence' 12
Black Sea Synergy 93, 95
Blair, Tony 66
Bolivia 28
Bolton, John 65
border controls: Central and East European
Countries (CEEC) 24, 104, 128; Eastern
Partnership 140; ENP 134, 140;
Mediterranean states 10, 11, 145, 149, 159;
Member States 20, 26, 30; Russia 83; as
security instrument 162; Treaty on
European Union (TEU) 21; Ukraine 136;
US 33
Borg, Joe 153
Bosnia-Herzegovina: conflict 7, 10, 22, 53,
121–2, 124; ESDP instruments 127; EU in
125, 129, 161; readmission agreements 25;
reconstruction 62; security 44, 124, 128;
Ukraine in 135; Union for the
Mediterranean 152; US in 64, 164
Britain 74 see also United Kingdom; relations
with Russia 94; as US ally 76; view on EU
security 53; Yugoslavian conflict 121–2
Broek, Hans van den 112
Bryza, Matthew 69
Bulgaria 97, 114–15
Bundeswehr 4
Bush, George H. 63, 68; Bush administration
59, 60–1, 64–6, 68
Bush, George W. 64, 68, 70, 106; Bush
administration 32, 64–6, 68, 70–1, 73,
107, 165

C4ISR 185(79)
Canary Islands 12, 24
Caribbean 28
Carrington Commission 120
Caspian energy sources 132–3
Central and East European Countries (CEEC)
115–17; accession to EU 10, 15, 21, 27;
costs of EU enlargement 107–9; EU
reform on enlargement
109–12; EU values 162; and hard security
103–7; immigration 24; organised crime 26–8; reforms prior to
joining EU 112–13; 'Return to Europe'
87, 101–3; risk of exclusion to EU 113–15

Chad 152, 161
Chechnya 10, 82
chemical weapons 144
Cherthoff, Michael 70
China 76, 95, 144
Chirac, Jacques 106, 122
'chocolate summit' 53
civilian power, Europe as 37–9
civilisation, Russian emphasis on 87–8, 91
climate change as insecurity 13
Clinton, Bill 63, 64, 105, 106, 122; Clinton
administration 64–6, 124
Clinton, Hillary 69
Code of Best Practice in the Supply Chain 45
Code of Conduct on Defence Procurement
45, 175(47)
Cold War, end of in Europe 3–6, 9, 18
Columbia 28, 29
Committee for the Civilian Aspects of Crisis
Management (CIVCOM) 6
Committee of Permanent Representatives
(COREPER) 51
Common Agricultural Policy (CAP) 13
Common Commercial Policy (CCP) 35,
39–40
Common European Asylum System 24, 34
Common Foreign and Security Policy
(CFSP) 35, 39, 40, 41–3, 46
Common Positions 20, 43
Common Spaces between EU and Russia
82–3
Common Strategies 43
Common Strategy for Russia 27
Common Strategy on the Mediterranean
region 149
Commonwealth of Independent States (CIS):
relations with EU 98, 125; relations with
Russia 53, 88, 89,
92, 95, 133
Community Assistance to Reconstruction,
Development and Stabilisation (CARDS)
25, 126
Comprehensive Plan to Combat
Illegal Immigration and Trafficking of
Human Beings in the European
Union 24
Conference on Security and Security in
Europe (CSCE) 53
Contact Group 53, 120, 121
Container Security Initiative 33
Conventional Forces in Europe treaty (CFE)
3–4, 91
Copenhagen Criteria 102
Copenhagen negotiations on climate
change 13
Cotonou Agreement 41
Council of Europe 52, 101

counter-terrorism 23, 30–4, 67
Counter-Terrorism Strategy 31
crime *see* organised crime
Crimea 5
criminal justice 21
Croatia: accession to EU 115, 128–9, 131,
  152; asylum seekers 25; conflict 104,
  121–2, 197 (19); EU in 125; NATO
  membership 71, 129; support for US 106;
  Union for the Mediterranean 152
Cyprus: accession to EU 104, 114, 117;
  attitude to Russia 97; EMP 152; relations
  with NATO 117; and Turkish EU
  membership 143
Czech Republic: accession to EU 114;
  attitude to Russia 97; Ballistic Missile
  Defence (BMD) 74, 87; EU trade 107;
  NATO 105; support for US 106; target for
  Russia 86; and US 106; view on EU
  membership 112

Darfur 9
data-sharing 33
Davignon Report 41
Dayton Accords 122, 125, 129
Declaration on EC-US Relations 61
defence equipment: EU 44–6, 164, 173(33),
  174(44), 179(116); EU-US collaboration
  74–6
Defence Technology Industrial Base
  (DTIB) 45
Delors, Jacques 120
Democratic Republic of Congo 9, 161
democratisation 149
Denmark 20, 21, 97, 112
Department of Homeland Security (US) 11,
  32–3
Developing Countries 40
Development Policy 35, 39–41
diplomacy as security instrument 11
disease as insecurity 12–13, 14
diversity within EU 109–12
drug trafficking: enlargement of EU 10, 104;
  globalisation 9; internal security 18, 28–9;
  Schengen Agreement 20

Eastern arc of instability 119–20
Eastern Europe and EU 15–16, 119–20,
  131–41
Eastern Partnership 35, 69, 95, 139–40, 163
East-West balance 3
economic deprivation as insecurity 12
economic immigration 10, 12
economic power as influence 162
Egypt 144, 146, 152
energy supplies 13, 16, 73, 97–8, 135,
  146–7

enlargement of EU 15–16 *see also* accession to
  EU; Central and East European Countries
  (CEEC); Balkans 21, 130; Central and East
  European Countries (CEEC) 117–18; costs
  107–9; 'deepening versus widening debate'
  109–11; diversity and reform 109–12;
  Eastern Europe 163; future of EU
  enlargement 115–17; and hard security
  103–7; impact on EU/Russia relations 82;
  internal security 18–19; limits to 163;
  Mediterranean States 143; organised crime
  26–8; preparatory reform of new members
  112–13; 'Return to Europe' 101–3; risk of
  exclusion 113–15; security challenges 17;
  security strategies 10; source of
  influence 162
enlargement of NATO 104–5
Estonia 94, 97, 99, 103, 111, 114
ethical considerations 7–8
ethnic cleansing 8, 20–1
EU-3 8, 53
EU Action Plan 30
EU Africa strategy 35
EU-NATO Capability Group 55
'Eurasianism' 84
euro-crisis 2009-10 15, 163
Eurojust (European Judicial Agency) 30, 33
Euro-Mediterranean Partnership (EMP) *see*
  Barcelona Process
EuropeAid Co-operation Office 40
European Agency for Reconstruction 126
European Arrest Warrant 31
European Capabilities Action Plan 43
European Coal and Steel Community
  (ECSC) 36
European Commission 33, 52; Albania 122;
  data-sharing 33; defence assets 44;
  Delegation to Washington 61; EU
  enlargement 114, 124, 131–41;
  Mediterranean States 146–55, 157;
  migration 24–5; relations with Russia
  82–3, 93–6, 98; representation 111; right
  of initiative 20, 21, 23; role in EU 105,
  108, 110; Yugoslavian conflict 121,
  125–31
European Community 61; Balkans 126;
  competencies and policies 36–42, 45–6,
  48, 57; development 4, 52; enlargement of
  EU 101, 103, 107; Mediterranean States
  148, 152, 156; relations with Russia 93,
  97; relations with US 61; Southern
  Caucasus 135
European Community Monitoring Mission
  (ECMM) 120–1
European Consensus on Development 41
European Council 46–7, 105, 110–11
European Court of Justice 23, 36–7, 121

European Defence Agency (EDA) 43–5, 51, 55–8, 75, 84
European Defence Community 36
European Defence Technology and Industrial Base (EDTIB) 43–5, 58
European Development Fund (EDF) 40
European External Action Service (EEAS) 43
European Gendarmerie Force (EGF) 6, 22
European Investment Bank (EIB) 40
'Europeanism' 74, 77
European Monitoring Centre for Drugs and Drug Addiction (EMCDDA) 28
European Neighbourhood Policy (ENP) 25, 92, 134–42
European Parliament (EP) 21, 23, 33, 45, 61, 111, 121, 131
European Partnership 141
European Police College (CEPOL) 27
European Political Cooperation (EPC) 36, 39, 41–3
European Refugee Fund 24
European Security and Defence Policy (ESDP) 17, 43–4, 50–1, 94, 162; attitude of CEECs 106–7; Balkans 127–8; Mediterranean States 156; NATO 57–8; Russia 94–5, 191 (100); Turkey 55, 117; US 68, 70–1, 74, 76–7
European security architecture 52–7
European Security Strategy (ESS) 5, 41–2, 47–52; climate change as insecurity 13; economic deprivation as insecurity 12; on preventative engagement 11; Russia 80; Southern Caucasus 132; terrorism 29; US 8
European Single Market 10, 142
Europol (European Police Office) 27–8, 30–3, 128, 146, 161
EU-Russian Common Spaces Report 94
EU Strategy against Proliferation of Weapons of Mass Destruction 8

Ferrero-Waldner, Benita 62, 91, 98
financial costs of EU enlargement 107–9
Finland 97
Fisher, Joschka 103
Foreign Policy Concept of the Russian Federation (FPC) 85–9
Former Yugoslav Republic of Macedonia (FYROM): asylum seekers 25; conflict 121–2; Greek sanctions 53; NATO membership 71; *Operation Concordia* 44; reconstruction 125–9; support for US 106; Ukraine in 135
fossil fuels 13
Fouchet Plan 36
FP7 Thematic Priority on Security and Space 44

France: Algerian terrorist attacks 145; anti-immigration parties 23; attitude to Russia 97; attitude to Yugoslavian conflict 121–2; defence procurement 75; EU counter-terrorism measures 31; EU/NATO 55; Georgia conflict 99; global military power 5; Iran nuclear programme 8; reduction in defence spending 164; relations with US 77; role in EU 105–6; Schengen Agreement 20; sharing of intelligence information 31; as US ally 76; view of Mediterranean States 144; view on enlargement 102, 108, 110, 115–16; view on EU security 53; view on Turkey 117; voting weights 111; Western European Union (WEU) 36
Fried, Daniel 71
Frontex (European Border Agency) 26, 128, 161
funding of Eastern Europe 139

G8 Global Partnership against the Proliferation of WMD 93
Galileo 77
Gaulle, Charles de 36
genocide in Rwanda 8
Georgia: accession of Turkey 143; conflict with Russia 68, 80, 83, 92, 95, 98–9, 164; ENP 131–3, 135, 137, 139–41; EU in 162; and membership of NATO 97; PCA 118; potential EU membership 89, 116; US policy towards 66, 71, 73; Rose Revolution 73
Germany: accession of Turkey 117; in Afghanistan 32; asylum seekers 20–1; attitude to Russia 97; Balkans 53, 121–2; civilian power 37; defence production 45; in EU 36, 51, 53, 111; foiled terrorism plot 30; and Georgia conflict 99; Iran nuclear programme 8; military power 5; in NATO 4; reunification 3, 4, 61; Schengen Agreement 20; sharing of intelligence information 31; and US 66, 76, 106, 164; view on enlargement 102, 108, 109, 110, 116, 143, 150, 163; view on EU security 53; voting weights 111
Gibraltar 24
Giertych, Roman 94
Global Approach to Migration 25
globalisation 9, 23, 160
global security 6–9
global security agenda 7
Global War on Terrorism (GWOT) 59–60, 64, 66, 68 *see also* War on Terror
Gorbachev, Mikhail 4
Graffy, Colleen 70

Greece: accession of Cyprus 104, 114, 117; accession of Turkey 117; attitude to Russia 97; attitude to Yugoslavian conflict 121–2; migration 24; near collapse of economy 163; view on EU security 53
Group of 6 31
Guantanamo Bay, Cuba 32

Hague programme 22–3
Hamre, John 76
hard security 17, 103–7, 144–5
Headline Goals 43–4
health threats 12
High Level Policy Dialogue on Borders and Transport Security 33
High Representative for Foreign and Security Policy 8, 46-7
HIV/AIDS threat 12
Homer-Dixon, Thomas 13
Hoop Scheffer, Jaap de 57, 74
Horn of Africa 152
Human Development Report 1994 (United Nations) 2
human rights 149
human security 12, 50
Human Security Doctrine for Europe, A 12
Human Security Response Force 12
human trafficking *see* people trafficking
Hungary: accession to EU 107, 114; aid to 61; attitude to Russia 97; border disputes 104; EU 125; North Atlantic Treaty Organisation (NATO) 105

Iberian Peninsula 146
illegal immigration 9, 14, 18–26
immigration: cause of insecurity 14; economic 12; and globalisation 9; illegal 145–6; internal security 23–6; policy development 18–23
individual security 2, 13–14
Indonesia 91
institutionalisation of internal security 19–23
Instrument for Pre-accession Assistance (IPA) 126
Intermediate-range Nuclear Force treaty (INF) 3
internal security 14, 18–19, 34; immigration and asylum 23–6; institutionalisation 19–23; organised crime and drug trafficking 26–9; transnational terrorism 29–33
International Monetary Fund (IMF) 66
Iran: chemical weapons 144; as EU neighbour 115, 124; EU/Russian convergence 90; exclusion from ENP 132; involvement of EU 156; nuclear programme 8, 73, 144,

164–5; regional ambitions 16; and Southern Caucasus region 133; US/Russia 68
Iraq: Britain in 76; British/Russian relations 94; chemical weapons 144; conflict 15; EU in 17, 73, 156; as EU neighbour 124; exclusion from ENP 132; lack of EU consensus 32; support for US in 106; US military intervention 8, 16, 63–5, 70, 74, 76, 87, 106, 145, 157; US/Russia 73; view of French 165
Ireland 5, 21, 24, 97, 108
Islam 124
isolationism 63
Israel 144, 147, 149, 152, 154, 156–9
Italy: in Albania 122; attitude to Russia 97; defence production 45; EU counter-terrorism measures 31; immigration 12, 23, 24; Mediterranean States 147; organised crime 19; sharing of intelligence information 31;
Ivanov, Sergei 86

Japan 37, 49
Jihadist terrorism 10–11, 23
Joint Action Plan (JAP) 61–2
Joint Actions 20, 43
Jones, Elizabeth 67
Jones, James L. 157
Jordan 147, 149, 152
judicial systems 19, 22
Justice and Home Affairs (JHA) 10, 18, 20–2, 24, 27
Justice, Liberty and Security (JLS) portfolio 16, 23

K-4 committee 20, 21
Kaldor, Mary 12
Kaliningrad, Russia 26, 124
Kazakhstan 95, 125, 133
Kennedy, Paul 63
Kerchove, Gilles de 30
Kissinger, Henry 69
Kohl, Helmut 61
Kornblum, John 55
Kosovo: conflict 7, 10, 22, 121–31; EU as security provider 161, 163–4; independence 68, 71, 130; US military intervention 64
Kozyrev, Andrey 84, 85
Kyoto Protocol 13, 90
Kyrgystan 95, 125, 133

Lake, Tony 105
Laos 28
Latvia 5, 97, 99, 103, 111, 114
Lavrov, Sergey 84, 98
Lebanon 152, 156, 157

Libya 144, 152, 165
Lisbon Treaty 23, 43, 46–7, 163, 166; and
    European security architecture 57
Lithuania 97, 99, 114
Litvinenko, Alexandr 94
Lomé Conventions 41
London terrorism attacks 23, 30–1
Luxembourg: attitude to Russia 97;
    Schengen Agreement 20
Lyne, Roderic 94

Maastricht Treaty see Treaty on European
    Union (TEU)
Macao 25
Macedonia see Former Yugoslav Republic
    of Macedonia (FYROM)
Madagascar 41
Madrid terrorism attacks 23, 30
Maghreb 152
Malmstrom, Cecilia 28, 31
Malta 12, 24, 97, 114, 143, 152
Marshall Aid 36
Mauritania 35, 146, 147, 152, 154
Mediterranean States: and the EU
    142–59; EU security contribution
    162; relationship with EU 16;
    security issues 7, 10
Medium-term Strategy 82, 92
Medvedev, Dmitry 16, 68, 71, 90–2,
    96, 100; and Russian foreign
    policy 83–9
Merkel, Angela 89, 152
Mexico 12
Middle East 7, 13, 144, 156–7
Middle East Peace Process (MEPP) 90, 156–7
migration 16, 23–6, 108–9, 198(28)
Military Capabilities Commitment
    Conference 43
military power 37, 38, 86, 162
military security 3–5
Military Staff of the EU 51
Milosevic, Slobodan 123
Mitterand, François 102, 121
Moldova 66, 124, 125, 131–3, 135,
    137, 141
Monaco 152
money laundering 28–9
Montenegro 21, 120, 123, 125–8, 152
Morocco 146, 147, 149, 152
Multidisciplinary Committee on Organised
    Crime 21
multilateralism 63, 65, 69, 90
Multilateral Nuclear Environmental
    Programme in Russia (MNEPR) 93
Muslims in Europe 10–11, 31
Mutual Legal Assistance Treaty 33
Myanmar 28

national interests of EU Member States 98–9
Netherlands 20, 23, 28, 30, 97, 115–16
New Transatlantic Agenda (NTA) 61–2
Nice Treaty 43, 46
9/11 terrorist attacks: 165 7; EU response
    29–30, 34, 41, 124, 142–4, 155; EU/US
    relations 32, 62; US domestic security 32–3;
    US foreign policy 59–60, 64, 77, 78, 160,
    165; US global security agenda 8
non-military security instruments 11–14
non-proliferation 68
normative power 37–9
North Africa 24, 25, 28, 145–6, 153, 162
North Atlantic Treaty Organisation (NATO):
    Afghanistan 7, 32; Balkans 71, 121–4, 129,
    161; Britain towards 74; capability
    development with 164; in the Cold War
    18; defence expenditure 45; enlargement
    106; enlargement of EU 104–5; European
    integration 36; European Security Strategy
    (ESS) 49, 50; EU-US relations 67; Georgia
    97, 132; Germany 4; Mediterranean States
    147; New Strategic Doctrine (NATO) 53;
    relations with EU 52–8, 76, 77, 164;
    relations with Russia 87, 89, 95–6,104,
    133;; relations with US 67, 71–3, 75;
    Turkey 107; Ukraine 86; US view of 17,
    59–60, 65–71, 79
North Korea 73, 144
Norway 76
nuclear proliferation 7, 8, 16, 144–5, 164
Nuland, Victoria 70

Obama, Barak 59–60, 65, 69, 70; Obama
    administration 16, 62, 65, 71, 73, 78,
    159, 165
OBNOVA (Programme for assistance to
    Boznia and Herzegovina) 125
Ohrid Framework Agreement 127
Operation Alba 122
Operation Artemis 44
Operation Concordia 44
Organisation for Security and Co-operation
    in Europe (OSCE) 89, 91, 122–3
organised crime: Balkans 129; Bulgaria 115;
    cause of insecurity 14; enlargement of EU
    10, 21, 104; ENP 134; and globalisation 9;
    internal security 18–20, 26–8, 42, 49, 128,
    161–2, 166; Mediterranean States 146;
    Russia 80

Pakistan 10, 28, 73, 99
Palestine 16, 20, 156
Palestinian Authority 149, 152
Palestinian Occupied Territories 161
Partnership and Cooperation Agreements
    (PCAs) 81, 118

Partnership for Peace (PfP) programme 67, 105, 129
Passenger Name Records agreement 33
people trafficking 9, 10, 23, 146
Perle, Richard 65
Permanent Structured Co-operation 46
Peru 28
Petersberg tasks 9, 17, 43, 51, 67, 123, 164
PHARE Programme of assistance (*Pologne et Hongrie assistance à la reconstruction economique*) 107, 125
Poland: accession to EU 76, 92, 93, 107, 114; aid to 61; Ballistic Missile Defence (BMD) 70, 87; Belarus 113; border guards 26; border with Germany 102; drugs 28; foreign direct investment in 107; and Georgia conflict 99; North Atlantic Treaty Organisation (NATO) 105; relations with Russia 94, 97–8; sharing of intelligence information 31; support for US 106; target of Russia 86; Ukraine 113; view on EU membership 112; voting weights 111
policies for EU external relations 39–47
policing 19, 21, 23
Political and Security Committee 51
Poos, Jacques 120
Portugal 97, 108
poverty 12–13, 14
Pre-Accession Pact on Organised Crime 27
Primakov, Yevgeny 84
Putin, Vladimir 68, 71, 82–9, 91, 94, 100

Qualified Majority Voting (QMV) 23, 110–11
Quint 53, 123

radicalisation 10–11, 16, 31, 145
readmission agreements 25
Readmission and Visa Facilitation Agreement (2007) 28
refugees 9, 10, 20–1
Rehn, Olli 112
Renovated Mediterranean Policy 147
Report of the High Level Panel on Threats, Challenges and Change (United Nations) 7–8
Revolution in Military Affairs (RMA) 74–6
Rice, Condoleezza 63, 64, 65, 66, 70
Ricketts, Peter 55, 74
Romania 89, 97, 104, 106, 113–14, 125, 130–1
Roma peoples 108–9
Rompuy, Herman van 47, 164
Royaumont Process for Stability and Good Neighbourliness in South East Europe 125–6

Rumsfeld, Donald 70, 106
Russia: arms supplies 144; Balkan conflict 124; conflict with Georgia 92, 98, 99, 116, 119, 135–6; drug trafficking 28; Eastern Partnership 140; energy supplies 13, 146; European security 57, 80–1, 99–100; EU strategic partnership development 81–3; EU-US relations 62; foreign policy 83–8; Frontex (European Border Agency) 26; Germany 3; immigration 25; importance to Eastern Europe 137–8; military modernisation 86; National Security Concept 85; organised crime 10, 26, 27–8; as outer Europe 131–4; readmission agreements 25; relations with Armenia 95; relations with Baltic States 5, 94; relations with Belarus 95; relations with Britain 94; relations with China 95; relations with CIS 95; relations with EU 14–17, 49, 73, 80–1, 103, 125, 139, 140–2, 164; relations with former Soviet republics 5, 13; relations with NATO 89; relations with Poland 94; relations with Ukraine 5, 13, 140; relations with US 16, 66–8, 70–3, 76, 78, 90; resurgence 160, 164, 166; as security challenge 163; Southern Caucasus 133; supplies to Middle East 144; view on EU enlargement 103–4; view on EU security 53–4, 57, 88–92; view on NATO enlargement 104
Rwanda 8
Ryan, Michael 56

Saakashvili, Mikhail 92, 99
Sabatié-Garat, Pierre 76
Safe Third Countries 25
Sarkozy, Nicholas 77, 89, 99, 116, 117, 150, 151
Saudi Arabia 10
Schengen Agreement 20–2
Schengen Information Systems (SIS and SIS II) 25–6
Schroeder, Gerhard 106
Secret Internet Protocol Router Network 76
securitisation process 1–2
security actor, EU as 2–3, 14–17, 57–8
security agenda: broadening 11–14; change in 9–11; global 6–9
Serbia: accession to EU 115; EU agreements 127–9; and Kosovo 123, 131; NATO air-strikes 198(28); organised crime groups 21; reconstruction 126; uranium 68; Yugoslavian conflict 120, 121, 124, 125
Sikorski, Radoslaw 97–8, 137
Single European Act (SEA) 41
Slovakia 97, 106–7, 114

Slovenia: accession to EU 114; attitude to Russia 97; as a CEEC 124, 125; support for US 106; Yugoslavian conflict 53, 104, 121
small arms and light weapons (SALW) 42
societal security 2
Solana, Javier 12, 47, 100, 127, 145, 158
Southern Caucasus 66, 119–20, 131–41
South Ossetia 89, 92, 94, 132, 139
sovereign democracy 85–6, 88, 91, 96, 97, 100
sovereign powers 27, 36
Spain: attitude to Russia 97; attitude to Yugoslavian conflict 121; EU counter-terrorism measures 31; illegal immigration 24; Mediterranean States 147; sharing of intelligence information 31; terrorism 20; use of structural funds 108
Sri Lanka 25
Stabilisation and Association Agreements 25
Stabilisation and Association Process (SAP) 126–7, 128, 141
Stability Pact for South Eastern Europe 126
strategic culture and the ESS 51–2
Strategic Framework Declaration 70
strategic partnerships 35, 95, 96, 100
Strategy for Combating Radicalisation and Recruitment to Terrorism 31
structural funds 108
Sudan 74
Sudarsano, Juwono 91
Sweden 5, 45, 51, 97, 106, 109
swine flu pandemic 12
Syria: EU co-operation agreement 152, 165; as EU neighbour 115, 124; inclusion in ENP 132; as nuclear power 144; in original EMP 152; relations with Russia 99

Tajikistan 125, 133
terrorism see also 9/11 terrorist attacks: 'bio-violence' 12; cause of insecurity 14; EU response to 165; and globalisation 9; internal security 20; international 8, 29–33; Jihadist 10–11; London and Madrid bombings 145; and migration 23; and organised crime 146; and Mediterranean States 145; transnational 18; US response to 165
Thailand 28
Thatcher, Margaret 110
timing of enlargement of EU 113–15
torture, US use of 32
trade as security instrument 11, 161
Treaty of Amsterdam (ToA) see Amsterdam Treaty
Treaty of Prum 23
Treaty of Rome 36, 40
Treaty on European Union (TEU) 4, 9–10, 18, 20, 40, 41, 42, 43, 109

TREVI (Terrorisme, Radicalisme et Violence Internationale) 20
tuberculosis 12
Tunisia 147, 149, 152
Turkey: accession of Cyprus 104, 114; accession to EU 71, 116–17, 143, 152, 163; drug trafficking 28; and EU/NATO 55, 56; in original EMP 152; Southern Caucasus 132
Turkmenistan 125

Ukraine: accession to EU 116, 137; dispute with Russia 94; as Eastern Europe 125; Eastern Partnership 140; energy supplies 98; ENP 141; EU neighbours 104; EU values 163; fault line 99; organised crime 10, 26; outer Europe 132–3; Partnership and Cooperation Agreements (PCAs) 118; readmission agreements 25; relations with EU 16; relations with Russia 5, 13; since inclusion in ENP 135–6, 138; target of Russia 86; trade with Poland 113; US policy towards 66, 71, 73
UNHCR 123
unilateralism 63, 69
Union for the Mediterranean 35, 150, 151–2, 155–6, 158, 163
United Kingdom see also Britain: anti-immigration parties 23; attitude to Russia 21, 97; defence collaboration 76–7; defence expenditure 164; EU internal security 20; global military power 5; intelligence information 31; Iran nuclear programme 8; legal migration 24; relations with EU 112; role in EU 105–6; sovereign powers 27; terrorism 20, 31; as US ally 76; view on enlargement 110; voting weights 111
Ukraine; Orange Revolution 73, 136
United Nations 7–8, 31–2, 36, 51, 121
United Nations Counter Terrorism Committee (CTC) 31–2
United Nations' Development Programme: Human Development Report 1994 2
United Nations Drug Control Programme (UNDCP) 28
United Nations Interim Mission in Kosovo (UNMIK) 123
United Nations Protection Force (UNPROFOR) 122
United Nations Security Council 8
United States (of America): attitude to Yugoslavian conflict 122; in the Cold War 18; counter-terrorism co-operation 32–3; criticism of EU 17; drug trafficking 29; enlargement of NATO 104–5; ESDP 106; EU/NATO 55–6; European security

59–60, 72, 78–9; European Security
Strategy (ESS) 49, 50–1; EU view of 72–8;
foreign policy 63–5; global security 6–8;
influence in Europe 77; leadership 36;
management of EU-US security
relationship 60–3; Mediterranean States
157–8, 159–61; Middle East 157; military
dependence on 77; National Security
Strategy (NSS) 48, 117; as normative
power 38; nuclear guarantees 36;
preventative military action 182(25);
relations with Britain 76; relations with
EU 3, 14–17, 164–5; relations with
France 77; relations with NATO 66,
67, 71; relations with Russia 16, 67–8,
70, 71, 90; Southern Caucasus 133;
view on European security and EU
53, 65–72
Uzbekistan 125

Vance-Owen Peace Plan 120
Van Eekelen, Willem 120
Verheugen, Gunter 112
'Vilnius Ten' 106
Visitor and Immigrant Status Indicator
Technology (VISIT) 33

Volker, Kurt 60, 67
Vries, Gijs de 30

War on Terror 8, 32, 106, 165 *see also*
Global War on Terrorism (GWOT)
Warsaw Pact 3, 4, 18
weapons of mass destruction (WMD) 8, 42,
68, 144–5, 155
West Africa 28, 146
Western Balkans Investment Framework 127
Western European Union (WEU) 36,
52–3, 104–5
Western Sahara 146
Wolfowitz, Paul 65
World Bank 66
World Trade Organisation 8, 66
Wörner, Manfred 53

Yanukovych, Viktor 140
Yaoundé Convention 41
Yeltsin, Boris 68
Yemen 10
Yugoslavia *see* Balkan conflict;
Balkans

Zakaev, Akhmed 94

Lightning Source UK Ltd.
Milton Keynes UK
UKHW022057310819
348939UK00005B/40/P